Environmental Choices

Environmental Choices
Policy Responses to Green Demands

Lawrence S. Rothenberg
University of Rochester

CQ PRESS

A Division of Congressional Quarterly Inc.
Washington, D.C.

CQ Press
A Division of Congressional Quarterly Inc.
1255 22nd Street, N.W., Suite 400
Washington, D.C. 20037

(202) 822-1475; (800) 638-1710

www.cqpress.com

Printed and bound in the United States of America

06 05 04 03 02   5 4 3 2 1

∞ The paper used in this publication meets the minimum requirements of the American National Standard for Information Sciences—Permanence of Paper for Printed Library Materials, ANSI Z39.48-1992.

Cover design: Karen Doody

Library of Congress Cataloging-in-Publication Data

Rothenberg, Lawrence S.
    Environmental choices : policy responses to green demands /
Lawrence S. Rothenberg.
        p.   cm.
Includes bibliographical references and index.
    ISBN 1-56802-630-7 (pbk. : alk. paper)
    1. Environmental policy—United States.   2. Environmental quality—
United States.   3. Environmentalism—United States.   I. Title.
    GE180 .R67 2002
    363.7'056'0973—dc21

                                                                    2001008314

In memory of Jeffrey S. Banks (1958–2000),
extraordinary scholar and dear friend

Contents

Tables and Figures

Tables

Figures

List of Acronyms

ANILCA	Alaska National Interest Lands Conservation Act of 1980
AUM	Animal unit month
BLM	Bureau of Land Management
CAA	Clean Air Act
CAFE	Corporate average fuel economy
CBO	Congressional Budget Office
CCC	Civilian Conservation Corps
CEQ	Council on Environmental Quality
CERCLA	Comprehensive Environmental Response, Compensation, and Liability Act of 1980 (Superfund)
CFC	Chlorofluorocarbon
CPSC	Consumer Product Safety Commission
CWA	Clean Water Act
DDT	Dichlorodiphenyl-trichloroethane
DOD	Department of Defense
DOI	Department of Interior
EPA	Environmental Protection Agency
EPCRA	Emergency Planning and Community Right-to-Know Act of 1986
ESA	Endangered Species Act
FDA	Food and Drug Administration
FIFRA	Federal Insecticide, Fungicide, and Rodenticide Act
FLPMA	Federal Land Policy and Management Act of 1976
FQPA	Food Quality Protection Act
FWS	Fish and Wildlife Service
GAO	General Accounting Office
GNP	Gross national product
LCV	League of Conservation Voters
NAAQS	National Ambient Air Quality Standards

NEPA	National Environmental Policy Act
NIMBY	Not in My Backyard
NPDES	National Pollutant Discharge Elimination System
NPL	National Priority List
NPS	National Park Service
OMB	Office of Management and Budget
OSHA	Occupational Safety and Health Administration
PRIA	Public Rangelands Improvement Act of 1978
PRP	Potentially responsible parties
RCRA	Resource Conservation and Recovery Act
SARA	Superfund Amendments and Reauthorization Act of 1986
SDWA	Safe Drinking Water Act
TMDL	Total maximum daily load
TRI	Toxic Release Inventories
TSCA	Toxic Substance Control Act
TVA	Tennessee Valley Authority
USDA	U.S. Department of Agriculture
USFS	United States Forest Service

Preface

Environmental policies in the United States often appear to be a perplexing morass—fragmented, contradictory, inconsistent, and rulebound. Although it is fairly easy to describe the policy system, it is far more difficult to gain a deeper understanding of what determines policy and the costs and efficacy of policy initiatives.

Despite the obvious importance of the environment and the policies that govern it, contemporary books that provide a unifying analytic approach are in short supply. *Environmental Choices: Policy Responses to Green Demands* fills this gap. It furnishes an important overview and perspective on research and issues while providing analytic tools that challenge students' intuitive understanding of environmental policy and public policy. Students using the book will be prepared to apply the knowledge gained from it to make sense of the world they observe. As well as being employed as a principal text, this book may be used in conjunction with a standard core text as a means of questioning conventional wisdom, shedding light on hard-to-understand policy features, and making connections more generally between environmental policy and public policy.

Although the book incorporates sophisticated ideas, it is written to be comprehensible. It offers and consistently applies a coherent framework that focuses both on the economic determinants of demand for environmental quality and on the nature of political supply in responding to such demands. In doing so, it provides a distinctive approach that shows how the U.S. political system produces higher environmental quality than would occur without government intervention but at a seemingly high cost.

More generally, *Environmental Choices* has two goals. The first is to provide a framework for understanding environmental policy that is derived from a general perspective on public policy. Environmental policy is a manifestation of more general processes that affect policy and is best understood that way. Drawing heavily on existing social science about public policy—and about how individuals, firms, organizations, and institutions make relevant choices—the various chapters accessibly introduce key ideas in economics and political science so that readers can easily understand where demand for environmental policy comes from and how political institutions supply it.

The second goal is to survey government's environmental policies in a way that closely ties in to the analytical framework. Consequently, rather than being presented with the history of environmental policy choices and their influences as a laundry list of accomplishments and failures, students are given a perspective from which to make sense of the political intervention observed, the policy instruments and agencies chosen, and the level of government and means of enforcement selected.

In communicating complicated and nuanced ideas, *Environmental Choices* employs a variety of helpful pedagogic tools. Key terms appear in bold face and are listed at the end of each chapter. Key data are presented in easy-to-digest tables and figures. And extensive references are provided to direct readers who are interested in exploring further.

Environmental Choices begins by laying out the general framework by which policies, among them environmental policy, are seen as a product of demand for goods and the nature of government supply. Chapter 1 explores how that demand for environmental quality has grown with economic prosperity and how the capacity of the United States to meet that demand has increased in a manner heavily influenced by a constitutional structure that produces fragmentation. This interaction—of rising demand with an expanding but fragmented political system—is a crucial element in the understanding of environmental policy. Chapter 2 lays out both the economic and noneconomic rationales for government intervention, and Chapter 3 applies the conceptual framework to the history of environmental policy in the United States. Chapter 4 investigates the impact of national political influences—voters and groups on the one hand and political institutions on the other—and shows how such demand- and supply-side forces interact. Chapter 5 surveys the implementation and enforcement of environmental policy and demonstrates that, although policy enforcement does seem to increase compliance, it also reflects the fragmented political process. Chapter 6 discusses federalism, providing an overview of the reasons for and against either localizing or nationalizing policies, and shows how the working of federalism in practice is profoundly related to the nature of supply and demand for environmental quality. Chapter 7 applies the conceptual framework to government policies with respect to the government's role as landlord, looking at the four principal land management agencies—the Forest Service, the Bureau of Land Management, the National Park Service, and the Fish and Wildlife Service. Chapter 8 applies the framework to government regulatory policies, focusing on the Environmental Protection Agency. Chapter 9, after demonstrating how the conceptual framework reconciles an often seemingly misguided political system with improvement in at least some elements of environmental quality, speculates on the many challenges that the future holds.

ACKNOWLEDGMENTS

This book has been a decade in the making, and I have incurred many debts along the way. Thanks principally go to my former students, graduate and undergraduate. My initial commitment to developing expertise in environmental affairs stemmed from a feeling of responsibility toward my graduate students, and special appreciation goes to Lucy Drotning, Todd Kunioka, and Marc Shapiro, among others. Thanks also to Randy Calvert for encouraging me to develop an undergraduate seminar in environmental politics and to the students who sat through the class as I educated myself.

Through the years, the University of Rochester's Department of Political Science and the Wallis Institute of Political Economy have been stimulating and congenial places to get my work done. Thanks to my colleagues and to the associated staffs. Thanks also to the administration at the University of Rochester for giving me a semester off as a Bridging Fellow to learn more about environmental concerns; Larry Lundgren of the Earth and Environmental Sciences Department proved a most gracious sponsor for that semester.

Several colleagues deserve special recognition. David Weimer, now of the University of Wisconsin, alerted CQ Press to the existence of my then-scattered manuscript and was a source of encouragement. Nathan Dietz of American University was willing to be co-opted into learning about grazing policy. Seth Goldstein provided able research assistance. Special thanks to Bill Lowry of Washington University for his support, his calming of my worries of being an intellectual interloper, and his valuable comments on the manuscript. Other very helpful comments were provided by Matthew Cahn (California State University, Northridge), Donald Haider-Markel (University of Kansas), Sheldon Kamieniecki (University of Southern California), Geoffrey Wandesforde-Smith (University of California, Davis), and Patrick Wilson (University of Iowa). After all this valuable feedback, I'm not even sure I recognize the finished manuscript any more.

Thanks also to the folks at CQ Press. Special thanks to Charisse Kiino for taking a flier on a manuscript that is admittedly a bit different from the press's norm, to Amy Briggs and Joanne S. Ainsworth for their patience with the author and their helpful editing of the manuscript, and to Gwenda Larsen for seeing the manuscript through production.

Finally, thanks to my family, particularly to my children, Daniel and Sarah, who are used to daddy carrying his laptop to art, swimming, and karate classes, on vacation, and to sundry other locations. Your love and affection make life something extraordinary.

This manuscript is dedicated to the memory of my dear friend and former colleague, Jeffrey Banks (1958–2000), whose extraordinary scholarship was, for those who had the privilege to call him a friend, overshadowed by his warmth and humanity. I count myself among those who are better for having known him.

Environmental Choices

1 | Environmental Policy in Context: Economic Demand, Political Supply

Not too long ago, swamps and bogs were commonly thought of as smelly, ugly eyesores. The wetlands recognized today as valuable resources for maintaining environmental quality were looked upon as expendable impediments to progress. Most people would have considered anybody draining them and creating economic activity as improving society both aesthetically and economically. Government policy aided wetlands destruction as a means of encouraging economic growth; for example, the U.S. Army Corps of Engineers routinely filled in swamps. Wetlands in the United States disappeared at a rapid rate, with more than half now destroyed.

But times have changed. For one thing, scientists came to realize that wetlands were extremely environmentally important and sensitive. Wetlands protect shorelines, reduce erosion, filter water, provide nesting and wintering areas for waterfowl, and act as spawning grounds for many fish species. The environmental benefits of maintaining these areas extend well beyond their owners, who, despite the ecological benefits of wetlands, frequently have economic incentives to transform these swamps in environmentally damaging ways. Given this state of affairs, environmentally concerned individuals and groups, of which there were a growing number, began paying more attention to wetlands preservation and restoration. These persons and groups began to advocate that government take a leading role in protecting these valuable natural resources.

Indeed, the government slowly redefined its role with respect to wetlands. Although preceded by some state-level efforts, beginning in the 1970s the national government assumed the principal government role in efforts to preserve them. There has been a considerable impact on wetland preservation, as the rate of loss of wetland areas has dropped by well over 80 percent.

Yet, rather than being applauded, wetlands policies have created much discord. Most notably, existing policies are highly fragmented and lack coherence or any rational, comprehensive, underpinnings. Laws, according to the Congressional Research Service, "do not add up to a fully consistent or comprehensive national approach" (Zinn and Copeland 2001, 3). Indicative of this situation,

1

wetlands policy involves a large number of agencies, with varying orientations: the Fish and Wildlife Service (FWS), the United States Department of Agriculture (USDA; through its Natural Resource Conservation Service), the Environmental Protection Agency (EPA), the Army Corps of Engineers, and the Bureau of Reclamation among them (on wetlands fragmentation, see Wenner 1993, Vileisis 1997, Fish and Wildlife Service 2000, Gaddie and Regens 2000). With so many agencies involved in an issue with wide-ranging impacts, many congressional committees and organized groups also attempt to guide, some might say to interfere with, wetlands policy. Those subject to the high costs of government restrictions have organized in opposition. One of the responses of these cost bearers has been to turn to the legal system. The courts, including the Supreme Court, have weighed in with a series of complicated decisions on whether certain restrictions are legal or are tantamount to illegal seizure of property, further adding to the impact of a disjointed policy. Presidents worry that, in relying too much on inflexible rules, wetlands policies are not as low cost as possible for the amount of protection offered and thus they burden the economy. For example, in 1993, in an attempt to produce more wetlands protection for the buck, the administration of President Bill Clinton (1993–2001) set out policies to create market-like **mitigation banking,** by which developers may create or purchase credits to use some wetlands by enhancing, restoring, or creating others (see Neal 1999, National Research Council 2001). And the states, in turn, have chafed at the restrictions and costs created by programs designed in Washington, D.C., and have pressed for more autonomy and assistance.

Heightened demand for environmental protection has seemingly generated a positive response by largely, if not completely, stopping the depletion of wetlands, but the resulting policy that is supplied seems amazingly fractured, conflictual, and costly. How can sense be made of a policy that appears both successful and deficient?

Answering such a question motivates this text. Specifically, a general framework is laid out that views policies, environmental policy among them, as a function of demand for goods and the nature of government supply. This framework is then applied to make environmental policy in the United States, both its methods and its effects, understandable.

Such an approach contrasts with that advanced by others. Those with strong personal concerns about a policy issue often approach their area of interest as unique to itself, but the larger economic and political circumstances in which public policies take place are typically crucial for understanding how they function. This is certainly the case for environmental policy and politics in the United States. Understanding both the historical development of the United States' approach to dealing with environmental ills and the current state of relevant policies requires appreciating how they have been shaped by the broader economic and political contexts that structure the choices that government routinely makes on public issues.

Although the latter statement may seem obvious, viewing environmental policy as unique is a conventional starting point. The assumption is that such policy is qualitatively distinguished from other government actions and, therefore, deserves different attention and unique analysis. For instance, one standard text begins: "Environmental policy is set apart from other policy areas by a simple but very important fact. Environmental policy has to do with sustaining the ecological basis of life. Other policy areas have to do with the quality of life" (Wells 1996, 1).

Although intuitively appealing, given the passion that many bring and the importance that they ascribe to environmental concerns, this perspective can be misleading. For one thing, the extent to which environmental policy differs qualitatively from other types of policy is debatable. Certainly other public policy areas involve life and death issues and not just the quality of lives. Is not regulating prescription drugs by the Food and Drug Administration (FDA), automobile safety by the Department of Transportation, or consumer product safety by the Consumer Product Safety Commission (CPSC) at least partially about sustaining and protecting lives? Analogously, other policies, like those affecting retirement benefits, such as Social Security, or education quality, such as student grants-in-aid, have long-term ramifications spanning generations. Even more germane, conclusions based on conventional analytic tools employed for conceptualizing policy generally will be more convincing because explanations will be systematic rather than ad hoc. As such, in a general sense, this text maintains that U.S. environmental policy has been guided by the interaction between an increasing, economically induced, demand for high quality of life and the political system's development of an institutional structure and resulting capacity to meet this demand within the context of a democratic society. Here **capacity** means the ability to manage resources directly or to influence production and consumption choices of societal actors; it may be a function both of formal authority and of effective and well-financed organization. The ability to gather, process, and act upon important information proficiently is a hallmark of political capacity. For instance, if an agency, legislature, chief executive, or court is confronted with highly technical environmental issues that they are in no position to understand, it is perceived as less capable, or as having less capacity. Focusing on capacity is important because capacity does not necessarily expand efficiently in a manner neatly corresponding to increased demand. Thus, understanding environmental policy requires considering the complex interplay between how much environmental policy is desired and the development of political capacity. Neither can be appreciated in isolation.

Economically, in the sense that demand is substantially induced by increasing prosperity, the United States has been characterized by gradually more strident calls for environmental quality. This growth in desires for environmental quality with increased economic success, such as for cleaner air or water or a toxic-free environment, is comparable to increased demand for all sorts of desirable **private goods,** whether they be housing, clothes, cars, or whatever else might be consumed (private goods are those that have clearly identifiable owners and whose consumption is rivalrous—if they are consumed by one actor they cannot be consumed by another). As advanced industrial democracies have financially prospered, pressure for government action has increased, although demand and prosperity do not necessarily increase in lockstep. In other words, the ability to pay for a more desirable environment may prove to be only one determinant of demand.[1] Nonetheless, citizens in wealthier nations indicate a greater willingness to pay for a cleaner, more pristine, environment than those in the developing world—despite the environmental harm done by high consumption levels and growing populations and the associated effects of congestion. In doing so, these citizens have also typically looked toward government to supply many of the answers.

Although political capacity has increased along with demand for environmental quality in other advanced industrial democracies, the nature of institutional development in the United States reflects its separation of powers and federated structure, giving environmental policy an especially fragmented and disjointed appearance. Specifically, heightened demand has interacted with a political structure that disperses power widely. Relevant policy systems, such as those associated with wetlands, appear fractured as a result. In turn, corresponding policies can lack comprehensiveness and sometimes appear incomprehensible or directed toward distributional considerations (that is, determining which societal groups are the winners and losers, financial or otherwise, from policy choices). For example, policies over cleaning the air may be more a product of determining whether auto manufacturers or large utilities pay the price of investing in cleaner technologies. At the same time, this fragmentation and dispersion of authority makes U.S. environmental policy more durable than in many other democratic systems because changing policy dramatically is made extremely difficult. Despite many drawbacks, the government has supplied improved environmental quality in a variety of instances.

As an initial foundation, this chapter lays out a basic logic that defines the relevant policy context: the joint effects of economically induced demand and politically determined supply. To a considerable extent, this context characterizes much of contemporary American public policy. Even though it may miss certain important nuances, analyzing policy from this perspective gets to the essence of the policy-making process and provides a general set of tools for understanding environmental policy specifically and public policy more broadly. Subsequent chapters show how this interaction of economic and political forces, conditioned, of course, by technical aspects (some problems are more or less difficult to solve or understand for purely technical reasons), manifests itself in a policy system and corresponding political processes and, ultimately, environmental quality.

Before proceeding, however, a note of caution: the approach adopted in this text provides only a general means of understanding the evolution, nature, and process of American environmental policy. Although it furnishes a powerful way of thinking about policy generally and environmental policy specifically, it cannot claim to predict how environmental policy *must* have developed in the past or will certainly develop in the future. Nor can alternative frameworks make such claims with confidence. Social scientists have produced numerous results indicating that, even with the existence of institutional structures, social choices (for purposes here, collective choices, given individual preferences) can have considerable randomness, and multiple potential outcomes (typically defined in terms of equilibria) are possible (for an introduction to this view of choice behavior, see Shepsle and Bonchek 1997). Here the analysis shows how to make sense of what is actually observed in a way that focuses on the features that are essential for understanding environmental policy and yet are general enough that they can be applied to understanding politics and policy generally.

The remainder of this chapter surveys the relevant economic and political contexts that will serve as the underpinning for the analysis of environmental policy through the entire book. In regard to the economic context, the fundamental point emphasized is that demand for environmental quality has grown with economic prosperity. With respect to the political context, the fundamental ideas are that the ability of the U.S. government to be involved in public policy has increased but that this growth is heavily influenced by a constitutional structure that produces fragmentation. An understanding of the interaction of rising demand with a more substantial but fragmented political system is crucial for understanding environmental policy.

THE ECONOMIC CONTEXT: ENVIRONMENTAL QUALITY AS A NORMAL GOOD

Perhaps the most basic point in terms of economic context is that, by and large, environmental quality appears to be a **normal good** (a good for which demand increases with economic resources), like many other government-supplied outputs, ranging from education to highways to libraries (for example, Coursey 1992). The alternative to a normal good is an **inferior good,** whose consumption declines as ability to pay grows; a classic example is cheap foodstuffs for which expensive commodities are substituted when prosperity increases. In the same manner, as for these other goods and for most private goods, environmental "consumption," or at least the demand for a high-quality environment, appears to increase with prosperity. That is, wealthier individuals demand more environmental quality. Quite naturally, then, as Americans have become more prosperous, their taste for environmental quality has grown along with, somewhat ironically, their preference for the myriad consumption goods that many self-styled "greens" condemn as major contributors to environmental degradation—gas-guzzling automobiles, large homes with corresponding space and energy requirements, disposable convenience products, and assorted consumer goods and services.[2]

Thus, it sometimes appears that in "postindustrial" society everyone is disposed to be a **free rider,** because it is quite natural to profess a desire for environmental quality but rationally realize that a choice not to reduce personal consumption of convenience or luxury goods is irrelevant for the overall state of the environment. Simply put, free riding involves failure to contribute to the provision of collective goods in the hope that others will do so. This failure can result in **suboptimal provision** (an **optimal provision** being how much of the good would be produced if there were no free riding, and suboptimal provision being an amount less than optimal) and have important ramifications for the type of interest group pressure felt by government as different societal interests, such as those that are more concentrated, are better able to overcome free-riding problems than others (for the classic work, see Olson 1965). The government's ability to influence such individual incentives to induce less environmentally damaging behavior is a potential rationale for political intervention.

Satisfying the environmental demands produced by increased incomes in a more technologically complex and congested world, and where private decision makers have incentives to pursue their own narrow self-interests, appears to require substantial government intervention. Stipulating a role for government is, however, not tantamount to maintaining that self-interested individuals cannot abate some environmental ills through their personal actions (for example, Kahn and Matsusaka 1997). For example, many wanting cleaner water invest in water filters or buy bottled water. Those desiring to avoid dirty air and many toxic substances may purchase residences in areas with favorable environmental characteristics (for example, one advantage of paying a premium to live by the Los Angeles shore has been that air currents push polluted air inland)[3] or invest in home air purification systems and remediate natural environmental ills, such as radon (a naturally occurring product of radium to which long-term exposure via occupation or residence may induce lung cancer and related diseases).[4] Those fearful of the effects of pesticides may pay extra for organically grown foodstuffs. Under certain conditions, private bargaining between parties where **property rights** ("the rights individuals appropriate over their own labor and the goods and services they possess" [North 1990, 33]) are well specified may also produce the optimal level of environmental quality.[5] Despite occasional calls, declining in recent years, by public and private environmental advocates to allow zero pollution (and statutes mandating this unrealistic goal), the text will typically consider there to be an optimal or a correct level of quality that policy might be designed to achieve; bargaining between two parties, independent of public policy, can also achieve this socially optimal level of pollution.

Still, high levels of environmental quality typically require the kind of **collective action** (joint action as compared with individual action) that is the province of governments. Ecosystems, formally defined as "organisms of a specific area, together with their functionally related environment . . . considered as a definitive unit" (Allen 1995, 270), are routinely beyond the means of any single actor or small groups of actors to purchase or control in entirety. For instance, even an area as large as Yellowstone National Park is considered by many environmentalists to be not big enough. When the park was established in 1872 seemingly essential parts of the ecosystem were omitted, such as lands over which its grizzly bears range, and thus many environmentalists call for expanding protection beyond the park's existing boundaries. Similarly, pollutants routinely cross property lines (transboundary pollution) in ways that are not easily amenable to private negotiation or avoidance. Indeed, some issues, such as global warming, have such a broad, cross-national, scope that remediation involves international bargaining. Others, such as the components of smog-producing stratospheric ozone, conventionally move across state lines. Completely dodging the impact of polluted air and water or exposure to toxic substances or pesticides in the food chain (given the many ways such substances work their way into diets) is impossible.[6] Also, not all government policy may be created to protect ecosystems from the evils of pollution. For instance, comprising a subset of America's national parks are unique "national treasures," which, by a rough consensus, must be made available for all to enjoy for perpetuity and kept from the clutches of private interests—although a minority, such as so-called free market environmentalists, might maintain that privatization, for example, ceding resources to private interests dedicated to preservation, would yield better protection (Lehmann 1995, Anderson and Leal 1997).

Given an apparent need for government intervention, the heightened demand for cleaner environments (along with the extremely expensive solutions often proposed) has transformed the relevant political context. Government has evolved over the last several hundred years from dealing with few or no demands, except to give away the nation's abundant natural resources such as government-owned land and minerals in the American West, to being seen as the keeper of the environmental flame over the course of the last thirty to forty years. Politicians and those to whom they delegate authority have been thrust into the position of managing how land is used, water quality is maintained, air is kept clean, pesticides are applied, and toxics are disposed of. In the process, and despite general support for the participation of government in environmental affairs, environmental politics and policy have become increasingly politicized and conflictual, involving thousands of groups, myriad politicians from all branches of the national government, and state and local governments as well.

This fragmented and contentious process is not unique to environmental issues. Other policy areas have been similarly transformed, with respect to both increasing government involvement and more complex and conflictual policy systems. Over the years, for example, as demand has grown, the federal government has played an increasing role in health care. Direct expenditures have increased greatly—for instance, in just the period between 1980 and 1998 income-tested medical benefits by the federal government increased by roughly 300 percent in inflation-adjusted dollars—as has the government's overall policy reach. Like environmental policy, health policy has involved growing numbers of politicians, bureaucrats, and organizations, and efforts to overhaul policy (notably during the early years of the Clinton administration) have ended in failure and frustration.

Despite such frustrations and in line with the proposition that wealth induces environmental demand, comparable public opinion data, when available, indicate that citizens in advanced industrial countries endorse environmental action more strongly than those in less-well-off nations. One note of caution: interpreting public opinion data in terms of demand for action must be done cautiously, in that expressions of support may not be tantamount to actual willingness to pay for environmental quality.[7] Despite this caution, and although such expressions may be partially endogenous—more active government involvement with respect to the environment in advanced industrial countries may strengthen citizen support for such involvement—they are consistent with the idea that economic well-being fosters a desire for environmental cleanliness.

For instance, in his survey of western European green parties (political parties organized around the environment), political scientist Russell Dalton summarizes public opinion in such nations as follows:[8]

> [T]he data . . . describe a [western] European public that is broadly interested in environmental protection and express a willingness to take significant actions to ensure and improve the quality of the environment. Although we should be skeptical that all who express support for environmental reform will agree when real choices are being made or real costs are incurred, these statements of support are still meaningful indications of how Euro-

peans view environmentalism. There are some national variations in environmental support—it is somewhat higher in Denmark and Luxembourg and lower in Britain and Ireland—but by the end of the 1980s the overall patterns speak of broad support that crosses national boundaries. Moreover, rather than being an issue that fades when economic problems revive, public support for environmental reform has endured over the past two decades. (Dalton 1994, 59)

In short, Dalton finds that advanced industrial democracies in western Europe, which have witnessed economic prosperity similar to that of the United States, are broadly supportive of environmentalism. The United States, to the extent that its citizens exhibit similar support, is not unique.

Examining American-specific public opinion data reveals several comparable features. First, there appears to be a rough consensus that government ought to preserve the environment (see Dunlap 1995; Ladd and Bowman 1995, 1996). For instance, answers to several basic questions posed in the General Social Survey over the years (Table 1-1) indicate that citizens want proactive government efforts on behalf of the environment. The General Social Survey, conducted by scholars associated with the National Opinion Research Center, is an almost annual personal interview survey of Americans about their opinions and behaviors. When asked to choose between government's making laws regarding environmental protection versus allowing either citizens or businesses to make their

Table 1-1 Attitudes toward the Environment

"If you had to choose, which **one** of the following would be closest to your views? Government should let ordinary people decide for themselves how to protect the environment, even if it means they don't always do the right thing, or government should pass laws to make ordinary people protect the environment, even if it interferes with people's right to make their own decisions."

Government should let ordinary people decide	19.0%
Government should pass laws	61.3
Can't choose	19.8
N = 2,865	

"And which **one** of the following [would be] closest to your views? Government should let businesses decide for themselves how to protect the environment, even if it means they don't always do the right thing, or government should pass laws to make businesses protect the environment, even if it interferes with business' right to make their own decisions."

Government should let business decide	8.6%
Government should pass laws	79.3
Can't choose	12.2
N = 2,864	

Source: General Social Survey (http://www.icpsr.umich.edu/GSS/).

own choices, the majority of survey respondents feeling capable of answering advocate legislative solutions. Less than 20 percent think that ordinary people should be delegated responsibility and less than 10 percent believe that businesses should be environmentally self-sufficient. Government is seen by the mass citizenry as central to environmental solutions.

Fundamentally, as Dalton indicates with respect to western Europe, the environment is widely trumpeted as a settled issue in the American political context. Although there are vehement opponents who view government policies as far too restrictive, as epitomized by the so-called **wise use movement** (for example, Arnold 1993, Helvarg 1994, Echeverria and Eby 1995), and others who believe that more radical solutions are required to avoid disastrous consequences (for example, Dowie 1995), most citizens believe that the government has appropriately settled on its general role as an environmental protector. Ironically, this approval of government intervention for the environment stands in stark juxtaposition to the skeptical view that most people have of the *efficacy* of government institutions in promoting good public policy.[9] Presumably as a result of this widespread consensus about government's role regarding the environment, and much to the frustration of many activists, environmental issues are rarely considered a key national problem (Ladd and Bowman 1995, 1996). Indicative of this, throughout the last several decades the Gallup Poll has found that, on average, a mere 2 percent of the population cite environmental concerns as the nation's most important problem.

However, as such endorsements of environmental intervention represent proverbial cheap talk (that is, there is no cost to an individual in advocating a clean environment), it is important to discern who might willingly sacrifice their private resources for the government to help clean up the ecosystem. Unlike the data reported in Table 1-1, people are more divided about their willingness to pay higher prices or taxes for the production of environmental quality (see Table 1-2). Furthermore, although the results are not dramatic (which may reflect measurement problems as well as the hypothetical nature of the tradeoffs in Table 1-2), a statistically significant relationship does exist between income and the measures of willingness to pay even when political preferences (liberal-conservative), education, and age are controlled. Significant numbers of Americans find the possibility of paying more for goods or, especially, higher taxes, distasteful. Roughly 50 and 35 percent of citizens state a willingness to pay higher prices and taxes, respectively.

A more concrete example of opposition to paying taxes for an improved environment occurred in 1993 when President Bill Clinton created a huge uproar when he proposed to raise gas taxes—a proposal opposed by many energy producers whose fortunes would be diminished, by many consumers not wanting to

Table 1-2 Willingness to Pay for Environmental Quality

"How willing would **you** be to pay **much higher prices** in order to protect the environment?"	
Very willing	9.6%
Fairly willing	39.0
Neither willing/unwilling, can't choose	25.7
Not very willing	17.7
Not at all willing	8.1
N = 2,863	

"And how willing would **you** be to pay **much higher taxes** in order to protect the environment?"	
Very willing	6.5%
Fairly willing	30.2
Neither willing/unwilling, can't choose	22.6
Not very willing	25.8
Not at all willing	15.0
N = 2,862	

Source: General Social Survey (http://www.icpsr.umich.edu/GSS/).

see their pocketbooks injured, and by numerous politicians who represented their interests. Although the administration originally considered increases as high as 50 cents, it eventually proposed just a 9 cent hike to Congress. In the end, only a 4.3 cents per gallon tax hike was put in place. Such results and examples prompt scholars, such as public opinion experts Everett Ladd and Karlyn Bowman, after conducting a survey of Americans' attitudes toward the environment (1995), to label America as a nation of "Lite Greens."

In short, Tables 1-1 and 1-2 highlight how general support for environmental protection does exist, but depth of commitment is questionable (for example, Dunlap 1995). The shallowness of support for further dramatic action is underscored by the modest intensity of preferences, the low priority of environmental issues relative to other national concerns, the hesitancy to confront the costs involved, and the unwillingness to contrast beliefs on advocating government intervention with convictions of government incompetence.

Perhaps more telling in revealing the level of actual support for the environment is examining behavior that comes at a personal cost—those more able to pay the cost (those with higher incomes) are more likely to pay the price to support environmental quality. For instance, like the vast majority of advocacy groups, environmental organizations are typically comprised of those who are relatively well off financially (see Rothenberg 1992). Consider a survey of five major environmental groups—Environmental Action, the Environmental Defense Fund (now known as Environmental Defense), the National Wildlife Federation, the Sierra Club, and the Wilderness Society—conducted in the late 1970s that found that well over half of respondents in all but one case (the Wildlife Federation, 45 percent) reported family income over $20,000 at a time when median family income was closer to $17,000 (these data were collected by Robert Cameron Mitchell and are reported in Shaiko 1989, 1998; for similar findings, see Mundo 1992, Jordan and Maloney 1997). It is important to note that the reported income figure represents a lower bound, as individuals tend to understate their income on surveys; indeed, state-level analysis finds that membership in environmental organizations per 1,000 residents increases significantly with per capita income (Pashigan 1985) and that per capita environmental spending increases greatly with such memberships (Couch, Atkinson, and Wells 1997). Furthermore, consistent with the notion that environmental group membership is a normal good for which demand fluctuates considerably, support for these organizations declines significantly in bad economic times (Richer 1995; see also Hansen 1985). Similar inferences are drawn from a study by economists Matthew Kahn and John Matsusaka (1997) in which they examine the relationship between income and support for California referenda that involve environmental spending; they discover that, generally, voters in wealthier counties are more supportive of these initiatives.[10]

In the same vein, although the relevant data are more aggregated (the preferences and choices of many actors are summarized with broad measures) and other factors certainly come into play, residents of more environmentally progressive states tend to have higher median incomes. For instance, Figure 1-1 displays a measure of the "pollution subsidy" per capita using data from the early 1990s and state median income in 1990 (this measure is presented in Templet 1995; see also Ringquist 1993). When analyzed, there is a significant negative impact of median income on subsidy both in a bivariate sense (when the relationship between income and subsidy is examined without respect to other potentially relevant factors) and when a measure of state political preferences is incorporated (that is, subsidies for pollution decline when income increases even after controlling for a state's being conservative or liberal). Wealthier states are less disposed to support polluters. Illustrative of the importance of economic demand, the results of an analysis of pollution subsidy per capita as a function of median state income and the percentage of vote for the Republican candidate George H. Bush in 1988 show that a $100 increase in median income translates to about $1.40 per capita decrease in pollution subsidy; by contrast, a 1 percent statewide increase in support for Bush produces a $3.94 increase in subsidy level. More intuitively, a $250 increase in per capita income has roughly the same effect as the change in preferences reflected by a 1 percent decrease in Bush support. Reflecting the relationship between environmental demand and wealth, almost all states subsidizing pollution had a per capita median income below $18,000 in 1990. Other measures

Figure I-I State Income and Pollution Subsidies

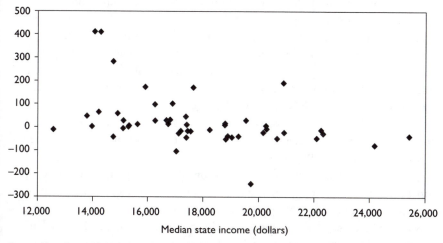

Sources: Templet 1995; U.S. Department of Commerce, *Statistical Abstract of the United States* (Washington, D.C.: Government Printing Office, 2000).

of state environmental commitment, such as those known as the Green Index, produced in the early 1990s by the Institute for Southern Studies, provide comparable results (Hall and Kerr 1991). For instance, an analysis corresponding to that for pollution subsidies, where the state's rank on the Green Index (ranging from 1 to 50) is substituted for the subsidy measure, finds that each $400 in per capita gross national product (GNP) translates into a one-place increase on the rankings. This equals a bit more than a single percent decline in the percentage of the vote in the state received by Bush. Analogously, studies employing measures of a state's fiscal health on its environmental expenditures draw comparable inferences. As one study puts it, "Understanding the fiscal health of a state provides a proven method for deducing its ability to acquiesce to interests pursuing finite resources" (Bacot and Dawes 1997, 358). Thus, the data illustrate that wealthier states are a good deal more environmentally receptive.

Corresponding findings are also discovered for nation-states. Some, such as those of economists James Murdoch and Todd Sandler (1997) in their analysis of voluntary reductions of chlorofluorocarbon (CFC) emissions, uncover a linear relationship between a nation's income per capita and pollution reduction as pollution declines with prosperity (a linear relationship means that pollution continues to be reduced at the same rate as per capita income grows). CFCs, useful for a variety of purposes, such as a coolant in automobile air conditioners, have diminished the world's stratospheric ozone layer by allowing higher levels of dangerous ultraviolet rays. Preventing emissions through substitution and careful recycling comes with significant benefits and costs.[11] Many other studies of environmental quality and development find a curvilinear relationship between income per capita and pollution reduction; in this instance, a curvilinear relationship means that pollution initially goes up and subsequently goes down, that is, with the so-called environmental Kuznets curve, pollution first rises with an initial burst of economic activity and then declines with modest per capita income growth (for example, Grossman and Krueger 1995, Rothenberg 2000). Even **post-materialist** scholars, those who emphasize values rather than economic circumstances, note that wealthier nations are better off on many environmental measures (Inglehart 1995).

In short, when a variety of evidence is considered together, there is ample reason to conclude that environmental quality is a normal good. Demand for a healthy environment roughly parallels the accrual of economic wealth. Not surprisingly, a broad societal consensus exists in affluent countries, such as the United States, for addressing environmental problems (and, as mentioned, these nations' environments do appear to be in better overall shape on many dimensions than they were 30, 50, or 100 years ago despite increasing populations and heightened consumption and congestion). Yet, among the citizenry, greater demand, if defined by an actual willingness to pay, is also a function of wealth to a significant extent. Analogous to most commodities, other factors such as political preferences do appear to mediate the relationship between clamoring for environmental quality and wealth, and thus influence the desire to purchase. Recognizing that environmental demand is not unique but roughly consistent with other kinds of goods is fundamental to understanding why demand has increased and how the policy process works.

However, such inferences do not imply that the political supply side responds mechanistically to heightened demand. The political system does not necessarily provide environmental quality in an efficient, low-cost manner in the way in which stylized views of the market (the stereotypical view in which the market works smoothly and without shortfall) for private goods might suggest. In other words, if demand for a private good increases, say for automobiles, the market may rather quickly and efficiently respond by increasing the supply of cars as cheaply as possible. In contrast, given that **public production** (production directly by government or heavily influenced by government policy) is involved and that the political supply side lacks the market's "hidden-hand," the relationship between demand and supply is mediated in its own special fashion as politics and all its vagaries become involved.

THE POLITICAL CONTEXT: CONSTITUTIONAL FOUNDATIONS AND THEIR POLICY IMPLICATIONS

Although the United States appears similar to its advanced industrial counterparts in regard to citizen demand for environmental quality, how its political system produces public policy to meet this demand is qualitatively different from many of them. The following two quotations—the first by two economists and the second by a political scientist—reflect the distinctive political system and its approach to public policy:

> "Fragmented" is the adjective that comes to mind when describing the U.S. pollution control regulatory system. The system is so complex and disjointed that no one person can fully understand it. It involves hundreds of laws and agencies and thousands of interested groups. It includes some general principles (such as the establishment of uniform national standards with states being allowed to set more stringent standards), but such principles only explain some of the laws and programs. Moreover, there are numerous exceptions even to the few principles that exist. (Davies and Mazurek 1997, 5; see also Davies and Mazurek 1998, Davies 1998)

> [F]ragmentation of power . . . [is] characteristic of American government. In the United States, political scientists regularly remind us, power is unsystematically divided between national and state governments, political parties are non-cohesive, and there has been high incidence (at least in recent decades) of politically divided government at both the national and state level. Such political fragmentation produces government and legislative processes that are unusually penetrable by interest groups and advocacy organizations, each seeking to make sure that regulatory policy will not be unduly influenced by their political opponents. Hence, American environmental legislation is implemented through many different agencies, national, state, and local [and it] often restrict[s] agency discretion by mandating detailed scientific analyses, deadlines for action, formal participation by business and advocacy groups, and judicial review . . . [and often] invite[s] private litigation to enforce environmental standards and hold agencies accountable (Kagan 1997, 874).

When examining policy from both an economic and political standpoint, the feature that fundamentally defines and distinguishes U.S. environmental policy is its relatively high level of political fragmentation. This fragmentation, by interacting with demand for environmental quality, has widespread ramifications for the way environmental policy is made and its eventual effectiveness.

Constitutionally, dispersed power defines American government. Most notable, of course, is that authority is separated among political branches at the national level and between the national government and subnational units in a federated structure. Nationally, the relevant actors vary in myriad respects, both in their powers and in their responsibilities. Presidents propose or veto policy and nominate appointees, legislators pass statutes and appropriations and approve appointments, judges decide a variety of constitutional and statutory issues pertaining to administrative processes, and bureaucrats promulgate rules and otherwise implement the specifics of public policy. Politically, presidents are responsible to a national constituency, legislators to a narrower geographic electorate, judges are protected from the electoral process once appointed, and, except for the small cadre of political appointees at the top of the administrative hierarchy, bureaucrats are largely insulated civil servants. Given these differences in authority and political situation, it is not surprising that fragmentation is the norm.

The federal structure leads to further fragmentation. Some responsibilities are reserved for national actors, others are delegated outright to states and localities, and still others are delegated to subnational governments following bargaining with national-level political actors. Relevant actors at different government levels are likely to manifest different preferences, produced by factors such as different sensitivities to local and national concerns, reinforcing the disjointed appearance of the policy process.

The resulting policy fragmentation contrasts with that found in many advanced industrial countries, where parliamentary regimes and centralized political systems result in more unified authority (see Moe and Caldwell 1994, Kagan 1999). Although concentrating authority does not necessarily produce more effective policy, as parliamentary regimes have their own institutional deficiencies and the combination of separation of powers and federalism its own virtues, the policy processes may be qualitatively different (for discussions, see Weaver and Rockman 1993, Moe and Caldwell 1994, Scruggs 1999).[12] For instance, in examining the representation of diffuse environmental interests (interests, typically pro-environmental, for whom the costs or the benefits of their actions are distributed widely among many actors), political scientist David Vogel summarizes the principal difference—or what he and his collaborators label the first-tier distinction—between parliamentary and separation-of-power systems.[13] As Vogel puts it, parliamentary leaders are more likely to be blamed for failing to keep commitments for collective goods such as the environment than those in separation-of-powers systems and are better at representing diffuse interests and resisting concentrated ones such as polluting industries while making policy. However, if they do not represent concentrated interests, such interests are not likely to have much political effectiveness. By contrast, presidential systems, given the separation of powers, provide diffuse interests with many places to influence policy. Because there are multiple points at which diffuse interests can try to affect policy, there is a greater likelihood than in parliamentary systems that interest groups ignored by the executive branch can, nevertheless, be influential (Vogel 1993).

Thus, American politicians are generally considered to be held less accountable for public policy than those in typical parliamentary regimes, which may provide U.S. elected officials with incentives to emphasize other, often inefficient, features of policy, most notably as related to distributional considerations. For example, politicians may not worry that they will be blamed for building cumbersome rulemaking provisions into a statute that serves the interests of supporters by ensuring that their interests are addressed. Such a lack of accountability tends to be particularly attributed to members of Congress, since they face certain collective action problems. Each member not only wants his or her colleagues to provide services for the good of the whole body but also possesses plausible deniability for the legislative actions of the whole. As such, numerous scholars assail legislators for their willingness to delegate authority with only vague instructions when more specific instructions are possible. In sending vague instructions to agencies for reasons beyond the sheer technical complexity of an issue, bureaucrats are put in a position to form alliances with private interests and to develop informational advantages to exploit their position for purposes such as budget expansion (for example, Lowi 1979, Schoenbrod 1993). Admittedly, others argue that, despite the tendency toward broad and seemingly vague delegation, legislators at least maintain more control over agencies and policy than such perspectives might imply (for example, Calvert, McCubbins, and Weingast 1989; McCubbins, Noll, and Weingast 1989; Bawn 1995).[14]

Additionally, widespread access to an institutionally fragmented political system allows many potential points for slowing momentum for change. Reflecting this, descriptions of policy formulation and adoption typically emphasize the length and almost randomness of the process and the multiple stages of the policy process, such as agenda setting, formulation, legitimation, implementation, evaluation, and change (for example, Kingdon 1995, Kraft 1996). Given this seemingly haphazard means by which policies get decided upon, implemented, and updated, it is not surprising that depictions of environmental policy note that how environmental risk is weighed, problems are defined, and strategies are adopted—and how the three, in turn, are integrated—is typically disjointed. For example, efforts at dealing with toxic cleanups have been deemed potentially less helpful for maintaining human health and the environment than those for dealing with water pollution coming from sources that are not at fixed points, such as agricultural runoff (for example, Fiorino 1995).

Another implication of how choices are made in this fragmented political system is that adopted policies tend to be highly durable and very slow-changing (on durability, see Glazer 1989). Durability, in turn, is a dual-edged sword, with positive and negative ramifications. Greater durability, for instance, facilitates private acts that will lead to successful public policy outcomes (on commitment problems, see, for example, Persson and Tabellini 1990; Glazer and Rothenberg 2001). Stated differently, to the extent that private actors have reason to expect that policy will be long- rather than short-lived, they are more likely to make the private investments required for ensuring a policy's implementation.[15] Private investment is often required for successful environmental implementation, such as for pollution-control equipment; durability thus proves to be a substantial asset. Conversely, economic actors investing to comply with a law prove an additional force to maintain a policy's credibility, making the status quo difficult to change even if it would mean a cleaner environment (for example, Zywicki 2000). Besides the U.S. political system's constitutionally built-in inertia, creating vested interests may make policies self-perpetuating. It can prove extraordinarily difficult to undo policies passed for private gain at public expense, discovered not to meet intended goals, or made obsolete by exogenous changes in the real world or in our understanding of how the world functions.

Change that does occur typically reflects compromise. Similar to durability, such compromise has both positive and negative characteristics. All things equal, incremental change will prove less disruptive and costly than dramatic change. However, when dramatic actions are needed, the tendency toward compromise is problematic. Additionally, compromise may produce policies and agencies that appear odd or even dysfunctional. This may particularly be the case given how politicians react to uncertainty about the political future (politicians in parliamentary systems are seen as having far less ability to build in such durability structurally). Political decision makers may worry about what will happen to policy if their successors have different preferences from their own. Thus calculating politicians can respond by designing policies more to ensure distributive consequences, to facilitate political control, or to ensure the interests of the enacting political coalition than to make policy flexible to changing conditions and efficient (McCubbins, Noll, and Weingast 1989; Moe 1989; Mashaw 1990; Hill and Brazier 1991; Moe and Wilson 1994; for a critique suggesting that cooperation may increase with electoral uncertainty, see de Figueiredo 1996). For example, in making new rules, agencies may be obligated to show that they have taken into account the comments of concerned parties, such as those favored by the enacting coalition of politicians.

As implied, the effects of fragmentation are felt throughout the various stages of the American policy process. They are reflected in how an agency is created structurally, how policies are written and whether and how they are revised, how a bureau implements policies, and how societal interests are organized and attempt to influence policy. Fragmentation thereby should result in policies that appear as fractured as the political system that creates them. Policies are often designed to provide distributional benefits more than effective policy outcomes; agencies' responsibilities and capacities will frequently seem mismatched and poorly integrated; and stated policy goals commonly appear difficult to attain in a competent and efficient manner.

OUTLINE OF ANALYSIS

It might seem intuitive to claim that environmental policy is unique, but it is best thought of as reflecting a general set of processes that influence public policies. Specifically, environmental policy can be conceptualized as a function of the interaction of economic demand and political supply. Using this framework makes both the growth of environmental policy and its distinctiveness relative to other advanced industrial countries understandable.

Demand for environmental quality has increased along with economic prosperity and greater awareness of environmental problems. In this sense, the experience of the United States corresponds to that of other advanced industrial nations. Although environmental quality typically involves government action, governments are neither well-functioning markets nor identical to one another. The capacity of the United States to produce environmental policy has risen dramatically, but it has been heavily influenced by the fragmented nature of the American political system, as epitomized both by separation of powers and federalism. Given the fragmentation built into the political system, environmental policy often has a disjointed if durable appearance.

The remaining analysis expands upon how economic and political contexts interact to make American environmental policy understandable. The next two chapters introduce both economic and noneconomic rationales for government intervention and provide a brief history of the evolution of environmental policy with respect to the periods before and after the Environmental Protection Agency's formation in 1970. The subsequent two chapters sketch what effects national political influences have on observed policies and supply an overview of how policy is implemented. Chapter 6 investigates the role of federalism generally and the conflicts that have arisen over issues of national versus local control. Chapters 7 and 8 consider how the contemporary environmental system has emerged by looking at government's role both as landlord—its control over roughly one-third of the land of the United States—and as environmental regulator stipulating guidelines for consumption and production choices via either rules and standards or market-based approaches, particularly with respect to the EPA. Finally, Chapter 9 summarizes the analysis and concludes by attempting to reconcile how a political system that often seems so misguided nevertheless appears to improve substantially elements of environmental quality. All in all, this book aims to provide a distinctive way to approach and to understand the calls for and the production of environmental policy.

KEY TERMS

Capacity (p. 3)
Collective action (p. 7)
Free rider (p. 6)
Inferior good (p. 5)
Normal good (p. 5)
Mitigation banking (p. 2)
Optimal provision (p. 6)

Post-materialist (p. 14)
Private goods (p. 4)
Property rights (p. 7)
Public production (p. 14)
Suboptimal provision (p. 6)
"Wise use" movement (p. 10)

2 Environmental Action, Environmental Caution: The Case for Government Intervention

A s stated in Chapter 1, the mere fact that demand increases for a good does not dictate that government will automatically step in to directly or indirectly produce it. Nor, given that rising demand interacts with political realities, does political action ensure that such production will even resemble the recommendations of politically indifferent policy analysts or benevolent social planners. Understanding American environmental policy requires identifying how increasing demand interacts with supply, particularly how distinguishing supply-side features such as political fragmentation affects the extent and nature of policy intervention given rising demand. More specifically, it is essential to detail the mechanisms that help to determine whether societal demands translate into government actions rather than fall upon deaf ears or precipitate private activity.

Although neither necessary nor sufficient for understanding why government might act, establishing the presumed reason for involvement is a first step in this direction. To this end, rather than jumping directly to how demands may induce actions from the political system, this chapter investigates the case for government intervention. Obviously, stated reasons for political interference to improve environmental quality may have little or nothing to do with the actual motivation for involvement or at least with the specific solution adopted. For instance, policies enacted legislatively by the federal government in 1977 that required coal-burning electric utility producers to install scrubbers to clean pollution had more to do with the narrow economic interests of high-sulfur coal producers and their political representatives than with a genuine desire to clean the air. Although allowing polluters to determine whether to install technology or to use clean coal might have produced cleaner air at a lower cost, eastern utilities and coal producers (high-sulfur coal is found in the East) emerged victorious over their western counterparts by making everyone install scrubbers, as the market for high-sulfur coal was strengthened and the production costs for western utilities were raised (Ackerman and Hassler 1981). Still, understanding why intervention might prove desirable provides a baseline for assessing what government actions are sensible and what are not.

TRADITIONAL JUSTIFICATION: THE TRAGEDY OF THE COMMONS

A casual discussion of why the political system ought to intervene can be found in Garrett Hardin's (1968) "The Tragedy of the Commons" (for a formal explication, see Moulin and Watts 1997). By Hardin's analogy, only a government's redirection of its citizenry's self-destructive behavior toward more productive activities can prevent environmental deterioration. In Hardin's depiction, the process behind the **tragedy of the commons** involves the inability of those with the right to consume resources to commit to limiting their behavior. The total destructive impact of a series of individual choices when such commitment is not feasible has dramatic repercussions for how resources get used and the social welfare of those consuming them. In this type of case, government can and should step in to solve the problem.

For example, a common pasture exists on which all herders can allow their cattle to graze. Like any such area, the pasture can sustain a given number of cattle over the long term. However, absent cattle owners' ability to coordinate their behavior and to limit voluntarily the number of their herd allowed, each producer lacks an incentive to limit his or her cattle grazing below what is profitable in the short run. Every farmer will incur only a small fraction of the cost of the long-term destruction that his or her actions cause at any point. As a consequence, each cattle farmer will overgraze the land. The effects may not be too damaging if only a few herders incapable of substantially expanding the number of cattle they graze are using the land, but the problem grows with the number of producers. With an increasing number of herders and cattle, the aggregate effect of individual choices is a gradual decline of the land's grazing capacity and the eventual destruction of the commons.

For those adopting this logic about using land effectively for production as a metaphor for understanding the environment, most environmentally damaging behaviors are the flip side of the grazing dilemma. Much like the commons example, each actor, such as a polluter, is unable to commit to behaving responsibly. However, the damage done to the environment is the result of adding a harmful element. Instead of removing something valuable from the commons (environment), such as those grazing livestock do when they reduce an area's grazing capacity, they introduce something harmful whose cost is shared by many (waste products dumped in international waters seems an especially apt example of polluting behavior precipitated by the existence of a commons). Analogous to a commons with few farmers, such actions are not particularly problematic on a small scale; for example, the effects of a few polluters living a subsistence lifestyle dumping into a vast ocean may be unobservable. But modern environmental problems emerge as both population and consumption grow. Unchecked behavior on the "environmental commons" reduces the ability to sustain its quality. Consequently, forceful government action is required to protect the environment.

As is the case with many metaphors, Hardin's powerful image is too simple to explain all the reasons for government intervention (for a critique, see, for example, the collection in Anderson and Simmons 1993). Actually, there exist a variety of potential **market failures**—the failure of markets to allocate resources efficiently—that present reasons for government intervention. Hardin's "Tragedy of the Commons" is just one example of market failure. Indeed, the solution to a standard commons problem typically involves specifying and enforcing property rights and not the more activist solutions often advanced for the market failures discussed here. However, given their complexities, these other market failures are not so easily solved by establishing rights and allowing market transactions. The three principal reasons seemingly justifying government intervention through environmental policy are public goods problems, the existence of externalities, and informational shortfalls (for a good discussion, see Kahn 1998).[1] Another reason sometimes provided for intervention may be labeled the moral imperative—despite a well-functioning market, situations may exist which government and its citizenry regard as intolerable. Any of these market failures or the moral imperative may be seen as creating the need for government intervention.

PUBLIC GOODS

Public goods are goods that are nonrivalrous and nonexcludable in their consumption. Put more simply, like Hardin's tragedy of the commons, excluding anyone from actually consuming such goods is impossible. However, whereas the tragedy of the commons is also driven by a rivalry over consumption concerning what are typically known as **common-pool resources** (that is, excludability is difficult but consumption is rivalrous; for an analysis, see Ostrom 1990), public goods are distinguished by one actor's consumption not limiting what is available to others because of the nature of the good. Environmental damage such as that caused by pollution may be a function of the failure to change behavior or to invest in environmental features that are nonrivalrous and nonexcludable.

In reality, most public goods are not "pure" public goods, but they do imperfectly approximate an idealized definition. For instance, clean air might be considered a public good—breathing pristine air takes nothing away from anyone else's breathing such air and, short of doing bodily harm, excluding anybody from enjoying the benefits of unadulterated air is hard. Yet, even air may not be a pure public good. If the air is cleaner in some places than in others and property values reflect such discrepancies, standard market processes may enable some individuals to consume cleaner air than others. Effects on peoples and nations can vary even when impacts felt worldwide make exclusionary behavior impossible. Global warming (the heating of the earth due to the production of greenhouse gases such as carbon dioxide) affects all populations because they are all subject to long-term global climate changes; however, individuals and nations may partially avoid its costs by investing in industries less likely to be harmed by global warming. For example, agriculture will be more severely affected by warming than other economic sectors (Schelling 1997, 1998; but see Mendelsohn, Nordhaus, and Shaw 1994). Even though one might argue that the industrial countries should pick up the financial tab for global warming because of their greater ability to pay, their historical use of fossil fuels, and moral considerations, the impact of warming is expected to hit the agricultural populations of the developing countries harder than those in the industrial- and service-oriented ones. Whether or not the industrial countries pay, they are somewhat excluded from the full impact of global warming because their industries are not harmed to the same degree.

Regardless, even imperfect public goods potentially provide normative grounds for intervention ("normative" refers to what ought to be done, rather than to actual reasons for what happens, which would be the positive grounds). Air quality or global climate may sufficiently approximate a public good so that domestic or international government intervention is justifiable. Given that exclusion from consuming such environmentally relevant goods (for example, cleaner air, more temperate weather) can be difficult or costly and that many can consume them because they are largely nonrivalrous, individual decision makers have a disincentive to take fully into account how their actions affect the provision of such goods unless they can coordinate their behavior with others. For example, they have a disincentive to make efforts to clean the air or reduce pollution at the source. As numbers of involved actors grow, voluntary coordination becomes extremely difficult. Typically, there is suboptimal provision of the public good, such as clean air (Olson 1965).

Put differently, because potential contributors cannot be excluded from consumption, they have an incentive to free ride, contributing less than they would allocate if consumption could be limited, and to enjoy the benefits of others' contributions. Of course, given that others are making the same calculations, all may be disappointed in the result. Consequently, the provision of public goods is likely to be less than desired and the cost of what is provided is likely to fall principally on **large members,** those receiving sufficiently high benefits from the public good that it is still in their interest to contribute at some level. If the good in question is a quality environment, such as an environment with clean air or unstressed by global warming, public good characteristics exclusive of government intervention can result in greater environmental harm than would otherwise be the case as costs and benefits are not fully internalized. The air may be dirtier or the temperature warmer than it would be if a private good were being considered.

As a result, there is a rationale for government to intervene to coordinate behavior with respect to public goods by having individuals contribute as they would after the removal of free-riding incentives. Although determining the size of contributions is a problem by itself, the existence of public goods is potentially—and has been argued to be in fact—a reason for intervention.

EXTERNALITIES

Externalities are market failures that provide the principal rationale for government intervention into environmental matters. They exist when the private costs and benefits of an action do not equal the social costs and benefits of the action (taking into account the sum of all costs and benefits imposed by and derived from the behavior). Although the precise definition involves many subtleties, here externalities are considered to be either the positive or the negative consequences, generally unintended, of an action that need not be taken into account by the relevant decision makers (whether they be citizens, firms, or even governments).

A host of examples of environment-related externalities immediately spring to mind. For instance, cigarette smokers who experience enjoyment of nicotine or satisfaction of nicotine cravings do not face the cost of making others sick or uncomfortable through exposure to secondhand or passive smoke (for example, National Research Council 1986, U.S. Department of Health and Human Services 1986; but see Misakian and Bero 1998). Similarly, a wealthy family constructing its dream house on a previously unspoiled wetland may realize few of the costs it imposes in threatening the quality of water that others drink, endangering the fish stocks that others eat, and disrupting the migratory patterns of bird species that others enjoy viewing. Another example would be a factory owner who generates revenues by producing goods that cause the dumping of industrial waste into an upstream body of water and is not held liable for reduced fishing stocks and diminished downstream water quality. Externalities can also affect the environment positively. For example, horticulturalists creating natural beauty by planting elaborate gardens may not consider others' enjoyment of the more visually pleasant landscape and the cleaner air. Similarly, profit-maximizing firms facing rising energy prices may adopt more energy-efficient production processes but not internalize the benefits others receive from breathing more easily.

In all these situations, each actor may act in a market characterized by externalities in which they do not fully pay the costs or completely realize the benefits of their actions. Why this happens when dealing with environmental characteristics is probably intuitive, such as with substances like air and water, whose natural flows often cross property lines and even national boundaries. Complex polluting behavior with many second- and third-order effects also makes it hard to realize costs and benefits, such as the application of pesticides whose impacts are felt throughout many layers of the food chain (for example, the pesticide DDT threatened bald eagles by accumulating in fish eaten by birds and, consequently, undermining the latter's reproduction by thinning their eggs). It is also natural to think that government should play an interventionist role in determining and equating private and social costs and benefits. Policy makers may mandate that polluters pay for the costs that they inflict on others or provide incentives to encourage potential producers of external benefits to behave as if they realize the benefits themselves. But moving forward from here, the government's role becomes a good deal more complicated than this description may imply; this conceptualization will be expanded in later sections.

THE RIGHT TO KNOW: INFORMATIONAL RATIONALES

The government may also have an interest in making sure that all actors have more accurate information before making any important decisions—whether they be to live in a particular neighborhood, build on a certain site, or accept a particular job. Private decision makers may lack sufficient data to make informed choices and to realize fully the costs and benefits of their actions as well as the choices of others (Magat and Viscusi 1992). The potential for such a rationale with respect to environmental issues is again probably intuitive, since keeping up with the latest research on environmental harm can be difficult for the average person. Even when information on risks is available, fully understanding technically complex choices can be difficult for decision makers, whether they be private citizens or even corporations (Slovic 1986). As such, providing easily digestible information may be desirable to ensure better decision making. Additionally, those holding valuable, environmentally relevant data may possess an incentive to withhold them from the public domain or to furnish them inaccessibly because easy availability might prove costly. In turn, such opportunistic behavior may undermine an efficient private market for information. Indeed, the potential for strategic withholding of information to subvert the market has been one critique of the advocacy (associated with the so-called Coase theorem discussed below) of allowing the free market's unfettered operation (for example, Farrell 1987).

Again, a litany of examples spring to mind. For instance, technical complexity may result in the average person's failing to recognize household hazards, such as the previously discussed threat posed by radon. Similarly, workers may not fully realize the long-term harm of substances that they work with—either because the issues are too complex or because employers have withheld the relevant information for fear of the cost and liability. Conventionally, if workers have an accurate understanding of the effects and the associated risks, they would have cause to obtain higher wages in exchange for accepting the risk, and a market shortfall would not exist (for example, Fishback 1992). Or companies might be loath to provide information about the release of toxics into surrounding communities because of fears that the adverse publicity generated, negative political responses, and rules defining liability would produce pressures to limit production, increase environmental safeguards, and provide financial compensation to those adversely affected (see the discussion of the impacts of the Toxic Release Inventories [TRI] in Chapter 7). Or individuals may find processing information about risks that will manifest themselves with extremely low probabilities difficult, for example, in choosing whether to live near sites where certain environmental toxics are stored. Whatever the reason for the inaccessibility of information, individuals nevertheless have an incentive to be aware of and understand the environmental risks they face.

In each instance, one might maintain that government intervention could produce more efficient outcomes. The provision of needed data at little or no cost to decision makers would result in more informed choices. Alternatively, market mechanisms could also solve many problems, although some proprietary private information might be withheld for strategic purposes. For instance, mortgage brokers wary of financing a suspect home and sellers of radon test kits attempting to expand their market both have incentives to make buyers aware of radon hazards. Unions trying to protect the rank and file or employers fearing civil litigation by workers have reasons to make employees aware of on-the-job risks. Lawyers looking for lucrative class action suits regarding the health effects of toxic exposure can also provide relevant data to those at risk, without any direct encouragement by policy makers. Despite these nonpolitical solutions, there may still be a need for the government to keep everyone honest by stipulating informational provisions. For example, the United States requires producers of toxics to report their emissions to the government, which then makes such data accessible to the public and their group representatives, so that residents know what is in the air that they breathe.

DO THE RIGHT THING: THE MORAL IMPERATIVE

Another, admittedly noneconomic, rationale for intervention can be termed the **moral imperative.** Some policies may exist that, although not motivated by an obvious market failure, are justified by the public and their political representatives as a reaction to behavior deemed too noxious to continue unabated. For instance, one perspective offered on the rise of modern environmental laws is that they represent a "republican moment," an instance in which public participation interacts with the effects of moral discourse or outrage, with respect to the public good (Schroeder 1998).

A good example of where the moral imperative comes into play involves secondhand smoke. In recent years, a movement to implement smoking bans in public places has been largely successful, even in some places where the rationale would seem to be the weakest. Whether in restaurants or aboard airplanes, this movement aims to combat environmental and health costs of secondhand smoke. Such bans are frequently promulgated on the grounds that nonsmokers have an inherent right to a healthy, smoke-free environment (for example, Rabin and Sugarman 1993). Yet, assuming that consumers and employees understand the costs of secondhand smoke and are consequently able to factor them into their choices, no obvious market failure would justify such a ban (Barro 1996).

Taking the example a bit further, if restaurant owners were unconstrained by government rules regarding smoking, they would possess the right to allow or prohibit smoking based on profitability and the knowledge that some smokers and nonsmokers correctly understand that secondhand smoke inflicts a cost on those breathing in these noxious fumes. They may reasonably assume that permitting smoking attracts smokers, repels nonsmokers, and raises labor costs because of a need to compensate workers for their exposure to smoke. Conversely, these owners likely believe that preventing smoking deters smokers from patronizing their restaurants, induces nonsmokers to use their services, and reduces wage demands. Alternatively, they will probably regard trying to placate smokers and nonsmokers alike as a middle ground, with corresponding impacts on smoking and nonsmoking customers and workers as well as perhaps some capital investment. They can install costly ventilation equipment to help clean the air of smoke, designate smoking and nonsmoking areas, or, maybe, offer inducements (such as reduced prices to smokers if their behavior is restricted or to nonsmokers if smoking is allowed). Given a diversity of preferences among potential patrons, a mixture of customer choices will likely arise as different establishments try to service various market niches, with some facilities advertising themselves as smoke free, others adopting intermediate solutions allowing smokers and nonsmokers both to face a minimum of inconvenience, and still others permitting unrestricted smoking. Illustratively, one telephone survey of more than 2,300 Massachusetts residents concerning the potential effect of smoke-free policies on (1) restaurant and (2) bar patronage finds that 61 and 69 percent of respondents predicted no change in their behavior, 30 and 20 percent predicted increased use, and 8 and 11 percent predicted decreased use (Biener and Siegel 1997). If such responses correctly measure future behavior, there is an incentive for some proprietors to ban smoking and for a lesser number to allow it. In this instance, not only may government intervention not be necessary as there is no market shortfall, but the market may create "havens" for all potential patrons.

Permitting the market to work and government to play a smaller role still sits poorly with many. Numerous individuals and organizations still push for smoking to be prohibited outright and have met with considerable success, as evidenced by the numerous restrictions on smoking in public places such as restaurants, buildings, and airplanes (for instance, on airline smoking bans, see LaRue and Rothenberg 1992, Krehbiel 1996; on tobacco control generally, see Jacobson and Wasserman 1997). The claims made in favor of such restrictive actions truly have a moral tone, since they aim to protect workers, children, and the inherent right to a smoke-free environment (arguments consistent with Landy's [1995] assertion that environmental policy has become rights-based). Ironically, children are still routinely exposed to smoke in other venues, such as in the home. Presumably there are workers who are willing to work in a smoke-filled atmosphere for a price, and, as smoking is legal, why the **utility** (for purposes here, the benefits or well-being) lost by smokers is trumped by that gained by nonsmokers is not immediately clear.[2] In other words, the ultimate rationale for smoking bans is likely, at least partially, that smoking is viewed as morally wrong and limiting the choices and the enjoyment of nonsmokers is inherently objectionable. Even if smokers pay for all of the externalities that their actions create (for example, through cigarette taxes providing for any and all health-related smoking costs), using cigarettes should be further discouraged. Interestingly enough, although many in society may hold smokers in low esteem, any number of others who harm the environment are certainly viewed with even greater contempt (for example, chemical companies producing toxic materials), suggesting that the moral high ground may be a significant rationale for government intervention.

Thus, another reason for the government's involving itself in environmental affairs is that some actions are so egregious (for example, producing toxics) that no documentation of market failure is needed. As one scholar puts it, "environmental questions . . . involve moral and aesthetic principles and not just economic ones" (Sagoff 1981, 1286). In other instances where there appears to be a strong argument for market failure, the moral imperative may dictate applying additional penalties (or building in added inefficiencies) by selecting one policy instrument over another (for example, bans on usage rather than the imposition of taxes that allow production) because the right individuals are being punished or the correct symbolic message is being transmitted. Indeed, with respect to policy instruments, one frequently encounters hostility to the notion that those willing to pay for the social costs of their actions should be allowed to harm the environment. A common argument employed against creating **pollution markets,** which involve changing decision makers' incentives and allowing them to act in their own best interests, is that they legitimize such acts. Thus, the well-known political philosopher and commentator Michael Sandel (1997) has complained that allowing the purchase of pollution rights removes the moral stigma from the act of despoiling the environment; similarly, philosopher Robert Goodin (1994) analogizes the selling of pollution rights to the sale of medieval indulgences to sinners to escape time in purgatory.[3] Along comparable lines, policy analyst Steven Kelman (1981, 154; see also Svendsen 1999 and the various replies in Stavins 2000a), after surveying the attitudes of environmentalists toward economic solutions to environmental problems, has passionately argued that:

> [m]icroeconomic analysis pays insufficient attention either to things that go on inside people's head or to the influence that the debates and decisions of political life have over people's values. The microeconomic agenda is one in which public policy making is denuded of some of the most important features of politics—politics in the best sense of the battle over what kind of society we are going to create.

In this vein, and although there are any number of possible explanations, the process of substituting market mechanisms for **command-and-control** policies, the utilization of rules and standards for regulation, has been time-consuming and painful.[4] Moral objections have only slowly given way even after positive market experiences.

SEVERAL NOTES OF CAUTION: THE CASE AGAINST GOVERNMENT INTERVENTION

Establishing rationales for government intervention is not tantamount to providing an unequivocal case that the political system *ought* to involve itself in environmental affairs. Rather, there are at least two reasons for caution. First, although there are economic justifications for government intervention, corresponding economic arguments do exist, particularly with respect to the all-important issue of externalities, for governments being only the definer and the enforcer of property rights. Second, even conditional upon accepting the idea that political intervention is called for, the means—typically referred to as the **instrument choice**—advocated for accomplishing such goals often varies significantly with what is realized in the real world (on the preferred solutions by economists, Pigou 1920 is the classic work; for more contemporary treatments, see, for example, Baumol and Oates 1988, Cropper and Oates 1992, Dijkstra 1999).

The Coase Theorem

The idea that government should define property rights, enforce contracts, and otherwise let the market function without interference is principally associated with the seminal work of Ronald Coase and his **Coase theorem** (1960; for discussions, see Milgrom and Roberts 1992; Kahn 1998; Viscusi, Vernon, and Harrington 1996; Farber 1997b; Medema 1999). Coase essentially argues that conditions exist under which externalities can be internalized into each decision maker's choice calculations. With the clear assignment of property rights, economically desirable choices will be made by the criteria of **efficiency** (that is, **Pareto optimality**—where increasing one party's welfare without decreasing that of another is impossible).[5] For instance, he illustrates that, under these conditions, the "right" (or economically efficient) amount of pollution is produced in a world in which there is a polluter and another actor suffering from its consequences. Put differently, the pollution level arrived at is that at which the benefits to the polluter from an additional unit of pollution are exceeded by the costs inflicted on others from that unit. Although who pays the costs and who receives the benefits is influenced by the assignation of property rights (Does the polluter pay off the actor subject to pollution or vice versa?), the choices made pertaining to how much pollution will occur are independent of bargaining power or upon initial ownership of rights. Rather, the possibility for free exchange leads to an efficient outcome regardless of the distribution of initial endowments. The combination of internalization of all costs and benefits with free exchange produces efficient outcomes as there is the Pareto optimal amount of production and pollution.

The working example from Coase's analysis (which is, admittedly, not specifically about the environment) provides further clarification of the theorem. There are two farmers on contiguous farms, one raising cattle and the other growing crops. No fence separates the properties and both farmers are trying to maximize their income net of costs. Not surprisingly, the first farmer's cattle wander over to the fields where the crops are growing, eat some and trample on others, and reduce the second farmer's crop output. In other words, the first farmer appears to inflict a negative externality upon the second farmer. Whether this seeming externality is allowed to continue, and to what extent, will cost one of the farmers income. What should be done and who should pay?

The intuitive initial reaction about who should pay seems unambiguous: the cattle farmer should lose income by taking the requisite measures to stop his or her herd from trespassing—either by spending money to erect a fence or paying the crop farmer to replace the crop loss. However, Coase argues that, under specified conditions, who actually pays is irrelevant because the outcome will be the same and efficient no matter what. In terms of efficiency or with respect to the ultimate solution adopted, whether the livestock owner is granted grazing rights that include the neighbor's fields or the crop grower is allocated the right to exclude cattle from roaming is irrelevant. If, for instance, the livestock farmer controls the right to allow the cattle to roam freely, the crop farmer can: (1) accept reduced crop production; (2) pay a fee sufficient for the cattle raiser to be willing to allow a fence that prevents the cattle from damaging his or her crops; or (3) pay a fee to induce the herder to reduce his or her number of cattle—lowering but not eliminating crop damage—to the point where marginal benefits equal marginal costs (that is, the value at the margin to the farmer of additional crops equals that of a single additional cattle to the herder). Conversely, if the crop farmer controls the right to order the rancher to keep the cattle away, then the cattle farmer could either (1) eliminate the herd; (2) pay for the fence; or (3) provide a fee to the crop farmer sufficient to allow the cattle free access, perhaps reducing the herd's size in the process in order to reduce the fee level. Although, clearly, who is better off depends upon whether the initial rights favor the crop farmer or the herder, the actual choice made between whether a fence is built or whether a cattle herd of a given size grazes where it pleases is identical under either allocation of property rights. Put another way, Coase shows that there are conditions under which seemingly obvious externalities do not exist, as costs and benefits are fully internalized into the choice process.

There is an obvious pollution analogue to this story. A nonpolluter and a polluter will efficiently choose how much pollution to allow regardless of whether the polluter has the right to pollute. Only who is better off varies. In the following example, a prospective factory owner purchases the land next to an upscale suburban home and starts polluting the air that the homeowner breathes. Despite the homeowner's moral outrage, whether or not he or she is positioned to tell the factory owner to cease is societally irrelevant as the same amount of production and pollution occurs. On the one hand, if property rights are well assigned and if it has been determined that the homeowner owns the air rights to his or her property, the factory owner can compensate the homeowner to be allowed to pollute at some level or shut down production completely. On the other hand, if the factory owner possesses the right to put what he or she wants into the air regardless of where the winds take it, then the homeowner can compensate the factory owner to reduce or eliminate the pollution or simply live with the consequences of the fouled air. Again, an intuitive reaction would be that the homeowner deserves clean air or compensation because the air was previously unspoiled, because the factory owner has chosen to pollute, or because nobody should pollute without at least paying an explicit price. But air cleanliness will be identical whether the homeowner or the factory owner possesses air rights. The same decision will be made about whether production is ceased or whether it continues at some level. The same amount of pollution will exist regardless of who is initially assigned which rights.

Obviously, as discussed with respect to the commons, under the Coasian scenario the government plays the role of "honest broker." It assigns property rights in a clear and detailed manner and enforces them so that it is universally understood that they cannot be ignored and will not be abrogated—it must be commonly recognized that government will uphold either a polluter's assigned right to pollute or the right of those subject to pollution to forbid the harmful activity and any contract stipulated between them. But there is no rationale for the polity to move beyond the honest broker's role and to adopt more activist policies, such as those routinely witnessed in the contemporary United States and other advanced democracies. Put another way, the government needs to assign rights, enforce contracts as it does for private goods and services, and proceed no further. According to the Coase theorem, the government does not need to decide environmental quality levels.

Although the Coase theorem advocates caution in seeing externalities where they might not actually exist, there are good reasons to believe that the conditions required for this bargaining solution to work are poorly represented in most cases of environmental degradation (a fact of which Coase was well aware). Such shortfalls might lead us to believe there is a rationale for government intervention.

The most notable problem with the Coase theorem involves **transaction costs,** which are simply defined as the costs of arriving at an enforceable agreement in an implicit or an explicit contract (for a discussion, see Farber 1997b; on some of the other problems associated with the Coase theorem such as strategic bargaining, incomplete information, and wealth effects, see Cooter 1982; Kahn 1998; McKelvey and Page 1997, 1999). Although there are numerous reasons for presuming the existence of transaction costs, two factors stand out:

- *Many actions can affect or be caused by large numbers of parties.* For instance, many upstream factories may dump pollution into a river and injure vast numbers of persons downstream, who, even if the costs being inflicted upon them are well understood, would find the problems and the costs of coordinating their actions to deal with this hazard formidable. Or air pollution may be generated by large numbers of fixed sources in small increments—for example, via the use of home fireplaces—making the cost of negotiating bargains almost certainly higher than the benefits.
- *Government may prove incapable of specifying all forms of property rights to the extent that would be necessary for the Coasian world to function smoothly.* Consequently, without other controls, there would need to be a constant process of government intervention, through courts or via administrative

agencies, for instance, for specifying the exact nature of property rights when new disruptions occur.

Nonetheless, despite all the difficulties associated with the Coase theorem, it serves at least two purposes in this discussion. First, it provides an ideal standard against which to judge real world outcomes. At a minimum, it highlights that, despite what those concerned with environmental quality might naturally feel, the "right" amount of environmental degradation, at least in terms of commonly accepted ideas of efficiency (not to mention technical feasibility, given production and consumption needs), is almost never zero. The Coase theorem is an interesting idealization of both the market and the government functioning in their assigned roles. Despite the attractiveness of this theorem, it is obvious that the real world does not correspond to its restrictive assumptions. But instead of disregarding the Coase theorem as "unrealistic," attention should be focused on how reality differs from theory and to what consequence (Dixit 1996).

Second, the Coase theorem underscores that there are reasons to exercise caution in assuming that detailed government solutions are always the answer. For instance, political scientist Elinor Ostrom and her colleagues have extensively analyzed, using real world situations (for example, fishing, irrigation, fuel wood, and groundwater) and experiments, the conditions and the rules by which the tragedy of the commons may be overcome (for example, small numbers of participants where monitoring of one another is easy) even without substantial government action for common-pool resources where consumption is rivalrous and not excludable (for example, Ostrom 1990; Ostrom, Gardner, and Walker 1994; and Ostrom and Walker 1997). For instance, they find examples of commercial fishers self-regulating themselves by agreeing to and enforcing rules (such as limits to where they can operate) aimed at reducing the tendency to overfish and enhancing the long-term viability of the local fishing industry (although, there are many examples where such overfishing takes place as well).

Instrument Choice

Another note of caution involves recognizing that economic rationales—by which the incentives of decision makers acting in their own best interests are changed through means for government intervention—typically emphasize adopting **market-based instruments,** such as taxes and **tradeable permits** and, perhaps, informational provisions, rather than specifying precise rules and standards, because market-based tools are deemed to be more economically efficient. For example, in a tradeable permit system, government may allocate rights to pollute and subsequently allow holders to trade them on an open market. Such a system potentially would provide those best positioned to reduce pollution cheaply an incentive to do so (since they will not need permits and can sell any that they might have); those who could not afford to reduce pollution might find it cheaper to purchase rights or even close down than to decrease their environmentally damaging behavior. Yet, as already implied, rules and standards associated with command-and-control have traditionally been the policy instrument of choice for politicians (on instrument choice, see Campos 1989; Hahn 1990; Spiller 1996; Stavins 1998, 1999, 2000b; Amacher and Malik 1998; Keohane, Revesz, and Stavins 1999). Nor, given an increase in the use of market tools in recent years, have those instruments chosen necessarily been those considered the most desirable by policy analysts.

In other words, the standard economic prescription to solving environmental problems involves equating social and private costs and benefits. The set of instruments recommended includes a variety of market-based tools, such as taxes and tradeable permits. Some solutions may be simple, such as placing a tax equivalent to the damage caused by given activities. For instance, if burning a gallon of gasoline produces pollution, then a properly set gasoline tax will help consumers realize the full costs of their actions. In turn, unless consumer demand is completely inelastic (that is, they will buy the same amount regardless of price), gasoline consumers will appropriately reduce the amount of fuel purchased by changing their behavior—whether by driving less, carpooling, buying fuel-efficient automobiles, or moving their place of residence closer to their workplace. Transportation producers will also have an incentive to provide new solutions to meet consumer demands for alternatives to the highly taxed gasoline—whether through investments in substitute fuel technologies, more fuel-efficient automobiles, or competing transportation modes such as mass transit. Alternatively, other market solutions can be more complex. For example, creating marketable permits allowing for a given level of pollution to be produced has proven more popular than taxes with politicians, perhaps because permits more effectively hide the costs of government intervention. Also, as already implied, efforts to provide information to relevant decision makers may be adopted. Yet, the basic premise remains the same: give those reacting in a manner that serves their best interests an incentive or an ability to internalize the costs and benefits of their environmentally sensitive actions.

To the exasperation of many policy analysts, and despite some movement toward adopting market-based solutions in recent years, governments in advanced industrial countries have relied more on standards and rules than on market-based solutions (for example, Stavins 1999). As might be expected, given their more unified political systems, certain western European parliamentary regimes have been somewhat more willing to implement market solutions (Anderson 1994). Many reasons could explain this peculiar preference for command-and-control, including politicians' desires to maintain control and garner political support through their right to intervene to address constituent complaints or to make policy credible and difficult to undo when occupants of key political offices change. Politicians may also want to create opportunities for specific interests (for example, corporations) to better themselves and to endorse the philosophic opposition to markets' seemingly validating negative behavior. Noting a substantial disconnection between implying that government ought to intervene, conditional upon adopting the right instrument, and the reality of instrument choice is sufficient grounds for caution in endorsing government intervention.

Additionally, and despite politicians' preference for standards and rules, in the few instances when they have adopted market instruments in the United States, tradeable permits, allocated to prior use, are their preferred solution (this ignores informational provisions for the moment). However, issuance of such permits may not always be the ideal choice. Two objections to this approach are (1) that when there is uncertainty rather than perfect information, taxes are sometimes the better solution, and (2) that when permits are used, although initial rights should be auctioned rather than allocated as a function of past behavior, rights have been assigned to those who previously inflicted more damage (Keohane, Revesv, and Stavins 1999). Again, for now, it is enough to recognize that a disjuncture between theory and practice in regard to instrument choice appears to exist and that it provides some additional grounds for caution in advocating government interference.

GROUNDS FOR ACTION AND CAUTION

There may be many reasons for government to intervene and create environmental policy. Despite the Coase theorem, few economic analysts, even the most vehement critics of contemporary policy, dispute the existence of a very strong case for a significant government role. Most economists, often critical of the general idea of government tinkering with the market, typically endorse intervention in environmental affairs. Paul Krugman (1997) states: "But my unscientific impression is that economists are on average more pro-environment than other people of similar incomes and backgrounds. Why? Because standard economic theory automatically predisposes those who believe in it to favor strong environmental protection."

To reiterate, and as the statement by Krugman, a well-known economist, highlights, by and large justifications for government intervention reflect standard reasons for political actors delving into policy affairs. Environmental quality may involve public goods for which consumption is nonexcludable and nonrivalrous and for which most actors have little incentive to contribute. Relevant actions may have externalities where the full costs or benefits are not internalized by decision makers, and the informational shortfalls on relevant issues may be of such magnitude (given the technical complexity or strategic situation) that government interference is often recommended. Absent any market shortfalls, a societal consensus can generate a moral crusade against polluters and potentially bring the government into the fray.

Yet, even without examining all the relevant political machinations very closely, the link between the normative rationale for the government to step in and actual observed political behavior should be viewed cautiously. Conditions may exist à la Coase under which seemingly obvious externalities will not exist; certainly, Coase demonstrates that the rationale for government intervention is not tantamount to saying that all despoiling of the environment is socially unacceptable. Additionally, the command-and-control solutions selected to implement environmental policy in the U.S. political system are not those typically designed by policy analysts to accomplish objectives at the lowest possible price. Rather, a heavy reliance on inherently cumbersome bureaucratic mechanisms rather than on the marketplace is favored in the United States. Even when market tools are employed, they are not necessarily the ideal ones.

Although it is not the point of this discussion to argue whether government ought to be involved in the business of regulating the environment, there is a plausible case for such intervention. However, particularly given that initiatives have deviated greatly from the usual analytic market prescription advocated for environmental ills, an understanding of how policies have evolved and what this path implies about the nature of environmental policy must be reached. Using both the economic and political contexts discussed earlier, the following chapters will address various government attempts to direct the course of environmental policy.

KEY TERMS

Coase theorem (p. 31)

Command-and-control (p. 30)

Common-pool resources (p. 23)

Efficiency (p. 31)

Externality (p. 25)

Instrument choice (p. 30)

Large members (p. 25)

Market-based instruments (p. 34)

Market failure (p. 23)

Moral imperative (p. 27)

Pareto optimality (p. 31)

Pollution markets (p. 30)

Public good (p. 23)

Tradeable permits (p. 34)

Tragedy of the commons (p. 22)

Transaction costs (p. 33)

Utility (p. 29)

3 A Brief History of U.S. Environmental Policy

Chapters 1 and 2 cover several basic propositions about environmental policy. Thematically, both societal demand for higher environmental quality and the fragmented nature of political institutions explain much of the production of U.S. environmental policy. Analytically, there are theoretical justifications for government intervention and creation of an environmental policy—which are accepted even among many of those who harbor suspicions toward political interference with the free market.

Given the contentions about demand and supply and the prima facie case for political intervention, what stance has the government taken in regard to the environment? The present chapter addresses this question by providing a brief history of environmental policy, emphasizing the period up to the creation of the EPA in 1970, with the years after 1970 only briefly discussed, to suggest how demand and supply interacted to broaden and deepen the environmental agenda. Subsequent chapters then focus on factors influencing how demand and supply combine in the present day to produce contemporary policy: national political forces (Chapter 4), determinants of policy implementation (Chapter 5), and the impact of the federal structure (Chapter 6).

THE EVOLUTION OF ENVIRONMENTALISM

Scholars typically define environmental policy's evolution in terms of periods distinguished by the changing goals and content of relevant initiatives and instruments, the nature of associated political conflicts, the government levels relied upon to develop and implement policies, and the principal proponents advocating and opposing intervention. For instance, Table 3-1 shows an adapted version of a schematic of environmental history developed by two respected political scientists (Costain and Lester 1995; other histories include Hays 1959, Dana and Fairfax 1980, Rothman 1998, Andrews 1999, Kline 2000). This chapter follows a similar organization in its discussion of policy evolution except that the "pre-environmental" period, encompassing the late eighteenth and much of the nine-

Table 3-1   Schematic History of Environmentalism

	1870–1920: Conservation-efficiency	1920–1960: Conservation-preservation	1960–1980: Environmental movement	1980–present: Contemporary
Issue scope	Preservation	Conservation	2d generation	3d generation
Dominant policy	Efficient use of resources	Multiple use of resources	Pollution abatement	Pollution prevention
Patterns of participation	Elite-dominated	Sub-government	Pluralism	Advocacy coalitions
Level of action	National government	National government	National government	Local and state government
Dominant concern	Environmental science	Technology development	Economics and politics	Philosophy and environmental ethics
Techniques of power	Technical negotiations	Corporate pressure	Middle-class politics	Participatory democracy

Source: Adapted from Costain and Lester 1995.
Note: Costain and Lester define the first environmental period as beginning in 1890; it is defined as 1870 here to correspond with the initial creation of America's national parks. The final environmental period is extended to the present.

teenth centuries, is also incorporated. As for environmentalism specifically, there are four stages of environmental policy evolution in the United States from 1870 to the present:

- *Conservation-Efficiency (1870–1920).* This era is typified by elite-driven attempts to induce rational government planning (hence the emphasis on technical negotiation in the context of elite domination). Sensible use of the nation's natural resources, rather than exploiting this bounty in an unthinking manner, was a defining goal.
- *Conservation-Preservation (1920–1960).* Although sensible employment of resources remained paramount, embodied by the idea of **multiple use**— defined as the "management of the public lands and their various resource values so that they are utilized in the combination that will best meet the present and future needs of the American people"—this period was characterized by increasing attention to preservation of resources, particularly to protection of lands.[1] The idea of multiple use was often combined with

sustained yield, the concept that a steady flow of resources should be available to those who consume them.[2] Decision making within the national government became more decentralized, prompting the rise of **subgovernments** (defined here as close, regularized, relationships between those being regulated, politicians, and administrators). Policy increasingly became subject to pressures from organized interests.

- *Environmental Movement (1960–1980).* The broadening of the issues, defined as second-generation issues, falling under the environmental umbrella (not to mention the creation of the EPA in 1970) was a highlight of this period. Politically, subgovernments broke down in favor of **issue networks** (defined here as porous, conflictual, and complex policy domains including many groups and other stakeholders with relevant expertise; for the seminal work on this concept, see Heclo 1978), leading to the depiction of participation as pluralistic. Environmental interest groups assumed increasing prominence, such as the ten major, mainstream, environmental groups that formed an alliance in 1980 (known as the "Group of Ten") because they feared the ramifications of President Ronald Reagan's (1981–1989) election. Efforts by groups such as those comprising the Group of Ten brought more middle-class influence to the forefront (Cahn 1985).[3]

- *Contemporary Period (1980–present).* A bit more difficult to define as qualitatively different from its predecessor, in many ways the contemporary period represents a continuation of the previous era. The increasing number and variety of issues encompass more localized concerns (for example, brownfields, or chemically contaminated industrial properties located in urban areas) and have been the impetus for grassroots mobilization (partially explaining why advocacy coalitions, environmental ethics, and participatory democracy are stressed). Supranational issues have also grown in importance as national governments struggle with such global problems as climate change and stratospheric ozone depletion.[4] Hence, this period is described as including third-generation issues. In more recent years, institutional capacities of states to intervene in environmental issues have also increased markedly if unevenly (Lester and Stewart 2000, Kraft 2000b), and the mix of policy instruments, in particular an increasing openness to informational and market approaches, has expanded (Portney 1999, 2000).

Not everyone will agree with this particular organization of U.S. environmental policy evolution, but the content of environmental issues, the formal goals pursued, the policies adopted, and the surrounding politics have clearly changed substantially throughout the years. Interpreting this evolution is the root issue.

Regarding such an interpretation, much of the history of environmental policy can also be understood as reflecting the interaction of increased demand for quality of life along with the development of the fragmented American political system and its institutional capacity. In this historical view, both technological constraints and possibilities relative to environmental threats must be recognized, in addition to the growing technological complexity of environmental problems and solutions and the increased technological sophistication of maintaining the environment, given increasingly diverse concerns. Nonetheless, focusing on societal preferences and how political institutions translate them into policy provides considerable insight into the pursuit of environmental quality in U.S. history. In this vein, as demand for government action has increased in a wide number of areas, the polity's role in environmental affairs meshes with broader developments in the American political system. Environmental politics, and the lack of it, is a manifestation of the development of the American political and economic systems. On the demand side, calls for environmental intervention increased during the late nineteenth century and most of the twentieth century in conjunction with economic development and related increases in competition for natural resources, congestion, technical complexity, understandings of environmental costs, and political organization of those with stakes in environmental policy. This development is broadly consistent with demands for expansion of desirable government-produced goods. Although the precise policies observed in the United States reflect the interaction of specific economic and political developments, experience in other advanced industrial countries suggests that heightened demand in the United States would almost certainly have precipitated a significant environmental policy. Lesser economic development (or basic constitutional differences) would, however, likely have led to a very different set of policies and administrative structures.

At the same time, on the supply side, government's willingness and capacity to intervene in public affairs, environmental and otherwise, increased. The national government rapidly expanded its portfolio of responsibilities affecting economic and social life. The form of such intervention, particularly with respect to environmental issues, reflected the increasing fragmentation of the U.S. political system, which, when coupled with the inherent problems of crafting policy in a democracy, created programs deviating considerably from the most efficient possible outcomes.

As a further complication, both demand generally and the preference for fragmented policy responses are, presumably, partially endogenous to these supply-side developments. Supply and demand feed each other in a mutually reinforcing manner, with fragmented policies leading societal interests to prefer the perpetuation of the status quo and similar solutions being adopted to other problems when they arise (for example, Zywicki 2000). Such self-perpetuating forces of demand and supply influence how much and what kind of policies are observed today.

Specifically, the interaction of supply and demand have helped produce a high level of intervention and policies noted for their fragmentation and lack of rationalization. At present, intervention in the environmental arena, both the management of government-controlled natural resources for environmental purposes and the regulation of consumption and production choices by economic actors, is pervasive. But diverse forms of environmentally relevant government action have been chosen, suggesting a lack of rationalization. A coherent, analytic vision of public policy appears lacking, which, beyond being a function of democracy per se, reflects the institutional structure of the United States and the related fractured nature of demand. Thus, on the one hand, environmental activism has corresponded to increased demand and increased government capacity; on the other hand, as this relationship is neither simple nor functional, the end product often appears dysfunctional.

BEFORE "ENVIRONMENTALISM": THE NINETEENTH CENTURY

Understanding environmental history requires a baseline of the world before government intervention. In the United States, the early years were not a period marked by conservation of natural resources or other environment-enhancing actions. (For a broader perspective, see Cronon 1995.) During most of the nineteenth century, environmentalism as understood in the twenty-first century was of little or no concern. On the demand side, there was a much smaller population that maintained a far more meager standard of living, consuming natural resources at a low rate relative to the nation's natural abundance. Concerns were far more likely to be directed toward using what nature had provided to achieve heightened economic prosperity than to environmental quality. There was little push for government involvement with environmental affairs and there were few worries about quality, even when objective conditions were problematic.[5] For example, consistent with the minimal development of the overall group system—few organized interests had formed to lobby over any set of issues—there was little organized political activity or lobbying for environmental concerns. The national government adopted a minimalist approach during the bulk of the nineteenth century and had a corresponding institutional capacity; changes in this situation occurred only slowly and haltingly after the Civil War along with changes such as rapid economic and industrial development and increasing demands from citizens and organized interests (Skowroneck 1982, Skocpol 1992, Sanders 1999).

Despite the small role played by government, the country's physical expansion resulted in the massive growth of the national government's natural resource cache. By acquiring many sparsely settled areas, the federal government at one point controlled roughly 80 percent of the land in the United States. There was an apparent mismatch. Although the national government neither faced societal demands to worry about the environment nor was positioned to do much with respect to conserving or improving the natural environment, it possessed an abundance of natural resources, including land, timber, water, and minerals.

In logical response, the government moved to rid itself of much of its bounty by giving it away, selling it at extremely low prices, allocating rights to exploit it at minimal cost, and providing required infrastructure such as roads (Libecap 1981, 1992). Consistent with the developing nation's materialist considerations (and despite the lack of confirming polling data or direct measures of demand), the American government's principal involvement in natural resource issues during the nineteenth century involved disposing of its holdings. Politicians promoted resource exploitation to encourage economic development rather than evidencing concern over environmental quality, resource conservation, or sustainable and efficient utilization of resources; the government preoccupied itself with facilitating consumption of resources by citizens and businesses (for example, Kline 2000).

The national government passed statutes through the years fostering the development and privatization of federal lands—typically in highly inefficient ways. At little or no cost to beneficiaries, public lands were placed in private hands, roads were built, water projects were constructed, and mining rights were allocated. Interestingly, only the **Mining Law of 1872,** which allows private actors to acquire mineral rights on open public land at extremely low prices (five dollars per acre) without regard to environmental standards or reclamation provisions, has been neither repealed nor dramatically amended (Humphries 1997; see also Chapter 7).

Given both the desire to have these valuable resources developed and the national government's lack of institutional capacity, it should not be shocking that much of this era of resource disposal during the nineteenth century (especially the second half) was marked by instances of impropriety and scandal (for example, Cubbage, O'Laughlin, and Bullock 1993). Indeed, national government corruption was a general problem in the post–Civil War era (see Thompson 1985). For instance, a company interested in acquiring title to vast tracts of land might build a log cabin to meet statutory requirements and move it from one land claim to another to receive property rights for settling the land in each instance. As with many progressive initiatives, widespread accusations of corruption and waste sowed the seeds for later government intervention.

Nonetheless, the government disposed of much of its natural resources. Reflecting such efforts, by transferring more than 1.1 billion acres into private hands, the federal ownership stake has declined to less than 30 percent of all land at present (Bureau of Land Management [BLM] 2000). Almost 300 million acres alone were distributed under homestead laws designed to develop vacant agricultural areas. Such laws, in place from 1862 to 1935, allocated plots in the American West to citizens or those intending to become citizens, conditional on settlement or cultivation.

In short, corresponding to the public's apparent demands for increased economic activity and government's small role at the time, politicians disposed of much of their resource abundance during most of the nineteenth and into the early twentieth centuries. Besides giving resources away, the federal government did facilitate development by providing a few services, such as roads and bridges, consistent with its traditional activities. Of course, not everything was disposed of. Particularly in the sparsely populated American West, the federal government to this day retains considerable territory (not to mention isolated Alaska, roughly half of which remains in the public domain), providing the foundation for enduring regional disagreements. "Environmentalism" began emerging only when debates began over what to do with such territories and their bounty.

BEGINNINGS OF ENVIRONMENTALISM: 1870–1920

From 1870 to 1920 the United States underwent a radical transformation. America's population soared from just under 40 million to over 105 million people. Although the exact numbers are debated, standard estimates of the per capita gross national product (GNP) indicated about a threefold increase, which means that the consumption level of a growing and wealthier population spiraled upward (Kuznets 1961). The resulting aggregate consumption increase of about 750 percent from 1870 to 1920 prompted fears that goods, such as forestry products, would become scarce. These changes, as well as political corruption, generated worries about employing resources sensibly and, to a lesser extent, preserving some environmental qualities, as at least certain societal elites gradually recognized that human development could damage lands.

This development coincided with the intensification, albeit piecemeal, of national government activities in the late nineteenth and early twentieth centuries. The federal government continued to do more of what it had done previously, such as building roads. Additionally, it began to absorb responsibilities from state governments, through a variety of statutory and regulatory initiatives, symbolized by railroad regulation and the Interstate Commerce Act of 1883. The government also assumed new previously ignored obligations, for example, the creation in 1906 of the Food and Drug Administration to regulate product safety and efficacy. With all these new responsibilities, the measurable size of government,

Figure 3-1   Growth in Federal Employment, 1871–2001

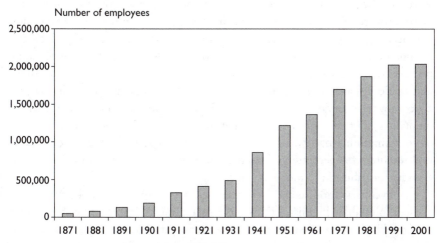

Number of employees

Sources: U.S. Department of Commerce, *Statistical Abstract of the United States* (Washington, D.C.: Government Printing Office, 1971–2000); U.S. Department of Commerce, *Historical Statistics of the United States* (Washington, D.C.: Government Printing Office, 1975); and Office of Personnel Management (http://www.opm.gov/feddata/html/empt.htm).
Note: Data measure executive branch employment minus Defense Department employment.

which had been slow to increase during the early years of the Republic, grew at a considerable pace. From 1871 to 2001, civilian employment in the federal bureaucracy increased more than forty times while the U.S. population went up roughly sevenfold. Employment was less than 50,000 in 1871 (roughly three-quarters being employees of the post office), grew to more than 300,000 by 1911, expanded to about 500,000 by 1931, and broke 2,000,000 by 1991 (see Figure 3-1). Furthermore, employment increases coincided with institutional changes, such as the initial development of the contemporary Congress (Cooper 1970), the inception of the civil service system (Johnson and Libecap 1994), and the emergence of the modern-day interest group system (Thompson 1985, Hansen 1991).

In this light, effectiveness-oriented cries for intervention into environmental affairs were consistent with broader "top-down" movements championed largely by middle- and upper-class interests that were defining government activities at the end of the nineteenth and the beginning of the twentieth centuries (Knott and Miller 1987). One of these movements, Progressivism (roughly 1890–1920), advocated implementing **scientific management**—the application of efficient, businesslike techniques to government endeavors—to use resources more effectively. Consistent with this ethos, preserving environmental and aesthetic qualities took a backseat to managing resources.

As such, two competing strains of environmentalism, under the rubric of conservation and preservation, respectively, emerged. Conservationists voiced utilitarian concerns about the wasteful consumption of the resources that government had been hastily giving away for most of the nineteenth century. They lamented the potential for timber shortages, pointed out the dire ramifications for economic prosperity, and insisted that government employ resources in a wise and sustainable fashion—both wise use and sustainable yield became conservationist mantras. By contrast, preservationists, essentially the forerunners of modern-day environmentalists, warned about the loss of nature in its most pristine state. They advocated maintaining natural and aesthetic qualities by setting aside important natural resources for perpetuity. The environment was to be valued for itself rather than its contribution to monetary gain.

Both conservationists and preservationists had a prominent spokesperson who assisted in establishing institutions for perpetuating and promoting their beliefs. Gifford Pinchot, the first American to receive professional forestry training in Europe, served as the primary conservationist proponent. He ultimately succeeded in establishing the United States Forest Service (USFS), writing the 1897 Organic Act laying out the agency's responsibilities, and situating the bureau in the congenial atmosphere of the USDA. He also helped to set up the Yale School of Forestry (with a gift from his well-endowed family) for training employees of the USFS imbued with the right tools and motivations to serve the agency's goals. John Muir, a Scottish immigrant from a farming family, was the main symbol of preservationist thought and ideals and a driving force in the formation of the National Park Service (NPS) in 1916 as the government institution with a preservationist ethos. Muir also was an influential force in the creation in 1892 of the Sierra Club as a private organization dedicated to preservation. Pinchot and conservationism won out over Muir and preservationism. The latter were relegated to a significant but decidedly secondary role throughout the first half of the twentieth century.

Like many policy initiatives, and consistent with constitutional fragmentation as well as with modest demand, environmental policy evolved slowly and haltingly during this period. Although it is difficult to date precisely the origin of the movement toward injecting the national government into environmental affairs, the creation of Yellowstone National Park, the first national park, in 1872 is a good starting point. More of a preservationist than a conservationist act, it was nevertheless a significant milestone. Yellowstone was the first of a series of such parks designated over a four-decade period, with the movement to set aside lands picking up speed in 1906. With passage of the 1906 Antiquities Act, Congress authorized the president to set aside lands, using the smallest possible area, that were historical landmarks or scientifically important, thereby streamlining the process (see Leshy 1998).[6]

The first significant move toward the conservationist goal of slowing massive land disposal is probably the passage in 1891 of the General Revision Act, which allowed the president to set aside lands as forest reserves (a right that would be revoked in 1907 by a Congress wary of a chief executive with too much power). Despite controversies over the act's application, fifteen parcels, totaling in excess of 13 million acres, were protected prior to the USFS's Organic Act in 1897, which effectively situated these reserved lands under the agency's control with the stipulation that they be protected, water flows be secured, and a continuous supply of timber be assured (note that the USFS was still within the Department of Interior [DOI] at this point). During Theodore Roosevelt's administration (1901–1909), the president worked closely with Pinchot, and such reserves almost quadrupled in size. The shift of the USFS and its lands to the USDA acted to further promote wise use (other lands remained the province of the DOI).[7]

Another decade would pass before preservationist interests achieved a governmental presence of their own with the creation of the National Park Service. Although the broader cause for this success can be linked to rising demand and the evolution of government and its institutions, the immediate precipitating event was a renowned battle that pitted those who believed in protecting such natural wonders as Yosemite with those who sought water for economic development. Specifically, in 1913, preservationist forces lost a political battle in Congress to ward off construction of a dam in Yosemite as part of an aqueduct system to funnel water to San Francisco. Construction of the Hetch Hetchy Dam in Yosemite National Park, putting a pristine valley under water in an area deemed so environmentally noteworthy, was the result. This catalytic event served as a rallying point for those believing that national parks remained vulnerable to wise use resource demands. The preservationists demanded a bureau dedicated to protect national parks and their resources. In 1916, in the aftermath of the controversial decision to build the dam and a splintering of preservationists and conservationists, national parks, assorted monuments, and a miscellany of other protected lands were retained in the DOI under the aegis of the newly created NPS to, according to its Organic Act, protect "the scenery and the natural and historic objects and the wild life therein and to provide for the enjoyment of the same in such manners and by such means as will leave them unimpaired for the enjoyment of future generations." The modern park system now had an institutional advocate.

Nonetheless, during this era, there was only modest demand for environmental protection, particularly of the preservationist variety. Consistent with this, the elite-driven conservationist movement largely won out over the elite-driven preservationist movement. Still, and corresponding to the evolution of organized groups and political institutions generally in the United States during this time, this period witnessed the founding of government agencies and the establishment of a variety of new environmentally relevant programs. In short, whatever the peculiarities of the policies put in place, the level and nature of demand for environmental protection roughly corresponded to the nature of political supply.

INCREASING SUPPLY AND FLUCTUATING DEMAND: 1920–1960

What is seen as the second major period of environmentalism, 1920–1960, is marked by several interesting features. Perhaps the most notable is that many environmentally relevant innovations were clearly tied to the expansion of government activity and institutional capacity more broadly. Indeed, numerous environmentally important policies during the New Deal era appeared to be little more than by-products of efforts to jump-start the economy and get people to work. Another notable feature, which occurred in the period of consumption and prosperity following World War II, is the seeming growth in demand for both natural resources and additional environmental protection. This put pressure on political decision makers to strike a balance.

Thus, particularly with the advent of the Great Depression and the election of Franklin D. Roosevelt (1933–1945) and a large Democratic congressional majority in 1932, many environmentally relevant policies were apparently produced by more economic considerations. Primarily designed to stimulate economic activity, environmental policies promoted environmental values as a byproduct. Confronted with the harsh economic hardships of the depression, the mass citizenry and political and economic leaders alike concerned themselves more with the economic decline and great future uncertainty of the time than with environmental quality.

Nonetheless, Roosevelt's New Deal, the spate of programs initiated to kickstart the moribund economy, spawned several important changes in environmental policy. Two of these programs, the Taylor Grazing Act and the creation of the Grazing Service within the DOI, addressed rapidly deteriorating public lands, long used by private livestock producers with no government oversight. The act stipulated uniform grazing fees, not even adjusting for features making one parcel of land more valuable than the other, originally at five cents per *animal unit month* (AUM), the forage needed to sustain one cow and calf, one horse, or five sheep or goats for a month. Not only had the livestock industry suffered like so many others during the depression but drought, moral hazards associated with ill-defined property rights, and commons problems undermined range quality (for example, Watts and Laurence 1994). **Moral hazard** is the proclivity of those holding insurance to reduce the care that they take to prevent losses for which they will be compensated (for example, Milgrom and Roberts 1992); here, it involves incentives of ranchers to invest less in caring for the land than they would if property rights were fully defined and there were no commons problem, since they do not necessarily accrue the benefits and costs created by their actions. It was hoped that in implementing the Taylor Act, the Grazing Service, which evolved into the modern-day Bureau of Land Management (BLM) when it and the General Land Office merged in 1946 during a government reorganization, would make grazing lands more productive and sustainable by eliminating the commons and by defining property rights (Libecap 1981).[8]

Another prototypical New Deal program was the formation in 1933 of the Civilian Conservation Corps (CCC), which put over a half million people to work on conservation-related projects. Planting almost three billion trees and building roughly one million miles of roads and trails (Andrews 1999), the CCC expanded labor force participation in times of extremely high unemployment. Other typical New Deal conservation policies included large-scale water projects, river basin management (epitomized by the creation of the Tennessee Valley Authority [TVA]), and soil conservation efforts. Also notable was the creation in 1940 of a predecessor to the U.S. Fish and Wildlife Service in the DOI to deal with issues such as wildlife conservation.

For the United States, this world changed dramatically after the end of World War II in 1945. The switch from wartime to peacetime was associated with a booming population, dramatic consumption increases, and a surge in individual mobility. Environmental ramifications were myriad. Tangibly, trends such as suburbanization meant an increase in housing construction, which consumed natural resources, such as timber, at an extraordinary rate. At first, the national government was responsive. For example, timber harvests from the national forest system increased rather steadily and substantially (sixfold) from 1940 until the middle 1950s (see Figure 3-2; Chapter 7 also elaborates on the policies behind this increase and the dramatic decline in the 1990s). Similar to this demand for natural resources, the desire to enjoy the nation's natural treasures, such as its national parks, soared: a precipitous postwar surge in number of visitors, only leveling off in the mid-1980s, put great pressure on the existing infrastructure (Figure 3-3). Less concretely, there is little doubt that demand for environmental protection, heightened consumption and competition for resources, and environmental awareness rose in the context of increasing prosperity (for example, Hays 1998). Environmental awareness, for example, is symbolized by Rachel Carson's *Silent Spring*, (1962) which discusses the dangers of growing pesticide use. It is also reflected by the federal government's first attempts, albeit rather ineffectual, to deal with issues such as air and water pollution (to be discussed in the next section).

Figure 3-2 Timber Harvests from National Forests, 1940–1997

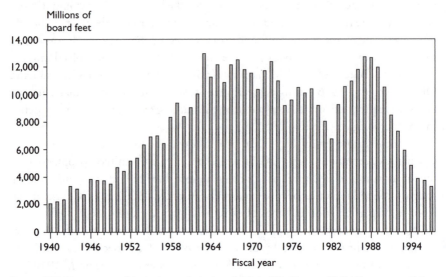

Sources: U.S. Department of Agriculture, *Agriculture Statistics* (Washington, D.C.: Government Printing Office, 1946–2000).

Note: Commercial and cost sales and exchanges; excludes free-use timber.

Thus, the period 1920–1960 was marked by many important changes—the role that natural resources played, the level of desired consumption, and concern for environmental quality all changed. Additionally, over these years, as implied in Table 3-1, the political foundations of environmental and nonenvironmental policies continued to evolve as institutional capacity expanded and fragmented. Environmental issues developed more of a modern-day political, "bottom-up," flavor and were often claimed to be functions of subgovernments—products of generally symbiotic relationships between agencies, producers (for example, ranching, logging, and mining interests), and congressional committees. Such politics reflected the development of interest groups, as organizations such as the National Wildlife Federation (1936) and the Wilderness Society (1935) were formed. Congress also further developed institutionally. Changes such as the growth in importance of committees and the increased resources (for example, larger staffs) controlled by individual legislators as authority became decentralized within the legislature highlighted this development. Agencies such as the BLM and the USFS, especially the former, would get the reputation of being "captured" by producer interests as they formed symbiotic alliances with the agencies and the increasingly influential committees (for example, Kaufman 1960, Culhane 1981; for the classic discussion of capture, see Huntington 1953).[9]

Figure 3-3   Visitors to National Park System, 1940–1998

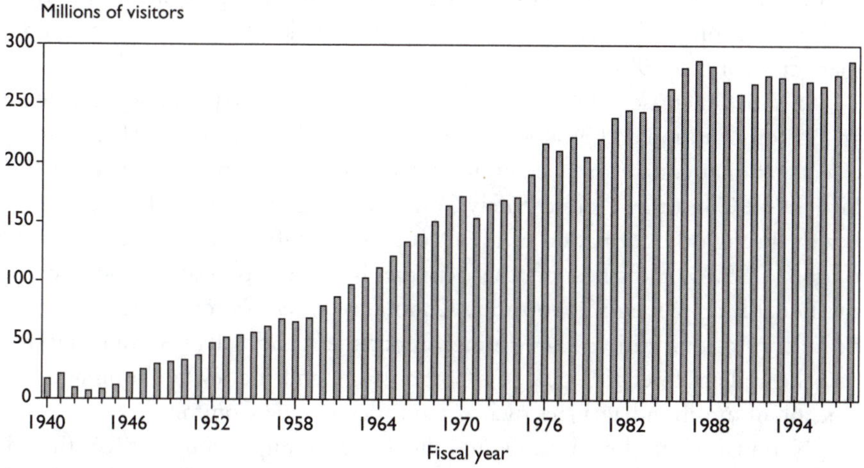

Millions of visitors

Source: National Park Service (http://www2.nature.nps.gov/stats/).

In brief, on the demand side, heightened consumption represented a threat to environmental quality. At the same time, the increased prosperity fueling such consumption also sparked concern about the environment. Institutionally, the government and its institutional capacity grew in general and with respect to the environment. During the New Deal, when there was little demand for acting on the environment, relevant policies were passed as part of efforts to keep the economy going. Afterward, the government tried to deal with the strains created by increasing consumption levels. With rising demands and increased willingness of the national government to assume an activist role, the stage seemed set for government to transform its relationship to the environment.

THE ENVIRONMENTAL MOVEMENT AND THE EPA: 1960–1980

During the early 1960s, changes brought about in the postwar era created a large shift in demand for political action on the environment. This coincided with the national government's further increasing its capacity and rapidly expanding its societal reach. Over time, such institutional developments increasingly influenced citizens' everyday lives, with the Great Society of the 1960s (the flurry of social welfare programs passed in the aftermath of John Kennedy's death), Lyndon Johnson's landslide 1964 election, and the creation of a large sympathetic Democratic congressional majority constituting the hallmark of increased activism. A quantum jump in the reach of environmentally relevant policies and the extent of environmental regulation and other social regulation—the managing of consumption and production choices as a result of claims of market failure—followed soon thereafter (Bryner 1994).

In short, increased environmental intervention occurred as policy expanded and as consumption and production were more regulated. The latter led to more direct national control over environmental affairs: consumer products via the birth of the Consumer Product Safety Commission (CPSC), workplace safety and health through the formation of the Occupational Safety and Health Administration (OSHA), and a host of other activities by the creation of agencies such as the Equal Employment Opportunity Commission, the National Highway Traffic Safety Administration, the Mining Enforcement and Safety Administration, and the Federal Energy Regulation Commission, and the revitalization and expansion of moribund agencies such as the Federal Trade Commission.

National political institutions and the interest group community continued to evolve as government came to influence more directly increasingly varied and technically complex topics such as product safety and the environment. National political institutions became more developed, capable, and specialized. Congress, for instance, evolved into an institution whose increasingly career-oriented members became more specialized in policy areas, controlled large staffs, belonged to powerful congressional committees, and relied less on their political parties. The presidency became analogously institutionalized, developing considerably more expertise and capacity in policy areas. The creation in 1969 of the Council on Environmental Quality (CEQ), which is controlled by the president and is designed to furnish environmental expertise, as an analogue to the long-established Council of Economic Advisors, reflected an increasing tendency to speak of the chief executive in institutional rather than in personal terms. As legislators and presidents became more institutionally capable, policy debates became even more politicized as each struggled to control bureaus with delegated authority. Such battles were over everything from structural choices over how agencies would be organized to agency appointments, budgets, and legislative statutes. Interestingly, the courts, led by the U.S Supreme Court, also developed a more activist impulse at times and exhibited a willingness to intervene in policy affairs, despite not necessarily keeping up with the increasing technical complexity of the issues (for example, Stewart 1975).

The interest group community expanded both in its numbers and its diversity. Perhaps the most notable compositional shift was the increasing prominence of so-called **citizen groups,** explicitly purporting to represent the public interest and to which membership was not confined to occupation or industry (for example, Berry 1977, Walker 1991). This important development for environmental policy introduced a wider variety of relevant issues and political tactics than previously found. Just as many—especially those with an environmental focus—have portrayed the 1960s as a period in which public interest groups moved onto the Washington scene or expanded, the universe of new groups with pro-environmental mandates included the Environmental Defense Fund (1967), the Friends of the Earth (1969), Greenpeace USA (1970), and the Natural Resources Defense Council (1970). Additionally, many prominent environmental groups with lengthier histories substantially increased their political activity, not to mention their memberships (for example, Vogel 1989). As symbolized by the first Earth Day, held in April 1970, the census of environmental organizations and the diversity of the group system increased substantially.

Thus, scholars went from viewing the modern group system as composed of narrowly based communities with common interests (that is, parts of subgovernments) to more porously defined and diverse issue networks. Perceptions of environmental organizations and associated policy processes evolved along these same lines (see Berry 1999). Whereas analysts had talked of congressional subsystems as defining environmentally relevant policy in earlier years (see Table 3-1), such policy was increasingly viewed as fluid and variegated, which is why politics of this era have been characterized as pluralistic.

The creation of the EPA reflected and accelerated this more free-form type of politics. (The early 1960s also saw substantial land management reform, notably the Multiple Use and Sustained Yield Act of 1960 and, especially, the Wilderness Act of 1964, which reflected, and provided for, a more diverse political environment; see Chapter 7). In merging and extending a large number of disparate operations, the EPA forged a broad, nationwide set of policies cutting across many interests and industries. The metamorphosis of environmental policy from managing specific industries (such as timber, ranching, and mining) to creating the rules and guidelines for both economy and society fundamentally changed the nature of the political process. The EPA's inception, although representing neither the first nor the last word in modern environmental policy, proved a galvanizing event that helped shape future outcomes as a result of the choices made and not made at the time.

Like many other agencies (although to a greater extent than most), the EPA did not spring up out of nowhere. It partially combined bureaucratic operations located elsewhere in government, such as in the Departments of the Interior and Health, Education and Welfare. Consistent with changes in post–World War II America, the national government had slowly begun broaching the idea of attacking water and air quality problems (see Chapter 8). These initial efforts generated little strident opposition, because they included **pork barrel/public works projects** that won supporters. (Pork barrel/public works projects are programs for which benefits are concentrated, typically geographically (for example, a congressional district), and are outstripped by costs, which are usually diffusely distributed [for example, across all congressional districts].) These edicts also lacked enforcement "teeth," and ultimate control essentially remained at the state level.

Before 1970, environmental statutes provided carrots rather than sticks in their efforts to clean up the nation's water and air. In 1948 Congress passed the Federal Water Pollution Control Act, followed by the Water Pollution Control Act of 1956, the Water Quality Act of 1965, and the Clean Water Restoration Act in 1966. These acts provided grants for the construction of water treatment facilities, rather than fines for not living up to clean water standards. In 1967 the first Clean Air Act (CAA) was passed. It required that states establish air quality standards based on scientific evidence provided by the federal government and that federal authorities set feasible automobile emission standards; state standards and enforcement were subject to federal approval. However, with an inadequate enforcement apparatus, this statute's inevitable failure was quickly apparent.

Finally, in 1969, with heightened environmental awareness, the demand for substantial changes building, and politicians eager to jump on the bandwagon, Congress passed the National Environmental Policy Act (NEPA). NEPA mandated in broad language the production of environmental impact assessments for public projects. As Section 101 of the act states, "It is the continuing policy of the federal government . . . to create and maintain conditions under which man and nature can exist in productive harmony." Thus began a process that produced much controversy over the years—although a controversial 1978 court decision known as *Vermont Yankee* [435 U.S. 519], has abated NEPA's impact somewhat—as such assessments and related judicial appeals often delayed, others would say obstructed, change (on NEPA, see Taylor 1984, Clark and Canter 1997, Caldwell 1998).

These incipient efforts in declaring increasingly nationalized goals and obligations could be easily criticized on many grounds. Among them, and most obviously, policies were not comprehensive and bureaucracies were not coordinated. Also, environmental quality often appeared to be a secondary priority to political considerations, and enforcement efforts lacked credibility. Given such shortfalls, although those representing the interests of business and others who gained a stake in the fragmented status quo may have been wary of the additional costs and distributional impacts of change, environmentalists wanted organizational structure rationalized, legislation strengthened, and enforcement invigorated.

The EPA, the Clean Air Act of 1970, and the Clean Water Act (CWA) of 1972 launched a new era of modern environmental regulation. Despite the institutional and statutory apparatus being ill-equipped to deal with environmental problems, politicians had strong incentives to appear pro-environment. On the surface, these three events marked a new direction for the federal government to create policy, yet each, in its own way, had substantial congenital flaws.

The EPA did not arise through a typical statutory process but via an internally contentious presidential reorganization that, nonetheless, required congressional acquiescence. The EPA's creation during the administration of Republican president Richard Nixon (1969–1974) was the product of an intensely political game played out between Nixon and his Democratic opponent, Sen. Edmund Muskie. There was a substantial movement to rationalize government structure to improve policy (for example, see the report of Nixon's Ash Council, President's Advisory Council on Executive Organization 1971). Although the administration reached no consensus about how to address environmental policy, a compromise emerged endorsing the creation of a separate independent agency (Landy, Roberts, and Thomas 1994). However, unlike most independent agencies, with multiple leaders immune from removal over fixed terms jointly making important policy decisions, the EPA would have a single presidentially appointed and removable head who would coordinate environmental activities and account for both the costs and benefits of environmental actions and instruments.

However, the eventual proposal sent to Congress failed to live up to these expectations. Created by a wary Republican administration in a politically volatile atmosphere, the new agency fell short of the lofty goals of comprehensive organizational authority and matching institutional capacity (Moe 1989; Landy, Roberts, and Thomas 1994). The structural choice was for an agency that, although grouping much environmental authority under one roof, had other, seemingly ill-conceived features.

On the one hand, the EPA did include a presidentially appointed, congressionally approved head in charge of many issues concerning water pollution, air pollution, toxics, and pesticides. On the other hand, structural impediments threatened the efficacy of the agency, as noted by political scientist Terry Moe (1989), who cited a litany of structural defects as guaranteeing future difficulties:

- *Lack of coherent organization.* Combining no less than ten bureaucratic operations, each with its own supportive constituencies, the EPA had a greater aura of separation than of integration (further reinforced by the nature of much subsequent environmental legislation).[10] Failure to integrate functions involves special perils because of the complex nature of environmental problems. Most notable is cross-media pollution where the means for solving one type of pollution can actually exacerbate another (for example, means of dealing with toxics can end up polluting the water supply). Many with different interests and perspectives continue to find common ground in criticizing the agency as fragmented and linking this state of affairs to the EPA's history.

- *Lack of scientific knowledge, complicated by major laws forcing quick action.* The EPA has been commonly accused of lacking the scientific apparatus to deal with the difficult set of issues and statutory demands to which it has been held (for a particularly damning indictment, see Wildavsky 1995; see also Powell 1999). Adding to difficulties associated with technical complexity have been statutes routinely calling for quick action and results (see Chapter 8).

- *Cumbersome rulemaking procedures.* Like many agencies in recent years, the EPA is saddled with burdensome rulemaking procedures that seem to impose considerable costs as well as various opportunities for political actors to manipulate the political process strategically (on rulemaking see Kerwin 1999; on EPA rulemaking, see Bryner 1987, McGarity 1991, Hamilton and Schroeder 1994, and Chapter 5). These procedures may both influence outcomes and raise transaction costs substantially.

- *Reliance on states and localities for much implementation.* Given its institutional heritage, the EPA was forced to use many states and localities to enforce its policies.[11] This provided the agency with an enormous set of actors whose behavior it needed to coordinate in a coherent and consistent fashion.

- *Disruptive judicial interference.* The courts, by exhibiting a willingness to interfere in agency deliberations, have slowed the speed of policy development and implementation both because EPA decisions are constantly being appealed and because a variety of time-consuming procedures must be utilized, such as creating long and detailed records justifying decisions. (Moe omits another potential problem associated with judicial interference—that the courts might simply make bad choices [see Chapter 4; but for a defense of the judiciary's role in environmental policy, see Rose-Ackerman 1995].)

Given the passage of two seminal pieces of legislation by 1972, the new agency had little time to get its house in order before confronting a host of additional responsibilities associated with the modern era of environmental politics. All in all, the EPA was placed in a trying position. For instance, the Clean Air Act of 1970 was extremely ambitious, reflecting the aspirations of its primary author, presidential-aspirant Muskie, and the apparent desire of other political leaders to be viewed as environmentally friendly (on this legislation, see Jones 1975). Originally proposed before the EPA's creation (it was to be administered by the Department of Health, Education and Welfare), the act was designed to establish

National Ambient Air Quality Standards (NAAQS) for pollutants constituting health risks and to allow states to develop their own implementation plans; as time went on, the bill that emerged gained a good deal of politically induced momentum and was more far-reaching. Similarly, the Clean Water Act was grandiose and convoluted, highlighted by explicitly technology-forcing mandates to meet ambitious, and essentially unattainable, water quality goals.

Ensuing decades have offered no respite. Rather, as subsequent chapters will document, government's reach has greatly expanded as a host of new environmental concerns have been added and efforts in traditional interest areas have widened.

CONTEMPORARY ENVIRONMENTALISM: 1980–PRESENT

The EPA's formation and new statutory mandates kicked off the modern era of environmental policy. Along with more environmentally sensitive laws and guidelines for the land administration agencies, the national government had taken the final step away from principally facilitating economic activity to balancing production and consumption on the one hand with environmental quality on the other.

In many respects, the process of continued growth in demand for environmental quality and corresponding changes in political institutions went on in fits and starts for the rest of the twentieth century and into the twenty-first century. Heightened demand was presumably a function of growing consumption and increasing awareness of detrimental effects on the environment and the ability to use technology to remediate or prevent them. Any number of galvanizing events over these decades received intense media scrutiny and widespread public attention. Whether by the nuclear accidents at Three Mile Island in Pennsylvania and Chernobyl in the former Soviet Union, worries about toxics at Love Canal, New York, or the massive oil spill caused by the Exxon tanker *Valdez* in Alaskan waters, the public became more familiar with and more aware of the potential dangers of environmental degradation.

As implied by the previously discussed distinction between second- and third-generation issues, growth in demand expanded from conventional concerns to a more diversified collection of issues at a more diverse set of government levels. Citizens and their organizational allies wanted more than national policies designed to clean air and water, reduce toxics and pesticides, and preserve land and species. Most notably, international issues, particularly those involving global warming and ozone depletion, came to the environmental forefront. Also, certain kinds of local matters, such as urban sprawl, by which metropolitan areas expand geographically with a variety of environmental, economic, and social repercussions, found their way onto the political agenda. Demand regarding action on second-generation concerns should not be construed as declining; rather, additional issues were added to the "policy stew."

Heightened demand has also been reflected in the interest group system. Interestingly, not only did environmental organizations continue to grow in important respects but other noteworthy changes occurred. First, the presence of corporations in the Washington interest group community rose substantially (Vogel 1989). Increasingly, as government continued to expand and social regulation continued to grow, corporations felt compelled to establish outposts to complement previous involvement in traditional trade and peak associations (**trade associations** claim to represent all or part of an industry, **peak associations** are more expansive by representing, for example, business interests generally). Spurred by environmental activity, the business community expanded political operations markedly in the 1970s and 1980s in a manner roughly paralleling the growth of environmental groups.

Second, as costs from environmental programs and restrictions continued to rise, explicitly anti-environmental movements and organizations, especially with respect to the use of natural resources, emerged, first under the rubric of the **Sagebrush Rebellion** (a term coined in the 1970s to refer to organized resistance to federal public lands policies in the American West, such as restrictions on grazing, logging, or mining; see Cawley 1993) and then in more conventional form as so-called wise use organizations (such organizations will be discussed in greater depth when organizations are surveyed more generally in Chapter 4). Beginning in the late 1970s, these environmental backlash movements and organizations (sometimes funded by corporate interests), tended to fight against additional environmental constraints on the use of natural resources, including those on federal lands, and became an institutionalized part of the local and national interest group scenes (Helvarg 1994, Echeverria and Eby 1995, Switzer 1997).

Finally, **Not-in-My-Backyard (NIMBY)** pressures rose. With increasing government intervention and requirements, local interests often mobilized to fight against incurring the costs of dealing with environmental woes, such as a landfill, when they are concentrated geographically. Although many might view this as a positive development because it allows local interests to have a voice, those concerned with **environmental justice** or racism, itself a greatly increased concern during this period, also worry that it leads to environmental costs falling disproportionately on the poor and on those historically discriminated against in American society, on the grounds that those in better-off communities are better able to mobilize and be heard.

On the supply side, political institutions continue to develop in capacity and to increase frequently in fragmentation and in politicization. The most notable

Figure 3-4   EPA Budget and Employment, 1970–1999

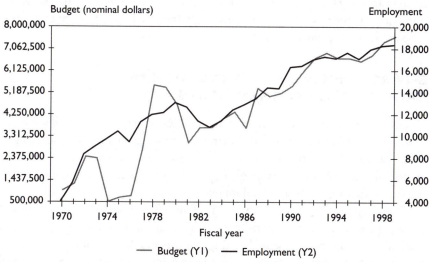

Sources: U.S. Department of Commerce, *Statistical Abstract of the United States* (Washington, D.C.: Government Printing Office, 1971–2000).

changes in environmental policy have been that responsibilities have continued to expand as part of a general, if halting, heightening of government activity; however, this has taken place in a disjointed manner, often layering one set of new policies on top of older sets of requirements. As such, institutional capacity has expanded, if in its own peculiar way, both at the EPA and other natural resource agencies and at their state-level counterparts. For example, despite a push for greater involvement of state and local administrators, the number of employees at the EPA went from about 4,000 at its inception to almost 20,000 toward the end of the twentieth century (see Figure 3-4). The agency's annual budget approaches $8 billion (with construction grants removed, this number is closer to $5 billion; see Warren and Weidenbaum 1999). Even efforts by conservative president Ronald Reagan and his administration (1981–1989), responding to high environmental costs and slow economic activity, to attack the agency—reflected, for example, in an employment dip at the EPA in the early 1980s—appear retrospectively to be a brief detour in a process of overall growth (see Chapter 4; by several conventional measures, societal regulation declined and environmental policy's onslaught was at least slowed if not stopped during the Reagan years).

Thus, American environmental policy reflects both heightened demand for environmental quality—which has occurred across advanced industrial democracies—and the highly fragmented, politicized, nature of U.S. political institutions. As depicted by the notion of **advocacy coalitions** (which consist of all the various actors pursuing a policy position within a subsystem), participation and influence patterns seem increasingly fractured (on advocacy coalitions, see Sabatier and Jenkins-Smith 1993).

ENVIRONMENTAL POLICY EVOLUTION: GROWTH AND FRAGMENTATION

Clearly, environmental policy has evolved considerably over the last century and a half. In general terms, increased demand has influenced many of these changes, which can be a function of wealth and the awareness of the costs of environmental degradation. So too has the nature of political supply, as evidenced by the U.S. political system's growth and development.

Thus, America began by using and selling off its natural resources, moved toward trying to use them responsibly, and eventually shifted toward searching for a balance between environmental quality and other demands. Government went from facilitating economic development to managing the nation's resources and then to guiding the consumption and production of its citizenry.

But American environmental policy has had its own distinctive feel, reflecting both the constitutional structure and the manner in which the country's political institutions and organizations have developed. Thus, the world of environmental policy seems fragmented, with a variety of resulting costs and benefits. During the same historical eras in which environmental policy has taken on greater prominence, so has the imagery of fractured policy making.

Comparing these different historical eras illustrates growth and fragmentation and their causes. In the pre-environmental period, demand for environmental quality was virtually nonexistent and government had little capacity to intervene in people's lives. The result was an effort to dispose of resources, which roughly corresponded to a desire to facilitate economic activity.

The period 1870–1920 saw the beginnings of policies with the purported goal of environmental protection and conservation. However, consistent with limited demand and the slow but gradual development of government capacity, calls for environmental action largely came from a narrow group of supporters, initiatives were modest, and conservation largely won out over preservation.

The subsequent period, 1920–1960, was notable in many senses. Demand for environmental initiatives certainly bottomed out with the Great Depression, but with the increasing economic activity and prosperity after World War II, stresses and advocacy for government intervention increased. Politically, government capacity grew relative to environmentalism and policy overall, but greater evidence of fragmentation, as personified by the growth of subgovernments, was visible.

During 1960–1980 environmental policy moved to the forefront of American consciousness and production of environmental quality, along with so many other concerns, became firmly established as a goal of the national government. Economic prosperity and heightened organizational activity fueled awareness and demand. At the same time, partly as a function of the growth of the organizational world, the political system itself appeared even more fragmented. Indeed, the very creation of the Environmental Protection Agency symbolized this fragmentation.

The years since have seen a growth in demand for environmental quality and an increase in political capacity. At the same time, the imagery of complexity and fragmentation has become even starker. Local and supranational issues (along with related governments and international organizations) have been added to the mix, relevant groups have grown more diverse, and overall policy appears even more fractured and politicized.

In short, the history of environmental policy is marked by the government's responding to demands by increasingly intervening in the lives of citizens, firms, and even other governments. This is consistent, to a great extent, with the general evolution of the U.S. government and with the increased intervention by advanced industrial democracies with respect to the environment. However, to reiterate, U.S. environmental policy has its own quality, which reflects the fragmentation that seemingly flows from constitutional structure and institutional and organizational development.

KEY TERMS

Advocacy coalitions (p. 60)
Citizen groups (p. 52)
Environmental justice (p. 58)
Issue networks (p. 40)
Mining Law of 1872 (p. 43)
Moral hazard (p. 48)
Multiple use (p. 39)
Not in My Backyard (NIMBY) (p. 58)

Peak association (p. 58)
Pork barrel/public works projects (p. 53)
Sagebrush Rebellion (p. 58)
Scientific management (p. 45)
Subgovernments (p. 40)
Sustained yield (p. 40)
Trade association (p. 58)

4 National Political Influences on Environmental Policy

The last chapter sketched an evolving environmental policy system with two defining characteristics, notably, growth in reach and breadth and fragmentation and lack of rationalization in design and execution. These features substantially reflect how growing demand for environmental protection interacts with the institutions supplying policy outputs. Societal demands are aggregated through various mechanisms and mediated by supply-side political institutions. Demand and supply are endogenous, one causing the other such that supply-side institutions are influenced by demands, as institutions themselves are malleable, and supply-side forces are affected by political institutions, as public opinion and their means of aggregation are manipulable. Policy outputs then emerge out of this reinforcing interaction of demand and supply.

This chapter will now focus on national political influences on both the supply and demand sides of environmentalism. Organized interests, Congress, presidential administrations, courts, and agencies all have different preferences and capacities. They push and pull at each other while trying to craft environmental policy. Although this chapter concentrates on EPA policy, this basic perspective applies to other environmentally relevant policies, such as those implemented by the four principal land management agencies. Broadly, in their contemporary incarnations, national political influences are fragmented, displaying contrasting incentives and preferences. Yet, most have developed increasing capacity over time. National influences appear as reflections and causes of evolving environmental policies and processes. Learning to appreciate these influences makes contemporary environmental policy more understandable.

THE DEMAND SIDE: ORGANIZED INTERESTS AND ENVIRONMENTAL POLITICS

What is the nature of the demands that policy makers confront? How have they changed over time? Answering these questions requires distinguishing between citizen opinions and organized interests. Characterizing the unorganized electorate's opinions is reasonably straightforward (recall Chapter 1), but analyzing the group system requires more subtlety.

Demand for environmental quality has grown through the years with economic prosperity, increased consumption, and awareness of environmental threats. At present, U.S. public opinion can be summarized as supporting a strong government role with four, related, caveats:

- Environmental problems typically receive a secondary emphasis, as other concerns (such as economic prosperity or educational quality) garner more attention.
- Expressions of support reflect general beliefs rather than specific opinions about either environmental issues or the means to accomplish them.
- General support typically lacks grounding in the trade-offs that are faced when making environmental choices.
- Knowledge levels about environmental issues are, rationally, low.

Indicative of the nature and limits of public opinion, although many strategic politicians are advised to support environmental policy, they are aware that choices regarding policy details can be more varied and reflect other factors, such as the goals of organized groups, personal preferences, or technological constraints.

The other principal element of demand, organized interests, is a highly visible force in trying to influence environmental policies. Policy-relevant groups may be officially dedicated to championing environmental concerns, the interests of individual corporations or industries and their workers, or the welfare of other governments (for example, states or municipalities) or their employees. By many definitions, individual corporations are not technically interest groups because they do not depend on voluntary contributions from many actors and, as such, suffer fewer resource problems. Here, they are included because both they and voluntary organizations play comparable roles in aggregating demand. Like environmentally relevant policy, the existing interest group system is far-flung and diverse and has spiraled upward in size, capacity, and complexity. Furthermore, changes in the tactical emphases of organizations, such as increases in the use of litigation, conform to the development of environmental policy.

More specifically, three interrelated elements of the group system stand out:

- *Endurance.* Traditional, environmentally specific organizations have proved to be long-lasting. Although experiencing ups and downs, they have typically been able to retain sufficient support to persevere through bad times. Endurance has surprised some who believe in a natural "attention cycle" by which issues, and presumably associated groups, rise and fall on the public agenda (Downs 1972, Dunlap 1995), but it is consistent with the growth and institutionalization of environmental issues.

- *Diversity.* Rather than unifying, environmentally specific organizations have become "a diverse collection of interest groups loosely connected to one another by virtue of their concern for some aspect of environmental protection" (Ingram, Colnic, and Mann 1995, 117). Reflecting changing policy substance and instruments, new groups have gained a foothold and existing groups have broadened to include emerging issues and means of policy influence (Baumgartner and Jones 1993).

- *Growth.* The universe of groups has grown in size. Environmentally oriented citizen groups, the fastest growing segment of the public interest group system, more than tripled in the almost four decades from 1961 to 1999 (Baumgartner and Jones 1993; see also Berry 1999). Additionally, the number and variety of organizations and corporations with political lobbying operations directed toward environmental issues have blossomed. Coupled with endurance and diversification, such growth creates an increasingly demanding but fragmented organizational system.

Considered jointly, these elements of demand indicate how issues of environmental policy and quality have become a permanent and growing part of the American policy scene. They also show that, given these changes, the extent and diversity of means by which citizens, firms, and governments articulate their preferences have grown in magnitude and diversity. As a consequence, political decision makers have an enormously complicated and conflictual policy environment to navigate.

The Environmental Group System

Several considerations make defining organizations with environmental interests tricky. One, which is generic to policy-specific group systems, is that the logic of collective action makes focusing on stated organizational goals problematic because contributors may provide resources for reasons other than the stated objectives of a group, and political goals may merely be a by-product of choices made for other reasons (Olson 1965). As alluded to in Chapter 2, in a world of many potential small contributors, the negligible impact of any single actor's potential contribution on environmental quality creates an incentive to free ride. When many actors have comparable incentives, fewer resources are available because fewer are volunteered than would be if free riding were not an option (indeed, there may be no contributions at all). However, additional funds may be donated for private, material rewards, ranging from discounts on consumer goods to valuable technical information, in which case group leaders may pursue political goals as a by-product of private choices.

Beyond such general features, additional problems arise in identifying interested parties with respect to the environment, particularly regarding EPA policies. These problems stem from the breadth of many policies that, driven by claims of market failure, aim at the social regulation of production and consumption choices (for example, policies from OSHA and the CPSC). Although land management agencies have focused on a small number of industrial and agricultural functions such as mining, timber, and grazing and have been typified by a narrow and relatively easily definable group universe, the EPA's widespread social and economic effects make the group universe, by extension, more amorphous. EPA policies affect virtually every industry, government, and consumer, and a wide array of group leaders may view their organizations as having a stake in these environmental policies. This broadening of the group community meshes neatly with the depiction in Chapter 3 of the evolution of policy from a dominance by narrowly defined subgovernments, corresponding nicely with single industry policies and narrow goals, to the preeminence of fluid and ill-defined issue networks and advocacy coalitions, consistent with industry- and society-wide policies and broad objectives.

Despite these cautions, the environmental group system can be broadly sketched by dividing environmental organizations into public interest groups, business and commercial organizations, and government associations (for example, Wenner 1990). Table 4-1 provides a very partial listing of groups from 1993 compiled by the Government Accounting Office (the *Encyclopedia of Associations* lists several thousand groups under "conservation," "ecology," "environment," and other relevant categories). The table also features contemporary data about the organizations' reported expenditures on congressional lobbying.

The public interest group system involves organizations with a wide array of specific concerns; the mix of business and commercial organizations includes prominent trade associations aligned with various industries, coalitions cutting across industries, and peak associations claiming to represent broad business and commercial interests. Government organizations include alliances of localities as well as occupationally based associations such as the National Association of State Foresters.

Public interest groups come in many shapes and sizes. Although public interest groups with broader agendas, such as Common Cause, sometimes weigh in on environmental issues, organizations with environmental concentrations typically take the policy lead. As indicated, the evolution of such environment-specific associations parallels the development of environmental policy. Many of these groups have widened their focus from traditional preservation and conser-

Table 4-1 Groups and Government Organizations Concerned with National Environmental Policy

Public interest groups	Business/commercial organizations	Government organizations
Alliance for Environmental Education	Alliance for Responsible CFC Policy	Association of Local Air Pollution Control Officials
American Rivers (5 lobbyists)	American Farm Bureau Federation (17 lobbyists, 2 others; $4,560,000)	Association of State Drinking Water Administrators
Center for Marine Conservation (12 lobbyists)	American Gas Association (9 lobbyists, 7 others; $356,087)	Association of State and Interstate Water Pollution Control Administrators
Citizens Clearinghouse for Hazardous Waste	American Mining Congress	Council of State Governments
Clean Water Action	American Petroleum Institute (39 lobbyists, 34 others; $2,982,188)	National Association of Conservation Districts
Defenders of Wildlife (12 lobbyists; $140,000)	American Trucking Associations (11 lobbyists, 12 others; $1,980,000)	National Association of State Foresters
Environmental Action (Defunct)	Chamber of Commerce (54 lobbyists, 2 others; $17,000,000)	National Association of Towns and Townships
Environmental Defense Fund (3 lobbyists, 3 others, $400,000)	Chemical Manufacturers Association (28 lobbyists, 28 others; $4,848,760)	National Governors Association
Friends of the Earth (2 lobbyists, $60,000)	Edison Electric Institute (29 lobbyists, 87 others; $11,020,000)	National League of Cities
Greenpeace USA	Hazardous Waste Treatment Council	State and Territorial Air Pollution Program Administrators
Izaak Walton League	Manufacturers of Emission Controls Association	State and Territorial Solid Waste Management Officials

Table 4-1 *(continued)*

Public interest groups	Business/commercial organizations	Government organizations
League of Conservation Voters	National Agricultural Chemicals Association	United States Conference of Mayors
National Audubon Society	National Association of Manufacturers (33 lobbyists, 5 others; $3,620,000)	
National Coalition against the Misuse of Pesticides	National Association of Water Companies (4 lobbyists, 6 others; $320,000)	
National Wildlife Federation (14 lobbyists, $220,000)	National Coal Association	
Natural Resources Defense Council	National Forest Products Association	
Rocky Mountain Mineral Law Foundation	National Solid Wastes Management Association	
Sierra Club (24 lobbyists; $130,000)	Public Lands Council (5 lobbyists)	
U.S. Public Interest Research Group (22 lobbyists; $407,860)		
Wilderness Society (9 lobbyists, $269,000)		

Sources: Group listings are from Schierow 1993; lobbying data are for 1998, reported under the Lobbying Disclosure Act and made available by the Center for Responsive Politics, Washington, D.C.
Note: When available, number of in-house lobbyists, number of other lobbyists reporting activity on organization's behalf, and lobbying expenditures are given in parentheses.

vation interests to include modern-day environmental concerns. Consequently, an organization such as the Sierra Club, originally defined by its preservationist goals, has become a major player in contemporary fights ranging from global warming to water and air pollution while still advocating such changes as cessation of commercial logging in national forests. Perhaps more notable is the emergence of groups taking up causes associated with global warming or brownfields or other newer environmental concerns. Organizations such as Environmental Defense and the Natural Resources Defense Council, created in 1967 and 1970, respectively, epitomize these groups both in their agendas (virtually the whole gamut of modern environmental issues) and in their tactics, which include a heavy dose of legalism. As an example of the expansive nature of such groups' agendas, in 1999, the Natural Resources Defense Council announced that it had won commitments from over 200 companies, including Kinko's, 3M, Starbucks, and Home Depot, to help save temperate rainforests by phasing out their use and sale of old-growth wood products. Beyond such major groups, a variety of smaller operations, including many functioning principally at the local level and a considerable number of wise use organizations opposing conventional environmental groups, have taken their place in the political world.[1]

In short, the public interest group system reflects and reinforces the growth and fragmentation of environmental policy. Organizations have increased numerically, diversified their interests, spread themselves across various levels of government, and broadened their tactical arsenal.

In addition to public interest groups, business and commercial organizations are also key components of the environmental group system. The most impressive feature of such groups is their expansiveness. By and large, these are peak and trade associations representing crucial sectors of the American economy; although many such organizations are neither new nor exclusively concerned with environmental policy, they nicely illustrate the breadth of contemporary policy. In the last three decades an increasing number of smaller operations of a type not represented in Table 4-1, down to individual corporations too numerous to name, have also involved themselves in environmental issues.

Analysis of government and quasi-government organizations produces similar inferences. Although intergovernmental lobbying organizations have roots in the Great Depression, as the national government began increasing federal grants available to states and localities for environmental policy and a wide array of other programs, the incentive for governments to organize got considerably stronger in the 1960s (Haider 1974, Cammisa 1995). Hence, a broad array of governments and their employees were increasingly vested in monitoring and influencing environmental policy. Consistent with the wide scope of contemporary environmental policy, organizations representing the interests of governments and those whose careers are tied up with government policy are diverse (Cigler 1995).

Support for Environmental Groups

Given collective action problems, determining the motivations behind support for the plethora of environment-specific groups can be difficult. Indeed, some assert that the rise and the endurance of environmentally focused organizations falsifies the logic of collective action and resuscitates the so-called pluralist ideal that shared political interests are key (for example, Ingram, Colnic, and Mann 1995). However, although the purest form of the logic of collective action might not neatly explain the existence of such groups, this logic makes many of their characteristics understandable, such as the amount of resources they control, the means by which they generate funds, the extent to which budgets are spent on fundraising, and the widely varying nature of fiscal support over time.

Consistent with problems associated with collective action, many environmental groups are short of cash and tend to receive small contributions from individuals who are financially well-off and feel strongly about improving environmental quality, meaning that these contributors almost certainly provide far less than they would if free riding was not an option. As an illustration, a Sierra Club membership in the year 2000 was obtainable for as little as $19 ($35 was the standard rate); although many may be motivated by so-called **purposive rewards,** the "warm glow" effect of giving, their willingness to donate is not commensurate with their high valuation of the environment and their generally well-off financial status. Presumably, those who are not as well-off might be willing to contribute something net of free riding but, instead, give zero (such an interpretation is consistent with experimental results such as those of Palfrey and Prisbrey 1997). Also, virtually every major organization provides some material benefit (magazine subscriptions, tote bags, and other items, with additional benefits for first-time contributors), suggesting that group leaders believe that citizens value such rewards and that these goods help overcome collective action problems. Thus, a Sierra Club member gets a backpack with initial membership, the group's magazine, and discounts and exclusive opportunities to participate in travel programs. In addition, many organizations offer so-called **solidary rewards,** by which members have opportunities to interact with others of a similar ilk. Beyond group travel and the like, a Sierra Club member, for instance, is promised invitations to local chapter events. Besides representing additional budgetary costs for groups, the extent of the "bells and whistles" deemed necessary by group leaders to induce citizens to join and to retain them as members highlights how tenuous organizational funding sources can be given collective action problems.

Accordingly, myriad environmentally specific organizations spend significant portions of their revenues trying to maintain their contribution streams. For example, in 1981 about $2 million of the Sierra Club's $7 million budget reportedly went to "studying and influencing public policy," whereas the remaining $5 million was directed at "outdoor activities, publications, and organizational functions" (Hardin 1982). Even a group like Friends of the Earth, which receives about 72 percent of its income from foundations, lists roughly one-quarter of its approximately $2.5 million expenses as being spent on fund-raising or management, with another 12 percent going for membership and "outreach" expenses (Friends of the Earth 1999). More generally, studies drawing on tax return data estimate that about 43.5 percent of the funds of large environmental groups are used for lobbying, advocacy, and similar policy efforts (Berry 1999, Lowry 1997).

Also, consistent with a world beset by collective action problems, support levels for environmental groups can vary greatly over time. Somewhat ironically, these associations tend to suffer when political times are good—reflecting the public's ephemeral nature. Contributors rally against perceived threats, such as those raised by Ronald Reagan in the 1980s (Hansen 1985, Richer 1995). Thus, most analyses of membership in key environmental organizations over time (although reliable data are often scarce) uncover a secular growth trend with a large spike in the 1980s and then a decline associated with the success of less hostile administrations (for example, Boerner and Kallery 1995). Not uncharacteristically, the Sierra Club's membership increased from 181,000 in 1980 to 600,000 in 1990 (it is currently about 630,000), and that of the Audubon Society went from 275,000 to 575,000 (it is currently about 550,000). Interestingly, there appears to be little evidence of a similar pattern with the creation of a Republican congressional majority to combat a Democratic president in 1994; apparently a conservative Republican congressional leadership did not draw the public's attention as much as the Reagan administration, when highly controversial appointees attempted to implement dramatic environmental policy shifts.

Another feature corresponding to the logic of collective action, and a partial explanation for endurance, is that environmental groups generate funds beyond what are furnished by those with strong free-riding incentives. Group survival is not completely a function of voluntary donations from the mass citizenry. One of the most notable funding sources is so-called patrons, such as foundations, representing the equivalent of large members with incentives to contribute whether anyone else gives or not (on patrons, see Walker 1991, Nownes 1996, Lowry 1999; for a critique by a wise use leader, see Arnold 2000). Figure 4-1 provides temporal data on foundation support of four major environmental organizations. Foundations undermined the issue attention cycle by raising their support precipitously just when such groups might have lost their financial edge after the initial environmental enthusiasm of the 1970s and the political threats of the 1980s abated. (As a point of reference, the 1999 *Encyclopedia of Associations* lists the budgets of these groups as: Audubon Society, $44 million; Environmental Defense Fund, $24 million; Natural Resources Defense Council, $27 million; Sierra Club, $43 million.) Enterprising organizations employ a variety of essentially commercial techniques to ensure that funds flow to their coffers. Consider the National Audubon Society, which receives 15 to 20 percent of its annual revenue from

Figure 4-1   Foundation Support for Environmental Organizations, 1974–1998

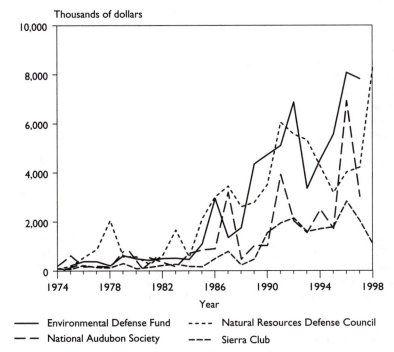

Sources: *Foundation Grants Index*, New York: Foundation Center, 1985–1999; and Bosso 1987.

earned income and royalties (roughly $9 million at last report for an organization spending a little over $5 million on "public policy and government affairs"). Beyond allowing Audubon prints on holiday cards and calendars—the group's namesake, John James Audubon, was a well-known wildlife painter—it receives licensing funds from companies as diverse as Avis Rental Cars and MCI Communications (National Audubon Society 1999). In the same vein, various corporations have increasingly engaged in what they term cause-related marketing, supporting, either directly or by matching employee contributions, environmental organizations viewed as nonthreatening to them (on such marketing see Meyer 1999; on its recent growth, see Halper 2001). For example, the National Wildlife Federation has a partial list of eighty-six major corporations willing to match employee contributions. Finally, to the chagrin of many on the political right or opposed to perceived government waste, government, including the EPA, is a nontrivial funding source for some groups. As Table 4-2 indicates, a variety of organizations receive government monies, and although they constitute only 4 to 5 percent of the budget of a major group, such as the Environmental Defense

Table 4-2   Government and EPA Support of Organizations, 1996–1997

Group	Government funding (percent of total revenue)	Cumulative EPA grant(s)
Alliance to Save Energy	$ 994,349 (33%)	$ 691,209
American Association of Retired Persons	79,430,000 (19)	20,937,108
American Farmland Trust	980,273 (11)	85,000
American Lung Association	649,000 (2)	166,883
Appalachian Mountain Club	15,242,293 (0)	5,000
Bicycle Federation of America	525,722 (42)	365,000
Center for Clean Air Policy	NA (38 over 5 years)	1,057,739
Center for Environmental Law	NA (NA)	40,000
Center for Marine Conservation	661,181 (10)	180,000
Citizens for a Better Environment	0 (0)	148,987
Clean Sites	1,231,270 (20)	815,712
Consumer Federation of America	636,699 (46)	380,275
Consumer Research Council	62,933 (22)	246,390
Earth Share	289,223 (3)	998,855
Ecumenical Ministries of Oregon	1,944,419 (38)	20,000
Environmental Defense Fund	1,082,760 (4)	1,310,000
Environmental Health Coalition	118,613 (14)	20,000
Lawyers' Committee for Civil Rights	81,391 (3)	81,391
League of Women Voters Education Fund	1,814,572 (35)	140,000
Minority Business Enterprise Legal Defense and Education Fund	334,862 (46)	1,100,000
National Caucus and Center on Black Aged	19,413,555 (99.6)	10,640,603
National Council on the Aging	38,327,686 (93)	5,560,670
National Rural Water Association	15,495,483 (79)	14,436,634
National Senior Citizens Education and Resource Center	36,216,787 (99.7)	6,074,800
Nature Conservancy	40,464,860 (10)	2,529,483
Surface Transportation Policy Project	326,671 (20)	425,000
Trout Unlimited of Pendleton, Oregon	171,444 (3)	20,000
World Resources Institute	4,180,702 (24)	310,000

Source: Citizens against Government Waste (http://www.govt-waste.org/publications/lookinglass/ pubs.looking.Phony-Phil.htm).
Note: Includes only those grants classified as for "Advocacy."

Fund, which receives about $1 million (see also Environmental Defense Fund 1999), they can be far more important for some smaller groups.

Although problems associated with the logic of collective action, and solutions for generating support, are most recognizable when observing organizations that represent neither specific industries nor specific occupations, they are relevant to other groups. For example, policies with diffuse impacts, meaning that they affect many commercial or government interests, make mobilization more difficult. Concentrated industries with a few principal firms have greater ability to form political action committees and to provide substantial sums to political candidates because collective action problems, by which one firm would like others to contribute to achieve mutual goals while giving less than its share, are easier to overcome (Grier, Munger, and Roberts 1991, 1994; Mitchell, Hansen, and Jepsen 1997). Similarly, even when individual interests are organized, coalition behavior is more difficult if there are many stakeholders and a common interest, such as limiting an environmental policy's cost; because of a desire to free ride, groups of a given genre find working together problematic, as they wish that other relevant interest groups would mobilize instead (for example, Libby 1998, Hula 1999). Alternatively, different commercial interests may have contrasting preferences and difficulties in coalescing around a common policy or set of goals (see Melnick 1998). Standard collective action difficulties have sometimes made it hard even for intergovernmental organizations to agree on resource contributions when they have attempted to work together (for example, Cigler 1995).

Taken in total, findings regarding support patterns for groups with environmental interests have three related implications:

- *Suboptimal political activity.* Political activity would be even greater if collective action problems were nonexistent. Despite the seeming omnipresence of organizations, free riding produces a suboptimal amount of political activity regarding environmental goods, lowering contributions and raising organizational costs.
- *Environment-specific groups are precariously positioned.* Although mitigated by innovations in procuring funds from foundations, governments, and commercial sources, environment-specific groups in particular confront collective action problems and find that their fortunes ebb and flow.
- *Broad concerns are especially problematic.* Organizations discover that broad issues of environmental concern are more problematic to mobilize around than specific issues.

Tactics for Influencing Environmental Policy

Tactics employed by organizations with interests affected by environmental policy, particularly environment-specific groups, are reflections and causes of the diversity of environmental policy and have changed in ways mirroring policy's evolution. At one extreme, a variety of organizations adopt a nonconfrontational, essentially research-oriented, approach by trying to create what they consider to be a more accurate understanding of technically complex issues. An organization such as the Environmental Law Institute prides itself on being a nonpartisan entity specializing in legal analysis but taking a back seat in explicitly political fights. Think tanks, some with a general policy interest (for example, the Brookings Institution and the Heritage Foundation) and others with an environment-specific focus (for example, Resources for the Future), also produce relevant information even though, for this discussion, they are not considered interest groups.

Others use conventional but more confrontational tactics. Groups may lobby, participate in electoral activities, or use litigation to influence government officials. As Table 4-1 indicates, many groups do lobby elected officials and bureaucrats on environmental issues. Such activities include "insider" lobbying, notably providing technical information about relevant issues, and "outsider" lobbying, principally grassroots mobilizing to signal information to concerned politicians about the electoral ramifications of their behavior. Although engaging in both types of lobbying, commercial and government organizations have a comparative advantage for insider lobbying, whereas public interest groups are better positioned for outsider lobbying (for example, for an illustrative application to forest policy, see Steel, Pierce, and Lovrich 1996). For instance, according to the Center for Responsive Politics (1999), for the 1998 calendar year reported lobbying expenditures on "Energy & Natural Resources"—not all of which involved environmental considerations—were approximately $144 million. By contrast, all "Ideological/Single-Issue" lobbying, of which environment-specific groups are only a part, totaled about $76 million. In short, business and commercial organizations lack the mass appeal (particularly) and the membership numbers of citizens' groups (although they may represent the interests of a large number of individuals in the form of workers, investors, and residents of affected communities) but control considerably more funds than exclusively environment-oriented groups.

As another strategy, numerous environmental organizations also provide campaign funds, endorsements, and assessments of electoral officials (given differences in tax status, not every group can legally engage in all such behaviors). Not surprising, given available resource levels, commercial and business organizations interested in more than environmental issues provide far more than environmentally specific organizations. However, as Table 4-3 shows, even the latter make campaign contributions. Additionally, the most prominent assessments and endorsements of elected officials come from these environment-specific organizations, which play on the citizenry's positive disposition toward the environment. Table 4-4 illustrates the kinds of issues that the League of Conservation Voters (LCV) uses to make rankings for members of Congress. Although endorsements and related actions might seem innocuous, theoretical and experimental research

Table 4-3   Environmental PAC Contributions to Federal Candidates, 1997–1998

Political action committee	Amount given (amount to Democrats)
California League of Conservation Voters	$ 31,163 ($31,163)
Clean Water/Vote Environment	6,504 (6,504)
Duck PAC	13,500 (11,500)
Forest & Nature Protection PAC	2,025 (2,025)
Friends of the Earth	3,587 (3,587)
Greenvote	4,000 (4,000)
Idahoans for the Outdoors	10,700 (10,700)
Keep Tahoe Blue PAC	2,750 (2,750)
League of Conservation Voters	70,926 (53,879)
Montana Conservation Voters	125 (125)
Natural Resources Policy	1,500 (1,500)
New Mexico Conservation Voters Alliance	1,844 (1,844)
New York League of Conservation Voters	250 (250)
Oregon League of Conservation Voters	1,496 (1,496)
Oregon Natural Resources Council	625 (625)
Sierra Club	236,708 (229,950)
Total	387,703 (361,898)

Source: Center for Responsive Politics (http://www.opensecrets.org/pacs/indus/1998/Q11.htm).

suggests that they affect individual choice behavior by providing information that citizens factor into their decisions, such as for whom to vote (McKelvey and Ordeshook 1985, 1986; Potters, Sloof, and van Winden 1997; Grossman and Helpman 1999; Sloof 1999, Wittman 2000).

Also, reflecting the contemporary love of complicated rulemaking procedures and the somewhat surprising willingness of courts to insert themselves into the policy-making process, groups have increasingly added litigation strategies to their repertoires. Organizations involve themselves in rulemaking and appeal administrative rules and actions to the courts. Indeed, as mentioned, several contemporary groups principally using legalistic mechanisms have sprung up; others employ litigation as part of an overall tactical strategy.

Finally, there is another layer of even more aggressive activities undertaken by a variety of organizations that, at the extreme, are even characterized by violence. There are well-known groups, such as Greenpeace and Earth First!, and more localized operations without such prominence, involving themselves in everything from peaceful demonstrations to acts of environmental sabotage known as **ecotage** (Abbey 1975 is commonly cited as the work inspiring calls to environmental sabotage); for example, environmental terrorism reared its head in Vail, Colorado, in 1998 when a group calling itself the Earth Liberation Front burned down a ski resort under construction on environmentally sensitive land, causing

Table 4-4 House Votes Used by the League of Conservation Voters to Rank Members of Congress in 1999

1. *Interior Appropriations Rider.* Amendment to reject riders that would "undermine efforts to protect and restore our cultural and natural resources." (Correct vote: YES; approved 218–199.)

2. *Interior Appropriations Bill.* Final version of bill, which included riders despite vote 1. (Correct vote: NO; approved 225–200.)

3. *Fighting Anti-Environmental Riders.* Attempt to ensure independent votes on anti-environmental riders to bills. (Correct vote: YES; rejected 203–216.)

4. *Land and Water Conservation Fund.* Amendment to provide $30 million in state grants for fund. (Correct vote: YES; approved 213–202.)

5. *Wildlife and Fisheries Management.* Amendment to transfer $23 million in USFS timber sales budget for wildlife and fisheries management. (Correct vote: YES; rejected 174–250.)

6. *Timber Revenues for Rural Communities.* Bill to increase timber revenues to local communities. (Correct vote: NO; approved 274–153.)

7. *Mining Waste.* Amendment designed to limit dumping of mining waste on federal government lands. (Correct vote: YES; approved 273–151.)

8. *Wild Predator Control.* Amendment to transfer $7 million of USDA funds from program that kills wild predators to programs that protect animals. (Correct vote: YES; rejected 193–230.)

9. *Wetlands Permits.* Amendment to provide more protection of wetlands via the Army Corps of Engineers permit process. (Correct vote: YES; rejected 183–245.)

10 & 11. *Mandates Information Act.* Two votes fighting efforts to extend unfunded mandates provisions, making it more difficult to implement environmental programs that impose costs. The first vote is an amendment that would weaken the legislation in question. (Correct vote: YES; rejected 210–216.) The second is the final vote. (Correct vote: NO; approved 274–149.)

12 & 13. *Small Business Paperwork Reduction Act Amendments.* Efforts to limit the burdens on small business owners, including environmental and public health laws. First vote is an amendment to reduce the extent of relief granted (Correct vote: YES; rejected 210–214.) The second is the final vote. (Correct vote: NO; approved 274–151.)

14. *Fossil Fuel Research.* Amendment to cut $50 million from fossil fuel research. (Correct vote: YES; approved 248–169.)

15. *International Family Planning.* Amendment restoring $25 million for international family planning. (Correct vote: YES; approved 221–198.)

16. *Funding for World Heritage Sites.* Amendment to prohibit funds for so-called World Heritage Sites. (Correct vote: NO; approved 217–209.)

Source: League of Conservation Voters, *1999 National Environmental Scorecard* (Washington, D.C.: League of Conservation Voters, 2000).

$12 million worth of damage. Although there is little systematic evidence that these actions have had a large effect in the United States, and for this reason they are largely set aside for the remainder of the analysis in this text, there are isolated instances where they do seem to have brought public pressure and political attention to an issue (for example, whaling in international waters).

Group Influence on Environmental Policy

Ultimately, determining the extent to which organizations influence policy is the principal reason why they are worthy of attention. Given the resources expended, there is a prima facie case that groups do matter but definitive statements are difficult (Baumgartner and Leech 1998). Compared with more sensationalist portrayals, the social scientific literature on group influence and analyses specific to environmental politics indicate that organizations are important but not dominant, because other aspects of demand and supply-side institutions also matter. It is also often true that groups increase the fragmentation and disjointedness of policy.[2]

Group influence has been most comprehensively studied with respect to the legislature. Consistent with the claim that organizational effects are at the margin, results are mixed. Understanding such influence requires distinguishing between **selection effects,** by which organizations influence which type of officials are elected, and **moral hazard effects,** by which groups affect the behavior of whoever is in office.

There is reason to believe, cautiously, that organizations can influence but not dictate which types of members are elected and presumably influence which nonelected individuals are appointed to key administrative posts. Perhaps the most convincing evidence involves campaign contributions, although, as mentioned, actions like endorsements may be influential. Consistent with selection, ideological compatibility between contributor and legislator is a key determinant for who contributes (Poole, Romer, and Rosenthal 1987; McCarty and Rothenberg 2000). Conservatives give to conservatives, liberals to liberals, and environmentalists to environmentalists, everything else being equal, and campaign spending, at least by challengers, significantly affects electoral outcomes. Why is there a need for caution? First, factors consistent with the purchasing of "access" to legislators who may not be ideologically compatible are also significant determinants of contribution behavior. For instance, there is a matching between contributors and committee memberships even if such legislators are not those whom groups might otherwise want selected (Romer and Snyder 1994). Second, and in line with the first point, giving for electoral reasons has theoretical problems; influencing selection is a public good because those of a similar disposition who do not contribute will, nonetheless, enjoy the benefits. Minimally, less money may be given for selection than would otherwise be the case (McCarty and Rothenberg 1996). Finally, for reasons that many believe to be methodological rather than reflecting the real world, documenting a linkage between money and incumbent electoral success is problematic (but see Erikson and Palfrey 1998).

Despite these data that committee memberships and the like matter for campaign support, evidence for moral hazard—that organizations can get legislators to change their typical behavior—is more mixed. Notably, support for the proposition that groups can "buy" relevant roll call votes with campaign contributions is weak. At most, such monies only move those who are nearly indifferent (Pashigan 1985, Rothenberg 1992). Although strong correlations between amounts of money received and roll call voting are typical, much of this is explained by contributors' giving money to those whose natural predispositions favor their interests. Similarly, echoing results generally, analyses of environmental lobbying tend to find real but marginal impacts on roll call voting (Pashigan 1985, Fowler and Shaiko 1987), reinforcing results of scholarly investigation that legislators follow a rather consistent behavioral pattern throughout their careers (see Poole and Rosenthal 1997).

Moral hazard effects may be subtler. Although voters or political elites, such as candidates challenging incumbents, may be able to closely monitor purchased votes (for example, Denzau and Munger 1986), organizational efforts behind the scenes may be more powerful. For instance, groups may determine who gets nominated to administer policy, which issues reach the legislative agenda, what details are contained in proposals being considered, and the nature of congressional oversight (see Hall 1996). In this vein, lobbying made a statistically significant difference on voting choices on Superfund issues in the House Ways and Means Committee—which has broad authority over raising revenues to finance the government (Wright 1990). Similarly, assertions that structural choice of how agencies are organized is interest group politics, because individual voters are not intimately acquainted with the details of how such bargains are cut, are consistent with the claim that the effects of moral hazard are nuanced.[3] Others maintain that many rewards from allying with organizations are long term. For example, as a function of the so-called "revolving door," relevant political actors (although not just those working in Congress) may be provided jobs by those whom they rule over—as a result, legislators, congressional staffers, or bureaucrats may find themselves subsequently working for organized interests affected by environmental policy. For instance, the Center for Public Integrity has developed case studies indicating that business and commercial interests use their finances to dominate various elements of environmental politics, such as those pertaining to pesticides and toxics (for example, Taylor 1994; Center for Public Integrity 1998; Fagin, Lavelle, and the Center for Public Integrity 1999). One such study claims that the chemical industry dominates the EPA through Congress by providing campaign contributions and hiring experienced members of government, especially former members of Congress and key staffers (54 of 67 of those in 1998 with revolving-door positions, leaving government and going to work for the industry, had legislative backgrounds).[4]

Although less intensively studied beyond the legislature, this theme of groups being influential but not dominant is echoed by the existing evidence. For example, a study by economist Amy Ando of organizational influence on decisions about whether a species should be protected under the Endangered Species Act (ESA) shows that groups can speed the process by which a species enters the protection process by filing a petition and, if the species is the subject of an FWS rulemaking by which the agency proposes a level of protection and asks for comments, can delay or hasten the process by formally protesting or supporting the action (Ando 1999). Similarly, by acting in support or opposition, groups can influence what courts consider or decide (Caldeira and Wright 1988) as much as nongroup adversaries (Epstein and Rowland 1991). Furthermore, although organized interests have often seemed to capture agencies with a single industry focus (see Rothenberg 1994), consistent with the greater diversity of the interest group system, organizations appear far less dominant in agencies with more varied mandates (as has increasingly typified, for example, natural resource agencies) and whose responsibilities cut across society and the economy (for example, the EPA). Additionally, while certain major interests receive some attention from incumbent presidential administrations, the chief executive often appears more hostile to organized concerns than do legislative or bureaucratic counterparts (Peterson 1992).

In summary, policy is not simply group politics. Organized interests do matter at least at the margins and may, in certain contexts, have considerably greater impacts; the findings of group impacts at the margin are consistent with analyses of intergovernmental organizations that also find modest influences on relevant policy (for example, Cammisa 1995, Nugent 1998, Smith 1998; but see Haider 1974). To the extent that organizations are important, they largely contribute to the imagery of fragmentation, inefficiency, and the preeminence of distributive concerns that pervades descriptions of environmental policy. In turn, such influence will reinforce the incentive of politicians to maintain and expand such a system.

THE SUPPLY SIDE: FORMAL POLITICAL INSTITUTIONS AND THE ENVIRONMENT

Demand provides only a partial explanation of policy. Political institutions are the "neglected side of the story" (Moe 1990). Explaining the policy process requires attention to the details by which supply-side institutions translate societally generated demands into policy.

There are many ways of thinking about whether political institutions independently affect the policy process. Social scientists elaborating general theories have developed various approaches with names such as the previously mentioned advocacy coalition, institutional rational choice (how institutional rules influence the behavior of rational individuals motivated by material self-interest), and punctuated-equilibrium (focusing on patterns of policy change, which are posited to be generally incremental but occasionally substantial) (see, for example, Sabatier 1999). Sketching key elements of national political institutions, without making fine academic distinctions, will provide a better understanding of the environmental policy process.

The basic features of Congress, the presidency, the courts, and agencies all affect the choices of policy, delegation, and implementation. This section focuses attention on three related institutional characteristics. First is the position in the constitutional system of separation of powers. Different institutional actors may play contrasting roles because of where they stand in the constitutionally specified sequence of decision making and the authority given to them. Second are preferences, since those with different ideal points (preferred policy choices) will tend to support different policies. Third is capacity, as different abilities to process and deal with complicated technology and information may have ramifications for policies advocated and roles played.

These features provide a general understanding of how the environmental policy process operates and how institutions influence the distributional and efficiency impacts of policy choices. Considered jointly with demand, they illuminate government's involvement in environmental policy, its successes, and its anomalies.

Congress: Agent of Parochialism?

Perhaps the obvious place to begin is Congress. Not only is the legislature in numerous respects the focal point of national policy making, but many relevant analytical models begin with Congress (for example, McCubbins, Noll, and Weingast 1989). Further, Congress is typically considered the institutional prototype of fragmentation, parochialism, and the triumph of distribution over efficiency— criticisms routinely leveled against the policy system generally and environmental policy specifically.

As is well known, Congress's most influential powers are likely its statutory and budgetary responsibilities and the Senate's approval rights over political appointments. In conjunction, legislators often engage in formal and informal policy oversight by holding hearings and inquiring into agency business as a means of monitoring, guiding, and punishing and rewarding policy makers. Congress can initiate legislation to change the policy status quo, which gives the legislature a "first-move advantage" of making other political actors react. However, because presidents can veto bills, courts may invalidate legislation, and agencies may be able to block implementation of stipulated changes in the right context, opportunities to manipulate the status quo do have limits. Congressional ability to unite to move policy through the legislative process also often appears to be a considerable impediment. Even net of the president's veto authority, the right of senators to filibuster and committees to keep bills unreported (that is, no vote gets taken on the floor of the chamber) means that programs and budgets require overwhelming support. Indeed, inaction, such as ignoring presidential proposals, often seems to be a greater source of influence than positive accomplishments (on the congressional gridlock claimed to result from the need for supermajorities and the existence of multiple veto points, see Brady and Volden 1998; to reiterate, such inaction may have the positive feature of providing policies with credibility).

In terms of preferences, members of Congress are typically interested in representing narrow, frequently concentrated, interests to enhance their reelection prospects. Such parochial preferences are induced from the interaction of the goal of reelection with a geographically based electoral system. It is frequently maintained that legislators willingly tolerate inefficient policies that bring their districts, or concentrated interests within them, benefits exceeding costs. For example, in 2001, Sen. John McCain, R-Ariz., a noted critic of such spending, cited the earmarking of $300,000 to remove aquatic weeds in the Lavaca and Navidad Rivers in Texas as an instance of inefficient spending with benefits specific to a narrow region endorsed by Congress.

Pursuing electoral security, members of Congress have built a considerable institutional capacity that reinforces specialization and fragmentation (with certain countervailing forces mitigating some of decentralization's most harmful effects to legislators). This includes well-developed party systems for coordinating members, large personal staffs, and various ancillary organizations for providing needed information (for example, the Congressional Budget Office [CBO], the Congressional Research Service, and the GAO). Perhaps most notable is the elaborate committee and subcommittee system that legislators have constructed; for instance Table 4-5 shows that, mirroring policy's fragmentation, the EPA must principally deal with five House committees and even more subcommittees with only slightly less dispersion in the smaller Senate. Although legislators lack perfect information, they can generate considerable data and potentially punish agencies with authority delegated for political or technical reasons if these agencies deviate from a given discretionary zone.

In light of legislators' constitutional position, preferences, and capacity, there are numerous prominent examples of their promotion of parochial environmentally relevant choices.[5] Congress has been accused of responsibility for cumbersome organizational structures, convoluted processes, and ill-conceived policy instruments governing land management agencies and the EPA that seemingly produce inefficiencies and misplaced priorities. In addition, critics and analysts alike claim that members tolerate fractured and unnecessarily rigid agency processes either because they provide a shield from blame and opportunities to intervene with the bureaucracy and claim credit for action or because they facilitate

Table 4-5 Congressional Committees and Subcommittees Dealing with the EPA

House of Representatives	*Senate*

Committees
  Subcommittees
  (Relevant policies where appropriate)
	Committees
	  Subcommittees
	  (Relevant policies where appropriate)

Agriculture
  Subcommittee on Department Operations,
    Oversight, Nutrition, and Forestry
  (For example, pesticides)
	Agriculture, Nutrition, and Forestry
	  Subcommittee on Research, Nutrition,
	    and General Legislation
	  (For example, pesticides)

Appropriations
  Subcommittee on VA, HUD, and
    Independent Agencies
	Appropriations
	  Subcommittee on VA, HUD, and
	    Independent Agencies

Energy and Commerce
  Subcommittee on Energy and Air Quality
  Subcommittee on Environment and
    Hazardous Materials
  (For example, hazardous wastes/toxics/
    Superfund/CERCLA)
	Environment and Public Works
	  Subcommittee on Clean Air, Wetlands,
	    and Climate Change
	  Subcommittee on Fisheries, Wildlife,
	    and Water
	  Subcommittee on Superfund, Toxics, Risk,
	    and Waste Management
	  Subcommittee on Transportation,
	    Infrastructure, and Nuclear Safety
	  (For example, water quality)

Government Reform
  Subcommittee on Energy Policy, Natural
    Resources, and Regulatory Affairs
  (For example, economy, efficiency, and
    management of agency)	

Science
  Subcommittee on Environment,
    Technology, and Standards
  (For example, new chemicals and
    technologies)
  Subcommittee on Research
  (For example, research and development
    funding)	

control. Thus, for instance, one well-known explanation for high congressional reelection rates is the availability of opportunities to aid constituents disgruntled with a rule-bound bureaucracy (Fiorina 1989; see, also McCubbins, Noll, and Weingast 1989; Schoenbrod 1993). Alternatively, Congress has been accused of writing legislation that is far too prescriptive (provides specific guidelines and instructions) and thereby accepting increased inefficiencies as the price for limiting discretion.

Beyond such choices, congressional parochialism affects the substance of delegated, environmentally relevant policies (for a somewhat backhanded defense of Congress in this regard, see Bailey 1998). For example, legislators are routinely blamed for the extraordinarily inefficient decisions about natural resources. Subgroups of members and their interest group allies are accused of being more interested in perpetuating policies maintaining the prosperity of concentrated local interests than in effecting changes that would realize economic gains from greater efficiency. For instance, the Mining Law of 1872 and its provisions allowed mining companies to profit from federal lands at virtually no cost, paying minimal attention to environmental laws. Assuming that 25 percent of the money goes back to the states, in 1999 the CBO estimated that an 8 percent mining royalty would realize the federal government alone $408 million in budgetary savings from 2000 to 2009. Yet, despite a close call or two, mining interests have stubbornly and effectively fought reform efforts that would reduce the profitability of their operations.[6] Similarly, for reasons appearing to stem from the interests of western legislators representing organized cattlemen and other interested parties, the AUM rate remains $1.35 despite efforts to overhaul cattle and sheep grazing rules on federal lands (Dietz and Rothenberg 2000). For example, when Bill Clinton's secretary of the interior, Bruce Babbitt, proposed increasing the rate to about $4 ("Rangeland Reform '94" 1994), members of Congress and cattle interests fought the plan by, among other things, filibustering the DOI's annual appropriation. Along the same lines, the distribution of water rights has been marked by inefficiencies and localized interests. For example, a mandate in the Water Resources Development Act of 1986 that localities pick up from 25 to 50 percent of the tab for water projects induced overall proposed project spending to fall by 35 percent. Price sensitive legislators and their constituencies value such projects at less than one-quarter to one-half of the actual price tag (DelRossi and Inman 1999).

Much EPA regulation is also shaped by parochial congressional incentives. Among the best-known examples of policy reflecting narrow legislative interests involves the battle over high-sulfur coal versus scrubbers in the debates over the Clean Air Act Amendments of 1977. In that battle, eastern utilities and coal producers dominated their western counterparts (Ackerman and Hassler 1981, Joskow and Schmalensee 1998). Along the same lines, regulation of automobile emissions has been marked by fights between those representing the narrow self-interests of automobile manufacturers and others having more to gain from taxing car companies. Similar allegations are made with respect to those favoring chemical and pesticide producers when it comes to Superfund and pesticide regulation, respectively.

Table 4-6 Estimate of Savings from Cutting Nine Congressionally Championed Programs that Have Possible Negative Environmental Effects (in millions of dollars)

Program (possible effect)	5-year savings estimate
Clean Coal Technology Program (actually encourages burning of coal)	$ 500
"Low-Level" Radioactive Waste Dump Promotion and Support Service (only promotes dump sites)	21
Swan Lake-Lake Tyee Intertie [Alaska] (project, which cuts through roadless area in Tongass National Forest, will damage pristine environment for little gain)	40
Irrigation subsidies (pricing water under market value encourages inefficient use of water, hurting wetlands, fish and wildlife populations, and producing pollution in the process)	2,200
Army Corps Flood Control Construction (many such projects increase pollution and encourage development near flood plains)	1,250
Sugar subsidies (disrupt water flows and add pollutants to Everglades)	n/a
Livestock Protection Program (killing predators has environmental damage and is not effective)	50
Highway Demonstration Projects (hurt environment without addressing important transportation needs)	6,900
National Flood Insurance Program (encourages development in environmentally sensitive coastal areas)	500

Source: Friends of the Earth, Taxpayers for Common Sense, and U.S. Public Interest Research Group, *Green Scissors '99,* (Washington, D.C.: Friends of the Earth).

Standing apart from resource management or EPA-style policy, other distributive programs marked by parochialism have negative environmental impacts. Indeed, the environmental community puts out an annual listing, known as *Green Scissors,* of allegedly wasteful spending that harms the environment. Almost all of these programs have considerable congressional support and focus heavily on energy, water, agricultural, and transportation projects. Although these projects may neither include all wasteful spending nor be without merits, many are commonly cited as wasteful and they jointly represent over $50 billion of spending over five years. A partial list of such policies and claims about available savings is shown in Table 4-6.

The President: Efficiency, the Environment, and Cross-Pressures

Popular discussions and many scholarly analyses frequently look to the president for environmental and policy leadership. Ironically, the chief executive's attempts to meet environmental expectations rarely satisfy anyone. This reflects the complex position that the chief executive occupies in the national political process.

Presidents can potentially influence, although not necessarily dominate, environmental policy. Formal vested powers include vetoing legislation, proposing appointments, and issuing executive orders. Sometimes such powers position the president to change the status quo and place the onus on others to redirect policy (for example, when executive orders can be employed). At other times they situate him to choose the status quo over proposed changes (for example, when vetoes are a threat), and in still other instances they allow him to make a strategic proposal and hope others acquiesce (for example, by suggesting appointments).[7] More subtly, chief executives may attempt to mobilize public opinion and to guide public discourse by appealing directly to the public and by proposing legislative initiatives for Congress. In general, presidents, like legislators, are better positioned to maintain the status quo or to undermine current policies than to make positive inroads through explicit adoption of new policy.

Presidential preferences tend to be oriented toward broad, national, concerns such as economic prosperity or environmental quality because, for one reason, presidents are elected nationally. Such national concerns are seen as fundamental for presidents if they are to maintain their popularity, secure their second-term election, and establish their historical legacy. Thus, the chief executive typically adopts a broader perspective in exploiting constitutionally assigned authority and in championing legislation and mobilizing public opinion. Given the chief executive's national constituency, even a president favoring core or electorally crucial societal interests (McCarty 2000) is, nonetheless, likely to adopt a more expansive perspective than his geographically limited congressional counterparts. Also, consistent with judgment by a national electorate, the general concerns on which presidents tend to be assessed include principally the economy's performance and secondarily, among other things, environmental quality.

As such, presidents exhibit common tendencies toward environmental policies as well as disagreements. Certainly, because of party, ideology, or other conditions, chief executives vary in their policy positions, particularly in their stance about how much societal and government resources should be allocated to environmental protection. For instance, President Reagan, a conservative Republican serving during a period of economic travail, emphasized the economy over the environment. This emphasis is evidenced by his attempts to emasculate the EPA and to steer natural resource policy in a direction advocated by Sagebrush Rebels, who desired more environmentally lenient rules governing public lands in the American West. Yet, the induced preferences of presidents in regard to the environment translate in two linked ways that are, to a considerable degree, invariant to their partisanship or ideology.

First, given joint concerns with economic prosperity and ecological well-being, presidents are more likely than other elected officials to advocate relatively efficient, market-based, policy instruments; analytic techniques such as cost-benefit analysis; and attacks on inefficient, environmentally harmful, pork barrel programs. Second, in regard to trade-offs between prosperity and environmental quality, chief executives exhibit a somewhat schizophrenic attitude on their preferred level of environmental protection (for example, Mintz 1995).

To illustrate the first point, Republican president George H. Bush (1989–1993) championed market-based instruments incorporated in the Clean Air Act Amendments of 1990. Despite ideological and partisan differences, President Bill Clinton, a Democrat, also advocated the adoption of market instruments, most notably as part of the December 1997 Kyoto Agreement on global warming (Skea 1999). Similarly, Clinton's successor, George W. Bush (2001–present), has made the use of market solutions for environmental solutions a principal commitment of his administration. Along the same lines, presidents have increasingly institutionalized information collection and the review of agency rulemakings for cost efficiency (Shanley 1992, Dudley and Antonelli 1997, Pildes and Sunstein 1999). Following the lead of his more conservative predecessors, in September 1993 Clinton issued an executive order, "Regulatory Planning and Review," stipulating that the Office of Management and Budget (OMB) produce an economic analysis of important regulations (see Figure 8-1; in recent years, the OMB has also been made responsible for a variety of other reports on regulatory costs). Similarly, presidents of various stripes have voiced displeasure with anachronistic, inefficient, natural resource policies despised by environmentalists, such as grazing and mining, and have attacked environmentally damaging pork barrel initiatives, such as water-related projects.

As for the second point, reinforcing what was said about the chief executive and interest groups, presidential "schizophrenia" is particularly notable for administrations that initially raise the environmental community's expectations, as the chief executive in question inevitably disappoints by making trade-offs. President Clinton is a prominent example (Vig 2000). Elected as an environmental champion, symbolized by the selections of Sen. Albert Gore as a running mate and pro-environmental leaders to head environmentally sensitive agencies (most notably Carol Browner at the EPA and Bruce Babbitt at the DOI), the realities of office induced some disappointing choices. For instance, Clinton's strong and successful advocacy of the North American Free Trade Agreement—initially championed by George H. Bush and supported by all the living presidents at that time—disquieted the environmental community because it feared that ratification would facilitate the exportation of pollution across national boundaries and induce a race to the bottom among nations in setting lower and lower pollution standards. Similarly, despite hailing Babbitt's appointment, many environmentalists condemned the DOI secretary for rejecting environmental values when political realities impinged. Evidence of environmentalists' reactions to the Clinton administration was a pronounced ambivalence regarding the president's 1996 reelection bid. Such a response was especially notable given the lack of any viable alternative. Although consumer advocate Ralph Nader expressed his disenchantment by accepting the Green Party candidacy for president, the environmental community disdained Republican nominee Robert Dole (for example, his 1996 LCV score was a 4 out of a possible 100, an improvement over a 0 in 1995). In its official magazine, the Sierra Club felt it necessary to pen an article titled "Bill Clinton: Does He Deserve Your Vote?" (Rauber 1996, 39), noting that the president deserved lukewarm support even though the environmental community's optimistic expectations about Clinton had "crumbled almost immediately."

As a somewhat fitting postscript, despite Gore's seemingly impeccable credentials prior to becoming vice president (for example, Gore 1992), his association with Clinton went into producing mixed reviews from the environmental community in his presidential quest in 2000, which was likely derailed in part by Nader's 3 percent of the vote being sufficient to tip key states in George W. Bush's favor.

Conversely, although the environmental community demonizes presidents whom they find threatening (Durant 1992, Soden and Steel 1999), these presidents do exhibit evidence of moderation. In 1982 the head of Friends of the Earth denounced the "Reagan wrecking crew" that was "destroying the institutions that give us the research and enforcement tools to protect the environment" (quoted in Taylor 1982, 57). Yet, presidential incentives, in conjunction with the negative publicity surrounding anti-environmental initiatives and inherent limitations on presidential authority (that is, the chief executive has an incentive to compromise), induced Reagan to modify this environmental stance. Not only did Reagan alter his most draconian policies to make them less extreme (and presidential actions sometimes precipitated legislative countermeasures limiting agency discretion), so that agencies could not implement policies favored by the president but opposed by Congress, but he acquiesced to the exit of his most anti-environmental appointees. The latter is exemplified by Reagan's reappointment of William Ruckelshaus, the EPA's first head and a man with considerable legitimacy, to lead the EPA after the disastrous rein of Anne Gorsuch [Buford] (Reagan also agreed to the exit of notorious DOI secretary and Sagebrush Rebel James Watt). Whereas Gorsuch was widely viewed as a loyal White House agent, Ruckelshaus received commitments of autonomy and independence and was credited with restoring much of the agency's lost luster, budget, and commitment to enforcement. Thus, budget and employment levels were put on an upward trajectory (recall Figure 3-4), administrative actions went from 864 in fiscal year 1982 to 1,848 in fiscal year 1983 and 3,124 in fiscal year 1984 (EPA 1998; see also Mintz 1995), and efforts were made to rationalize environmental priorities. Rather than continuing a frontal attack on environmental and natural resource policy, Reagan proved content principally to block additional, expensive programs, such as new acid rain controls championed by environmentalists (Matlack 1988)—although even in this case he modified his stance and acknowledged that acid precipitation constituted an environmental problem. Similarly, George W. Bush, who was widely attacked by the environmental community for some of his initial policies, most notably his refusal to go along with international global climate change agreements, proceeded to ratify other pro-environmental policies, such as a costly cleanup of sediments from the upper Hudson River opposed by many in the business community.

Finally, despite not always realizing environmental objectives, chief executives have developed a considerable information gathering and processing apparatus to help pursue their goals and respond to increasingly politicized choices. This includes, importantly for environmental affairs, both the CEQ and the OMB (which deals with the environment as part of its considerable budgetary and regulatory responsibilities and is often seen by the EPA as its mortal enemy). The broad scope of presidential authority and the rapid turnover and politicized nature of appointees often lead to administrations being portrayed as somewhat in the dark regarding agencies' day-to-day operations; however, the institution has considerably more information and technical wherewithal than it had several generations ago.

The Courts: Strategic Political Actors

The courts have come to occupy a prominent role in modern environmental policy's evolution. Indeed, as environmental attorney David Sive puts it, "In no other political and social movement has litigation played such an important and dominant role. Not even close" (cited in Polsky and Turner 1999, 34).

In the contemporary world, none of the agencies discussed earlier seems positioned to make a significant move that is unchallenged judicially by some government, business or its group representative, or environment-specific interest group. Business and environmental groups sue when the Bureau of Land Management promulgates rules on grazing rights; court cases follow when the EPA issues new National Ambient Air Quality Standards stipulating acceptable levels of pollutants such as particulates, and aggrieved parties often respond with judicial action when the FWS employs the Endangered Species Act (for example, many prominent cases regarding **takings** issues—claims that government was unconstitutionally expropriating property—have been heard and, because of agency claims of budgetary shortfalls, the FWS has actually adopted a policy of not proceeding with any ESA listing *unless* it is court ordered). A widely cited statistic of the 1980s is that 80 percent of the 500 or so annual EPA regulations get tied up in the legal system (for example, Wilson 1989, but see Coglianese

1994)—although this figure likely varies somewhat with time in response to judicial rulings and the payoffs in terms of policy influence yielded by alternative means of influence, such as organizational lobbying of agencies, legislators, or presidents. Regardless, such statistics imply that those filing cases believe that judicial remediation will produce positive net benefits, that is, in contrast to the courts' passive stance developed during the New Deal period toward many of Franklin Roosevelt's programs, judicial activism is possible. Hence, even casual examination suggests that justices of all predilections, including those on the U.S. Supreme Court, act strategically and that their choices have policy-related designs. In this vein, conservative critics lament the judiciary's metamorphosis from administering the common law, essentially enforcing specific property rights and contracts, to a broader view in which values regarding policies such as environmental protection are central (Greve 1996, Meiners and Morriss 1999, Schoenbrod 1999).

Yet, the ability of courts to deal with this responsibility is questionable. As the following quotation by a famous member of the District of Columbia Court of Appeals underscores, the prima facie case for benign judicial influence is weak because of the judiciary's lack of technical capability: "The path that lies ahead is to improve the capability of the courts to apply the rule of administrative law to the environmental area, in which special problems of complexity are presented" (Leventhal 1974, 555). In many respects, the capacity of federal courts and the technically complex nature of policy, coupled with extremely involved administrative processes, appear mismatched. Unlike other political institutions, the judiciary's ability to generate and process information has not remotely kept up with changes in responsibilities. Because courts seem ill-equipped to analyze numerous environmental policies effectively, they might seem advised to let other political actors work out the substance of policy if agency processes follow administrative guidelines.

In broad scope, and analogous to the trade-off between specific and vague delegation, judicial actions, given a lack of capacity on the part of the judiciary, have dual ramifications. There are distributional consequences because, depending upon judicial preferences, interests with stakes in environmental policy, be they business, environmental, or government, are helped or harmed. In addition, inefficiency is heightened as costs are raised and fragmentation and complication are reinforced. Indeed, the judiciary's geographical fragmentation, allowing multiple courts to rule on the same issues, is ready-made for fractured policy (see Cross 1999). As one scholar puts it, despite all the conflicts between various sides, there is general agreement that the courts produce even more fragmentation than would otherwise exist: "[W]hen subjected to constant litigation, even the most coherent policy agenda will disintegrate. . . . [T]his consideration suggests that the courts should not exacerbate the fragmentation of environmental policy and, if possible, play a positive, integrative, role" (Greve 1996, 92–93).

How, then, does the position of the federal courts, the preferences of its members, and judicial capacity produce this state of affairs? With respect to the former, federal courts deal with three types of environmental cases: (1) those essentially national in scope and decided in the District of Columbia Appeals Court; (2) rules or decisions principally affecting localities or regions, which go to the regional appeals courts; and (3) cases involving violations of standards and administrative rules, which are left to district courts (Wald 1992). After initial decisions, cases may go to the Supreme Court, which sets precedents that guide other environmentally relevant judicial choices. Broadly, the courts can rule on the constitutionality of given actions, whether agencies are properly using their delegated authority, and what interests can be heard in court (**judicial standing**).[8]

Scholars have found that depending on the preferences of other political actors, such authority can have an important effect on policy (for example, Ferejohn and Shipan 1990, Epstein and Knight 1998, Tiller 1998, Tiller and Spiller 1999). In the same spirit, those involved with environmental policy believe that the courts have been a major actor in its evolution, with the judiciary varying its policy choices, the extent to which it makes policy rather than protecting agency discretion, and the breadth of standing (on judicial impacts by environmental policy area, see McSpadden 1995).

More concretely, courts can move the status quo given several conditions:

- *Cases are brought to them.* The courts lack agenda control, with the exception of the Supreme Court, which can decide which small number of cases it will hear of many possible cases. The judiciary depends upon issues being brought before it. Admittedly, justices may signal receptivity toward dealing with certain policies through various rulings, precipitating interested parties to turn to them.
- *Decisions are implemented.* Just because the courts rule does not mean that other political actors will implement their decisions: "[T]he federal judiciary is institutionally dependent on Congress and the president for jurisdiction, rules, and execution of judicial orders" (Ferejohn 1999, 355). Relative to other institutional actors, the ability of courts to enforce their rulings is limited.
- *Political actors are disposed to uphold judicial rulings.* Unless they wish to have their decisions overturned legislatively, judges will only make rulings that they believe will be upheld by other political actors. Courts are occasionally overruled; for example, Congress overturned seven different court cases in writing the Clean Air Act Amendments of 1990 (Eskridge 1991, Spiller and Tiller 1996).[9] Admittedly, fragmented political authority produces many situations in which efforts to override court rulings, particularly statutorily, will be stymied.

In short, the judiciary occupies a reactive position in the decision-making structure. It depends on its edicts being implemented and its choices being sustained politically. However, whether ill-advised or not, institutional fragmentation and the constitutional position of judges are such that the courts can influence environmental policy by changing the status quo.

What, then, are judicial preferences? Defining them is more difficult than determining an elected official's preferences. Rather than being electorally selected, justices are negotiated choices between the Senate and the president (Segal, Cameron, and Cover 1992; on the impact of judicial partisanship and ideology, see, Kovacic 1991, Revesz 1997a, Cross and Tiller 1998) and, unlike elected officials, essentially receive lifetime appointments. Although possible, removal is a modest tool for political control at best (for an explanation, see Ferejohn 1999). Consequently, a judge's behavior will somewhat reflect the preferences of initial selectors but may correspond poorly to those of current elected officials (but see Eskridge and Ferejohn 1992).

Nonetheless, for our purposes, judicial preferences can be thought to have legal and policy dimensions. On the one hand, judges have a view of what role law and the courts should play and a valuation of legal precedent. For instance, they may believe in dramatic judicial policy intervention or in a reserved judiciary, with precedent also weighted. On the other hand, judges may have a policy bent leading them to want more or less environmental protection.

How these two dimensions interact depends on the policy preferences of other political actors. For example, judicial preferences for more environmental protection and judicial restraint may be consistent if politicians and bureaucrats prefer environmentally friendly policies and the courts create a **deference** precedent by which there is a presumption in favor of the implementing agency in its statutory interpretations and implementation choices. By contrast, if others are hostile to such policies, then the courts need to decide how to balance their legal and policy preferences. Thus, the 1970s and 1980s can be seen as largely a time in which there was a rough consistency between the courts' legal preferences and its policy preferences regarding environmental policy. The 1970s was an era of generally activist, environmentally sympathetic, judges (for example, Wenner 1982), and the 1980s was a period when the courts, especially the Supreme Court, were less activist judicially and more conservative politically (for example, Wald 1992). In the 1970s the courts pushed an EPA that was sometimes hesitant to act (which was consistent with choices made at the agency's creation) at a time when elected political officials were not positioned to overrule many judicial dictates. In the 1980s, with agencies and the chief executive becoming more conservative and Congress remaining comparatively liberal (as did the appellate courts), the now conservative Supreme Court could suggest that agencies be given broader delegation and show both judicial restraint and facilitate preferred policies.[10]

Interestingly, the advent of the more liberal Clinton administration in the 1990s proved a more difficult time, because a conservative Supreme Court could no longer rely on protected agencies implementing preferred policies. Consequently, many judicial rulings of the 1990s and early twenty-first century can be seen as efforts to maneuver around such roadblocks.

With respect to judicial capacity, perhaps most notable are judicial limitations in dealing with technically complex issues.[11] Not only are judges generalists like other elected officials but, despite some urging that the situation be remedied, they lack staffs and ancillary organizations to provide and confidently process the requisite information. Put differently, courts receive data and analysis regarding environmental policy from interested parties. Although such information is valuable, judges lack the ability to make low-cost, high-benefit court rulings on environmental affairs, particularly given the complex choice of regulatory instruments that other policy makers typically settle on. Consequently, given the apparent efficiency costs of judicial intervention, it might be believed that justices would be well advised to let politicians and bureaucrats work technical issues out as long as they both follow proper procedures.

Yet, the judiciary has, to a considerable extent, adopted a policy-oriented role regarding environmental affairs and other social regulatory issues. Consistent with the so-called *new administrative law* (a doctrine justifying a more activist judicial stance to control agencies' exercise of discretion; see Stewart 1975), judges have often proved to be an active force, contributing to the fragmented, inefficient depiction of environmental policy. Indeed, as implied, even judicial moves toward deference can be interpreted as reflecting efforts to achieve policy goals.

Specifically, the courts' environmental policy impact has principally worked through three mechanisms: (1) determining whether agencies should be given the benefit of the doubt regarding whether they have followed stipulated decision-making procedures; (2) deciding if the statutory interpretations of agencies should be deferred to; and (3) ascertaining whether a narrow or broad set of societal interests have standing and thus the right to judicial appeal. Interestingly, for seemingly strategic reasons related to controlling policy outcomes, the Supreme Court has changed its course in applying the latter two mechanisms, pushing the judiciary toward a secondary role that would appear to correspond more closely to its capacity.

As for procedural choices, courts can allow bureaucrats to behave as they choose as long as they comply with the Administrative Procedures Act (a set of rules governing administrative decision making; see Kerwin 1999), providing them with discretion and presumably reducing their costs, or they can insist upon careful and detailed review, which may raise the price of doing business and induce agencies to adapt their policies in a judicially palatable manner (for example, Tiller

1998). With the evolution of modern environmental policy, the courts decisively selected the second option by, most notably, insisting upon applying a "hard look" doctrine by which agency adherence to procedural requirements is carefully examined, often with great substantive implications (Leventhal 1974, Banks 1999). For instance, the courts may decide that the EPA has insufficiently considered available evidence when determining the strictness of an environmental standard and remand the case back to the agency, providing the bureau both with an incentive to create a judicially acceptable record and to make choices less likely to incur judicial wrath. Thus, although they may seem policy neutral, procedural rulings can allow for judicial policy control at the expense of building additional transaction costs into the policy process.

With respect to substantive rulings, the courts' adoption of more interventionist and reserved stances in the modern environmental era is also interpretable as means of control. The judiciary was active in the years following the EPA's creation. For instance, the courts essentially stipulated a standard preventing significant air quality deterioration for areas exceeding quality levels mandated by the 1970 Clean Air Act, which was then ratified by the 1977 Clean Air Act Amendments. But attitudes changed. Thus, in its landmark 1984 *Chevron* case (*Chevron USA* v. *Natural Resources Defense Council* [467 U.S. 837]; see Starr 1986), the Supreme Court attempted to reverse judicial course by stating that administrative agencies should be accorded deference, meaning there should be a strong presumption in favor of the agency. In practice, *Chevron's* impact seems to be real but principally at the margin, reflected by the government's winning more court cases (Wenner and Ostberg 1994). Consistent with the discussion above, this switch toward deference is explicable as a function of more liberal interests in the Congress and the appellate courts (Cohen and Spitzer 1994, 1996). Deference would allow agencies to move policies in a conservative direction, with President Reagan and conservative legislative allies preventing overruling. As such, the Court directed authority away from the appellate courts and toward the agencies when the ability of the legislature to punish bureaucrats was limited.

Issues of standing are especially important for environmental policy, given its frequently diffuse cost bearers and beneficiaries. Courts possess a continuum of options, ranging from restricting standing to interests that are central and basic to granting rights to any group claiming that government actions affect their well-being. More concretely, for example, can national environmental groups petition to protect a waterway, a forest, or the air? Or, as Supreme Court Justice William O. Douglas phrased it, do trees (or at least their representatives) have standing? Narrowly conceptualizing standing can limit the sample of cases courts can choose from and the arguments heard.

Consistent with the Supreme Court's activist stance, beginning in the 1960s the courts drastically expanded environmental standing, allowing a wide variety of interested parties to go to the courts or to threaten lengthy judicial proceedings as a bargaining tool (for example, *Scenic Hudson Preservation Conference et al.* v. *Federal Power Commission* (354 F2d. 608 [1965]) and *Sierra Club* v. *Morton, Secretary of the Interior, et al.* (405 U.S. 727 [1972]); on the "ossification" of regulation created by granting such wide standing and broad judicial review, see Cross 1999). In the 1990s, however, the conservative Supreme Court, led by Justice Antonin Scalia, moved to restrict standing (Manus 1999; see also *Bennett* v. *Spear* 117 U.S. 1154 [1997]). This change, while perhaps consistent with the Court's judicial philosophy, also seemingly reflected the fact that agency discretion threatened to produce more liberal outcomes at this time as agencies (and appellate courts) turned in a liberal direction; even the advent of a more conservative Congress in 1994 did not ensure that policy initiatives would be held in check. Put differently, limiting standing was a seemingly attractive way of guiding policy, especially environmental policy, in a more conservative direction at a time when agency discretion was insufficient. For example, in 1998, in *Steel Co.* v. *Citizens for a Better Environment* (111 U.S. 1003), the Court ruled against citizens' being able to sue a pickle plant failing to file TRI reports because the fines that could be assessed would not redress the harm to such individuals (see also *Lujan* v. *Defenders of Wildlife*, 112 U.S. 2130 [1992]). Admittedly, by stating that an offender merely coming into compliance after the commencement of litigation did not undermine a citizen group's standing (*Friends of the Earth Inc.* v. *Laidlaw Environmental Services Inc.*, 98 U.S. 822 [2000]), the Court has proved to be unwilling to go as far as Scalia would like. Nonetheless, rights of standing have been restricted.

In short, the courts have used the three principal means strategically and there is every reason to believe that they will continue to innovate if circumstances dictate. Perhaps the most notable aspect of judicial manipulation is the considerable efficiency and transaction costs traded off for influencing policy direction. To a considerable degree, and to a different extent at various times, distribution has triumphed over efficiency.

Environmental Agencies:
The Zone of Discretion and Informational Advantages

As discussed earlier, environmental agencies have grown in their capacity but have been hamstrung by their construction, their assigned responsibilities, and their designated means for realizing their assigned goals. The picture painted is often troubling, as rationalized and integrated decision making is not typically the rule of the day.

Delineating strengths and weaknesses is easy compared with answering questions about causality. Do agencies independently affect environmentally relevant policy and, if so, how and to what effect? As agencies are constructs of other political actors, with possibilities of punishment or even elimination, much bureaucratic behavior may be at the behest of politicians and their allies or the product of politically determined structural and statutory choices. Put differently, although agency employees make mistakes, at least some faulty selections reflect not administrative deficiencies per se but, rather, decisions made by politicians and judges.

The crucial issue is whether bureaus sometimes steer policies in a direction favorable to them but not selected by other institutional actors. Upon close examination, it does appear that bureaus can have some impact, because political choices in the separation-of-powers system provide agencies with a zone of discretion and because technical complexity furnishes bureaucrats a strategic advantage that politicians can partially but not completely overcome.

For example, political scientists Kenneth Shepsle and Mark Bonchek nicely summarize how bureaucrats may operate within a discretionary zone when all political actors in the separation-of-powers system cannot act as one:

> The problem for the politicians . . . is that bureaucratic agents have missions, interests, and objectives of their own that may conflict with those of the politicians. Indeed, clever agents will take into account that, in order to sanction a bureau . . . the component members of that coalition must act *in unison*—this is the constitutional requirement in the separation-of-powers political order of the United States. As long as the agent makes sure that no alternative is preferred by all component members of the enacting coalition to whatever it does, it will be spared punishment. (Shepsle and Bonchek 1997, 367)

From the perspective of bureaucrats, then, the key is to find a new policy that they prefer to that currently in place and for which they will not be penalized.

The strategic advantage associated with technical complexity stems from the greater expertise of bureaucrats. Although politicians can give agency members strict marching orders, this will be costly if there is a lack of understanding of how policy works. The alternative is to provide agencies with discretion, which can allow them also to steer policy in a direction not favored by politicians. As economist Kathleen Bawn puts it, politicians face a trade-off between expertise and control: "[There is] a trade-off between control and expertise [that] affects the degree of independence delegated to any agency. A legislative coalition's choice of agency independence . . . depends on technical uncertainty about policy consequences, as well as uncertainty about the political environment" (Bawn, 1995, 71).

Although hard to prove definitively, discretionary zones appear to have been more important in recent years, because of the problems of gridlock and divided government, whereas the impact of the trade-off between expertise and control on agency autonomy was likely to have been more relevant earlier, when informational sources were fewer and less diverse even in the context of lesser agency responsibilities. Furthermore, for the EPA and at least for the historically preservationist natural resource agencies, these impacts generally, if not always, produce stricter environmental policy.

The role that agencies play within the separation-of-powers system is a function of political choices. Consistent with judicial and scholarly ambivalence over whether politicians can assign broad, quasi-legislative responsibility to agencies, such authority is delegated rather than constitutionally derived. As mentioned, politicians might find delegation, particularly where bureaucrats have substantial discretion in making choices and policies, desirable for political and technical reasons. Politically, it can deflect unwanted policy responsibilities from elected officials (at the expense of some control) and yet provide these same politicians with opportunities for intervening on behalf of constituents and organized interests. Technically, delegation allows more expert bureaucrats to deal with the issues at hand, which would seem quite important for many environmentally relevant concerns. Regardless, although there has been a movement toward greater specificity in political instructions, agencies must frequently translate their authority into precise plans. For example, the EPA must determine how to produce new gasoline blends that will reduce air pollution produced by trucks; the NPS must decide how to operate new areas given varied designations; and the FWS must choose a policy to protect migratory birds. Although such outcomes cannot be assumed to be solely the work of these agencies, these initiatives leave open the possibility of bureaucratic influence.

In the separation-of-powers system, possible agency-induced changes to the status quo are contained within a zone of discretion. Given this zone, other political actors, especially the president and the legislature, are unable to respond effectively. Figure 4-2 graphically illustrates this logic through an example in which a statute directs the EPA to develop a clean air policy; the agency, House of Representatives, Senate, and president have ideal policy mixes that represent preferences for (a) absolute reduction levels, and (b) reductions from producers of stationary and mobile pollution sources such as smokestacks and automobiles (for a more complete development, see McCubbins, Noll, and Weingast 1989, and for a simple exposition, see Shepsle and Bonchek 1997). A Republican-controlled Senate prefers low reduction that asks high relative contributions from the automobile industry, a Democratic president prefers more reduction with roughly the same contribution from both sources, and a Democratic House prefers even higher reductions with greater emphasis on stationary sources (for example, key Demo-

Figure 4-2 Agency Zone of Discretion: An Illustration

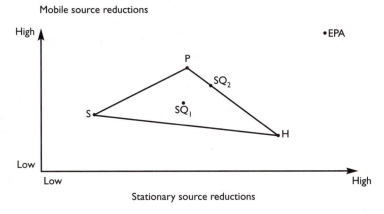

Note: H = House of Representatives; P = President; S = Senate; SQ_1 = policy chosen by H, P, and S; SQ_2 = policy implemented by EPA.

cratic leaders are highly supportive of automobile interests). The strongly pro-environmental agency desires very high reductions while favoring stationary pollution reduction. Politically, any solution contained by the triangle linking the ideal points of the House, Senate, and president is a possible or feasible outcome. For illustrative purposes, assume that SQ_1—the policy chosen by the House, Senate, and the president—is selected and, as mentioned, the EPA decides how it will be precisely achieved (for one reason, because the agency's technical expertise is needed). The agency, however, knows all the actors' ideal points and is aware that any policy that it implements that falls on or within the triangle will be sustained politically. Thus, it chooses and implements policy SQ_2, which is closer to its ideal point than SQ_1, and politicians are unable to coordinate a response. Consequently, assuming a modicum of discretion, the agency can move policy within limits, the extent to which is a function of the distribution of other institutional players' ideal points.

Related to advantages stemming from agency actions in a stylized decision-making sequence, bureaucrats have been posited to influence policy as a result of their informational advantages. If agency members can mislead politicians on matters of fact, they can influence policy by affecting the induced ideal points of elected officials (for the classic work, see Niskanen 1971; for reviews of informational models, see Mueller 1989, Shepsle and Bonchek 1997). For example, if bureaucrats exaggerate the number of lives that a given NAAQS will save—a charge leveled against the EPA in its setting of standards on ground-level ozone—they may win more political support for a stricter standard than they would if they had possessed perfect information. If politicians find verifying such statements difficult, if they have monitoring problems, then bureaucrats may color the truth and affect policy. More will be said about such possibilities later.

Like judges, defining the preferences of agency members is more difficult than doing so for legislators or presidents. First, political appointees and civil servants must be distinguished (Johnson and Libecap 1994). Appointees are selected via a bargaining process between the Senate and the president and can represent an important means of political control (Calvert, McCubbins, and Weingast 1989). They may be preselected to reflect the policy preferences of political actors, who presumably also wish to choose someone technically competent, and are subject to removal. As civil servants are almost impossible to fire, politicians' means of control, such as rules governing promotions and overall agency budgets, are blunter and likely to be less effective than for political appointees. Generally civil servants prefer agency growth and expansion. However, they may also favor policy instruments that provide them with more responsibility, like command-and-control instruments, despite efficiency costs. Civil servants' preferences may also be influenced by their professional orientations. For instance, biologists may be more sensitive to the environmental importance of species and de-emphasize economic costs, whereas economists may be oriented toward using efficient policy instruments along with cost-benefit and risk analyses. Preferences of political appointees are likely to be more variable; appointees may also put a greater value on efficiency, since agency effectiveness can be a high priority for them.

Clearly, assessing agencies' capacities can vary, depending on one's perspective. On the one hand, some members will have more specialized expertise. Also, absolute agency capacity has grown with time. On the other hand, as the number of tasks and responsibilities have grown and become more complex and technical, agency capacity relative to responsibilities frequently seems insufficient. Given agency position, preferences, and capacity, how important have the environmental agencies been in steering policy and by what means? Although these agencies have probably played some role in moving policy, the importance of various mechanisms has likely changed over time. In earlier years, gridlock was less troublesome, because legislators and the chief executive were better able to come to agreement. During that time, information, whether provided by partisan interest groups, government agencies, or other sources, was less plentiful and more costly because groups were fewer and institutional capacity to produce information was less developed. Bureaus could have used monitoring difficulties to push somewhat more extreme policies. Agencies such as the BLM, which was viewed as having a cozy relationship with ranchers, were positioned to make informational statements that elected officials might find too costly to validate given the potential returns. For example, the BLM could make statements about the efficacy of grazing policies in maintaining the land and keeping the agricultural industry healthy that might have gone unchallenged.

In later years, however, the interest group explosion and the growth of presidential and congressional institutional capacity have dissipated monitoring problems and made it more difficult for agencies to get away with serving their own purposes. For example, in the recent ground-level ozone and particulate standard debates, numerous opponents arose when the EPA was seen as making scientifically exaggerated claims (see also Chapter 5). But, at the same time, gridlock increased notably for reasons having little to do with environmental policy, and beginning in the 1980s cooperation among political decision makers became more problematic (Kraft 2000a). This probably created opportunities for agencies such as the EPA to use their zones of discretion without punishment in trying to manipulate policy. For instance, if the EPA orders a particularly expensive reformulated gasoline to reduce pollution, polarization of politicians' preferences may make punishment more problematic than before. Elected officials may try to counter increased agency discretion by providing more detailed instructions when they can agree on a statutory compromise, as was the case with a good deal of environmental legislation of the 1980s, but such prescription often comes with efficiency costs.

So not only may agencies such as the EPA further appearances of fragmentation and inefficiency, they may push the policy boundaries and actually cause more fragmentation and inefficiency in the process. For the EPA, except during rare times, this has meant stricter but not necessarily more efficient regulation, for natural resource agencies it has presumably meant pushing their de facto mission—whether it be species preservation, promotion of national parks, or some variant of multiple use, for example. Elected officials have countered these opportunities in various ways. Informational obstacles would appear to have been substantially overcome with the growth of the interest group system and the development of greater informational capacity; agency abilities to move the status quo within the zone of discretion have been countered with more prescription, but the possibility of greater inefficiency tends to mitigate the attractiveness of such a response.

LINKING DEMAND AND SUPPLY: IMPLICATIONS FOR PUBLIC POLICY

A variety of specific insights is produced by the detailed examination of national political influences that have important implications for environmental policy. Considered jointly, these detailed conclusions provide a broader understanding of how demand and supply operate to produce the environmental policy system.

On the demand side, public opinion has been heavily supportive of increased environmental protection and has been a major factor in policy expansion. However, although voters have an incentive to prefer more efficient solutions to less efficient ones, they have few strong views on whether efficient policy instruments are adopted. Compared with the general support of the public, interest groups have contrasting preferences over how much environmental policy is promulgated. The environmental interest group movement has certainly pushed for more protection, but opposition interests, such as business interests that must pay many of the costs of policy, have also arisen. In toto, organizational effects seem to be substantial but not generally dominant, particularly for EPA-style policies. Given both the preferences of the unorganized and the efforts of interest groups, environmental policy often seems a somewhat awkward combination of the organized and unorganized efforts of those with a genuine desire for a better world and those promoting narrow self-interests (Yandle 1989). Additionally, with some exceptions where interests have coalesced over the use of more efficient instruments in conjunction with a given level of protection, organizational efforts have contributed to inefficiencies and the failure to approach policy solutions systematically.

But supply matters too in influencing how societal interests get reflected in policy. The intermeshing of political institutions appears to have had a substantial influence on the extent and nature of environmental policy. The prototypical disjointed institution, Congress, has helped to promulgate inefficiencies when responding to perceived demand. By its very nature, Congress promotes representation of narrow interests, and legislators lack an overriding interest in promoting efficiency. As such, although legislators have responded to spiraling demand for environmental protection by increasing efforts to improve quality, they have not proved to be strong proponents of efficient policy instruments. By contrast, and often in opposition to the legislature, presidents have tended to advocate more environmental protection, echoing public opinion on such matters. They have been notable for championing more efficient instruments as they have tried to plow ground between pursuing economic prosperity and meeting demands for protection. Yet presidents rarely satisfy environmental advocates (or opponents), as the former's incentives seldom mesh with the latter's preferences.

To make the situation even more disjointed, courts have served as strategic political actors rather than as dispassionate interpreters of the law. Sometimes this has led justices to push toward more environmental protection and at other times toward less. Most striking, judicial intervention in the environmental policy process has added inefficiencies by making the courts de facto policy makers in a technically complicated policy area where they lack the requisite capacity to make informed choices.

Agencies then find themselves in the middle of all this political gaming. Moreover, although they are the symbol of many problems as well as the medium of success, and although they substantially reflect the choices of other political officials, they have a real but limited independent influence on policy. To the degree that agencies have such an effect, they tend to push for their expansion and have relatively little incentive to advocate efficient solutions. Whereas in earlier times, when other institutional players had less analytic firepower and organizational actors were less diverse and capable, informational advantages were likely a prominent element of bureaucratic influence, currently agencies probably rely more on the zone of discretion associated with the separation-of-powers system. Given divided government and political gridlock, this zone has seemingly widened somewhat. To the extent that political actors have responded in recent years to such agency manipulation with greater prescription, more inefficiency almost certainly results.

It seems clear that the strong demand for environmental quality has induced political decision makers, despite the fragmented system in which they operate, to increase markedly the extent of environmental policy in the United States. But given supply-side institutions, the slowness of politicians to remedy policies' deficiencies, despite a constant barrage of criticism, and the increased politicization of policy, are also understandable. All in all, environmental policy has increased in the United States as it has in other advanced industrial democracies, but the way in which American environmental policy has grown seems to be influenced substantially by specific organizational and national institutional factors.

At a more general level, two features stand out. First, national political influences result in and reflect a fragmented policy with significant effects. An amorphous public opinion and a variety of diverse organizations produce demand while the American separation-of-powers system, with political actors negotiating the nature of delegation, generates the supply. The interaction of demand and supply seems bound to generate fractured policies—fraught with inefficiencies, misplaced priorities favoring one interest or region over another, and poor integration. Such policies, in turn, reinforce the fractured condition of political organizations and institutions. Second, a variety of feedback loops exist. Institutional fragmentation provides an incentive for a plethora of interests to organize and gain a stake in current policy, and the existence of such interests provides political officials with incentives to maintain the disjointed nature of political institutions or to make them even more fractured.

KEY TERMS

Deference (p. 91)
Ecotage (p. 75)
Judicial standing (p. 90)
Moral hazard effects (p. 77)

Purposive rewards (p. 69)
Selection effects (p. 77)
Solidary rewards (p. 69)
Takings (p. 88)

5 Developing and Enforcing Environmental Policy

Implementing environmental policy is clearly problematic. Almost every principal agency entrusted with enforcing environmental policy has been assailed for not carrying out its mission. Natural resource agencies are often cited for poor care of their resources, giving away valuable goods at below market costs and not fully integrating economic considerations into their decisions, catering to special interests, violating the Constitution by taking private goods belonging to others, and lacking coherent goals and policies. Similarly, the EPA is criticized for poor integration, inept employment of scientific knowledge, incoherent policies defying commonsense, delays, and burdening itself and others with enormous transaction costs.

Such condemnations might seem endemic to policy implementation where there are winners and losers, where agencies are dominated by civil servants, or where complex organizations are needed (see Miller 1992). But other, interrelated, reasons for such disappointments stand out that are intimately linked to the fragmented nature of political supply and the resulting lack of integration produced when political decision makers respond to political demand. Although agencies have their faults, appreciating implementation requires a far broader perspective on political supply and the problems created in translating rising demand into policy. In particular, four features—the choice of policies and instruments, the strategic interplay between enforcer and those needing to comply with policy, the willingness of politicians to interfere with the process, and problems of credibility by which political promises and threats are deemed unlikely to be realized—combine to give implementation its unique character.

Thus, among the problems facing those charged with the task is that the policies that are chosen are commonly difficult to implement. Complex policies are frequently selected over seemingly simpler, not to mention more efficient, alternatives. In particular, selecting command-and-control over market mechanisms makes implementation inherently more difficult, since command-and-control requires more active policy development, monitoring (detecting violations), and punishment. Additionally, as products of political bargaining, many policy provisions delegated to agencies are designed with a goal of appeasing contrasting interests rather than of facilitating implementation.

Implementation also involves intrinsically complicated strategic issues. Most notably, a cat-and-mouse game is often played between the agency and societal actors, with bureaucrats searching for the right mix of monitoring and penalty levels to deter individuals, firms, and even governments calculating to minimize their costs in response. Further complicating this situation is that societal actors may plead ignorance, claiming that a lack of knowledge rather than calculated evasion leads to their violations, which may or may not be the case. In developing an implementation strategy, an agency must decide, with political input and preferences in mind, whether to emphasize an adversarial **deterrence strategy** (punishing offenders to induce compliance) or a conciliatory approach focusing on cooperation and provision of information.

Adding to these complications is political interference. Political actors may involve themselves in minute details of the implementation process. Thus, an agency charged with policy enforcement may contend with a variety of interests from all corners of the political system. Competing interest groups, local office-holders and agencies, national political officials, and the courts can seek to guide implementation, and the agency may press its own concerns. At the same time, given these potentially competing interests, there is limited political ability for dramatically reforming implementation, meaning that change tends to be incremental, marginal, and layered on top of existing rules.

Finally, credibility problems arise, as those subject to implementation may doubt that agencies or interested politicians will follow through on promised rewards and threatened punishments. Put differently, the inability to write credible contracts threatens to subvert implementation. Even pledges regarding punishment made in statutory edicts may be discredited by an inability or unwillingness of political actors to carry out threats.

Although not rendering policy completely ineffective, these related factors can complicate environmental policy implementation. They contribute to policy's haphazard and disjointed image and to the inference that achieving goals involves costs beyond those dictated by technical constraints. Increasing demand for environmental quality does not mean that the political system supplies easy-to-implement policies.

This chapter will explore the problems of developing and enforcing environmental policy and attempt to explain them further. Emphasis is placed on difficulties associated with the mandates for implementation that agencies are given—including a heavy focus on difficult-to-implement command-and-control instruments and cumbersome rulemaking procedures—the amount of enforcement activity that takes place and the alternative strategic choices that agencies and politicians must make, the impact of political interference on implementation, and the importance of credibility for the success of implementation.

MANDATES FOR IMPLEMENTATION

A difficulty plaguing bureaus in the American political context generally, and certainly those implementing environmental policy, involves their mandates. Directions given to agencies implementing environmental policies, typically in legislative statutes, are frequently recipes for problems, indeed, some might say for disaster. Implementation difficulties often appear preordained before agency members make a single choice.

Tensions between policy mandates and bureau implementation have two levels. Both stem from the preferences of political decision makers. First, when choosing policy instruments, these decision makers have exhibited a preference for command-and-control. Stress on command-and-control rather than on markets greatly raises the likelihood of major implementation problems because the former are inherently more difficult to implement than the latter. Furthermore, the specific command-and-control policies that these decision makers select are often more difficult to implement than alternatives. Unattainable goals and convoluted procedures are specified, not to mention that insufficient budgets for achieving specified tasks are frequently allocated, often hamstringing implementation.

Command-and-Control versus the Market

Simply put, economic instruments are far easier to implement than command-and-control mechanisms. As complicated as implementing any environmental policy might appear, that politicians prefer command-and-control makes the process that much harder.

Market-oriented policies do have potential implementation problems. For instance, government must ensure that the market is respected by enforcing property rights and transactions or it will not function properly. For example, in trying to reduce pollution in a low-cost manner, authors of the Clean Air Act Amendments of 1990 specified that producers of the air pollutant sulfur dioxide operate via a market. Although polluters must hold appropriate permits that they are free to trade as if they were stocks (the actual market is located in Chicago), if government does not make sure that all polluters have permits or fails to enforce contracts to exchange such permits when a dispute arises, the market for pollution will not function properly and many of the theoretical gains to society from pollution markets will be lost as implementation is undercut. Additionally, there may be credibility problems, because economic actors may believe that market instruments will be discontinued and, as a result, not make market trades that would otherwise take place (Carlson and Sholtz 1994, Foster and Hahn 1995). Indeed, such credibility issues can be especially prevalent for markets because, unlike command-and-control, where specific fixed costs are involved (for example, investing in mandatory pollution abatement equipment that is cheap to operate once purchased), there may be less political endogeneity by which those affected support the status quo and help perpetuate its continuation. In this vein, it took a considerable number of years after the creation of market rights to emit sulfur dioxide for vigorous trading to occur, probably at least partially because of fears that the market would not last. Although the market did not become efficient until mid-1994, it is now a success story (Joskow, Schmalensee, and Bailey 1998). Along the same lines, certain market solutions, such as taxation, may be more prone to credibility problems than others, such as emissions trading, because the latter may more successfully induce investment (Gersbach and Glazer 1999).

Yet, when all is said and done, markets are transparent and self-sustaining compared with command-and-control mechanisms. Markets are easily observable by affected parties and do not require much active management to work effectively. As economist Robert Stavins (1998, 74) puts it, "Market-based instruments do not require the same kinds of technical expertise that agencies have developed under command-and-control regulation; and market-based instruments can imply a scaled-down role for the agency by shifting decision making from the bureaucracy to the private sector." Indeed, to reiterate, experiences with market mechanisms, such as with sulfur dioxide markets, although having a few bumps in the road, have been largely favorable, and implementation issues are not especially noteworthy (see Portney 1999, 2000). Additionally, successful operation of informational provisions (a cooperative form of implementation) involves more agency intervention than markets but requires more limited technical expertise or monitoring than command-and-control. Put differently, although informational approaches are based on unobtrusively overcoming market shortfalls, the implementation issues involved are subtler than those for standard market mechanisms such as tradeable permits or taxation.

As for the specific command-and-control policies selected, it is the nature of political choice often to produce decisions not clearly laying out a set of achievable goals. There are many instances where defined objectives, and the prescribed mechanisms for their achievement, virtually ensure implementation problems or failures. Natural resource agencies, whether they be the BLM, the NPS, or the USFS, are provided with conflicting directions regarding preservation, recreation, and resource exploitation. Also, many statutes and goals for which these agencies are responsible are layered on top of one another and do not integrate trade-offs or remove tensions. Consequently, implementation seems almost certain to fail in its goals.

Unattainable goals, either in an absolute sense or given available resources, plague a wide variety of EPA programs (and the FWS in implementing the Endangered Species Act). For example, the goals of the Clean Water Act of 1972 were that water be "fishable" and "swimmable" by mid-1983 and subject to zero discharge of pollutants by 1985. Such goals were simply unattainable on technical grounds even for a perfectly designed and implemented policy (see Chapter 8). Alternatively, achieving the goal of a program such as Superfund, to rapidly clean up toxic sites, is severely hamstrung by funding provisions that generate high transaction costs, such as judicial challenges, and slow progress. Regulators spend much time and money on infighting with those who will bear the cost rather than on actually cleaning waste sites (see, once again, Chapter 8). Despite seemingly good intentions, Superfund is perhaps the most notorious example of legislation ill designed for agency implementation.

In short, politically determined mandates to pursue environmental quality given to agencies seem destined to make implementation problematic. Goals are often conflicting and unattainable. Selection of command-and-control instruments, and difficult to implement ones at that, complicates matters from the outset.

Rulemaking

Additionally, procedural rulemaking requirements are notoriously cumbersome and can produce delay and debilitating court battles (see Chapter 4) (Kagan 1995, 1997, 1999; Ando 1999; Kerwin 1999). Although the absolute number of regulations taking effect would seem large—the EPA alone develops in excess of 500 each year—and arduous to implement, the strategic and technical processes of developing rules are tortuous and certainly deter agencies from being proactive.

A somewhat atypical but prominent example occurred when the EPA attempted, as it is directed to do under the Clean Air Act of 1970, to develop a standard on air particulates 2.5 microns or less in diameter (for overviews, see Blodgett, Parker, and McCarthy 1997; Meltz and McCarthy 1999). These small particulates result from combustion and chemical reactions in the atmosphere and have been claimed to have negative health consequences, including respiratory disease, heart attacks, and asthma, as well to reduce visibility and add to haze. Under the Clean Air Act, as amended especially by the 1990 Amendments, the EPA is required to review its National Ambient Air Quality Standards every five years with the goal of protecting the public health with a margin of safety. Such reviews are to be without reference to costs, technical feasibility, or nonhealth criteria (although Executive Order 12866 governing major rules dictates that a cost-benefit analysis be produced—a contradiction that has never been formally addressed). Despite such edicts, the Reagan-Bush EPA, being more conservative than its predecessors, was reluctant to review particulate and ground-level ozone standards, precipitating the American Lung Association to lead a judicial charge to force adherence to statutory obligations. Induced to act by the courts (the particulate case was filed in 1993, four years after one was filed regarding ozone, but the two were essentially joined), the agency began its review process by preparing a 4,000-page "Criteria Document" for ozone and particulates assessing current scientific knowledge, then having it reviewed by an independent Clean Air Scientific Advisory Committee. Subsequently a "Staff Paper" by the agency translated what was learned into policy options. In November 1996, led by EPA head Carol Browner, the EPA proposed rather aggressive particulate and ozone standards (although many environmentalists wanted even tighter standards), and in accordance with the dictates of the Administrative Procedures Act filed them in the *Federal Register* for a sixty-day public comment period and planned a public hearing. Most notably with respect to particulates, the agency recommended focusing on finer particles to supplement existing rules on coarser particulates (adding a strong "2.5" standard to supplement the existing "10" standard), claiming that by 2007, when much of the implementation would be realized, annual benefits of $57 billion to $119 billion would be achieved for a $6 billion price tag.

Claims of vast improvements in social welfare based on more than three years of intensive deliberation might produce expectations that the ensuing rulemaking procedure would be smooth sailing, but this was anything but the case. Instead, a firestorm of controversy followed. Lobbyists for the oil, coal, electric, and auto industries swarmed Capitol Hill, drumming up opposition to the standard, coordinating their attacks with national radio ads and the like to energize the public. Intergovernmental groups, particularly representatives of areas that would be out of compliance with the new rule and bear substantial costs, mobilized in opposition. Also—echoing comments in Chapter 4 of difficulties for modern-day agencies to use informational advantages—much to opponents' delight and sometimes with their encouragement, numerous scholars, such as Brookings Institution economists Robert Crandall and his colleagues (Crandall, Rueter, and Steger 1997, 43), questioned the scientific evidence underpinning the agency's particulate standard:

[T]he entire body of available scientific evidence strongly leads us to question whether ambient PM [particulate matter] is a major causative agent for mortality and morbidity. In addition, the ambient concentrations of the airborne substances that probably are the principal causative agents—namely, bioaerosol and chemical allergens emitted from indoor sources into the indoor air—have not been reduced. Accordingly, the sizable health benefits that the draft report has attributed to reductions in ambient PM concentrations in its benefit-cost analysis are highly speculative. The true health benefits from reducing ambient PM levels undoubtedly are much smaller.

Yet, although opposition took its toll as numerous congressional figures, even Democrats, requested that the EPA be forced to back off, President Clinton endorsed a rule in 1997 only slightly modified from that of the EPA. Congressional opposition was insufficient to do anything about this choice. But, rather than being settled, the battle moved to another arena in the separation-of-powers system as the American Trucking Associations, quickly joined by many others, filed suit in the District of Columbia Court of Appeals. Two years later, the court made a potential landmark ruling, arguing that the agency's actions, in conjunction with those of Congress, violated the nondelegation doctrine associated with Article I of the Constitution. If the Supreme Court did not deem otherwise, Congress would have to approve each standard directly unless the EPA developed an "intelligible principle" for its choices (for a critique, see Pierce 2000). However, in early 2001, the Supreme Court refused to role regulation back sixty-five years and affirmed the EPA's right to develop its standards and, indeed, to pay little explicit attention to costs in a manner consistent with the CAA's language (*Whitman* v. *American Trucking Associations*, 99 S.Ct. 1257; see Meltz and McCarthy 2001). But, with a new president in office and the rule still tied up in litigation on more conventional grounds (for example, that, according to the U.S. Chamber of Commerce, it was made "arbitrarily and capriciously"), it is likely that this judicial action will merely instigate a new round of debate over the right standard.

Thus, the EPA has essentially lost a decade in developing and implementing a particulate standard, at least partially because of the rulemaking process (for example, the agency is not given a clear rulemaking standard, such as equating costs with benefits, with assurance that its rules will take effect given a demonstrated good faith attempt to meet the standard). A new particulate standard, should it be developed, will reflect not merely technical consensus but a complicated and convoluted political process and will not be fully implemented until well into the second decade of the twenty-first century.

In light of this tortuous process, agencies such as the EPA, frequently pushed by their political overseers, would seem to have an incentive to develop alternative coping strategies. However, in practice, such changes appear marginal and do not rationalize the underlying process.

The most notable rulemaking innovation, **negotiated rulemaking,** is used by various agencies but is primarily associated with the EPA (for example, Harter 1982, 2000; Susskind and McMahon 1985). Under negotiated rulemaking, a committee of interested parties is consulted to forge a consensus prior to a rule's formal proposal, thus, it is hoped, saving time and reducing litigation. Once consensus is reached, the rule is proposed and the notice-and-comment period proceeds. Originating in the 1980s, Congress officially endorsed this process by passing the Negotiated Rulemaking Act of 1990 (permanently reauthorizing it in

1996), and the Clinton administration's efforts at agency reform through its National Performance Review were strongly encouraging. Yet, although many find this process appealing, its use so far has had only a modest impact. For instance, such efforts do not effectively overcome the adversarial process, at most substituting one form of conflict for another, and not surprisingly rulemaking takes roughly the same amount of time (about three years on average) and has a probability of subsequent litigation comparable to nonnegotiated rules (Coglianese 1997). Also not surprisingly, this method has been used sparingly. For example, from 1980 to 1996 the EPA employed it only eighteen times, with only twelve proposals actually becoming finished regulations (for an argument on why negotiation is inapplicable for environmental policy, see Rose-Ackerman 1994).

Thus, besides the preference of politicians for command-and-control over market mechanisms, generally making implementation more difficult than is necessary, their specific choice of rulemaking procedures makes translating mandates into policy fraught with difficulties even beyond technical hurdles. For the most part, efforts to change this situation have been incremental and piecemeal, with matching results.

ENFORCEMENT: DETERRENCE, COOPERATION, INFORMATION

Despite what has been said about mandates, given the delegation of authority, agencies must go about their business of implementation nonetheless. This process has many aspects, but perhaps the most crucial for environmental quality is dealing with those who are, or who may be, violating rules and regulations. One legal scholar describes the situation and the EPA's approach to it as follows:

> Deterrence-based enforcement is the prevailing societal approach for controlling unlawful individual and corporate conduct. This theory underlies the EPA's current enforcement system. The agency's enforcement approach is legalistic, and its extensive enforcement policies stress the use of formal enforcement actions . . . . The agency has traditionally measured the success of its program by the number of inspections conducted, the number of enforcement actions initiated, and the number and size of penalties assessed—all indicators that some type of formal enforcement action has been taken. (Rechtschaffen 1998, 1188–1189)

As the above quotation implies, assuming formal markets are not selected (but including informational provisions), any agency or politician has a rough continuum of strategies available. Some are extremely adversarial and combative, others are cooperative, and still others are informational. Adversarial approaches, although typically inflicting higher penalties, tend to involve greater transaction costs, such as lengthy administrative and judicial proceedings, and more difficulty with detection. Cooperation reduces transaction costs and, perhaps, problems in monitoring but potentially results in less fear of penalty and detection and lower remediation levels. Information depends on the goodwill of those subject to policy or on less direct political and market pressures. Some advocate more conciliatory approaches (for example, Church and Nakamura 1993), and others claim that they work less well than adversarial approaches (for example, Harrison 1995).

Put differently, the continuum of strategies that agencies, particularly regulatory operations such as the EPA, choose from are anchored at one end by strategies based on ideas of deterrence and at the other end by those focused on education, with a host of intermediate options (Scholz 1994). Deterrence emphasizes developing a monitoring plan to detect violators and sufficient, credible penalties for providing potential violators with incentives to follow statutory dictates (Heyes 1998). **Educational strategies** involve furnishing information so that potential violators either can or are made to comply with specified rules and regulations (for a general overview of EPA enforcement, see Mintz 1995).

Not surprisingly, given the fragmented political context and its various responsibilities, environmental agencies, particularly the EPA, have seen themselves pushed and pulled between adversarial and cooperative approaches. Over the years, the EPA's approach to violators has changed with the times. Relatively confrontational in the 1970s, the EPA developed a strategy labeled as **adversarial legalism** to pursue violators (see Kagan 1995, 1997, 1999). Corresponding to the ethos of the Reagan administration, the EPA adopted a more passive stance for much of the 1980s while beginning to innovate with informational approaches. In the 1990s (and continuing through the first part of the next century), the EPA became somewhat more adversarial, but this stance was overlaid with efforts to forge collaborations with business where firms had incentives to comply with regulations and fix problems on their own initiative (especially with Republican control of the U.S. Congress after the 1994 elections) and to make greater use of educational strategies. Given varying signals, the agency's leaders are often criticized as lacking a clear vision and a coherent implementation plan for carrying out their mandates. Nonetheless, out of all this emerges implementation that, ostensibly, is designed to get relevant actors to conform and, ideally, to raise environmental quality.

The Amount of Enforcement

Before turning to the impact of enforcement, it will be helpful to explore the mechanics and scope of such actions (particularly their adversarial elements). Since the EPA's implementation efforts are more nuanced than, for example, those of the natural resource agencies, they will be the main focus here. Principally, the EPA carries out enforcement either directly through ten regional offices or via the states with these offices acting as overseers. As with many agencies, informal mechanisms often overlay formal processes.

The inner workings of the standard EPA compliance program are the product of a series of strategic choices. First, the agency/state decides what inspection strategy to follow, which, in turn, determines who is inspected and at what depth—making the choice and potential determinants of inspection strategy intriguing. An inspection strategy can mean prioritizing which policies, as well as which actors (be they individuals, firms, industries, or governments), will be targeted; regarding the latter, industries that may have a large impact on environmental quality, for example, pulp and paper with respect to water quality, are often given special attention as are companies deemed most likely to engage in violations. Regardless, if those inspected are found to be in violation, the agency/state has the option of dealing with the issue informally by providing a Notice of Violation or proceeding directly to more formal means. If a Notice of Violation fails to induce the requisite response, more formal enforcement efforts, either administratively (essentially quasi-judicially) or judicially, may commence. Such a formal action will begin with the agency or state stipulating required changes to meet compliance, a timetable for action, and the possible consequences and legal penalties for failing to comply. Then there will either be satisfactory compliance or further action. Eventually, an administrative compliance order will lay out a compliance schedule or an administrative penalty order (essentially a fine), or both. If the agency or state turns to the Department of Justice to initiate a civil judicial action (states operate through their attorney generals), the result may be penalties and court orders for remediation and actions to prevent future violations. Generally, judicial actions are a more severe means of sanctioning the offending party (and hence appropriate for more egregious cases) than administrative actions and tend to involve higher transaction costs (this description follows from GAO 2000c). Criminal prosecution is chosen over civil action where noncompliance is seen as deliberate and creating particularly serious public risk.

As mentioned, in practice, environmental enforcement is more flexible and somewhat less adversarial or rigid than this description implies. Put differently, informal means are often incorporated to get around some of enforcement's harshest elements. Nonetheless, the noncooperative approach, depending upon formal mechanisms associated with adversarial legalism, continues to underlie, and be the dominant means of, agency enforcement.

The EPA has often focused on measuring enforcement effectiveness by observable outputs (on efforts to change this focus, see Garrett 1998). This itself

Table 5-1 EPA Inspection Activities, Fiscal Year 1997

Policy	Number of inspections
Clean air (stationary sources)	2,844
Clean air (mobile sources)	104
Asbestos demolition and restoration	653
NPDES (minor and major inspections)	1,702
Clean water (other)	2,195
TRI	911
FIFRA	207
RCRA	2,165
Drinking water	5,490
Toxic substance control	1,014
Miscellaneous/underground storage tanks	1,421
Total	18,706

Source: EPA 1998.

may be distorting. A focus on observable characteristics may direct attention toward maximizing what is easily measured rather than improvement in environmental quality per dollar spent. For example, concentrating focusing on observable features such as number of enforcement actions may lead to emphasizing relatively unimportant and cost-ineffective minor violations over more relevant actions (Scholz 1984).

Nonetheless, available data provide an idea of the underlying dynamics of implementation. Table 5-1 reports the number of EPA regional inspections for fiscal year 1997 by policy (state inspections, which are not reported, involve a far larger number of inspections than the EPA)—clean air stationary (fixed) sources, clean air mobile sources, asbestos demolition and restoration, clean water via the National Pollutant Discharge Elimination System (NPDES), other clean water policy, the Toxic Release Inventories passed via the Emergency Planning and Community Right-to-Know Act of 1986 (EPCRA), the Federal Insecticide, Fungicide, and Rodenticide Act (FIFRA) that covers pesticides, the Resource Conservation and Recovery Act (RCRA) that regulates the current production of hazardous waste, drinking water, toxic substance control, and policies regarding underground storage tanks (many of these policies are discussed in more depth in Chapter 8). The inspections reported in Table 5-1 reflect the first step in implementation once a strategy has been decided upon. Almost 19,000 regional inspections were made that, although dispersed, focused on drinking water, stationary source air pollution, various features of the Clean Water Act, and RCRA. As for the next step, administrative actions, Figures 5-1 and 5-2 provide data on EPA actions by statute and state actions by program area. Statutes include the CAA;

Figure 5-1   EPA Administrative Actions by Statute, 1974–1997

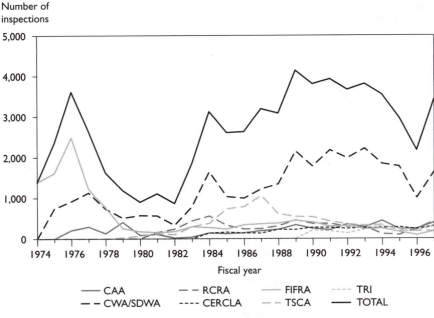

Source: EPA 1998.

the Comprehensive Environmental Response, Compensation, and Liability Act of 1980 (CERCLA), which established Superfund; the CWA and the Safe Drinking Water Act (SDWA), RCRA, the Toxic Substance Control Act (TSCA), and the TRI. Clearly, in order of magnitude, most problems involve water (especially) and air pollution. Also, although the EPA reserves principal authority over a number of programs, there is a reflection of how much more enforcement states actually do than the EPA itself. Here, the process by which the agency delegates authority as policy has become established for a program such as FIFRA, where a rise in state enforcement has more than compensated for declining EPA enforcement, is also observable.

Figure 5-3 shows that the alternative option of using the judiciary is employed but with some hesitancy. Interestingly, the level of EPA civil referrals has remained rather constant from the middle 1980s on, while the states' reliance on the courts declined.[1] This increased use of the courts on the national level appears to represent the general push for a more activist enforcement agenda in the 1990s, whereas the decline in the states seems to reflect the push for less adversarial approaches. In a controversial move, the EPA has also resorted to criminal enforcement more

Figure 5-2 State Administrative Actions, 1987–1997

Number of
administrative actions

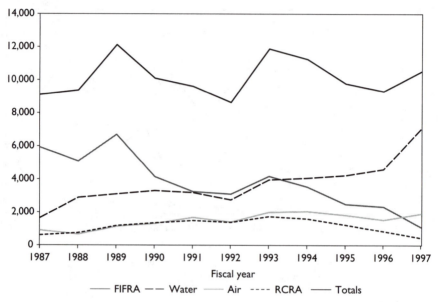

Fiscal year

——— FIFRA — — Water ········ Air ---- RCRA ——— Totals

Source: EPA 1998.

frequently in recent years (Frater 2000); illustratively, there were 65 criminal referrals in fiscal year 1989 and 278 in 1997. Occasionally, a single case has large ramifications, for example, Refrigeration, U.S.A., a Florida firm, was fined $37.4 million in 1997 for illegally importing CFC refrigerants.

These actions combine to produce some combination of penalties and additional expenditures to meet obligations (obviously, it is also hoped that they produce improved environmental quality). As Table 5-2 shows, the EPA reports exacting over $2 billion from its fiscal 1997 enforcement efforts. The agency itself currently expends close to $400 million on those efforts with, except for the CAA and TSCA, injunctive relief, by which those out of compliance act to redress problems, accounting for the vast majority of expenditures. Although comparable data for states are lacking, EPA expenditures likely dwarf state levels.

As indicated, some of the initial luster of modern environmental policy has worn off in recent years. The EPA is criticized for adopting an "enforcement first" strategy of penalizing those out of compliance without distinguishing between those wanting to do the right thing and falling short and those being deliberately evasive (for example, Hawkins 1997), whereas many states have been advocating

Figure 5-3   EPA and State Judicial Referrals

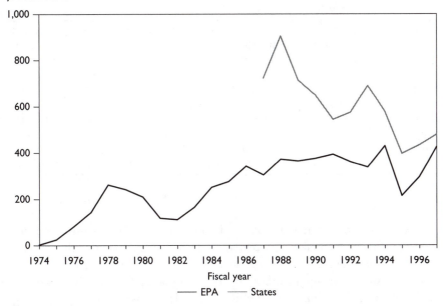

Number of
judicial referrals

Source: EPA 1998.

more cooperative approaches. Partially as a response, more conciliatory and less adversarial implementation has gained popularity. One major step in this direction began in the 1980s with the push for greater use of informational provisions to shape policy (another movement about this time, to be discussed in Chapter 8, was for greater use of risk analysis in establishing agency priorities). The principal, although not the only, example of informational environmental regulation is the TRI, a database of firm emissions initiated by Congress in 1986. This database makes data summarizing toxic releases relatively easy to access so that even individual residents may obtain reliable information about their polluting neighbors. As such, polluters may have greater incentives to reduce their emissions levels than would otherwise be the case. The TRI has proved to be so popular with certain political interests, such as those in the Clinton administration, that the number of toxics on which companies must report has been nearly doubled (to more than 600) and the number of industrial facilities required to report information has been increased about 30 percent (to well over 30,000). With encouragement, the EPA has pushed the informational envelope in other areas, such as safe drinking water, surface water, clean air, and hazardous waste (EPA 1999a).

Table 5-2 Dollar Value of EPA Enforcement Actions by Statute, Fiscal Year 1997

Statute/ penalty type	Criminal	Civil	Administrative	Injunctive relief	Supplemental environmental programs
CAA	$ 54,077,526	$13,792,299	$ 3,093,055	$ 38,245,378	$21,966,583
CERCLA	4,623,918	314,966	42,239	778,912,089	0
CWA	94,194,123	22,142,408	4,256,948	949,026,967	38,798,563
EPCRA	0	0	5,183,747	2,435,393	7,646,285
FIFRA	102,174	66	1,453,885	10,346,787	816,265
RCRA	11,683,721	9,698,368	8,246,082	50,611,488	13,001,323
SDWA	40,000	18,500	369,552	38,335,856	159,500
TSCA	2,003,824	0	26,501,272	5,405,879	3,004,053
Other	2,557,610	0	31,714	20,004,000	50,350
Total	$169,282,896	$45,966,607	$49,178,494	$1,893,323,837	$85,442,922

Source: EPA 1998.

As also mentioned, in the 1990s, and consistent with efforts at forging greater consensus in the rulemaking process, the agency began exploring other ways of making enforcement somewhat less adversarial. For example, in 1995 the EPA, under pressure from, among others, the new Republican Congress, announced a policy allowing for regulatory **self-audits,** by which firms identifying, reporting, and correcting violations would have penalties reduced or eliminated (EPA 1999a).[2] Essentially, for those employing self-audits, the agency does not seek penalties based on factors other than economic damage caused and eschews recommending criminal prosecution. The intuition behind such a policy is straightforward: a firm will have an incentive to fix problems if doing so makes it better off than it would be if it waited until they were discovered through agency/state monitoring. However, this depends on making sure that the violator has incentives to be forthcoming and proactive. Otherwise, the policy will not have the intended effects. For example, in conducting a 1992 self-audit, the Coors Brewing Company discovered it was emitting about 17 times more air pollution than earlier thought when brewing beer. But, rather than simply being allowed to address the problem, Coors was fined $1 million for volunteering the information (later reduced to $237,000). From the company's perspective, it was being punished because it came forward and revealed information that regulators lacked. This case is often linked to the beginning of a push for so-called privilege and immunity for self-reporters. Like negotiated regulations, self-audits are controversial from a number of perspectives. Environmentalists are wary of self-policing because of the ability of firms to hide their damaging behavior and to determine how they will remediate problems that are uncovered (which may be contrary to the solution preferred by the environmentalists), and business criticizes the agency's self-audit policy as too modest. There appears little reason to believe that self-audits will result in anything beyond marginal changes (for example, Freedman 1998). Indeed, self-audits have also degenerated into a political quagmire, as the EPA has found itself vigorously blocking states from using them leniently and extensively (twenty-three states have adopted such policies at this writing); ironically, advocates of auditing have also clashed with proponents of informational approaches, as corporate preferences for "polluter secrecy" in audits clashes with environmentalists' championing of the public's right to know.

Thus, the general point regarding the mechanics of implementation is that, to date, adversarial enforcement has dominated. Various national political actors, many states, firms, and some environmentalists believing in more cooperative approaches are pushing for expansion of the use of more consensual mechanisms. But the political response has been only to experiment with such techniques at the margins, sometimes in ways that seem ill-designed, generating frustration from those wanting bolder steps.

The Adversarial Approach

The effects of standard punishment and deterrence are well documented. Although nuanced, virtually all systematic analyses show that deterrence works in that enforcement does produce greater compliance. However, monitoring and "being caught" matter more and penalty levels matter less than most theory predicts.

Thus, on the one hand, monitoring and penalties result in more compliance with rules and regulations (Gray and Deily 1996, Helland 1998a, Magat and Viscusi 1990, Nadeau 1997); whether this means that these actions improve environmental quality or result in more cost efficiency is another issue (Adler 1998). On the other hand, small penalties do not seem to lead to low compliance levels to the extent that theory suggests (the seminal work is Harrington 1988; this phenomenon has also been noticed for agencies such as OSHA [see Scholz and Gray 1997]). Put another way, in much of its enforcement activity, the EPA has been reluctant to penalize violators heavily because of political pressures (often only a Notice of Violation without penalty is given). Design of an optimal enforcement strategy would likely suggest far higher sanctions (although high penalties may lack credibility). Yet, potential violators, principally firms, have complied at a greater rate than theory might dictate (for conditions under which low penalties may generate optimal compliance levels, see Lear and Maxwell 1998).

Several explanations have been offered for this anomaly. For example:

- The EPA makes it more attractive to be in the compliance group (Harrington 1988; but see Raymond 1999).

- The agency looks the other way and does not enforce some regulations in exchange for compliance with those that it does enforce (Heyes and Rickman 1999).
- Potential for bad publicity induces those with greater consumer contact to comply (Arora and Cason 1996).

Also, it is possible that such an outcome arises out of repeated play—that the agency and its charges go through the same dance many times and the two learn how to cooperate. Repetition facilitates the effectiveness of low penalty levels.

Nonetheless, direct and indirect evidence suggests that auditing inspection strategies is important. Analysis of pulp and paper mill compliance with the NPDES provisions of the Clean Water Act provides one form of direct evidence (Helland 1998a; see also Magat and Viscusi 1990). These mills produce much water pollution and are, thus, good candidates for empirical analysis. Specifically, targeting inspections of mills that are more likely to violate the CWA not only uncovers violations, resulting in a direct penalty, but induces the same firms to self-report their own violations, presumably to demonstrate their willingness to cooperate and to deter future, unwelcome, inspections and penalties.

Less directly, several other types of evidence reinforce the implication that inspections and penalties motivate regulatory compliance. For example, higher EPA enforcement budgets induce firms to purchase more pollution control equipment (Seldon et al. 1994). This suggests that enforcement is effective and that the prospect of more inspections, everything else being equal, increases fear of detection and penalty and, thus, induces anticipatory compliance. In the same vein, firms found out of compliance with EPA regulations are penalized by the stock market in the form of lower stock prices, inflicting an additional cost on them beyond any agency-imposed sanctions and providing them with an extra incentive to comply (Badrinath and Bolster 1996; see also Bosch, Eckard, and Lee 1998).

Thus, without demonstrating that deterrence is optimal or cost efficient, substantial evidence indicates that it works to establish compliance. Potential violators, notably firms, have reason to act as if they fear enforcement activities and react accordingly (individuals may be less sensitive than firms to the effects on factors such as public and investor perceptions that may induce the latter to comply).

Although well established by some criteria that punishment works, a detailed analysis is lacking of whether, or under what conditions, more cooperative intermediate approaches (such as regulatory self-audits) would be as, or more, effective. Punishment's efficacy undermines certain claims made to promote and explore these less adversarial enforcement efforts. In other words, although some studies extol the virtues of cooperation, whether or when it works better than credible deterrence remains an open question.

The Educational Approach

The efficacy of informational approaches, at least under certain conditions, can be ascertained. Indeed, providing information that is otherwise difficult to acquire results in considerable improvements, with those advantageously positioned to apply political pressure being even better able to take advantage of opportunities presented by additional data than others.

As discussed in Chapter 2, informational mechanisms are intuitively appealing. By having more data available, decision makers should be better positioned to make their choices. Additional information should be especially helpful for those dealing with issues that are technically complex (which characterizes many environmental woes), for small more than large economic decision makers (for example, for individuals more than large corporations), and in situations where those with relevant data may have strong incentives to hide them.

In regard to implementation, informational policies may have dual impacts. First, they can lead to higher environmental quality as increased surveillance discourages those who would otherwise damage the environment, because their neighbors, consumers, and investors will become aware of their actions. Additionally, there may be distributional consequences in that where environmental degradation takes place may change. For example, if wealthier citizens are better (less) able to take advantage of these data, they may be more (less) advantaged compared with poorer citizens than when information is more costly or impossible to obtain.

For example, has the TRI, as emblematic of informational approaches, made a difference and if so of what form? Many analyses suggest that the program has been important and that toxic releases have declined (see also Chapter 9). For example, chemical companies that the TRI reveal to be emitting high levels of toxics receive a negative reaction from the stock market and, presumably in response, reduce their on-site emissions (Khanna, Quimio, and Bojilova 1998; see also Hamilton 1995a, Konar and Cohen 1997).

Interestingly, however, rather than redressing differences in ability to mobilize, greater drops in toxics are also associated with a heightened ability to apply pressure (Brooks and Sethi 1997, Arora and Cason 1999, Shapiro 2000). In other words, although the TRI has seemingly made environmental quality better for all, its disproportionate benefits exacerbate environmental inequity. Such experience runs counter to the hopes of those who might wish that informational provisions would improve the distribution of environmental costs between wealthy and poor, resulting in greater environmental justice.

The more general point is that policy outputs are affected by informational provisions. Low-cost information induces those who might otherwise harm the environment to behave in a more environmentally friendly manner, particularly when dealing with those who are better able to mobilize politically. To repeat, this latter point does not mean that those who typically bear the brunt of environmental problems are worse off, just that their lot improves less dramatically.

POLITICAL IMPACTS ON IMPLEMENTATION

As a good deal of the discussion has already highlighted, another factor further complicating implementation is that political pressures may be brought to bear. Consequently, not only may promulgated policy be a function of political forces, but similar influences may affect the details of its implementation. Given a fragmented political system, it stands to reason that these forces pull agencies in diverse directions. Indeed, to a considerable extent, scholars have been absorbed less with whether political forces disrupt implementation, which they largely accept as given, and more with determining which political forces are influential. Do national political actors guide policy and, if so, which ones, or do local political actors have an impact, or some complicated combination of the two?

Empirical studies have examined these issues with reference to various aspects of EPA policies and have come up with somewhat contrasting results. Again, the EPA will remain the focus of this discussion because of the availability of high-quality data; however, analyses of natural resource agencies, mainly qualitative, confirm that government actors or their interest group allies do influence implementation. Consistent with other studies of regulatory agencies, such as those examining OSHA, virtually all EPA-specific analyses conclude that political actors of one sort or another influence enforcement (for example, Wood 1988, 1991, 1992; Wood and Waterman 1991, 1994). Various scholars have emphasized local political officials, presidential administrations, legislators, interest groups, and even the courts. Given the previous discussions of national political actors, it ought not to be too surprising that findings vary, given differences in subject matter, political conditions, research designs, and the like. Regardless, the key is that implementation is complicated by overt political influence in addition to features such as delegation and monitoring.

Thus, for example, interest group efforts have been found to influence the severity of observed enforcement of CWA provisions, as enforcement is adjusted to reflect group preferences (Hunter and Waterman 1996; for further study see Van Houtven and Cropper 1996). Similarly, interest groups have been found to influence decisions about whether to cancel or to continue registration of pesticides and to affect the finding of carbon emissions violations in metropolitan areas (Mixon 1995; recall also that groups influence regulatory delay in the FWS's implementation of the Endangered Species Act [Ando 1999]). By contrast, broader examination reveals that a host of political actors, principally Congress and the president but also others, seem to influence policy implementation of four

EPA programs related to air, water, toxics, and pesticides (Wood and Waterman 1994). Congress is also found to play a role in the implementation of Superfund, the program designed to clean up toxic waste sites, although only for a site's transition from proposed to final status on the National Priority List (NPL), which enumerates potential cleanup candidates (Hird 1990). Additionally, counties with higher voter turnouts, states with more environmentalists, and senators with stronger environmental voting records are found to have stricter cleanup targets at their Superfund sites (Hamilton and Viscusi 1999). To foreshadow Chapter 6, from a more explicitly federalist perspective, local interests as well as national policy makers seem to alter substantially implementation of NPDES standards for regulating water pollution from fixed sources via permits (Helland 1998b). Further, as implied in Chapter 4, the agency may itself be able to have an independent if frequently difficult-to-measure effect on outcomes; for example, the EPA has been found to employ its rulemaking authority strategically on RCRA, the program designed to deal with toxic waste currently being produced, to advance its own interests (Hamilton and Schroeder 1994).

In summary, although identifying one political actor as dominant is problematic—which is consistent with theoretical models and with the government's constitutional structure—research suggests that external political actors partially drive implementation. To reiterate, this jibes with the general description of the variation in environmental policy over time and with the tendency to impose low penalties. The impact of political forces provides yet another reason why it should not be surprising that the implementation process is met with hostility by those advocating an impartial, efficient administration of policy.

CREDIBILITY

As this discussion of deterrence implies, imposing penalties is a key weapon of bureaus seeking to implement policy. This suggests that, in general, the higher the penalty, the greater the compliance level. Such an effect should be found in environmental regulatory policy or in nonregulatory activities such as natural resource policy.

As also mentioned, one problem with this notion is that the empirical literature fails to establish clearly a positive relationship between penalties and compliance. This may be for many reasons, such as the failure of observers to take into account all possible sanctions that fall on violators or because potential violators and bureaucrats interact repeatedly. But, given that government cannot easily rely upon an agent to enforce its own punishments, the lack of efficacy of real and threatened penalties may be because violators deem that stated punishments lack credibility. In the end, there is a belief that punishments will not be carried out. A similar argument is that high penalties provide a greater incentive to contest them and, therefore, their effects are indeterminate (see Nowell and Shogren 1994).

Presumably, credibility issues such as the willingness to carry out punishments are most relevant for exceptionally severe penalties. Yet, interestingly, they are also found with respect to penalties that are not intuitively extreme. Credibility problems help explain why polluters are routinely given Notices of Violation rather than more costly penalties within the EPA's purview; it is commonly believed that politicians would undermine a more aggressive policy of levying fines. Even more starkly, various studies show a tendency to enforce laws with less vigor on troubled firms or industries than on those that are more robust and, presumably, have the means and willingness to redress violations. For instance, less prosperous mills are more likely to remain uninspected for NPDES violations, as the EPA tends to look the other way when troubled firms and industries are involved (Helland 1998a). Along the same lines, in enforcing air pollution regulations, the EPA has shied away from plants likely to close, particularly where the firm in question was a major community employer (Deily and Gray 1991). Obviously, this tendency to vary enforcement activities may also reflect political pressures brought to bear on the EPA. Thus, assuming that vulnerable firms and industries know the EPA's enforcement pattern and the bureau's reluctance to enforce its rules in certain circumstances, the credibility of the agency's policies in relation to these economic actors is undermined and these firms and industries will more likely ignore costly rules.

Also, as would be predicted, the effectiveness of more dramatic, draconian penalties has probably been even more severely undermined because of an absence of credibility. Perhaps the best-known example of dramatic credibility problems involves implementing **corporate average fuel economy standards** (CAFE standards; for a general overview of this program, see Crandall 1992). Created by the 1975 Energy Policy and Conservation Act, these standards mandated that each car manufacturer's fleet of passenger cars achieve a specified average fuel efficiency (18.5 miles per gallon in 1978).[3] Because this legislation was passed as much to save energy as to improve air quality—although in more recent years the program has also become attached to concerns about global warming—the fleet requirement was to be set by the secretary of transportation (and not, for instance, by the EPA head) according to various specified factors. Fines for noncompliance were $50 per car per mile per gallon that a company fell under the CAFE standard so that, for example, a manufacturer selling 4 million passenger cars and falling 3 miles under the standard—because people only desire larger and less fuel efficient models, for instance—would incur a $600 million fine.

From an implementation standpoint, the problem with this policy is that manufacturers might not believe that the government will impose penalties or raise the required CAFE standard to levels that will induce substantial investment. This is particularly likely if policy makers view manufacturers' own threats of economic hardship and potential plant closings as credible. Would the government willingly throw employees at marginal plants or vulnerable factories out of work?

Such credibility problems have haunted CAFE. For instance, on multiple occasions during the 1970s, despite its stated commitment, the U.S. government was unwilling to punish American automobile manufacturers for failing to meet standards. This lack of resolve was, apparently, a product of fears that shutting down manufacturing facilities would cause too much economic havoc. Targets were missed and, after being raised to 27.5 miles per gallon for 1985, the standard was actually temporarily reduced for 1986–1989 when it became clear that mandates would not be met—demand for smaller cars had fallen in conjunction with declining gas prices—and has remained at 27.5 subsequently. In recent years, environmentally minded political actors called for a standard of more than 40 miles per gallon in response to the multinational agreement reached in Kyoto, Japan, to deal with global warming and in reaction to skyrocketing gasoline prices. Their requests have fallen on deaf ears, as evidenced by the increasing importance of sports utility vehicles, which are classified as light trucks and not subject to the 27.5 limit. Including sports utility vehicles, average vehicle fuel efficiency has fallen by more than 1 mile per gallon from its height of 26.2 miles per gallon (DOT 2000).

The CAFE enforcement problem has been simple. Firms most likely to fall short of standards, particularly stringent ones, have been American manufacturers threatening to shut domestic plants and lay off American workers. Such repercussions significantly deterred vigorous implementation of CAFE as federal regulators and the wary politicians from whom they took cues backed down despite their statutory authority. Put another way, the car companies and the U.S. government played a high-stakes game of chicken. The government blinked first.

Experiences with technology-forcing provisions of air pollution regulation, which dictated that manufacturers develop then-unavailable technology to meet looming standards, were analogous to those with CAFE (see Chapter 8 for further discussion). For instance, politicians had a problem with respect to enforcing mandated emissions standards required by the Clean Air Act and its Amendments, as automakers consistently failed to meet requirements and faced ever larger fines if policies were enforced (for example, $10,000 per car failing to meet standards). But politicians proved unwilling to hold the manufacturers' feet to the fire.

This is not to say that credibility problems created by edicts such as promulgated deadlines cannot sometimes be overcome. Models indicate that, through repeated play, an agency or relevant elected officials can establish a strident reputation, and implementation can proceed smoothly. For example, if government had stood up to the auto companies the first time they fought over CAFE and established a willingness to assess maximum penalties and steadily hike the fleet standard, automobile companies might have made the requisite choices and investments to conform. Similarly, as mentioned, in the early days of the pollution markets created by the Clean Air Act Amendments of 1990, there was rather little trading activity in emissions rights, based, presumably, on the belief that the government was uncommitted to the market approach and the current set of rules. However, given experience and a continued lack of interference, trading picked up and the market operated more in its originally envisioned manner.

Or, less abstractly, in his insightful analysis of air pollution deadlines, political scientist R. Shep Melnick (1992, 93) distinguishes between selective and broad actions in discerning what is and is not credible:

> It is quite clear that the EPA's threats do become credible and produce results when the agency demands that states and polluters take selective actions (installing scrubbers or instituting auto inspection and maintenance programs) that Congress has clearly endorsed and, thus, will most likely stand behind. Conversely, neither threats nor cajoling work when regulators make open-ended demands that states do absolutely everything and anything necessary to attain national standards or insist on the use of expensive or disruptive controls not clearly supported by Congress. The reality of pollution control is that regulators and polluters bargain over what controls are "reasonably available," with each side keeping in mind the extent of its political support. If application of these "reasonably available" controls fails to result in the attainment of national standards by statutory deadlines, then Congress either provides new deadlines (as it did for the steel industry in special legislation passed in 1982) or it lets the deadlines quietly slip by.

In short, implementation may suffer when credibility is at issue. Although theoretically and empirically it is difficult to lay out when credibility will and won't exist with certainty, it is possible to suggest a variety of conditions—the severity and breadth of sanctions—where it is more likely. Otherwise, given the short-term costs that they face, politicians are likely to back down.

THE PERILS AND PITFALLS OF IMPLEMENTATION

Although demand for environmental quality has risen along with capacity, this has not typically resulted in a well-designed policy process. The themes of fragmentation and lack of integration carry over to implementation and enforcement, where different strategies have also produced mixed results.

Thus, while environmental agencies have their foibles (although structural choices and leadership selection are political choices), and there are basic technical problems involved with delegation, many implementation difficulties are inherent in the nature of delegated responsibilities, the willingness and desire of interest groups and political officials to intervene, and a lack of credibility exacerbated by the nature of political regimes. Consistent with a system beset by fragmentation, changes have been incremental and layered on top of one another.

Put differently, although bureaus, whether they be the EPA or the natural resource agencies, are often portrayed as the villains, understanding frustration with enforcement and implementation requires a broader perspective. These agencies have to implement difficult or impossible mandates with complicated policy instruments. Politicians intervene, push for innovations that may or may not improve things, and are often reluctant to provide sufficient resources. Bureaucratic fears that politicians will not stand behind them, associated with the very nature of democracy, may undermine an agency's ability to punish and, hence, to ensure compliance. Ironically, at least measured by compliance rather than environmental quality (see Chapter 9), enforcement actions, whether they be deterrence or education oriented, do seem to have an impact, providing at least some optimism that policy produces a significant return.

KEY TERMS

Adversarial legalism (p. 110)

Corporate average fuel economy (CAFE) standards (p. 122)

Deterrence strategies (p. 103)

Educational strategies (p. 110)

Negotiated rulemaking (p. 108)

Self-audits (p. 116)

6 National or Local Control: Conflicts over Environmental Federalism

The development of a strong national presence in environmental affairs has not meant that state and local governments, and the forces trying to influence them, have become irrelevant. Indeed, they continue to play an active role in environmental affairs. As established in Chapters 3 and 4, a variety of more localized environmental issues and interests have developed as part of the evolution of environmental regulation. And, as the discussion of implementation in Chapter 5 made clear, state and local forces may substantially influence policy enforcement, adding to implementation's fragmented appearance.

In addition to that created by its system of separation of powers, the American federalist structure, which involves multiple levels of government, builds in another source of fragmentation with respect to demand and supply. Interestingly, though, whereas the effects of fragmentation created by separation of powers are typically agreed upon, those produced by the federalist structure are often disputed.

Indeed, in the United States, **federalism**—the division of authority across levels of government (for example, local, state, national)—arouses passionate debates among scholars and practitioners when environmental policy is at stake. Some strongly argue for states and localities retaining all but a few circumscribed responsibilities, whereas others advocate keeping vast amounts of responsibilities nationalized. Each perspective is based on different assessments of what effects federalism produces.

This debate could appear curious in light of the need for government intervention (see Chapter 2). After all, externality and public goods issues seem to indicate centralization's desirability. Centralization, typically thought of as national government control, would encompass the geographic area covering the vast majority of the costs and benefits of a public good or externality; a more localized or devolved policy, typically associated with state or local autonomy, would not necessarily internalize all of these factors. However, the theoretical case for centralization is actually more nuanced. Centralization may have its own costs, such as

126

a lack of appropriate information, which can be overcome by more decentralized or devolved policies allocating responsibility to a more localized government. Also, while the association between the two is often made, centralization is not necessarily tantamount to national control, as costs and benefits may not always be national in scope. Further, many touting centralization focus not simply on internalizing costs and benefits but on avoiding the so-called **race to the bottom,** the process by which local political leaders bid against one another for economic investment by reducing environmental restrictions and, in the extreme, drive policy to the lowest common denominator. Additionally, arguments for centralization may appear less intuitive, given the already delineated gap between the conceptual case for intervention and its execution, much of it directed from the national government.

Consequently, the theoretical and empirical link between centralization and dealing with public goods and externalities is more ambiguous than the initial discussion of policy action might imply. Many do consider centralization necessary for thwarting harmful political competition and ensuring effective environmental policy even when environmental effects are largely localized. Others tout the possibility of decentralization's moving policy closer to its beneficiaries and its cost bearers. Indeed, potentially important advantages in leaving numerous policies localized exist.

Although it is difficult to sort these competing visions out without some ambiguity, this chapter will provide theoretical and empirical insights into these alternative perspectives. Through a broad empirical overview and two intensive case studies where local and centralized control appears more or less attractive—one of drinking water regulation and the other of ground-level ozone standards—the chapter will survey the conceptual issues that mark the debate over environmental federalism and indicate how such a distribution of authority influences environmental policy in practice.

Despite contrasting viewpoints and evidence that is difficult to interpret, two themes emerge:

- *Although federalist structures affect policy, in many respects their effects seem counterintuitive because they are not the ones anticipated by either opponents or proponents of federalism.* The involvement of subnational political actors can influence whose preferences go into policy formulation and implementation. But evidence of far greater innovation and efficiency, benefits trumpeted for federalism, is weak. Nor are federalist opponents' worries about a race to the bottom, by which local political competition for economic activity mechanistically guts public or environmental policy, realized. Still, and consistent with the discussion of implementation, local decision makers, with at least tacit approval of national political actors, can successfully influence outcomes.[1]

• *Although centralization could offer more possibilities for efficient policy outcomes in certain situations, the environmental policy status quo fails to correspond closely to the textbook recommendations of conventional policy analysis.* Centralized policies are not necessarily those in which national political actors have an obvious comparative advantage and are often not implemented in an integrative and comprehensive manner that accounts for externalities or the nature of public goods.

Hence, federalism does affect environmental quality. Its importance reflects and further reinforces the political system's fragmented appearance, because, as a result of political choices, the status quo is not rationalized to take full advantage of the virtues of federalism or, for that matter, of centralization. However, as indicated by the general overview and the specific case studies, many of the alleged evils of policy devolution such as the race to the bottom are also not manifested.

THE CASE FOR POLICY DEVOLUTION

From a policy analytic point of view, to realize efficient outcomes, public services should generally be assigned to the smallest unit encompassing all relevant costs and benefits (Oates and Schwab 1988, 1992; Inman and Rubinfeld 1997a,b; McKinnon and Nechyba 1997; Oates 1998; Besley and Coate 1999; Levinson 1999). In specific circumstances where costs and benefits are at a subnational level, the national government might also want to establish limits on how far local interests may go in implementing this authority (Ferejohn and Weingast 1997). A clear-cut example of such a circumstance occurred during the last third of the twentieth century when the U.S. national government stepped in to combat local discrimination against African-Americans in the southern states. Just as the national government must protect the civil rights of its citizens, there may be local environmental policies so strict or lax that they justify the involvement of the federal government. But, otherwise, internalization of costs and benefits should be paramount.

Although advocates of decentralization might agree that extreme situations do warrant national intervention, these same advocates would argue that decentralization produces better policy on the whole because devolving authority includes a trio of advantages:

• *Superior information.* Local decision makers may know more about the specifics of the situation than those further removed. If, for example, the subject is cleaning up the Great Lakes, those with local experience may have a greater insight into efficacious remedies. Assuming that policy makers have the incentives to respond to issues confronting them, this presumably makes an effective response easier to accomplish.

• *Flexibility.* Factors varying geographically can be integrated into the decision-making process in ways that policies designed for broad application cannot (for example, Bardach and Kagan 1982). For instance, U.S. federal environmental laws are criticized for being too uniform in specifying treatment requirements and discharge levels (Rose-Ackerman 1995) and for not incorporating the tastes of local residents and other unique local conditions that are important to consider in addressing policy problems (Pashigan 1985, Scholz and Wei 1986, Lester 1995).

• *Innovation.* Devolving authority can offer the potential for greater innovation than keeping it centralized in a single actor's hands. More perspectives are brought to bear on a problem and, given competition, there will be greater incentive to experiment and for others to adopt successful innovations (on employing states as innovation laboratories, see, for example, Nice 1994). Certainly, the states trumpet their environmental innovations, such as through the Environmental Council of the States (for a list of innovations, see http://www.sso.org/ecos/publications/innovate.htm).

This enumeration of benefits implies that the analytic case for devolving decision making is strongest for policies with predominantly or exclusively local effects (Inman and Rubinfeld 1997a). For instance, if the costs and benefits of a river's pollution are experienced exclusively by residents of a given state or if the impact of an air pollutant is felt only within a metropolitan area, then the problem may be best handled by the local authorities. Even when effects spill over to a small number of entities it is possible that, if property rights are established and transaction costs are small, a Coasian-type negotiated solution is a preferred alternative to national regulation (Quigley and Rubinfeld 1996).

Some also find devolution attractive because it brings policy closer to the people. Thus, as mentioned in the discussion of environmental history in Chapter 3, one element of the environmental devolution movement comes under the rubric of **civic environmentalism** (for example, John 1994), which has been summed up as a means of returning authority to the citizenry.

Civic environmentalism differs from both of these standard models (command-and-control and market-based) in that it puts democracy back at the centre of environmental policy-making. It argues that the policy-making process should help citizens and representatives deliberate and hopefully achieve greater enlightenment as to what their interests are, rather than assuming those interests are either irrelevant (the environmentalists' model) or fixed (the economists' model). People are more likely to take this responsibility seriously when they are able to elect representatives at a local level who have real power. Rather than defer to . . . specialists . . . they will need to develop capacities and knowledge of their own, and these are likely to be different in kind from those that elites bring to the table. (Teles 1997, 29)

Whatever the reasons, the contemporary lure of devolving public policy constitutes a vivid reaction to the previous massive centralization epitomized by the birth of the EPA in 1970 (Rivlin 1992). Subsequent to the agency's creation, for instance, a burgeoning devolution movement arose, championed typically by those who were more conservative and Republican, who disapproved of the growing activism of the national government, although to reiterate, there are liberal interests who view devolution as allowing for citizen-level, grassroots, control. Under the guise of the **"New Federalism,"** a range of devolutionary administrative reforms were created in an effort to return power to the states and localities, including attempts to have policy implemented at more local levels and funds redirected back to localities; passage of the State and Local Fiscal Assistance Act of 1972 highlights this move toward devolution (Conlan 1988). With Ronald Reagan's election and the ascendance of those conservative Republicans suspicious of Washington policy expansion, including the growth of environmental policy in response to heightened demand (as well as other policies, such as welfare), the 1980s experienced another strong federalist push to delegate authority to state and local governments. More recently, this movement continued with an added concentration on discouraging **unfunded mandates,** the placing of responsibilities on one level of government by another without paying the costs of carrying them out, typically by the national government on the states or localities. Notably, the Unfunded Mandates Reform Act of 1995, spurred on by the Contract with America endorsed by many Republicans running for Congress in 1994, required that new information be produced for use in the legislative process, such as cost-benefit analyses by the CBO, and that new procedures intended to make creating new unfunded mandates more difficult be used. Unfunded mandates have been widely built into key environmental programs such as the Clean Air Act. George W. Bush, who ran for president on a platform supporting the devolution of policy authority, supports additional discouragement of unfunded mandates and has announced a federalism initiative designed to reduce federal constraints on the ability of states and localities to act, for example, to allow a state such as California to move quickly to meet its energy needs by streamlining environmental permitting requirements.

THE CASE FOR POLICY CENTRALIZATION

Despite the seeming desirability of decentralization for many environmental concerns, several factors potentially complicate its attractiveness and may heighten the appeal of policy centralization. One of the most prominent is the possibility that states and localities seeking to be economic development engines compete to attract business activity by systematically lowering environmental quality standards. Just as competing geographic polities may offer tax incentives and reductions to lure firms and produce economic activity, they may also relax environmental standards. Such a bidding war could create a race to the bottom, in which the weakest environmental standards are adopted across the board, or at least standards are set suboptimally. Put another way, this perspective (which is somewhat in the spirit of the pioneering work of Tiebout [1956]) implies that individuals vote with their feet and locate in the area that they find most advantageous, creating a race to the bottom, as dueling local jurisdictions weaken environmental protections to outdo one other in creating favorable business conditions (for a critique, see Revesz 1992, 1997b; see also Stewart 1977, 1997; Esty 1996; Swire 1996; Farber 1997a).[2] Later analyses of similar models have more benign implications, suggesting that there exists a real potential for determining which types of individual are likely to move and which are likely to stay—for instance, those with a lesser willingness to pay for a cleaner local environment may separate themselves out from those with a greater willingness to pay—which would reduce the likelihood of there being a race to the bottom (for example, Epple and Romer 1991). Despite such theoretical findings, the possibility of jurisdictional bidding wars to induce economic development in spite of environmental degradation remains a possibility and is certainly a powerful image.

From a policy analytic perspective, bidding between localities may result in the choice of an efficient level of environmental protection for each locality and in the fostering of policy innovation (see Oates and Schwab 1988, 1992). Additionally, jurisdictional competition may create incentives to adopt more efficient policy instruments to facilitate economic activity and keep the citizenry happy. Theoretically, the veracity of such claims depends on specific modeling assumptions (Levinson 1997).[3] Regardless, many environmentalists find competition over environmental standards disturbing because it may force quality down (although examples are imaginable where jurisdictional competition produces greater environmental quality).[4] Additionally, as mentioned with respect to implementation, states' institutional capacities vary considerably, opening up the possibility that some lack the means for effective implementation (Lester 1995, Rodriguez 1996, Lester and Stewart 2000). Alternatively, such a shortfall may reflect a general absence of will and, therefore, environmental outcomes are explained not by capacity per se but by its determinants. In a similar vein, some environmentalists seem to prefer environmental centralization at least partially because of the belief that equity requires comparable treatment of individuals (certain other related issues are discussed subsequently). Hence, such scholars as respected legal analyst Richard Stewart (1977, 1997) have argued that national environmental policy helps preserve national moral ideals.

A second, rather obvious, potential problem is that decentralization may produce more unaddressed externalities. Local policy makers may lack requisite incentives to deal with interstate externalities and find little reason to confront negative behavior, such as by coal-burning utilities that affect the residents of other states downwind or downstream. Additionally, policies adopted by these policy makers may actually create externalities. A tempting "solution" can be to export problems across political boundaries. For instance, locating large smokestacks near jurisdictional borders and allowing wind currents to carry their emissions to another state could be an attractive option. Consequently, such incentives must be eliminated if federalism is to operate in an efficient manner. Along these lines, the "right" concerns must be delegated from and retained at the national level—"right" being defined by the match between the geographic area over which environmental costs and benefits occur and the smallest government that encompasses the vast majority of these costs and benefits. Then, assuming policies are correctly sorted between government levels, such concerns need to be addressed with appropriate instruments and incentives. Federalism will be problematic if, beyond the inherent difficulties posed by any policy whose choice is subject to political bargaining, significant interstate externalities exist and authority over damaging behavior is delegated to local jurisdictions while power over actions for which costs and benefits are localized remains nationalized. Federalism will also be problematic if interstate externalities are not redressed or prevented even if the right regulatory activities are sorted between government levels.

Another analytic concern is that various state restrictions may prevent private actors from taking advantage of scale economies in producing environmental quality, that is, the benefits of coordination may be lost. **Economies of scale** involve reducing the average cost of a good when that product is made in large quantities.[5] If, for instance, various states mandate different technologies for car emissions, auto production costs may rise because the average price of producing a given emission reduction technology for a small number of cars will be far higher than for a large number of autos. This will be reflected in prices and even in exit by producers from small market states, limiting the sales by firms and the choices of consumers. Not surprisingly, only California and, much later, New York—two of the largest and wealthiest states—dared veer off the focal point of national automobile standards by dictating that car manufacturers meet different, more stringent, requirements (a third large market state, Texas, recently considered and rejected a move to California standards after strong auto industry lobbying; see Chapter 8 for more discussion). Thus, a uniform compliance standard, more easily produced with centralization, may be attractive, given substantial private investment for a national market (see CBO 1997a).

Linked to the logic making centralization a desirable means of coordination, the national production of scientific and technical knowledge that local policy makers can share may involve substantial economies. Whether knowledge is produced directly by government or indirectly with its support, there may be a substantial case for national retention of control over knowledge generation as a method of producing more valuable information for each dollar spent even if policy mechanisms and implementation are decentralized. For example, the exact same research done by twenty different states would not be the best use of their time and resources.

Additionally, and related to a race to the bottom, devolution may create efficiency but be a less successful tool for redistributing the negative impacts of environmental degradation from one group in society to another (Peterson 1981, Musgrave 1997). If environmental policy is designed to redress inequities by which the poor or those historically discriminated against are more subject to negative environmental effects, as many opponents of environmental racism and NIMBY-like activities are apt to want, then allowing small government entities to control the process is not likely to work well because those who are well-off can choose to move to a different jurisdiction with policies' favoring them. Hence, policy designed to achieve distributive objectives (which many would find a highly dubious goal for numerous environmental policy issues) would seem to warrant a much stronger central government role.

Finally, state political processes can simply prove less (or more) successful than those at the national level. For instance, states may lack the institutional capacity to deal with relevant issues. Additionally, the sensitivity of local politics to constituent desires, which may be greater than the national government's, can be damaging (see Kagan 1999). For example, local governments can facilitate the kinds of choices associated with NIMBY and environmental racism by catering to well-off individuals, who are likely to be better able to oppose any program that may inflict some costs on them (on the impact of differences in collective action for local environmental choices, see Hamilton 1993, 1995b). Decentralization may be seen as resulting either in stalemate or in environmental injustices, such as asking the poor and disenfranchised to shoulder an unreasonable amount of policy's costs (for example, Swire 1996; for a discussion of how such arguments are undeveloped and untested, see Stewart 1997).

Thus, some states appear unresponsive to environmental problems within their borders because of these problems associated with decentralization (Lowry 1992, Rabe 2000). For instance, some states fail to monitor or report accurately in implementing environmental regulation because they lack the requisite capacity; alternatively, there may be "vast differences in likely state receptivity to governmental efforts to foster environmental improvement" (Rabe 2000, 41). Assuming that states are implementing policies with principally localized effects, complaints of insufficient vigor in policy making or enforcement are based on very specific beliefs that quality should not be chosen by cost bearers and beneficiaries.

Thus, it can be maintained that centralization is just as attractive as devolution, given the right situation. Arguments for centralization associated with externalities and scale production are consistent with conventional wisdom about allocating responsibilities to internalize costs and benefits and produce environmental quality at the lowest price (and, of course, depend on allocating responsibilities properly to begin with) but only apply to a subset of environmental issues. Indeed, the case for centralization is most compelling when policy effects extend widely across jurisdictions or where bargaining involves high transaction costs (for example, Peterson 1995). For instance, emissions from the considerable number of Midwest utility operators linked to East Coast acid rain would appear to require centralized control if negotiated solutions prove unfeasible. The product of nitrous oxide and sulfur dioxide combining in the air with oxygen and moisture, acid rain acidifies the soil and water bodies on which it falls; a particularly notable feature is that it can travel considerable distances—pollution from a midwestern power plant can cause acid rain on the East Coast of the United States and Canada. Similarly, because pollutants interacting to generate smog may travel considerable distances, such as along the East Coast, centralized, or at least regionalized, intervention may be needed. This logic actually suggests a supranational solution for some environmental issues, such as gases threatening the ozone layer or determinants of global warming (see Chapter 9).

Other arguments for centralization, such as those linked with the race to the bottom and differing political capabilities, elicit more debate because either their effects are disputed—for example, whether a race to the bottom occurs—or the inferences drawn, given agreement on effects, differ—for instance, whether jurisdictional competition over environmental quality is a good or a bad thing.

FEDERALISM AND ENVIRONMENTAL POLICY

How, then, does environmentalism correspond to contrasting portraits of federalism? Many policies regarding air, water, toxics, and pesticides originated at the state and local level, with the national government assuming a principal role in the last third of the twentieth century (Percival 1995; Butler and Macey 1996a, b; Esty 1996). Indeed, critics of EPA environmental policies often maintain that quality improvements began prior to 1970 and, hence, national policies have been ineffectual (for example, Goklany 1999). Moreover, much American environmental policy is still conducted at least partially at the subnational level—alternatively labeled **cooperative** or **conjoint federalism** (by which policy is jointly determined by the national, state, and local governments)—including the regulation of hazardous waste, industrially generated air pollution, and virtually all water pollution. Whatever its virtues, such dispersed authority seemingly reflects and contributes to the fragmentation of the U.S. political system.

Regardless, from the viewpoint of those concerned with cost-effective environmental quality, the empirical reality of American federalism provides both good and bad news. To a substantial extent, decentralization has not proved to be especially problematic, although the centralized political system has implemented federalism in a somewhat inept manner. Put differently, federalism does generate variance in policy outcomes with little evidence of a competition-induced race to the bottom. It seemingly fosters at least some creative and innovative policy making. Unfortunately, the system is not rationalized in the manner that mainstream theories of federalism or public economics would recommend so that many of the advantages, such as internalization of costs and benefits, at the lowest level are not achieved. Consistent with a view of politics emphasizing political fragmentation and associated difficulties in policy making, the status quo does not yield an abundance of the benefits that federalism's proponents would typically advertise it producing.

Jurisdictional Influences

Although no clear race to the bottom exists, jurisdictional differences are important. Indeed, there seems little dispute that the federated structure influences policy by producing stricter environmental policies in some places and weaker policies in others.

In this vein, quantitative studies virtually all indicate that local forces matter. For instance, one study finds that although national political actors remain capable of influencing CWA enforcement in states where authority has been delegated, state and local interests also influence how policy works. National political officials, in exchange for passing on costs to the states, cede some of their authority and accept uneven implementation of laws, which presumably explains why national political actors willingly allow a federal structure to continue rather than striving to appropriate policy authority (Helland 1998b; see also 1998c). Another study discovers multiple influences at all government levels of the CAA's enforcement and concludes that federalism may impede national initiatives meant to change the status quo in either a pro- or an anti-environmental direction (Wood 1991, 1992). Further results from another inquiry show that state environmental policy responds to public demands, both from organized interests and the public at large (Hays, Esler, and Hays 1996). Employing states as the unit of analysis, another study concludes that federalism allows discretion by those at the state level. Interestingly, some state leaders are willing to exceed national guidelines, rendering states potential catalysts for increased environmental protection (Lowry 1992; see also Vogel 1995).[6] Finally, a study focusing directly on pollution outcomes finds that organized political interests, state political capacity, and economic conditions such as wealth are all important determinants (Ringquist 1993).

Similarly, states differ considerably in the nature of observed demand and supply. Generally, they vary in the demands of their citizenries and in their interest group systems as well as in the capacity of political institutions (for a general overview, see Gray, Hanson, and Jacob 1999). Not surprisingly, in the spirit of the analysis of pollution subsidies in Chapter 1, state environmental expenditures, either per capita in absolute terms or as a percentage of the overall budget, exhibit wide discrepancies. For example, Table 6-1 presents such state-level data and shows differences of several orders of magnitude. Although expenditures have a variety of determinants, such data show substantial disparities on a state-by-state basis. Nor are these outlays exclusively a function or product of environmental need—"sometimes [but not always] the states with the worst pollution spend the least to correct their problems" (Hall and Kerr 1991, 135)—indicating that a diversity of effort and outcomes is the norm.

Clearly, as Table 6-1 shows, these results do not imply a race to the bottom. Indeed, although not an unambiguous test, as the national government may play a constraining role, that some states are more vigorous than others in pushing an environmental agenda suggests that bidding for economic activity is not enough to drive down the strictness of policy and certainly not to the lowest common denominator. Such results make sense in light of evidence that environmental restrictions only marginally influence a firm's choice of location (for a literature review, see Jaffee et al. 1995). Almost all analyses of new plant locations, for example, find virtually no impact associated with environmental compliance costs (for example, McConnell and Schwab 1990, Levinson 1996; for a review, see Stewart 1993, and for similar evidence with respect to the international arena, see Kahn 2000). Rather, they suggest that different citizen preferences are mediated through varying state and local political institutions to produce contrasting policies.

Federalism and Innovation

As mentioned earlier, an alleged benefit of federalism is that it fosters creative solutions. Indeed, empirical evidence appears to indicate that the federal system does induce a modest level of innovation (Davies and Mazurek 1997). Many actions by subnational governments are certainly touted as innovative (environmental policy is also claimed to spur many firms to innovate by commercially applying new knowledge). For example, in the late 1990s, Texas governor George W. Bush championed an effort for government to provide suggestions on how older polluting industrial facilities, exempted from state regulations, might voluntarily reduce their emissions.

Unfortunately, measuring the success of a new policy approach remains difficult. Success can be defined as delivering net returns exceeding those provided

Table 6-1   Variance in State Environmental Expenditures, Fiscal Year 1996

State	Per capita spending (percentage of state budget)	State	Per capita spending (percentage of state budget)
Alabama	$28.07 (1.09%)	Montana	$107.93 (3.47%)
Alaska	400.19 (4.74)	Nebraska	54.10 (2.06)
Arizona	17.65 (0.72)	Nevada	74.26 (2.95)
Arkansas	50.71 (1.96)	New Hampshire	39.18 (1.60)
California	83.28 (2.69)	New Jersey	25.25 (0.78)
Colorado	57.98 (2.49)	New Mexico	38.66 (1.06)
Connecticut	49.09 (1.37)	New York	39.54 (1.04)
Delaware	103.86 (2.57)	N. Carolina	24.15 (0.91)
Florida	41.40 (1.78)	N. Dakota	62.00 (2.14)
Georgia	28.52 (1.13)	Ohio	18.64 (0.73)
Hawaii	45.99 (1.04)	Oklahoma	39.19 (1.63)
Idaho	91.12 (3.51)	Oregon	65.60 (2.18)
Illinois	30.74 (1.21)	Pennsylvania	51.27 (1.86)
Indiana	35.39 (1.43)	Rhode Island	52.10 (1.51)
Iowa	32.57 (1.13)	S. Carolina	37.45 (1.30)
Kansas	31.89 (1.23)	S. Dakota	70.92 (2.81)
Kentucky	47.59 (1.74)	Tennessee	40.79 (1.68)
Louisiana	50.79 (1.75)	Texas	27.47 (1.26)
Maine	84.07 (2.79)	Utah	70.70 (2.52)
Maryland	42.38 (1.61)	Vermont	86.95 (2.66)
Massachusetts	32.78 (0.88)	Virginia	37.00 (1.51)
Michigan	45.37 (1.40)	Washington	57.33 (1.80)
Minnesota	50.91 (1.50)	W. Virginia	70.48 (2.28)
Mississippi	52.17 (1.90)	Wisconsin	104.74 (3.53)
Missouri	42.54 (1.94)	Wyoming	212.95 (5.66)

Source: Council of State Governments 1999.

by previous means rather than as simply implementing a new and creative way of tackling an environmental concern. For instance, it may be difficult to determine whether the voluntary Texas approach is more cost efficient than a traditional regulatory strategy. Following are a few examples of places where scholars and practitioners maintain that innovation has provided a more efficient response than previous means to environmental policy concerns.

- New Jersey and Minnesota have adopted pollution prevention programs with particular emphasis on integration and dealing with cross-media pollution in innovative ways. Efforts in the Great Lakes region have generated similar innovations. For example, inspectors in Minnesota have worked together to deal with cross-media pollution, by emphasizing it in enforcement and inspection activities where it had been previously ignored, and to provide additional technical assistance for prevention, a shift from traditional emphases on dealing with pollution once created (Rabe 1995, 1996, 1999b).

- Southern California has creatively attacked its air pollution problems, most notably via a market-based program known as RECLAIM, which commenced in 1994. Designed to reduce nitrous oxide and sulfur dioxide from stationary sources, RECLAIM uses a declining emissions credit allocation with a sophisticated emissions trading model that accounts for a variety of regional characteristics such as geographic differences (Foster and Hahn 1995, Johnson and Pekelney 1996). The results, although not perfect, have been successful in reducing pollution in a seemingly low-cost manner (Bearden 1999).

Thus, there are certainly cases where innovation would appear to be successful. However, the broader issue of the extent of innovation produced by states remains indeterminate.

States do develop novel approaches when given the opportunity, and some of these initiatives appear to be successful innovations. But federalism does not seem to have been the hotbed of successful innovations and their diffusions that strident advocates would claim. Rather, innovations have been modest. Devolution's supporters would likely claim that states would be far more innovative if the national government involved itself less in environmental affairs. Although this would be an interesting experiment, the outcome is far from certain. For instance, the highly decentralized Canadian system has been found to exhibit less local innovation than the more nationalized American system (Rabe 1999a). If this discrepancy reflects decentralization rather than other factors, which is difficult to discern, it would suggest that turning the states loose might not produce an abundance of worthwhile innovation.

FALLING SHORT

Decentralizing authority does result in some integration of local preferences into environmental policy and some policy innovation, but the current federated structure is assailed by a wide variety of policy practitioners and scholars. Admittedly, such commentaries are often mingled with complaints about command-and-control instruments, making it sometimes difficult to disentangle whether the primary grievance involves a policy's governmental level or the means employed. Nevertheless, contemporary environmental federalism generates frustration on the part of those analyzing the efficacy of American environmental policy, whether they favor more national control or less.

Critiques of Nationalized Policy

Perhaps the strongest critiques come from those who favor state and local delegation. For example, well-known legal scholar David Schoenbrod (1996, 24; see also 1993), frustrated with the status quo, has argued for a radical redefinition of the EPA:

> The Environmental Protection Agency should be stripped of its power with four exceptions. First, it should gather and publicize information on pollution and its consequences, both on the national and the local level. Second, it should propose to Congress rules of conduct to control types of interstate pollution that are not adequately addressed by the states or that require special protection, such as the Grand Canyon. Third, it should propose to Congress rules of conduct for goods, such as new cars, when state-by-state regulation would erect significant barriers to interstate commerce. Fourth, it should draft model state environmental laws and conduct policy studies that states could use when considering whether to enact such laws. States, however, should be free to amend or reject federal proposals in favor of different approaches to pollution control.

If Schoenbrod had his way, the EPA's authority would be reduced to little more than an advisory function except when economies of scale are extremely high (and Congress would delegate far less than currently if the agency were given responsibility). As his comments imply, advocates of state authority principally complain that centralized control in Washington is insensitive to local needs and preferences; a barrier to states functioning as innovative laboratories for policy experimentation, as the national government acts as an unresponsive monopoly; plagued by poor integration (Scheberle 1997); and poorly attuned to interstate externalities (Anderson and Hill 1997, Merrill 1997). Many would also echo the view that Congress should be more active in the delegation process when agencies are given authority. States and localities, whatever their abilities to undermine the achievement of policy goals, are considered the preferred default and should be preeminent.

The first trio of complaints should not be surprising. First, Washington's unresponsiveness to local needs and preferences is a natural criticism, given the inherent nature of command-and-control policy instruments. Innovation is slowed by seemingly inflexible rules, which has caused the EPA itself to recognize the need to "apply common sense, flexibility, and creativity in an effort to move beyond the one-size-fits-all system of the past and [to] achieve [outcomes providing] the very best protection of public health and the environment at the least cost" (cited in GAO 1998a, 2). However, in the same report, the GAO notes that a large number of obstacles—complexity, the recalcitrance of key decision makers, and the EPA's institutional abilities—make realizing considerable innovations in the future problematic. Indeed, in 1993, when the national government, under the leadership of Vice-President Albert Gore, undertook its National Performance Review in its effort to rationalize government it, too, highlighted such problems with respect to the EPA:

> Local governments cite examples where failure to devise better ways to pro-
> tect the environment affordably may result in just the opposite of the in-
> tended effect. In the Southwest, one city reports an increase in desert dump-
> ing of solid waste by citizens because of a refusal by the citizenry to pay to
> expand the local landfill in accordance with federal regulations, which re-
> quire installation of double liners and a leachate collection system to com-
> ply with RCRA groundwater laws. The city questions whether the require-
> ments are necessary in this case because of its geology and arid climatic
> conditions. (National Performance Review 1993, 5–6)

Finally, the lack of integration between programs is consistent with the fragmented political system and the choice process, which produces the structure for policy implementation.

The federated structure's inability to deal with interstate externalities is an especially damning criticism against national authority in environmental affairs. Yet, for instance, neither air nor water pollution regulations provide enough in-
centive for upwind and upstream polluters to behave appropriately; that is, there is often insufficient punishment or incentive for those upstream or upwind not to export their pollution (Revesz 1996). A market-oriented solution might solve the problem here, but it is hard to believe that the failure by politicians to deal with externalities is accidental rather than purposeful, as politicians are certainly aware of the environmental implications of their choices.

Critiques of Localized Policy

In looking at the efforts of states and localities in the federated system, others see grounds for centralization:

> [S]tates face inherent limitations in environmental policy. Rather than a
> consistent, across-the-board pattern of dynamism, we shall see a more un-
> even pattern of performance than the current conventional wisdom might
> anticipate. This imbalance becomes particularly evident when environmen-
> tal problems are not confined to the boundaries of a specific state. Many
> environmental issues are by definition transboundary, raising enduring ques-
> tions of interstate and interregional equity in allocating responsibility for the
> burden of environmental protection (Rabe 2000, 40).

In the spirit of the above quotation, three arguments favoring centralization are at least partially based on empirical observation of the contemporary federated system. *Whether or not states actively compete to sell their environmental quality to the highest bidder, state environmental quality varies, and, hence, centralization is a positive in regard to constructing a level playing field (Stewart 1977, 1997).* Although those favoring localized authority might counter that an efficient system should look like this, one might add that localities have not proved to be especially adept at sidestepping NIMBY woes. Many have fallen prey to problems of environmental racism because their group systems are less balanced and they are unable to act collectively while those able to so act do so to prevent environmental cleanup and siting.

Like the national government, states too have difficulties defining goals, developing proper institutional capabilities, avoiding special interests, and integrating means for improving quality. Although examples of state cooperation do exist, such as that discussed above regarding Great Lakes cleanup, innovation is unsuccessful when the situation more closely approximates a zero-sum rather than a positive-sum game. This occurs when, rather than gains from cooperation being possible, one side's gain equals another's loss (and agencies such as the EPA certainly claim to be innovative as well). For example, one study that examined the ability of eight southern states to settle on a solution for radioactive waste dumping found that the socially desirable solution was not reached (Coates and Munger 1995; see also Rabe 1994).

Essentially the flip side of the externalities argument, the specter of environmental spillover remains troubling and, therefore, authority should be centralized without states having the opportunity to opt out. Whether a strong case is made that environmental policy does, or within the feasible set of policy options can be made to, address these concerns effectively and efficiently is the obvious cutting point between the two perspectives.

In short, one way of summarizing empirical observations is that there is enough for both proponents of devolution and advocates of centralization to grab onto. Devolution advocates point to the failings of the national government; centralization proponents suggest that states and localities do not do such a great job, so giving them more responsibility is a bad idea.

CASE STUDIES

Examining actual cases in some depth provides additional insight into environmental federalism. The first case concerns drinking water, for which decentralization would appear justified because costs and benefits are largely confined to small geographic areas. The second case, ground-level ozone, seems to warrant more nationalized policy because costs and benefits are geographically widespread. Although supplemented with other sources, these two cases were initiated by the CBO (1997a). In both instances, political decision makers reacted by creating a policy to improve environmental quality. Each case will show the extent to which the status quo corresponds to the ideal type of federalism, by which the smallest government unit encompassing costs and benefits is provided principal authority.

Drinking Water

Control over drinking water is a classic example of the national government playing a prominent role despite local policy effects and producing, until recently, unfunded federal mandates. It is also an instance of how responses are typically incremental when an initiative falls well short of its goals, as the national government's involvement has not been globally reexamined but, rather, problems have been addressed by marginal changes.

In 1974 Congress passed the Safe Drinking Water Act (SDWA), and the federal government transferred state and local authority over drinking water to the EPA (see Chapter 8). The law has been amended over the years, principally in 1986 and 1996. The agency establishes, given the best available technology, maximum contaminant level goals and feasible corresponding standards. States and localities have been generally expected to implement these standards and to pay the associated costs (with some help from the national government since 1986). Specifically, the 1974 legislation authorized the EPA to announce and subsequently revise water contaminant standards. In conventional EPA fashion, this process moved slowly, so that when the 1986 amendments were enacted only 23 (out of as many as 600) contaminants had been addressed. Consistent with much later legislation, the 1986 statute, widely seen as responding to frustration with the EPA's lackluster progress, was very specific. It enumerated 83 contaminants that required standards based on best available technology within three years—typically, the EPA fell far short of the prescribed time frame—and mandated further standards (for example, 25 new water contaminant standards every three years beginning in 1991). Although a small federal subsidy was authorized, the amount paled compared with the financial obligations these mandates put on local water authorities. And, consistent with legislation in the 1990s, the 1996 statute responded more to criticisms about risk and flexibility; the statute emphasized prioritization of contaminant risks and allowed state and locality exceptions where achieving certain standards was extremely expensive. Also consistent with 1990s approaches, the statute included a right-to-know provision requiring that water quality information be made public. Additionally, reflecting pressures to combat unfunded mandates, more financial support was provided, notably via a $10 billion state revolving loan fund provided at below-market rates (GAO 1997a), which, while perhaps easing the states' burdens somewhat, creates incentives to overuse capital-intensive technologies (see CBO 1997b). Finally, stress was put on a greater national government research role, which has proved to be a mixed bag as the EPA regularly asks for *less* money than Congress wants to provide (see GAO 1999a, which curiously blames these small requests on poor budgetary processes; on the operation of science generally at the EPA, see Powell 1999).

What is striking about the overall trend toward nationalizing and strengthening the standards for drinking water quality is that corresponding costs and benefits are almost exclusively local. On the one hand, although external benefits from reducing the potential for waterborne diseases are imaginable (for example, fewer health complications for travelers and reduced federal government medical costs, given current policies), such returns are negligible in the larger scheme of things and given the obvious incentives of local citizens to have potable water. On the other hand, because any drinking water system supplying either 25 people or 15 homes and businesses falls under the EPA's aegis, assuming control over roughly 200,000 public water systems nationwide is a huge task.

Of course, net of other considerations, few would disagree that safe drinking water is a highly desirable policy goal. Everyone wants water free from diseases with a minimum of negative long-term health effects. Yet, while all Americans deserve healthful drinking water, the key role assigned the national government may seem puzzling from a conventional policy analytic perspective. Beyond the lack of interjurisdictional externalities, the rather high cost for improving drinking water— in 1995 the EPA (1999c) estimated required infrastructure investments through 2014 at $138 billion, more than the value of existing infrastructure—varies substantially from place to place, most notably in conjunction with the size of the system involved. The cost of attaining nationally mandated standards for small systems, which are numerous (about 85 percent of systems serve 3,000 people or less) but provide water to only about 20 percent of the total population, is frequently extraordinarily high. For example, consider Table 6-2, which shows 1995 estimates of the average cost per household of three proposed rules under the SDWA by the size of affected water systems. In all three instances, system size and cost estimates strongly correspond.

Stated differently, a standard federalist viewpoint indicates that locales are best positioned to decide how to maintain their drinking water and at what purity level as clean water is a matter of degree and not an absolute quality. Citizens uncomfortable with their water's quality could adjust their own behavior, from drinking bottled water or buying certified water filters to moving to a different

Table 6-2 Average Household Costs for Proposed Rules by Size of Affected System, in 1992 Dollars

Size of system (number of people served)	Disinfectants	Surface water treatment	Radon
25–100	$223	$445	$260
100–500	204	250	99
500–1,000	199	212	47
1,000–3,300	164	72	26
3,300–10,000	186	45	17
10,000–25,000	57	29	15
25,000–50,000	44	23	10
50,000–75,000	40	20	9
75,000–100,000	36	17	8
100,000–500,000	31	18	7
500,000–1,000,000	27	16	87
1,000,000+	26	15	5

Source: CBO 1995.
Note: Costs estimated for systems in category affected by rules.

town or state. Unless society holds clean water of the highest purity as an inherent right, thus making it worthy of redistributive subsidies from those who are better off, and believes that the national government is markedly superior than the local government at ensuring such clean water supplies, then the case for across-the-board national level standards is weaker than for many environmental concerns. Reasonable arguments might be made that the national government could help lower some transaction costs (perhaps brokering bargaining so that small systems might merge to take advantage of economies of scale), disseminate information, or fund basic research into ways to improve water systems, but little else seems appropriate.

Yet, the roots of strong political pressures on the national government for controlling drinking water policy are easy to identify, since unclean water fraught with diseases and parasites is very frightening. The EPA's initial case for control in 1974 was made by citing substandard water in areas such as New Orleans, Louisiana, where carcinogenic contaminants due to chlorine treatments were found in the drinking water supply. More dramatically, events in Milwaukee, Wisconsin, in 1993 were part of the impetus for the 1996 SDWA Amendments. When the intestinal parasitic Cryptosporidium oocysts found their way into the drinking water, roughly 400,000 residents became ill, about 2,000 seriously, and anywhere from 1 to 40 died in a metropolitan area of about 1.5 million. Treatment at one of the two city water treatment plants failed to eliminate the bacterium, which was not subject to any EPA standard at the time. In light of events such as those in New Orleans and Milwaukee and associated fears, wary national political actors might feel compelled to try to act even if it means assigning higher and more expensive standards for water quality than cost-benefit analyses and risk assessments might suggest. Additionally, of course, various private and public health community interests, supportive of the national government's forcing high levels of water quality on communities, even given few if any spillover effects, have incentives to use frightening events to their strategic benefit.

In predictable fashion, political responses to complaints about national drinking water policy have been incremental, allowing a bit more flexibility and easing financial burdens somewhat by providing loans and other assistance to locales. Fundamentally rethinking the relationship between government levels is not part of the equation.

From an economic perspective large welfare losses are associated with nationalizing drinking water policy. To reiterate, because cost-efficient standards for large systems may have price tags far exceeding benefits for smaller systems, forcing the latter to adopt them is not generally considered advisable from an analytic perspective.

The end result is that, although informational responsibilities might best be nationalized, the case based on conventional criteria for the EPA to control drinking water quality is weak. Yet, for more than a quarter of a century nationalized policy has been the status quo and, rather than addressing the system's fundamental inefficiencies, national leaders have reacted by making policies somewhat more accommodating, assuming more of the costs, and removing some objections by institutionalizing what to some appears to be a pork barrel system.

Not surprisingly, the SDWA, particularly after 1986 amendments gave it much more enforcement teeth, has generated considerable frustration. Subnational units such as state and local governments view it as representing a prime example of unfunded mandates by which the national government, without sufficient fiscal support, has given localities costly standards to achieve; there are roughly ninety such standards, some for multiple contaminants, with more promised (Tiemann 1996, EPA 1999c). Conversely, many in the public health community voice frustration because they do not perceive federal efforts as sufficiently effective or rigorous to achieve crucial goals and protect future water quality.

Ground-Level Ozone

In regard to whether policy should be nationalized, regionalized, or localized, ground-level ozone involves more complicated issues than safe drinking water, and it has generated far more recent political attention. Although many of the nuances about its formation and dispersion involve uncertainty, ground-level ozone is formed by a chemical reaction between volatile organic compounds and nitrogen oxides with sunlight in the atmosphere; utilities and motor vehicles largely produce man-made nitrogen oxides; motor vehicles and small area sources such as dry cleaners principally generate volatile organic compounds. Ground-level ozone differs from stratospheric ozone, associated with concerns about protecting the earth from ultraviolet radiation and involves different scientific, economic, and political issues. From the perspective of federalism, ground-level ozone is interesting because it is a case in which government beyond the local and state level would appear appropriate if costs and benefits were properly internalized.

First, some background. Although the exact extent is debated, there is little doubt that ground-level ozone is costly. It is a significant component of the smog plaguing many Americans, particularly urban residents. For humans, especially those with breathing difficulties, such as asthmatics, smog affects short-term respiratory health, although long-term effects are disputed. Additionally, ground-level ozone affects vegetation by reducing the growth rate of agricultural crops and placing plants and trees at greater risk of disease.

Although the federal government's role regarding ground-level ozone corresponds reasonably well to that implied by standard federalist theories in some respects, it fails considerably in others. More precisely, there would be a substantial place for national government activism, but the role that the national government has chosen to play does not quite correspond to that advanced by policy analysts because costs and benefits are not effectively internalized in the policies that have been developed. There have been some efforts to adapt at the margin, but policy has not been systematically overhauled in the manner that would seem desired.

Like so many environmental issues, the federal government assumed a gradually more central role in dealing with ground-level ozone. Although the Air Pollution Control Act of 1955 specified that the federal government should only provide research and technical assistance and financial support, with primacy responsibility reserved for localities, the national role first increased a bit with the enactment of tailpipe emission controls in 1965 and escalated with the 1970 Clean Air Act and its subsequent amendments. The CAA gave the EPA authority over new and existing large stationary or fixed source emissions with the intent of creating uniform standards. Amendments in 1977 required that if states failed to meet ozone standards by the end of 1983, then they must provide a specific schedule for implementing a vehicle maintenance and inspection program to remedy the ozone problem. Amendments in 1990 differentially regulated areas according to their degree of compliance (providing stricter regulation for areas more out of compliance but giving them more time to meet the standard). The latter statute also created an Ozone Transport Commission to address the regional flows of ozone in the northeastern United States (recognition that ground-level ozone was not merely confined to urban airsheds and was, indeed, a regional problem began in the 1970s).[7] Although standards were to be reconsidered every five years, it would actually take seven years and a court case led by the American Lung Association to induce such a reconsideration in the 1990s, producing a standard that would then get tied up in the courts.

Given both the regional differences in problems associated with ozone, the differential treatment of areas since 1990, and the need to reevaluate policy periodically, it is probably not surprising that different states and localities have reacted differently to policy regarding ground-level ozone. For instance, for reasons that are a bit perplexing most northeastern states and California supported efforts to change the ground-level ozone standard (many of them were having a hard time meeting the old standard), whereas midwestern states, which had largely attained the goal but would have to institute costly controls to meet the new proposed standard, were in opposition (McCarthy 1999). Overall, about half of all Americans live in areas violating the ozone standard of 0.12 parts per million (over one hour) that was in effect until the middle of 1997, when it was announced that the National Ambient Air Quality Standard would be replaced by an eight-hour standard of 0.08, setting off a firestorm of controversy and judicial appeals.

Given externalities, there is a policy analytic case for regulating ground-level ozone on a fairly large jurisdictional scale. Otherwise, some costs of polluter actions may be ignored. Particularly as evidence has grown on the regional effects of ground-level ozone, some of which seems to have spurred the initial national regulation of ozone, the case for incorporating downwind and upwind areas has been strengthened (for a discussion, see Wilcox 1996).

Nonetheless, situating policy at the lowest possible jurisdiction suggests that regional-based control would be ideal if proper political authority could be structured to incorporate externalities. Doing so would introduce more information to treat the problem effectively and more ability to innovate. Alternatively, states could negotiate with one another if transaction costs were low enough.

The question then is, does the EPA, and the statutes it must implement, properly incorporate externalities into EPA policy? The evidence indicates that they do not. Specifically, localities have been judged by how much ozone is found *in the immediate area;* the more ozone, the greater the abatement effort, which implies that upwind areas actually pay a greater cost than those downwind because property rights are implicitly assigned in a manner benefiting downwind producers (and a Coasian solution is not easily achieved). In other words, politicians and the EPA have not rigorously addressed externalities, even though this is the primary conceptual underpinning for federal involvement. Some of the changes in the 1990 Clean Air Act Amendments, such as the creation of the Ozone Transport Commission, and efforts in the form of the Ozone Transport Assessment Group, established in 1995, to provide a forum by which states (including those not part of the commission) could negotiate cost-efficient solutions, have induced some progress but have encountered considerable roadblocks, such as a lack of authority to make states and localities accept proposals integrating cross-border externalities (Parker and Blodgett 1999). Additionally, attempts to delegate further authority to such regional bodies may face legal obstacles (Trinkle 1995).

In short, one theoretically trades off local informational and innovative advantages with national ability to encompass externalities for regional opportunities to function as an intermediate solution that can effectively deal with transaction costs. The national government and regional organizations might play a considerably greater role for ground-level ozone than they do for safe drinking water. In practice, the federal government has tended to set standards not adequately accounting for externalities and, recognizing the problems, to nibble away at the margins. This probably should not be surprising given the many regional considerations that politically affect environmental decision making. In particular, once a policy that favors upwind producers is enacted, overhauling policy over objections will likely prove difficult.

Thus, conceptually, there is an important place for the national government in dealing with ground-level ozone. In practice, given the vicissitudes of the political process, the appropriate role of the national government might be characterized as indeterminate.[8] A nationalized policy failing to internalize externalities does not unambiguously trump merely delegating authority to localities.

FEDERALISM IN THEORY AND PRACTICE

The choice between greater emphases on national or local control is a difficult one. Making this decision is complicated for both theoretical and empirical reasons. Theoretically, the national government would minimally possess authority where environmental policy has large cross-boundary effects, not easily amenable to bargaining solutions between the affected local parties. Also, the federal government could play an important role in providing scientific and technical information and realizing the benefits of coordination. The contribution of the national government in other situations is more subject to dispute, depending upon whether local and state governments produce better and more innovative policies and whether a race to the bottom exists and to what effect.

Empirically, as cases such as drinking water and ground-level ozone illustrate, how demands are translated into policy by the institutional system makes it difficult to realize the greatest efficiencies from federalism. Distributional considerations are again important and, once policies are in place, their wholesale reform is problematic as interests arise wanting to perpetuate and extend the status quo. Nor are instances of local control either the panacea or the disaster that those with different perspectives envision. There is no clear race to the bottom and there is some innovation, but much local policy seems to fall short. As such, many of the findings about federalism's impact have seemed counterintuitive.

To reiterate, two things are clear. First, the federal structure matters because its existence influences who benefits and loses from policy and policy effectiveness. Whether authority is retained at the national level, the local level, or shared, affects outcomes. As one scholar comments, "Americans pay for a brand of federalism that tries to guarantee local responsiveness and central control at the same time" (Kagan 1999, 732). This often creates an awkward combination of choices.

Second, the correspondence between the federalist ideal and empirical reality is rather weak. Specifically, a clear, rationalized division of responsibilities is not evident. Even when the seemingly correct issues are kept at the national or local level, the policies adopted may not take advantage of the alleged virtues of either.

More generally, although federalism may help accomplish goals such as preserving markets and property rights, it is not working in a textbook fashion. Rather, as stated initially, it reflects and reinforces the fragmented nature of the American political system. Fragmentation, and features stemming from it, such as a bent toward regionalism and institutional choices that produce policies that fail to rationally address problems such as interstate externalities, all make national control less attractive. As such, federalism appears to contribute to the seeming lack of coherence and efficiency costs that characterizes the American response to environmental affairs. Given this political structure, it should not be surprising that national and local authorities are frequently at odds and frustrated with one another. The former wants adherence to its policies, the latter wants recognition of local differences and compensation for federal mandates. In the process, choices are often complicated, convoluted, and delayed. That the political will to overhaul such a situation dramatically will be fast coming is unlikely.

KEY TERMS

Civic environmentalism (p. 129)

Cooperative (conjoint) federalism (p. 134)

Economies of scale (p. 132)

Federalism (p. 126)

"New Federalism" (p. 130)

Race to the bottom (p. 127)

Unfunded mandates (p. 130)

7 Land Use Agencies: Government as Landlord

The previous chapters have laid out a means for understanding environmental policy. They have provided a general perspective for understanding and justifying policy, a historical perspective on how policy has evolved and is influenced by national and local forces, and an overview of the processes determining policy implementation. They have shown that there is a seemingly ever-increasing wealth of players making competing demands on government and the environment and a growing, highly politicized, and fragmented political system responding. Additionally, they have demonstrated that demand and supply are endogenous to one another.

With this foundation, the current chapter and Chapter 8 examine actual outcomes. The present chapter focuses on the land management agencies, Chapter 8 on the EPA. They indicate that the heightened demand, increased supply, and fragmented policy system are all reflected in the policies that are observed in the present-day United States. Environmental policy is much more ambitious and far-reaching than it has ever been but in a highly fragmented, and sometimes dysfunctional, way.

As described in Chapter 3, much of the initial evolution of environmentally relevant policy in the United States involved stewardship of the land and related resources. Largely through elite demand, agencies were created with the stated purpose of managing and protecting the nation's portfolio of resources. Before analyzing contemporary innovations in environmental policy beyond land management, a discussion of these traditional concerns provides an interesting and helpful comparison with these other prominent environmentally related responsibilities.

Several contrasts and commonalities between land policy and EPA-style environmental initiatives will become evident later. However, one qualitative difference and another similarity, both already foreshadowed, are central and deserve immediate recognition. The distinction is that land management principally involves administration rather than regulation. The EPA regulates air, water, toxics, and pesticides primarily through rules and standards with command-and-control instruments and secondarily by enhancing or creating markets designed to influence private behavior.[1] By contrast, the land use agencies principally manage the nation's lands while also defining rules and standards affecting the use of privately held land to some extent. These agencies tend to be preoccupied with the use of the federal lands and resources put more directly under their control. Thus, for reasons that some find appalling and others consider common sense, the federal government retains ownership of almost 30 percent of the United States' acreage and is considering adding to these holdings through actions such as the so-called Lands Legacy Initiative and the Land and Water Conservation Fund (Zinn 2001; states also own almost 7 percent more of the nation's land).[2] As Table 7-1 shows, the extent of government holdings in each state varies; among the forty-eight continental states, national government holdings range from Connecticut, where it owns less than 0.3 percent of all land, to Nevada, where it retains almost 80 percent. Given such a huge portfolio, and with so many competing demands for the lands and the resources on them, government agencies must put much energy into their stewardship as both owner and landlord. Besides managing certain lands directly, federal agencies rent out other areas and assign associated rights to interested parties for mining (including energy sources), grazing, logging, and recreation. All activities substantially affect the environment and merit careful attention.

Conversely, with respect to basic similarities with EPA-style policy, and consistent with the fragmentation of the political system, the bureaucratic system characterizing federal land management reflects its piecemeal evolution as a product of heightened demand and growing political supply. Created at different times in response to different sets of demands and reflecting different political choices, agencies of various stripes, scattered around the federal government, administer a bevy of statutes that have historically been layered one on top of the other rather than comprehensively rationalized and integrated. Relations are not particularly warm between these agencies and they do not interact a great deal, certainly not in a concerted attempt to forge a coherent policy. Neither do they appear to actively compete much with one another, their priority seeming to be managing their own domains in light of conflicting political demands. Diverse management and statutory foundations create an overall contradictory policy, with some features costing more than the benefits, whether costs and benefits are measured from a narrowly economic or a broadly environmental perspective. For example, the Forest Service may antagonize firms and workers who depend on wood products for their livelihoods by preventing logging to ensure that waters will not be damaged by sediment; yet the Bureau of Land Management may create sediment runoff by allowing ranchers to graze arid lands when such grazing is not economically justifiable. Interestingly, despite this wide dispersion of authority among different land management agencies, the EPA's managerial role is indirect even for the most envi-

Table 7-1   National Government Ownership by States, 1997 (in percentages)

State	Land ownership	State	Land ownership
Alabama	3.30%	Montana	27.32%
Alaska	47.00	Nebraska	1.05
Arizona	43.11	Nevada	79.82
Arkansas	8.15	New Hampshire	12.70
California	44.67	New Jersey	2.11
Colorado	36.29	New Mexico	33.71
Connecticut	0.22	New York	0.64
Delaware	0.15	North Carolina	6.46
District of Columbia	23.45	North Dakota	3.18
Florida	7.62	Ohio	1.07
Georgia	3.92	Oklahoma	1.54
Hawaii	8.53	Oregon	51.64
Idaho	62.33	Pennsylvania	2.16
Illinois	1.13	Rhode Island	0.46
Indiana	1.70	South Carolina	4.82
Iowa	0.83	South Dakota	5.27
Kansas	0.67	Tennessee	5.90
Kentucky	4.24	Texas	1.19
Louisiana	2.58	Utah	64.33
Maine	0.97	Vermont	6.34
Maryland	2.49	Virginia	8.94
Massachusetts	1.04	Washington	27.96
Michigan	10.91	West Virginia	6.99
Minnesota	7.95	Wisconsin	4.95
Mississippi	4.22	Wyoming	49.53
Missouri	3.75		

Source: Bureau of Land Management (http://lm0005.blm.gov.80/natacq/pls98/98PL1-3.PDF).
Note: Additionally, more than 3 million acres of nonfederal land are controlled via leases, agreements, easements, and permits by the four major land management agencies, and about 52 million acres are retained in trust for Native Americans.

ronmentally sensitive lands (for example, for **riparian lands,** which are vegetated areas bordering rivers, streams, and other bodies of water especially vulnerable to overgrazing, as elimination of vegetation harms surrounding water, with secondary impacts including damage to the health of species).

Put another way, land policy is a crazy quilt of activities, administered by a diverse group of government entities, reflecting a variety of increasing demands and changes in political institutions. Although wide differences of opinion about the remedy exist, liberals, conservatives, and policy analysts alike largely agree that the government has significantly failed in its custodial role (much the same is said for EPA policies). There is also consensus that, in the process of making such errors, politicians and the relevant agencies have inflicted substantial environmental harm on the land and induced poor economic use of resources.

The government's duties and institutional capacity to act as landlord have evolved in ways consistent with heightened demands and increased but fragmented capacity. With demands for resources, recreation, preservation, and environmental quality all increasing, government has assumed more responsibilities, but in a manner accentuating the American political system's fragmentation and politicization. Hence, political conflict, a lack of coordinated policy making, and the triumph of distributional over efficiency considerations constitute hallmarks of government's custodial role.

THE LAND USE AGENCIES

Principal supervision of most federal land is dispersed among four agencies mentioned in Chapter 3: the Bureau of Land Management, the Forest Service, the National Park Service, and the Fish and Wildlife Service.[3] These bureaus differ in many ways, have varied (if increasingly overlapping) mandates, operate in different institutional settings, and have developed contrasting bureaucratic reputations.

In regard to land quantity, the two largest agencies, the USFS and the BLM, currently control about 190 million and 270 million acres, respectively (GAO 1995b). However, reflecting increasing environmental demand and the conservationist roots of the USFS and the BLM, the amount of land allocated to these agencies has declined significantly as environmentalists and their political allies have successfully moved some lands to agencies whose aim is more toward preservation. Also, the distinction between the types of land each bureau controls has blurred as, given increased politicization, choices about responsibilities have been made more for political reasons than as a result of a well-thought-out division of labor. Initially the Forest Service handled wooded areas and the Bureau of Land Management controlled rangelands (and the lucrative minerals lying beneath all federal lands), but now both agencies are responsible for lands that would seem best allocated to the other. The BLM controls 47 million acres of forests and the USFS has substantial grazing authority. Indeed, calls for combining the two agencies on the grounds of eliminating wasteful duplication and facilitating coordination have become frequent (Gorte and Cody 1995).

By contrast to the Bureau of Land Management and the U.S. Forest Service, the National Park Service and the Fish and Wildlife Service have more preservationist orientations and control less land, although many of the FWS's responsibilities extend to non-FWS lands. Largely as a result of policy changes toward

Alaska, the amount of land that both agencies control has risen several-fold in the last few decades. NPS holdings have gone from 27 to 78 million acres, and FWS lands, which include the National Wildlife Refuge System and the National Fish Hatchery System, have expanded from 22 million to 93 million acres. Perhaps even more than the USFS and the BLM, both agencies have felt the political pressures associated with preservation in a world where such actions come with high costs.

An analysis of each agency will provide a sense of overall policies toward land management, emphasizing both common and unique experiences and shared and distinct features. Some of the major controversies associated with these units highlight the tensions surrounding them—timber sales for the USFS, grazing and mining for the BLM, balancing preservation and recreation for the NPS, and takings issues (agency actions that reduce the value of property, typically without providing compensation for those adversely affected) for the FWS.

These agencies have been caught up in the increasing fragmentation and diversity of pressures characterizing the American political system. Administrators are tugged in every direction and end up pleasing very few. For environmentalists, this increased pressure is not all bad. Agencies such as the BLM and the USFS that were traditionally seen as industry lapdogs or too commercial now place greater weight on environmental considerations. However, efficiency costs may be considerable, as government is not necessarily realizing the most environmental quality bang for its considerable number of bucks.

The United States Forest Service

Gifford Pinchot may have clearly defined the Forest Service's mission as the embodiment of multiple use. Although some would say that timber was the first among equals (for example, Clary 1986), this is no longer the case due to increased demands and greater politicization of policy. The Forest Service's positive "Smokey the Bear" image has come under attack during the last few decades because the agency has had a multitude of problems to address—problems that Pinchot could not have conceived of in his time. Most notably, the agency has discovered that the resource management choices resulting from juggling vigorous, conflicting demands offend many and please few.

Emblematic of this state of affairs is restrictive legislation deadlocking the Forest Service. A 1993 Forest Service document, "The Principal Laws Relating to Forest Service Activities," outlines 226 laws, some of which are in direct conflict with each other. As a result, the agency "cannot move in any direction without breaking one or more laws" (Jordan 1994, 17). Asked to accomplish myriad goals and given incentives and rules guaranteeing inefficient use of its resources, the

USFS and its more than 40,000 employees, roughly 30,000 full-time, are almost assured of harsh critiques of its administration of 155 forests, 20 grasslands, and well over 100 other units. One analysis outlines the agency's predicament this way:

> The Forest Service . . . expanded after World War II in order to manage the public forests for use by predominantly commercial clients. In so doing, its personnel developed a strong commitment and conformity with the initial organizational goals. In the last two decades, public awareness, changing values, and legislated policy goals have changed perceptibly from those prevalent in the days of Theodore Roosevelt and Gifford Pinchot. The agency may have had difficulty shifting its organizational beliefs and responses from predominantly single use to multiple objectives, but it has capitalized on its enlarged constituency by increasing clients, agency power, budget, and size. However, this has not been achieved without increasing confrontation, administrative and legal challenges, and declining agency morale. Adapting to new public values and attendant desires for the national forests while maintaining agency power and influence will continue to challenge the Forest Service for years to come. (Cubbage, O'Laughlin, and Bullock 1993, 173)

Thus, in broad brush, there is a huge disjunction between the first and the second halves of the twentieth century. The first half placed fewer and more easily handled demands on the agency's resources such as meeting modest commercial needs for timber. During the second half, the agency ran into conflicting societal and political pressures. Most notably, its increasing exploitation of forest resources in light of rising demand sat poorly with the expanding number of interests concerned with either the environment or recreational opportunities. Contesting forces sparred back and forth in the political arena. In recent years, more preservationist-oriented concerns, such as those represented by environmental groups like the Sierra Club, appear to have at least temporarily moved the status quo in their direction while commercial interests and their political representatives seem to have lost ground. Not that preservationists claim victory—for instance, they have grown irate at compromises that they maintain redefine the definition of salvage timber, whose harvest is not subject to many environmental provisions, from wood that is dead and dying, to include "green" timber. In the midst of tumult and conflicting mandates, the USFS has found itself knocked off its administrative pedestal as those championing commercial, recreational, and environmental usages, as well as policy analysts, all find features of the agency and the policies it implements wanting.

The process underlying this evolution reflects how economic demands have been mediated by the political system in ways satisfying few participants. For instance, both environmentalists (for example, a coalition of groups and activists known as the American Lands Alliance) and market-oriented interests (for example, the American Forest Service Association) have attacked the Forest Service's handling of timber sales. Although some beneficiaries would beg to differ, it is generally recognized that timber rights are sold well below what an efficiently operating market would yield, producing an overexploitation of resources with few rewards for the government (for example, O'Toole 1988). Additionally, although a wide variety of environmental restrictions have been put into place, incentives to fully incorporate all the societal costs of logging, especially as they pertain to the damage inflicted on the environment, are lacking. For the timber industry, the results are frustrating rules that exclude many lands from harvesting, and a financial windfall at the expense of America's forests, the environment, and society's welfare.

Returning to themes from the earlier chapters, the USFS's situation appears to reflect how the American political system has tried to mediate rising economic demands for both goods and environmental protection. Timber sales increased dramatically until the 1990s (recall Figure 3-2) because of growing economic demand for wood and paper products after World War II and policies that allowed increased harvests in the national forests. Harvesting increases coupled with moral hazard problems, created by the lack of strong incentives for timber companies to sustain government-owned forests (that is, it is in these firms' interests to treat their forests better than government-owned forests), generated considerable environmental costs. For one thing, timber production requires disrupting forests by constructing roads—although such building probably disturbs environmentalists more because it makes logging possible rather than for the actual environmental or aesthetic damage that it produces. For another thing, tree removal may damage watersheds by allowing sediment to build up, as occurs especially when harvests are done by **clear-cutting.** This method, begun in earnest in the 1950s, involves cutting down entire timber tracts rather than selectively harvesting trees and is despised by many for its environmental and aesthetic damage. Consistent with moral hazard, timber companies may clear-cut public lands because they do not own them and need not pay much attention to their future value. Additionally, as forests may be habitats for otherwise threatened or endangered species, their destruction or alteration can be costly. This concern has been highlighted with respect to so-called **old growth forests,** roughly defined as areas with substantial portions of trees at least two hundred years old, which are commercially valuable and typically have unique environmental attributes such as being the home to species that would otherwise be extinct. Controversies have resulted, such as that over preserving the northern spotted owl on private and public lands in the Pacific Northwest (most of the relevant forest is public), which led to a titanic conflict between commercial and environmental interests in the first half of the 1990s.[4] Additionally, commercial exploitation and resulting environmental dam-

age to the national forests collide with increasing demand for recreational opportunities as, for example, visitors to national forests will not want to experience the
ravages of clear-cutting. Responding to increased recreational use of the national
forests (visits to national forests are expected to surpass one billion per year early
in the twenty-first century), given policies facilitating commercial usage, produces
additional stress for the Forest Service.

Instead of carefully sorting through competing, skyrocketing demands from
the wood products industry, recreationalists, and environmentalists, politicians
gave the USFS mandates increasingly at odds with each other. Politicians trying
to satisfy different constituencies directed the agency to promote environmental
values and to facilitate recreational opportunities on the one hand while simulta-
neously providing it with incentives and directives to sell timber at below market
cost on the other. If not contradictory, these obligations increased tensions, producing stress at the Forest Service and working toward undermining both its external reputation and internal morale.

From the perspective of the USFS, timber is especially alluring because it is
lucrative in ways that the other activities of the service are not. Under various laws
that politicians have not felt compelled to change, the agency is allowed to keep
substantial amounts of its timber revenues. Additionally, because the Forest Service does not pay many of the costs of producing timber, it has an incentive to sell
logs when prices fall below the marginal cost of production.[5] Thus, a 1995 GAO
report (1995a) shows that the USFS sold almost $3 billion worth of timber from
1992 to 1994 and applied more than $1 billion of this revenue to building and
maintaining roads and trails on its lands, reforestation, and miscellaneous items
like erosion protection. Other monies from such sales principally went for salvage
sale preparation and administration, reimbursement to the states where the forests
are located, and directly to the national Treasury.

But increasing demands from other quarters have limited the agency's timber sales. Most obviously, as mentioned in Chapter 3, many high-profile, environmentally related, legislative initiatives directed the agency toward protecting less
developed lands. After a long battle, notably in the aftermath of a successful 1956
effort led by the Sierra Club to protect the Dinosaur National Monument (a sand-
stone edifice on the Colorado-Utah border) from the construction of a dam that
would put it under 500 feet of water, the preservationist-oriented Wilderness Act
of 1964 was passed. Described as "the most important change in national forest
policy since the formation of the Forest Service" (Klyza 1996, 92), this legislation
initially designated 9.1 million acres of Forest Service land as wilderness and
directed the USFS (along with the NPS and FWS) to examine the suitability of
protecting all areas under its control that lacked roads or could be defined as prim-
itive (this Roadless Area Review and Evaluation is known as RARE I). In the after-

math of a second review in the 1970s, RARE II, the Forest Service found itself managing more than one-third of the newly created National Wilderness Preservation System, since about 35 million acres under USFS control were now designated as wilderness. Removing these lands from developmental activities was a blow to timber and other commercial interests. Encouraged by environmentalists writing more than a million supporting letters and postcards (Israelsen 2000a), the Clinton administration moved to set aside another 40 million acres of currently roadless area and to decommission some of the 380,000 miles of existing roads as part of a revised roads policy. The future of this initiative is uncertain with the election of George W. Bush. The subsequent resignation letter of Forest Service chief Mike Dombeck was highlighted by a plea not to oppose roadless protections and, at present, the USFS insists that it will move forward with a "responsible" roadless policy.

Similarly, although the FWS is a much bigger player, the USFS has found itself trading off environmental and timber interests in Alaska. Symbolic of this balance, the Alaska National Interest Lands Conservation Act in 1980 (ANILCA) purported to balance economic and environmental needs by allowing timber harvesting on some environmentally sensitive lands while protecting others. ANILCA was passed after a high-stakes bargaining between environmentalists and their allies (including former president Jimmy Carter) and commercial interests and their supporters (including Alaska's congressional delegation) in the U.S. Congress. Additional environmental constraints, such as those involved with implementing the Endangered Species Act, have hindered commercial efforts, particularly given the opportunity of environmentalists to use rulemaking procedures and direct their pleas toward the judicial system.

The end result has been that, while timber harvesting has not been systematically reformed, it has become more problematic for the timber industry as substantial tracts of forested lands have been removed from commercial use. Especially in light of judicial intervention in the Pacific Northwest, and an inability or an unwillingness of elected politicians to sort out the disputes, harvests on USFS lands fell precipitously in the 1990s to about 4 billion board feet (see, again, Figure 3-2). Along the same lines, the percentage of USFS harvests from clear-cutting, as compared with more selective harvesting, has declined somewhat, and new road construction mileage has been greatly reduced (USDA 1997). With political encouragement, and despite the ire of environmentalists, salvage sales have become an increasingly important part of the overall harvest and the USFS budget.

Not surprisingly, given conflicting incentives to sell wood and pressures to protect lands, most agree that the USFS timber program lacks much logic. Those representing loggers and the timber industry are exasperated with the constraints they face while those with a populist, environmental orientation consider current policies exploitative, reflecting payoffs to organized interests (for example, Hodges 1996).

From a policy analytic perspective, two obvious alternatives to the USFS's current policies exist. First, timber sales and the use of other resources could be rationalized so that marginal costs, including those inflicted on the environment, equal marginal benefits. The amount of timber consumed (at least on those lands currently being harvested) would be reduced as would environmental costs in the process. Alternatively, much of the land deemed suitable for timber production, like most areas on which wood is harvested in the United States, could be privatized, with the environmental consequences treated the same as for private forests employed for logging. Those favoring such an approach argue that this would result in more efficient use and care of valuable lands; those opposed typically maintain that corporate interests will gain control of forests and the end result will be environmental degradation.

However, at present, neither reforming timber pricing nor privatization appears to generate sufficient political support to alter the status quo qualitatively. Timber producers seem capable of blocking efforts to make public harvesting more efficient, and privatization has little chance of overcoming the objections of environmentalists. Rather, conflicts between the variety of interests concerned with USFS properties will probably produce changes that are only incremental and piecemeal.

The Bureau of Land Management

Although different in many respects from the USFS, the BLM was assigned a similar multiple use/sustained yield orientation. Instead of forests, the BLM is principally responsible for rangeland, of which mining and grazing are the predominant commercial uses. Originally created to serve agricultural interests by combining programs designed to ease moral hazard problems plaguing the rangelands, at present, the agency controls 264 million federally owned acres (164 million authorized for grazing), spread over 139 resource areas. It is also in charge of underground mineral rights covering more than twice that acreage.

As mentioned, despite their similarities, the bureau has been traditionally viewed in a far more negative light than the Forest Service. Whereas the USFS historically has had a positive image, the BLM has been stereotyped as the quintessential captured agency, dominated by the interests whom they are supposed to control—the ranchers and the miners receiving rights to natural resources at prices far below their market value (for example, Culhane 1981). Although some of the agency's problems may be blamed on the statutes it must implement, BLM stewardship has nonetheless been criticized for providing those with the rights to exploit the land incentives to treat it poorly either through overuse or by taking few precautions against damages caused by use. Only with the 1976 Federal Land Policy and Management Act's (FLPMA) stern call for multiple use and the passage of other laws, such as the NEPA and the ESA, has the agency been considered to have become more balanced in dealing with competing interests (see Cody and Baldwin 1997). However, this is not akin to saying that BLM popularity over the last quarter of a century has risen. Quite the contrary, the agency remains under assault from all sides.

Environmentalists and more conservative interests often agree on problematic elements but have different emphases and draw contrasting inferences. Environmentalists lament how 23,000 livestock owners' overuse of federal lands places rare and endangered species at risk, produces soil erosion, creates runoff threatening water and fish supplies, and degrades the quality of the landscape. They similarly decry the environmental impact of a variety of BLM-sanctioned mining activities—as well as the tens of thousands of abandoned mining sites scattered on federal lands (GAO 1996)—that pollute rivers, poison land, destroy aesthetic value, and produce toxins. More economically oriented observers largely agree with this assessment but interpret it differently. They focus on nonmarket pricing, which, they believe, results in the inefficient use and the overuse of land and other natural resources and in revenue shortfalls. They also zero in on the moral hazard problems of failing to protect and invest in the land adequately created by granting short-term ranching leases (ten years) that may disappear in the future or be subject to changing terms (for example, Dobra 1994).

As for solutions, environmentalists are inclined to raise prices, make administrative processes more hospitable to environmentalists, and remove some lands, especially riparian lands, from use entirely. Those who are more market-oriented frequently argue that, beyond estimating the correct market price and trying to write improved contracts so that land is correctly employed, most or all such lands and mining rights should be privatized to provide the correct incentives for investment and care. Once again, externalities could be accounted for as they are for private lands and mining operations. Some also adopt a federalist perspective by arguing, using the logic developed in Chapter 6, that land should be given to the states, claiming that local units more closely reflect the preferences of those with the most to gain or lose. Regardless of such condemnations, government has again been slow to act decisively to remedy these ailments as the fragmented political system's many veto points have provided ample opportunities to maintain the status quo. Rather, policies toward mineral and grazing rights change only incrementally. A quintessential example is the before-mentioned Mining Law of 1872, a costly and antiquated vestige of the settling of the American West. Despite ire created by sporadic stories of expensive rights being bought for little or nothing by companies that are not even based in the United States, this law continues to form the basis of hardrock mining (the mining of nonfuel minerals including gold, copper, and silver) on the public lands. The price of inaction is high. For example, the DOI (1998) claimed that, from January 1993 until April 1998, the Mining Law had forced Secretary of the Interior Bruce Babbitt to deed $15 billion worth of mining assets in return for $24,000. In a symbolic gesture, using a pen owned by President Ulysses S. Grant (in office when the Mining Law was passed), an angry Babbitt signed away an estimated $1 billion of rights covering more than 110 acres of public land in Clark County, Idaho, to a Danish mining company for a mere $275 in 1995. The repeal of the law is the obvious first step, but Congress has been loath to do so. Although environmentalists and their allies wish to eliminate the law, as may others, such as chief executives and groups against government waste, who prefer more efficient policy, repeal arouses little passion in the mass citizenry. By contrast, mining interests that would lose a great deal by repeal do appear to have enough political strength and allies to take advantage of multiple legislative veto points and thus bog down proposed changes. Therefore, Congress has addressed environmental concerns in characteristically piecemeal fashion by modifying the statute's impact in several ways. For instance, the passage of the Wilderness Act in 1964, while allowing continued mining on land declared wilderness until 1983, but not after that date, by and large removed such land from the domain of miners (Klyza 1996). Thus, a mining policy has been allowed to continue despite a consensus that it is environmentally *and* economically unsound. A stalemate exists, with the principal exception that land has been removed from the mining system and reallocated in the American land management morass.

Many have also been frustrated with failed attempts to overhaul the administration of animal grazing on the roughly 260 million acres of USFS and BLM land devoted to such purposes (Dietz and Rothenberg 2000). Environmentalists complain that such grazing damages the ecological condition of the land and local waterways, as well as reducing recreation activities, scenery, and fish and wildlife habitats (see Cody and Baldwin 1997). For example, they point to the poor condition of many riparian lands, particularly in the American West, where numerous areas are viewed as at-risk or nonfunctional. Table 7-2 reflects this point of view, although the assessments presented are sometimes claimed to be biased. Even more galling to many environmentalists and policy analysts is that the price charged to numerous ranchers is an order of magnitude below market rates (and, as Figure 7-1 shows, the amount charged in real dollars has declined significantly with time for the past several decades); moral hazard induces grazers to overuse the land; and the system provides an incentive to forsake land uses that are more appropriate than grazing (see Hess and Holechek 1995).

Table 7-2 Condition of Riparian Areas (in percentages)

State (miles)	Proper condition	At-risk/nonfunctional	Unknown
Alaska (140,361)	91%	8%	0%
Arizona (860)	34	53	13
California (3,590)	52	36	12
Colorado (4,347)	46	50	4
Idaho (3,883)	29	40	31
Montana (4,853)	42	57	1
Nevada (2,244)	25	53	22
New Mexico (456)	35	64	1
Oregon (6,714)	32	26	42
Utah (4,922)	35	38	27
Wyoming (4,762)	27	58	15

Source: BLM 2000.
Note: At-risk areas are deemed susceptible to degradation; nonfunctional areas lack adequate vegetation, landform, or large woody debris to dissipate stream energy associated with high flows.

Yet, western legislators routinely beat back calls for overhauling market rates and addressing the negative impacts of grazing. Analogous to mining laws, a variety of incremental adjustments have layered changes on the existing system rather than rationalizing it as policy analysts might prefer. As mentioned, general environmental legislation like the ESA and the NEPA, along with the FLPMA, placed more pressure on accounting for environmentalist and recreationalist interests and moved the BLM toward a more traditional multiple use orientation and away from placing ranchers first among equals. Similarly, regulations promulgated under the Clinton administration included modest provisions for heightening public participation, emphasizing ecosystem health and protection, and creating conditions that might reduce the number of livestock allowed to graze. Attempts to challenge these regulations judicially have largely failed (see Baldwin 2000 and the Supreme Court's decision in *Public Lands Council* v. *Babbitt* [98-1991]). Additionally, reflected by the growth of NPS and FWS holdings, nontrivial amounts of land have been transferred away from the BLM into more protective custody. As illustrated by Figure 7-2, which shows the trend in AUM authorization since 1960 for Section 3 lands, constituting approximately 150 million acres of BLM grazing lands, grazing has declined (Figure 7-2 should be viewed a bit cautiously, as the increasing size of animals somewhat decreases the impact of the decline). Yet, as of this writing, the nominal AUM rate remains at $1.35 despite attempts to increase it several-fold and, at least for the time being, it appears that more dramatic reform efforts—for example, withdrawing substantial additional lands from grazing and further revamping local oversight as a means of continuing to reduce

Figure 7-1 Real Grazing Fees, 1946–1999 (1982–1984 Dollars)

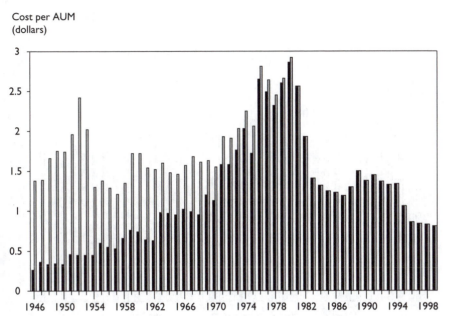

Cost per AUM
(dollars)

■ Bureau of Land Management (BLM)   ☐ United States Forest Service (USFS)

Source: Consumer prices available at ftp://ftp.bls.gov/pub/special.requests/cpi/cpiai.txt.
Note: BLM and USFS grazing fees are identical by statute beginning in 1981. Also, as the size of animals has increased with time, the amount of forage that an animal unit month (AUM) entails has increased somewhat over the years (the decline in real prices in the last twenty years is somewhat underestimated).

the number of authorized AUMs—have been abandoned as politically unrealistic. The more drastic alternative, privatizing land whose principal value is grazing or recreation (for example, Lehmann 1995) and deeding areas deserving preservation to appropriate groups (for example, the Nature Conservancy), has never even reached the political agenda.

The result is that the grazing program is attacked by environmentalists, recreationalists, and marketeers alike. Like many depression-era policies designed to prop up ailing and developing industries (for example, trucking, airlines), it is criticized for lacking a legitimate economic justification and for introducing economic distortions by charging a price so low that overgrazing relative to what a market might produce is ensured. The price is far too low whether market prices, grazing fees on state lands, or federal agency administrative costs are used as a yardstick for comparison. The program also gives a lesser status to alternative uses, such as recreation or preservation, particularly for riparian areas.[6] But, unlike

Figure 7-2 Authorized Grazing AUMS, 1960–1998 (Section 3 Lands)

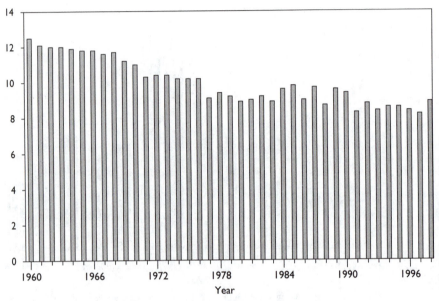

Authorized AUMs
(in 100,000s)

Year

Source: Bureau of Land Management, *Public Land Statistics* (various years).
Note: Animal unit month (AUM) is defined as the required forage for feeding one cow and calf, one horse, or five sheep or goats for a month. Data through 1982 are for calendar year or grazing fee year (March 1 through the end of February); after 1982, data are for fiscal year. Data for 1988 are listed as incomplete for Colorado, Nevada, New Mexico, and Oregon.

many of these other industries, grazing has not been marketized (on such deregulation, see Derthick and Quirk 1985, Rothenberg 1994). Also, given remaining moral hazard problems, there is a disincentive to care for the land and an incentive to employ it in ways that degrade its environmental value.

As the case of grazing illustrates, the BLM is likely to continue to operate in a minefield in which the agency alternatively alienates one interest and then another without rescue by politicians. Thus, the BLM will antagonize grazers and recreationalists when it closes off a section of the Mojave Desert to protect an endangered turtle, as occurred in 2001, and environmentalists when it attempts to allow cattle to drink from a "unique water," a spring in Arizona's Arrastra Mountain Wilderness Area, as happened in 2000. In dealing with such tensions, the agency should not expect its political superiors to clarify how it is to respond to a multiplicity of demands or to provide it with more efficient policy instruments to ease the process, as the fragmented political system promises incremental changes that may only further complicate matters rather than simplify them.

The National Park Service

Although probably the least subject to vociferous criticism of all the land use agencies, the NPS is far from immune from attacks (for example, Pritchard 1997). An assessment of the Park Service voiced in the *Economist* ("Managing Paradise" 1993, A31) at the beginning of Bill Clinton's first term in office summarized some of the key problems facing the agency:

> The [National Park] service, now 76 years old, is one of the country's most revered institutions. Yet it is in a parlous state. The parks can barely cope with current demand—in 1990 around 252m [million] people elbowed their way in. . . . Such numbers take their toll; a third of the parks' 7,900 miles of roads need repairing. . . . And dams and other irrigation projects are diverting water from the parks, while worsening air pollution obscures the majestic views.
>
> The park staff, known as the ranger corps, are also in a bad state. [They are poorly compensated and] spend more time controlling traffic, or rescuing visitors from crevasses, than explaining and looking after the natural wonders around them. They are leaving the service at a fast rate, and replacements are becoming harder to find.

In short, John Muir's legacy of a preservationist agency is beset with problems. Although still primarily associated with the stewardship of the nation's "crown jewels," such as Yellowstone or the Grand Canyon, over the years the agency has become increasingly saddled with projects that fall far short of such a description, such as a collection of railroad artifacts in Scranton, Pennsylvania, known as "Steamtown." Rather than being created at the behest of environmentalists, Steamtown was the pet project of powerful local congressman Joseph McCade. It has been derided as "park barrel" for its dubious merit and called "the god-darndest boondoggle joke you ever saw" by McCade's fellow congressman Joel Hefley (cited in Satchell 1995, 24; see also O'Toole 1995). Pressure to increase the range of NPS holdings is likely to continue. For example, in February 2001, New Jersey's two senators joined forces to advocate a national park for the Great Falls (a series of factories around a seventy-seven-foot waterfall) in Paterson, New Jersey, claiming that it would bring millions of dollars of development into an area needing economic growth ("National Park Status Sought for Paterson Waterfall Site" 2001). In 2000 the NPS controlled 382 diverse sites (only 56 of which are actually labeled national parks), ranging from urban parks, to his-

Table 7-3 Diversity of National Park Service Holdings, by Type and Acreage, as of December 31, 1999

Type of area	Number of Acres
International historic site	22
National battlefield parks	8,060
National battlefield site	1
National battlefields	11,877
National historic parks	114,727
National historic sites	20,122
National lakeshores	145,644
National memorials	8,041
National military parks	35,170
National monuments	1,880,659
National parks	4,985,333
National preserves	21,445,909
National recreation areas	3,403,577
National reserves	10,932
National rivers	311,093
National scenic trails	157,938
National seashores	478,282
National wild and scenic rivers	72,780
Parks (others)	37,723
Parkways	164,039
Total	78,165,932

Source: National Park Service (http://www2.nature.nps.gov/stats/acreagesum99CY.pdf).

toric homes, to large national parks, to dubious creations à la Steamtown, designed to spur economic activity. Indeed, Table 7-3 shows twenty different designations for areas making up the agency's 78 million acres (83 million including nonfederal holdings). This growth and diversification reflects both the increased demand for protection of natural wonders and the ways in which supply-side choices have become politicized, with enterprising politicians attempting to place lands under the NPS umbrella for reasons far from those originally envisioned.

Tensions facing the NPS appear to revolve principally around three related issues: balancing individual demands to consume environmental and recreational opportunities on NPS properties with environmental preservation; the need for funding levels corresponding to the current size, scope, and usage; and a blurring of the agency's preservationist mandate to include other goals. Combined, these three factors result in a bureaucracy asked to do more in an absolute sense and to engage in a greater variety of tasks than previously without comparable increases in financial support.

The first of these tensions stems from heightened demand for park use (recall Figure 3-3). Visitations have risen from 79 million in 1960 to approaching 300 million as the twenty-first century begins. Although the increase is partially a feature of park system growth, many properties have experienced attendance surges. For example, Grand Canyon National Park had approximately 437,000 visitors in 1941, 682,000 in 1951, 1.3 million in 1961, 2.2 million in 1971, 2.5 million in 1981, 3.9 million in 1991, and 4.5 million visitors in 2000. Such heavy usage has significant consequences, especially for those entities that represent nature's beauty. Surely the more people who visit the national parks, wishing to enjoy their pristine beauty, the less pristine such areas become without significant expenditures to redress the damage done, leading to conflict between pressures for maintaining the environment and usage demands (Lowry 1994). Although the obvious market-oriented solution to such conflict—substantially raising prices to produce revenue that can be used to maintain the properties and to reduce attendance (only half of all parks charge anything at all)—has met obvious political resistance, there have been some tentative steps at some of the most visible national parks to innovate in ways that may provide some protection. For instance, some modest pricing increases as well as the development of other income sources have been allowed, although whether over the long term the federal Treasury will simply keep such receipts or the monies will be plowed into park maintenance is a matter of contention.

Encroaching development often adds more tension to the mix (Freemuth 1991). Preferences of residents living outside park boundaries create considerable turmoil, particularly with respect to the agency's most famous parks, where desires to maintain and restore natural features have run into heavy local criticism. For example, reintroducing and maintaining native species, such as gray wolves and wild bison, respectively, that threaten cattle around Yellowstone, have produced widespread objections from neighboring cattle ranchers who fear the costs to their herds (on Yellowstone, see Primm and Clark 1996).

Lack of NPS funding has exacerbated many problems. The National Park Service produces little money on its own and relies on federal government appropriations. Perhaps because a strong, well-organized constituency is lacking, as the agency does not serve specific industries like the USFS or the BLM, by virtually all accounts funding is insufficient for the agency's delegated obligations. Horror stories of raw sewage running through parks and substandard facilities, to a considerable extent attributable to the lack of funds for necessary upgrades, abound. For example, the amount needed for the NPS maintenance backlog is currently claimed to be about $5 billion, and this total has been steadily building as the maintenance done in any year has not kept up with the additional needs created by time and usage (GAO 1998b). The agency's chief public affairs officer remarks in frustration that "we are an agency with an annual budget of $2 billion and sometimes $100 to $200 million goes toward the maintenance backlog. It doesn't matter if [the maintenance backlog] is $3 billion or $5 billion. That budget is never going to do it" (cited in Shaw 2000, 1).

Further compounding these difficulties, the agency's core mission has been blurred by political decision makers, serving their own needs by forcing the NPS to manage areas not otherwise candidates for agency preservation (see Kunioka and Rothenberg 1993). Not only do local environmentalists favor giving lands to the NPS because of its pro-environment reputation, but, since association with the agency is considered prestigious, those interested in tourist-based economic development tend to favor NPS management against the wishes of agency leaders. Thus, the bureau's mandate has evolved from protecting a few isolated national parks to a wide range of obligations. Additionally, expenditures for less central activities such as running a park like Steamtown seem to reduce available funds for projects that the Park Service considers higher priority. The image of a park ranger roaming the wilds characterizes fewer and fewer employees with each passing year because rangers are not only dealing with more and more visitors but are forced to manage areas lacking such pristine qualities.

Politicians have charged the NPS with too many duties given its resources, hampering a system that cannot be adequately run at its present funding levels. Politicians have further complicated matters by including lands that correspond poorly to the agency's traditional mandate. Indeed, the NPS itself has fought against its own expansion and lost on numerous occasions while seemingly more worthy lands, some of which the NPS advocates making parks, have been excluded. Efforts toward rationalizing park policy have mostly met with frustration, as politicians, particularly members of Congress, seem content to use the agency in strategic ways to achieve their own objectives.

The Fish and Wildlife Service

Originally created in 1940 as a way of combining several disparate programs at the urging of wildlife conservationists, the FWS was then constituted in much of its present form by the Organic Act of 1956. After extended conflict between commercial fishing and conservation interests had marred its first three decades, its responsibilities for commercial fishing were removed in 1970. Like the other land management agencies, the FWS receives a great deal of strong criticism as well. But, as mentioned earlier, designed to protect endangered and threatened species and to restore them to a secure status in the wild, the FWS's regulatory role distinguishes it from its fellow land use agencies by giving it substantial authority in setting rules and standards that affect lands beyond those which it directly controls. Notably, in some circles, the agency's implementation of the

ESA has been widely criticized both for not balancing the benefits of species protection with the economic costs inflicted on individuals, firms, and society and for failing to move vigorously enough to protect and promote endangered species.[7] Despite criticism, the FWS has increased its landholdings, especially in Alaska, as part of the expansion of the national wildlife refuge system (notably 49 million acres from the BLM between 1979 and 1980). More than 91 million acres spread over all fifty states now include more than five hundred refuges and more than eighty other areas concentrated on north-south corridors by which species migrate, as well as in Alaska. Although the agency's land management mission is primarily to protect fish, wildlife, and related habitat, other uses such as recreation (for example, hunting and fishing), mining, grazing, and timber harvesting are allowed when claimed not to interfere.

In truth, the FWS's role in managing land is not heavily clouded by controversy (Clarke and McCool 1996). Rather, it is the agency's implementation of the ESA—applied not only to FWS-controlled lands but to other public and private holdings—that has generated the most controversy with environmentalists for its ineffectuality and with those with economic interests for its financial costs:

> Virtually all interested parties agree that the ESA can be significantly improved, despite their vocal disagreement as to how this should be achieved. As currently structured, the ESA imposes large and unnecessary costs and uncertainties on a broad range of property owners. At the same time, its effectiveness in saving and restoring endangered species is, at best, mediocre. (Thompson 1997, 321)

In fairness, although FWS bureaucrats implementing the ESA are frequently criticized as either having so strong a biological orientation that they are impervious to other costs or for not moving expeditiously to protect species, many also consider the nature of the legislation itself as a major, even as the principal, problem. In other words, choices produced by the political bargaining process, and the inability to update them, precariously position the agency.

From the perspective of those commonly considered conservative critics, there are, essentially, two standard and related criticisms of the ESA, one based on efficiency and the other on distribution. The efficiency argument is that the law fails to accomplish its goals in a low-cost manner or in a way that balances costs with benefits (for example, Polasky and Doremus 1998). The distributional complaint is that private property values are diminished without compensation, which, such opponents claim, is unconstitutional according to the takings clause of the Fifth Amendment of the Constitution, which states that "nor shall private property be taken for public use, without just compensation"; in modern-day application, the relevant issue becomes whether actions such as those associated with the ESA—rulings not appropriating property but substantially reducing its value without compensation—are takings (see Blume, Rubinfeld, and Shapiro 1984; Epstein 1993; Wise 1994; Fischel 1995; Hermalin 1995; Innes 1997). Efficiency and distributional complaints are linked in that many believe that compensating losers from endangered species protection would provide incentive to change the extent, mix, and tools of species preservation.

Inefficiencies can be traced to the passage of the ESA in 1973 (an apparent response to several earlier, ineffectual statutes); in that law costs were specifically prohibited from being considered in protecting endangered and threatened species. Interestingly, legislative debates were not marked by the type of battles that highlighted other major environmental regulatory initiatives of the decade, because the congressional supermajority supporting the bill essentially viewed it as protecting only large, impressive wildlife such as the bald eagle. What fights occurred had little to do with the issues that would arouse controversy in implementation. But, along with the ESA's expansion via judicial interpretation, once scientific understanding of the scale of threatened extinction and what can be done to prevent it grew, and the demands for and politicization of environmental policy increased, the statute's importance and associated controversy heightened (Petersen 1999).

The end result has been widespread delegation of responsibility to FWS biologists for determining allowable human activities on both public and private lands. Cases such as the controversy precipitated by FWS protection of the northern spotted owl distressed both marketeers and environmentalists alike. The former complain that:

> Like other dedicated people, Fish and Wildlife officials would like to believe that their mission transcends all others. And, at least as currently interpreted, the law appears to support them. It appears to authorize the protection of endangered species as "trumping" all other missions. But until the conflict between the fact of scarcity and the apparent ability to disregard scarcity is resolved, the ESA will not work effectively to save species. (Stroup 1995, 3)

Although statistical analyses discerning which species get listed for ESA protection actually indicate that costs and benefits are one determinant of protection (Ando 1997, 1999; see also Coursey 1994), the lack of full integration of costs into decision making has helped produce a litany of stories for critics to seize upon. For instance, there is the case of the "Riverside Rat," where protecting a small rat in Riverside County, California, put residents' homes at risk. The FWS told homeowners in 1992 that, to protect the Stephen's kangaroo rat, they could not plow their lands to create firebreaks to stop the movement of oncoming fires; the following year, fire destroyed twenty-nine homes, presumably because of the lack of firebreaks (Stroup 1995). Furthermore, those favoring market solutions point out that the ESA may lead to peculiar anticipatory behavior. Private landowners, responding to legislative incentives offering penalties but not rewards, may deliberately undermine the ability of their lands to sustain endangered species, degrade their land's biological value, and reduce the likelihood of FWS intervention.

Related complaints by environmentalists center on problems of protecting species and helping them thrive. Although environmentalists tend to believe that the law has had a more positive impact than do more conservative critics (see, most notably, the National Research Council 1995), it is generally recognized that, overall, the number of species whose situations have significantly improved as a result of legal protection is less than desired. This may not be too shocking given the conflictual situation created under the ESA. Thus, for example, cost bearers have incentives to delay implementation by strategically using FWS rule-making and judicial suits to delay actions. Not surprisingly given such transaction costs and, like the NPS, lacking a strong unified constituency such as a single industry to aid in persuading politicians to provide a far larger budget, the agency, in turn, claims that it lacks sufficient financing for responding to all the petitions for species protection (the agency has traditionally been viewed as cash poor as a result of a lack of political support; see Clarke and McCool 1996). Indeed, when sued by the Center for Biological Diversity to determine the status of the Colorado River trout, the agency's reaction was to state: "They [environmentalists] petition faster than we can do our status reviews. . . . [W]e just don't have the people and money to get the job done" (Israelsen 2000b).

The distributional critique of the ESA follows straightforwardly from these efficiency complaints. Because protecting species against the will of private landowners or those potentially using public lands for other purposes involves an uncompensated economic cost, the ESA is said to be unfair because it abolishes rights without remuneration. Economists, legal scholars, and market-oriented political activists who believe the result is unconstitutional takings argue that the FWS should compensate firms and individuals and perhaps even other government agencies whose fortunes are diminished. Presumably, this would provide the FWS with a reason to choose actions with high benefits relative to costs. For landowners certain that future restrictions would be compensated, the incentive to destroy areas of high environmental value preemptively would be largely eliminated.

Not too surprisingly, environmentalists reject arguments that costs should be factored into choice behavior and are suspicious of takings claims. Presumably, such opposition is strategic. Even if destruction of environmentally sensitive areas were prevented in some instances, compensation provisions would likely drive down the level of resources devoted to the environment generally and to species protection specifically.

In the last two decades, high-profile efforts to incorporate takings—which advocates believe should be applied to any environmental action reducing property values substantially—have largely failed legislatively and in popular referenda. Those championing change have been frustrated by the institutional features producing policy durability and the popularity of environmental causes juxtaposed with the fear of additional tax obligations. For instance, following their "Contract with America" after their 1994 congressional landslide, Republicans fell short of producing statutory reform when the Senate failed to even vote on takings legislation given a Democratic filibuster threat. Although efforts at reform continue, the fragmented political system provides environmentalists and their political allies multiple points at which to stop change and retain the status quo, and thus no takings legislation has been forthcoming, proving policy very durable. Similarly, a 1995 Washington State referendum was defeated by a 3-2 margin amid environmental opposition and fears of program cost, effectively wiping out efforts by that state's legislature to establish a strict landowner compensation scheme.

However, judicially, and consistent with the willingness of courts to take an activist stance, discussed in Chapter 4, takings advocates have realized at least mixed success on constitutional grounds, and the courts loom as a potential major obstacle for environmentalists. Most notably, in a series of cases in the 1980s, the Supreme Court ruled that regulations may so completely deprive property owners of value as to require compensation. Although these decisions have not had nearly the impact as would more sweeping proposals offered legislatively or via referenda, they imply that there are limits, albeit unclear ones, on what policy makers can do without compensating property owners. They also mean that political actors must live with courts that are less deferential with respect to such issues than previously (see Wise 1994).

Nonetheless, despite the widespread belief that the ESA does not supply much bang for the buck, there seems to be at most room for modest reform (Pope 2000). For example, it might be possible to slightly weaken the prohibition on including economic factors so that the law better reflects reality or to somewhat streamline the tortuous administrative processes involved (for a discussion of current reform proposals, see Buck, Corn, and Baldwin 2001). But without sweeping judicial rulings, interested parties appear positioned to stymie more significant change.

In short, like other agencies, the FWS can be interpreted as reflecting demand increases in the context of a political system that supplies goods in non-intuitive ways. Efforts to respond to heightened demand for environmental quality, particularly maintaining the health of various species, have been tangible. But the supply-side response, particularly the promulgation and interpretation of the ESA, has perplexing features that appear to reflect distributive concerns. Furthermore, political gridlock has stymied efforts to change the system substantially. Only ambiguous judicial changes to the status quo have resulted.

CONCLUSIONS: GOVERNMENT AS STEWARD

With the exception of the ESA, government stewardship of the federal lands is considerably different from the EPA's explicit regulation of the environment. Yet, four basic, related inferences may be drawn:

- *Demand has spiraled upward.* Demand for much of what the federal lands provide—recreation, resources, natural beauty—all went up in the last half of the twentieth century with no end in sight. Such heightened demand is reflected in consumption increases and in intense political conflict between environmentalists, recreationalists, and economic interests such as those associated with the timber, logging, and mining industries. Similarly, demand for species preservation has markedly jumped, as has the intensity of reactions of those standing to pay the price for protection.
- *Supply has increased notably.* Roughly mirroring the American political system's general development, a variety of land management agencies has developed throughout the twentieth century: first the USFS, then the NPS, subsequently the BLM, and finally the FWS. In this sense, institutional capacity involving land management, like that of the overall political system, has increased substantially. Although, given the nature of the political system, this has not always meant that these agencies have been able to achieve the numerous goals given to them, over the long term the absolute capacity of land management agencies has grown.
- *Policy has become more fragmented, both in the underlying process and in regard to actual choices.* The interaction of heightened demand with the development of myriad land management agencies reflects the nature of the American political system. Not only does the policy formulation process appear more fractured than previously, as numerous societal interests are brought into the fray, but so do the resulting policy choices. Rather than a neat division of labor, with agencies rationally dividing up tasks (or a single agency integrating such tasks), land management is characterized by increasing fragmentation. A lack of integration, rationalization, and coordination appears to typify resulting policies, and different agencies deal with overlapping issues in contrasting ways (for example, Clarke and McCool 1996). Thus, although, in theory, each agency has its own domain—the USFS has timber; the NPS, preservation; the BLM, mining and grazing; and the FWS, habitat—reality is far murkier. Elected officials

may have analytic and explicitly political reasons for preferring multiple agencies (Landau 1969, Bendor 1985, Wilson 1989, Kunioka and Rothenberg 1993), but the result is a system about which few are very positive.

- *Distributional concerns often seem to receive priority.* Given the nature of statutes and other mandates, it should not be surprising that resources are often used in a manner that seems perplexing and policy instruments are adopted that are not intuitively sensible. Distributional issues about who receives policy benefits often appear to take precedence over efficiency. As such, it seems that many programs have costs far exceeding benefits. Indeed, the inference that efficiency gets short shrift is buttressed by the argument that it is often not obvious why government in many instances functions as landlord. To advocates of this perspective, only political explanations—such as the path dependence of history (by which choices at one point in time influence those made later) and resulting political endogeneity, as interests wishing to sustain and reinforce the land management status quo are first created and then strengthened—can account for this government role.

In short, this study of land management agencies illustrates many of the basic themes of the analysis of environmental policy foreshadowed. Government policy is a function of political demands for goods such as environmental quality, recreational opportunities, and government-controlled natural resources as mediated by the supply characteristics of the political system. Consequently, policies, after initially being oriented toward the needs of economic producers for raw materials, have evolved to incorporate the desires of others for recreational opportunities and environmental protection. However, change has typically been agonizingly slow, policies have been fragmented and often at cross-purposes, and the methods employed have frequently involved layering one startlingly inefficient means on top of another in ways appearing more aimed at satisfying distributive goals than at meeting stated objectives.

KEY TERMS

Clear-cutting (p. 156)
Old growth forests (p. 156)
Riparian lands (p. 152)

8 The EPA:
Government as Regulator

Although the government's principal policies toward the environment in the first half of the twentieth century involved its functioning as a landlord, in the second half of the twentieth century, and continuing to the present, they increasingly entailed its acting as a regulator. Government took on the role of setting policies to direct the specific production and consumption choices of individuals, firms, and even other governments. At the national level, the lead agency for environmental regulation is the Environmental Protection Agency. With the exception of the FWS implementing the ESA, the mission of the EPA, to set rules and guidelines or operate markets to make the choices of decision makers more environmentally favorable, is qualitatively different from those traditionally assigned to the land management agencies discussed in the last chapter.

In numerous respects, the EPA embodies modern American politics and policy. Many point to the agency as emblematic of post-materialist politics, by which quality of life rather than economic survival is brought to the forefront of public policy, that they claim are coming to dominate the political agenda (for example, Berry 1999). Reflective of modern social regulation, which has thrived as government's commitment to economic regulation has waned, the EPA's jurisdiction spans a vast array of activities. Literally thousands of organized concerns—national groups with broad policy portfolios, local grassroots organizations, groups with an exclusive environmental focus, firms, government-sponsored organizations, and unions among them—believe that a single agency importantly influences their well-being.

As implied, the EPA's creation in 1970 symbolically redefined the national government's relationship to the natural environment. Washington bureaucrats no longer principally managed the use and protection of the nation's abundant natural resources. Civil servants now influenced the minutiae of specific production and consumption choices of individuals, firms, and even governments. For individuals, environmental policy affects the types of cars they drive, how they care for their lawns, and even how they barbecue their food; for firms and governments, it affects the production processes they use for everything from making automobiles to running zoos, investment choices, and disposal of the by-products produced from their activities.

Additionally, the EPA is typified by a lack of rationalization. Rather than being comprehensively planned, it appears to be an amalgamation of ill-fitting parts, which both reflects and reinforces perceptions of the American political system's fragmentation in the face of heightened demand. Despite efforts by some political actors to make more integrated, goal-oriented, risk-sensitive, and efficient policy, the EPA continues to display this fractured quality more than three decades after the agency's creation.

This chapter outlines the modern environmental regulatory policy context to show both how large and how fragmented the government's environmental authority, particularly as represented by the EPA's activities, has become. Policies toward air, water, toxics, and pesticides at the time of the EPA's creation are reviewed first. The chapter then surveys the principal laws administered by the agency with respect to these media and pollutants before covering general trends characterizing environmental regulation.

To reiterate, the interaction of demand and supply, given the nature of the American political system, provides the foundation for this conceptual analysis. Heightened demand is reflected in the sheer breadth of contemporary environmental regulation. Its interaction with political supply features is vividly demonstrated in the imagery of fragmentation and diversity on myriad dimensions produced when the agency's policies and responsibilities are reviewed. EPA policy mirrors both those surveyed with regard to government as landlord and the variegated structure of the American political system.

ENVIRONMENTAL REGULATION CIRCA 1970

The period between the end of World War II and 1970 saw a rise, first gradual and then more dramatic, in demand for environmental quality just as the federal government began to expand, if cautiously, its role as an environmental regulator. Still, environmental laws were modest at the time of the EPA's creation (see Chapter 3). The agency received dramatic mandates, more consistent with the environmental impulses that seemingly symbolized its formation, only subsequent to Nixon's executive order creating the agency.

During the post–World War II era, various government agencies and statutes started to address air pollution, water pollution, pesticide use, and the management of toxics. Consistent with the slowly growing demand for environmental quality and with the national government's propensity to increase supply by expanding its reach, these issues began to make their way onto the national political agenda in a limited form. Even when environmental awareness seemed to be rising during the tumultuous 1960s, the national government continued to request rather little from firms, individuals, or other governments. To the extent that subnational governments were leery of national encroachment, payoffs, notably but not exclusively financial assistance (for example, money to build water treatment plants), provided a salve for their wounds (see Chapter 3). These programs in departments such as Agriculture, Interior, and Health, Education and Welfare were not huge impediments.

With demand and supply increasing, the postwar/pre-EPA period defines when the government, despite not significantly changing institutional arrangements, began to intrude upon state environmental regulation of individuals and firms. Specifically, from the end of World War II through the era culminating in the passage of the first round of landmark environmental legislation (roughly 1970–1980), with a few minimal exceptions the federal government collected information, offered technical assistance, and financially aided state and local governments on environmental matters. To the marginal extent that rules and regulations existed, they lacked enforcement mechanisms. Bureaus did not possess the will, the resources, or the authority to catch violators and assess substantial penalties.

As a result, through 1967, air pollution legislation involved only information collection, research, and technical assistance. Through 1970 federal water pollution statutes provided state and local governments with technical assistance funds while attempts to link such aid with federal enforcement programs failed. Pesticide regulation through 1972 involved, initially, producing labeling information (for example, to impede fraudulent activities) and, subsequently, limiting residues on food; toxics regulation until 1976 focused on research, demonstration projects, and training, along with reclaiming energy and materials from solid waste. By and large, the federal government hardly proved a thorn in the side of polluters or subnational governments. But just as control of lands went from periods of relative harmony to controversy, the national government moved from times of chiefly facilitating the efforts of other governments and private concerns to making them responsible for meeting strident, difficult to achieve, and expensive goals.

Rising demand for environmental quality from both the mass citizenry and organized interests coincided with the general expansion of the national government's willingness to interfere with a wide range of production and consumption choices that had previously either been beyond the reach of government or left to the states. The political bargain bringing the EPA to life by mixing and matching a variety of existing government agencies was struck. Republican and Democratic politicians alike wanted to show their commitment to the environment but, given political compromise and worries about the future political control, they created an agency that they knew was awkwardly constructed for such a daunting task (see Chapter 3).

GROWTH AND FRAGMENTATION

If the EPA were created simply to administer environmental statutes as they existed circa 1970, its inception would likely be considered significant but not overwhelmingly important. But the same set of forces that seemingly induced the agency's creation led to the expansion of social regulation generally and environmental regulation specifically. A flurry of initiatives, starting with the Clean Air Act and the Clean Water Act, placed national government in a more intrusive and combative position in relation to producers, consumers, and state and local governments and other federal agencies. In time, laws were revised and frequently (but not always) strengthened, a product of changing politics and technologies, increasing demand for environmental quality, and frustration by all sides with initial results and the nature of political supply.

Further, environmental policy grew in a manner reflecting heightened demand mediated by fragmented supply-side institutions. Consistent with rising demand and understanding, policy became more intrusive. But growth has been fragmented, disjointed, and often inefficient rather than coherent and integrated. Just as the EPA's formation emerged from political haggling, environmental initiatives sprang from bargains and compromises.

Reflecting this political birthright, the resulting policy was sometimes centered on media such as air and water and at other times on pollution type, such as pesticides and toxics (both of which can be on land or in the water or air). Different problems were regulated in qualitatively different ways and in a manner sure to cause confusion. For example, how can water quality be regulated under one policy, but pesticide regulation, which can also affect water quality, be managed separately? Also, analogous to natural resources policy, changes tended to be layered on top of existing regulations.

Consequently, the EPA's disparate pieces, cumbersome procedures, and restrictive statutes made it difficult to develop comprehensive solutions to complicated environmental problems. For example, regulations across media and types of pollution have been and continue to be poorly integrated. As a result, solving problems in which a pollutant involves more than one medium has been difficult. Manifestations of cross-media pollution, such as mitigating acid rain, have proved to be very problematic given acid rain's ability to travel long distances in the air and acidify both the soil and water bodies on which it falls (see Chapter 6). Although many scientists believe that acid rain poses less of an environmental risk than other problems that receive less attention and fewer government resources, it may slow forest growth, quicken the deterioration of human-made materials, and affect water ecosystems. Generally, the effects on waterways, particularly the dramatic imagery of dying lakes and streams, are claimed to be responsible for the prioritization given acid rain (for example, Breyer 1993). Among the difficulties in finding a solution to acid rain is that, although policy specific to the problem has focused principally on large, stationary sources such as power plants, it is caused by fossil fuel combustion such as that by automobiles. Designing a policy that addresses the sources of acid rain and effectively accounts for the processes by which acid rain has negative environmental consequences is daunting, to say the least. Policy has reduced some sources of acid rain, notably from utilities, but others have increased, principally from vehicle emissions. The total amount of acid rain has increased (GAO 2000). Often, pollution has seemed to be moved physically around rather than reduced or prevented.

Beyond differences across media and types of environmental threats, various programs discernibly deviate from each other. Among the most notable variations are:

- *Means of regulation.* Although command-and-control policies have been generally emphasized (straining EPA capacity in tangible ways, given the budgets allocated by politicians), in some instances the agency declares standards, in others it requires permits, and in still others it issues rules governing usage. Additionally, in various instances tight statutory reins are kept on the agency, and in others much discretion is given. Perhaps more notably, over time the agency has been somewhat directed away from command-and-control techniques and toward informational and explicitly market-based mechanisms.
- *Acceptable criteria.* For command-and-control policies, there has been a continuum, anchored on one end by edicts that are essentially **technology-forcing**—dictating that technology superior to that available at the time a goal is set must be developed—and secured on the other end by requirements that costs meet benefits (cost-benefit analysis). Less onerous than technology-forcing are mandates for use of the best available control technology regardless of costs. Somewhat less restrictive still is a set of intermediate criteria that might be labeled as "risk-based," stipulating quality improvements until some level of risk reduction, typically to humans, is achieved (for example, one death per one million persons).
- *Means of funding.* Funding government programs is politically sensitive and has resulted in a variety of choices. For some programs, general tax revenue is employed; others rely on user fees; and, for still others, funding schemes only describable as convoluted are mandated.

• *Level of regulation.* As discussed in Chapter 6, in some instances the EPA retains principal authority on the national level, in others hybridized versions are used, in which subnational political units such as the states play significant political roles, and in still other instances almost all authority remains at the subnational level.

There is great variation even within the context of a single agency. Of course, diversity would not be especially notable if it reflected the best policies, given a set of objectives, relative to the tasks at hand. However, this does not seem to be the case, as a basis beyond the political for many discrepancies between policies is not obvious. One extremely comprehensive evaluation of EPA legislation concludes that the situation is "Byzantine" (Davies and Mazurek 1998, 2). Examining each and every reason behind each delegation choice is beyond the scope of this chapter. Still, the explosion and diversity of environmental policy can be documented by examining how the EPA has been, and is currently, addressing environmental quality. As such, the agency's main areas of involvement—air, water, pesticides, and toxics—and general policy trends will be covered.

THE EPA'S MANY RESPONSIBILITIES

Table 8-1, summarizing principal statutory laws, reflects the sheer number and variety of the EPA's vast responsibilities. Per modern social regulation, the agency's considerable breadth covers a wide array of industrial, agricultural, government, and consumer behaviors. Not surprisingly, as Figure 8-1 illustrates, the EPA accounts for a full 10 percent of all proposed new major rules by the national government; strikingly, the FWS accounts for *another* 10 percent in its regulatory role. Major rules, defined statutorily, are proposals with annual economic impacts over $100 million (only about 1.5 percent of all rules are defined as major). To illustrate, EPA rules recently under consideration covered arsenic in drinking water, cleaning of transportation equipment, municipal sewers, water quality standards for the state of Kansas, centralized waste treatment, land disposal of aluminum, air toxics, highway diesel emissions, reformulated gasoline, handheld engines, "significant new alternatives" concerning air pollution, organic chemicals and air pollution, light trucks and air pollution, ozone standards, high production volume chemicals (two rules), and acrylamide grouts (a human carcinogen used to seal manhole and sewer leaks). The heavy emphasis on command-and-control combined with inherently technical issues, plus a plethora of burdens created by politically dictated constraints on rulemaking and decision making, results in a prodigious agency workload. It is not surprising that the EPA legitimately seems short of the requisite funds for implementing its mandates despite its growing size. Real spending and numbers of staffers having increased roughly 450 and 600 percent,

Table 8-1 Summaries of Environmental Laws Administered by the EPA

Legislation (year of enactment)	Description
Clean Air Act (1970; key amendments in 1977, 1990)	Requires EPA to set mobile source limits, ambient air quality standards, hazardous air pollutant emission standards, standards for new pollution sources, and significant deterioration requirements; and to focus on areas that do not attain standards.
National Environmental Policy Act (1970)	Requires EPA to review environmental impact statements.
Clean Water Act (1972; key amendments in 1987)	Establishes sewage treatment construction grants and regulates/enforces waste discharge into U.S. waters.
Federal Insecticide, Fungicide, and Rodenticide Act (1972; key amendments in 1988, 1996)	Governs pesticide products.
Ocean Dumping Act (1972)	Regulates disposal of materials into ocean water.
Safe Drinking Water Act (1974; key amendments in 1986, 1996)	Establishes primary drinking water standards, regulates underground injection disposal practices, establishes groundwater control programs.
Environmental Research and Development Demonstration Act (1976)	Authorizes EPA research programs.
Resource Conservation and Recovery Act (1976; key amendments in 1984)	Regulates solid and hazardous waste.
Toxic Substances Control Act (1976)	Regulates chemical use and testing.
Comprehensive Environmental Response, Compensation, and Liability Act ("Superfund") (1980; key amendments in 1986)	Establishes a fee-maintained fund to clean up abandoned hazardous waste sites.
Emergency Planning and Community Right-to-Know Act (1986—Title III of Superfund Amendments and Reauthorization Act)	Requires industrial reporting of toxic releases and encourages planning to respond to chemical emergencies.
Pollution Prevention Act (1990)	Seeks to prevent pollution through reduced generation of pollutants at their point of origin.

Source: Adapted from Lee 1999.

Figure 8-1 Major Regulatory Rules, October 1, 1996–September 30, 1999

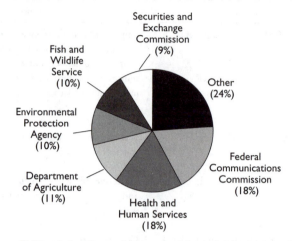

Source: Angela Antonelli, "Regulation: Demanding Accountability and Common Sense," in *Issues 2000: The Candidate's Briefing Book,* ed. Stuart M. Butler and Kim R. Holmes (Washington, D.C.: Heritage Foundation).
Note: Percentages are in relation to the total number of major rules proposed by all agencies for the three-year period.

respectively, since 1970, making it the largest U.S. regulatory agency (Mintz 1995; also recall Figure 3-4). Efforts to increase agency capacity have not kept up with the combination of increasing demand, reflected by a bevy of statutory mandates, and burdensome choices of regulatory instruments and procedures.

Air Pollution

Air pollution issues are probably the most politically sensitive of all those within the EPA's purview. Relevant policy debates routinely set regions in opposition, pit major industrial sectors against those who are environmentally conscious, and place industries and firms at odds with one another. Several additional features of air pollution policy are especially noteworthy. First, air pollutants are essentially regulated on a substance-by-substance basis. Rather than applying a general criterion that can be equally applied to each air pollutant, such as cost-benefit analysis or use of the **best available technology** (available regardless of cost), every pollutant is basically viewed in isolation. Even though the pollution criterion contained in the CAA with respect to the National Ambient Air Quality Standards—which cover sulfur dioxide, particulate matter (both 2.5 and 10 microns), nitrogen dioxide, carbon monoxide, ground-level ozone, and lead (added in 1978)—is technically protecting the public health with an adequate margin of safety, the standards have not led to consistency. This is not surprising because factors such as costs cannot be considered in calculating each standard. Indicative of this lack of consistency was the appeals court ruling rejecting proposed ozone and particulate standards that stated that the EPA lacked any "intelligible principle" in making its recommendations.

Second, air pollution policy has witnessed the greatest innovation with respect to policy instruments, as highlighted by a greater willingness to adopt market approaches in recent years. Most notably, a small amount of air pollution regulation related to problems of acid rain has been marketized through a tradeable permit system allowing polluters flexibility even to increase their pollution levels if they pay the price.

Finally, states are allocated a substantial portion of the responsibility for dealing with air quality, particularly pollution generated from stationary sources. As such, air pollution has proved to be a major battleground for scholars debating the wisdom of federalism and for those involved in the policy process who prefer contrasting levels of, and diversity in, environmental quality.

Much of the current system is still traceable to the Clean Air Act of 1970, which, to reiterate, was a product of many of the same forces that produced the EPA the same year. Furthermore, like the EPA, the CAA was not designed to attack the problems of air pollution in a cost-effective, or indeed in a realistic, manner. Rather, it was the product of a set of complicated political bargains and the desire of many politicians to show that they were pro-environment even if it meant choosing features that were unattainable. Of the variety of remarkable elements associated with this statute, the three that were perhaps most impressive were extreme optimism (in that only under the most positive of scenarios could stated goals possibly be met); technology-forcing; and scant consideration of costs to the individuals, firms, and governments that would incur them. These features were reflected in the act's two principal mandates, National Ambient Air Quality Standards and automobile emissions standards (the two other important provisions allowed the EPA to develop a program to regulate air toxics and strengthened regulatory enforcement).

Thus, for NAAQS concerning pollutants constituting health risks, it was optimistically decreed that the vaguely stated adequate margin of safety criteria was to be met by 1977. Under this system, the EPA would announce initial standards that specified the amount of a pollutant allowable in the air, presumably matching its assessment of how much pollution was acceptable given an adequate margin of safety (also, the agency was to update, presumably to strengthen, these standards every five years). Thus, for example, the agency would decree how much sulfur dioxide was permissible to be in the air from all sources. It was then largely up to the states to come up with an industry-by-industry implementation strategy approvable by the EPA, its state implementation plan, to detail how it would meet these standards. However, although there was room for state flexibility, the EPA retained authority to decide how much pollution new stationary sources (for example, a new factory) could produce. For major new pollution sources, the act also commanded adopting the best available control technology, that is, even if an area would be in compliance with a lesser technology, the better, and presumably more expensive, alternative was to be adopted. In combination, the early deadline, ambitious goals, and best available technology provisions reflected a seeming disregard of costs relative to benefits.

Automobile emissions policy was similar but relied more heavily on technology-forcing. Rather than using best available technology, new technology would have to be invented. Within five years, emissions had to be cut by 90 percent; in contrast to the great deal of delegated authority for NAAQS provided to the EPA and the states, legislators directly specified automobile pollution levels, with states allowed to adopt only stricter standards. As discussed in Chapter 6, there is an efficiency-based justification for insisting upon uniform standards for car emissions, because building automobiles with the same technology provides economies. Allowing each state to dictate its own technology to solve emissions problems could have proved to be a nightmare for automobile manufacturers as they tried to meet requirements from fifty different states. Regardless, technology for meeting the ambitious 90 percent reduction was unavailable, so this stipulation dictated that new technology be quickly developed (see Bailey 1998). Also, these high aspirations and the need for expensive technological innovation meant, almost by definition, that cost considerations were poorly integrated. It was quite likely that, after some portion of mandated reductions were achieved, additional costs would exceed additional benefits.

In light of this optimism, technology-forcing, and inattention to costs, not to mention heavy reliance on command-and-control techniques, controversy and disappointment in the CAA's aftermath were unavoidable. Most notably, with those charged with meeting the statutory deadlines—including local politicians, industries, utilities, union leaders, and auto manufacturers—screaming of technological impossibilities and high price tags that would prove a drag on a struggling American economy, most targets went unmet. Even if air quality improved, many regions and municipalities failed to attain different NAAQS, and new automobiles polluted more than the law permitted. Furthermore, conflicting congressional and judicial interpretations marred implementation, particularly with respect to whether despoiling air that was previously cleaner than the common standards was a legitimate means of achieving goals. For example, there were disputes about whether scattering pollution around (with higher smokestacks that took pollution a greater distance so that one area below a standard was now in compliance and another that was above the standard was now just at compliance) was consistent with the law. Was moving pollution around geographically to meet standards without aggregate pollution reduction acceptable (Melnick 1983)?

In the wake of such costs, failures, controversies, and increased political pressures, Congress relaxed some deadlines in the CAA reauthorization and adopted rules originally promulgated by the courts to prevent significant deterioration of currently clean areas. Finally, as described in Chapter 2, reflecting the regional nature of environmental debates by which elected officials and their allies from one region battle those of another to protect their parochial interests, the 1977 legislation benefited eastern over western coal and utility interests by mandating that new coal-burning power plants install scrubbers instead of allowing for burning low-sulfur coal when economical.

Consistent with political fragmentation and the forces leading to policy durability that mark environmental policy, for more than a decade the statute stayed the same—despite considerable unhappiness over costs, slow progress toward maintaining and enhancing air quality, the instruments being used to accomplish these tasks, and failure to confront emerging issues such as acid rain and the stratospheric ozone layer's erosion. Finally, the CAA was amended during its 1990 reauthorization with the Clean Air Act Amendments of 1990 (for an in-depth discussion, see Bryner 1995; see also Drotning and Rothenberg 1999). Although in many ways extending the 1970 and 1977 statutes, this legislation also differed in important respects. First, like much environmental regulation of the time, it was far more detailed. Legislators favored control over flexibility, with some exceptions. Also, a trade-off was seemingly made between more efficient instruments and a greater level of pollution abatement: those tending to oppose stricter policies because they bore many of the costs agreed to tighter standards in exchange for policy instruments that reduced their per unit cost in diminishing emissions (a kind of trade-off discussed in Hahn 1990, Amacher and Malik 1998).

Among the highlights of this complicated bill were:

- A host of new regulations for the states to follow in dealing with the NAAQS. Specifically, nonattainment areas, those not meeting a standard, were classified according to their extent of nonattainment with an eye toward bringing them into compliance. Areas more out of compliance were given stricter regulations but additional time.
- Stricter emissions standards and provisions for the production of clean fuels and clean-fueled vehicles.
- Use of the best demonstrated technology within given industries, as determined by the EPA, to regulate 189 air toxics.

- Reductions in sulfur dioxide and nitrogen oxide and, quite notably, creation of a market mechanism for dealing with acid rain.
- Establishment of a new state-administered permit system for stationary polluters.
- Elimination and recycling of CFCs as a means of dealing with the disappearance of stratospheric ozone, putting the EPA in compliance with the Montreal Protocol's mandate that CFCs be recycled and phased out in quick fashion. (The Montreal Protocol was the 1987 international agreement in which industrial countries agreed to address CFC production and usage.)

Basic features of air pollution policy since 1970 that are consistent with the general themes of the analysis of environmental policy stand out. In line with rising demand for more environmental quality generally, demand for better air quality has increased. Despite economic ups and downs and changes in public support of political conservatives, policy initiatives have, for the most part, become more severe. But the fragmented nature of supply-side institutions as well as demand has meant that the approach taken to the myriad problems of air pollution, indeed even within a given bill such as the 1990 amendments, has varied notably, and not exclusively for technical reasons. Thus, some policies were explicitly technology-forcing (automobile emissions) and others were not (stationary air pollution using the best available control technology). Similarly, some (most) employed command-and-control techniques and others created markets (acid rain). Further fragmentation was evidenced in enforcement and the impact of federalism. Hence, some issues, along with their implementation and enforcement, were federalized (for example, stationary sources of air pollution), whereas others were nationalized (with a few exceptions, such as automobile emissions in California). Although there were some economic justifications for this division, in practice these choices made enforcement even more fractured (for example, by adding local political actors to the mix of those implementing policy), as discussed in Chapter 5. Also, as illustrated in Chapter 6, policy was often not structured to take full advantage of the benefits of centralization or decentralization but did add to the picture of disjointed policy.

Water Pollution

Statutorily, most water quality issues involve either surface water or public systems providing drinking water. Of the two, surface water quality has garnered the most attention. Moreover, with respect to surface water, issues involving **point source pollution**—that generated from a discrete, identifiable, place such as pipes from factories or sewage treatment plants (roughly corresponding to stationary source air pollution)—have traditionally been of primary concern. By contrast, issues concerning **non–point source pollution** (analogous to mobile source pollution) have been secondary, especially until recently. Non–point source pollution is produced more diffusely than point source pollution, for example, via storm water runoff from farms, forests, and urban areas. A major distinction between non–point source water pollution and mobile air pollution is that many remedial efforts for the latter involve dealing with a small number of automobile manufacturers. Reducing non–point source water pollution involves millions of individuals and firms; everything else being equal, this makes the mitigation of non–point source water pollution far more difficult.

Many forces behind the Clean Air Act of 1970 also drove the Clean Water Act of 1972 (for a description of the latter, see Copeland 1999), making these initial post-EPA efforts strikingly similar. Admittedly, for water, even more ambitious goals were set than for air, technology-forcing was more fundamental, and delegation to states and localities was in some instances more complete. Yet, similarities outshine the contrasts.

Again, the legislation expressed great optimism in its stated goals and delegated broad authority to the EPA, states, and localities to meet them—as discussed in Chapter 5, the 1972 legislation stipulated that there was to be zero pollutant discharge by 1985, with all waters being "fishable" and "swimmable" by 1983. In line with these ambitious objectives, much emphasis was placed both on using the best existing technologies and on technology-forcing; relatively little was put on overall costs to citizens and firms for cleaning the water or maintaining its quality relative to benefits that go along with having water that is fishable or swimmable. Thus, industries were directed to implement, by 1977, the best practical control technology, the best technology for pollution control available at reasonable cost and operable under normal conditions (municipalities faced analogous requirements, with the national government to pick up 55 to 75 percent of the costs), and to have the best available technology, which, to reiterate, is the best technology for pollution control available regardless of costs or other obstacles to implementation in place by 1989. In practice, **best practical technologies** are applied to conventional pollutants, such as bacteria- and oxygen-consuming materials, whereas the more ambitious best available technologies are implemented for toxic pollutants, such as for heavy metals, pesticides, and other organic chemicals.

First the EPA issues regulations concerning technologically achievable effluent standards for categories of industrial sources (for example, by industry or groups of industries). States deemed qualified by the agency may then enforce these regulations through permit programs such as the National Pollutant Discharge Elimination System; the national government may pay as much as 60 percent of the tab. Under the NPDES, nobody can discharge effluents into the nation's water without permission—each of 65,000 industrial and municipal dischargers require a five-year permit specifying the control technology to be used for each pollutant, the effluent limitations, and appropriate deadlines. Depending upon the type of violation, failure to comply with an NPDES permit can cost from $25,000 to $50,000 per day or even lead to jail time.

As mentioned, regulation of point and non–point source pollution of surface water is substantially distinguished by government's more vigorous efforts and the EPA's more intense involvement in curbing point source pollution. Although hard to establish definitely, besides the obvious opposition of interests such as agriculture that would incur substantial costs, non–point source pollution was probably dealt with much later than point source pollution both because it is less politically visible—it is easy to see a large pulp paper plant despoiling a river and much harder to see the causal effects of agricultural fertilizers—and because point source pollution is easier to monitor and address.

Whatever the reason, despite evidence that non–point source pollution presented a major impediment to achieving ambitious statutory goals, the Clean Water Act of 1972 principally addressed point sources. Not until 1987, with the Clean Water Act amendments, did states have to implement programs to tackle non–point source pollution (states were provided financial incentives from the national government to help defray the costs). By this time, non–point sources made up 50 percent of the remaining water pollution problem. Also, as part of the contemporary effort by environmentalists to attack non–point source pollution, an overlooked provision of the Clean Water Act of 1972 has come to the forefront in recent years. Under this provision, states were to develop programs to limit their total maximum daily load (TMDL) of pollutants into water bodies through the use of "best management practices." However, despite the need to set an estimated 40,000 TMDLs, the EPA did not even issue guidelines for the states until 1985 and little happened afterward. But, spurred by a plethora of lawsuits filed by environmental organizations in the early 1990s, notably by the Natural Resources Defense Council, the EPA developed clear and, from the perspective of opponents, strict rules in the late 1990s, and the Clinton administration strategically avoided congressional attempts to prevent their implementation in 2000 (GAO 2000b). However, in August of 2001, the Bush administration proposed delaying implementation of the new TMDL rules and requirements, originally set to begin in October, until May of 2003 so that they could be further studied. The future of TMDLs remains an open question likely to be fought on judicial, legislative, and administrative fronts for quite some time.

Drinking water has had its own somewhat idiosyncratic set of rules and regulations with several notable features. First, under the 1974 Safe Drinking Water Act (SDWA) and its subsequent amendments (principally in 1986 and 1996), the national government via the EPA has tended to issue specific standards, to be met by localities, with respect to waterborne contaminants in drinking water (recall the case study of drinking water in Chapter 6). The 1986 amendments represented an attempt to accelerate the pace of contaminant regulation in a manner consistent with both increasing demand and heightened fears of tainted drinking water (Tiemann 1999). Second, except for financial support from the national government, to a very great extent, states and their public water systems have maintained primary implementation and enforcement authority. Third, in a spirit somewhat analogous to the 1990 acid rain provisions, authors of the 1996 amendments attempted to add some flexibility to standard setting to go along with many detailed instructions and to pay attention to costs by requiring cost-benefit analysis for new standards.

Thus, water quality policy has, indeed, been diverse. Overall, a secular trend reflects a greater demand for higher quality despite the appearance of forces, such as consumption and population increases, that might otherwise threaten maintaining quality. Consistent with the nature of political supply, overly ambitious goals have frequently been set, division of labor with subnational governments has varied, the extent of political control by statute has fluctuated, a variety of means have been employed, and costs have been differentially integrated into decision making.

Pesticides

After World War II, use of pesticides, products that kill, repel, or control pests, increased greatly and, in many respects, were a boon to social welfare. Farm production levels grew immensely (to this day agriculture accounts for roughly three-quarters of pesticide usage). Disease control efforts effectively used pesticides to stop transmission of disease by pests. Sensitivities to harmful public health or environmental effects remained low in this era. Pesticides were regulated by the USDA, and the original Federal Insecticide, Fungicide, and Rodenticide Act (FIFRA) passed in 1947. FIFRA aimed to prevent ineffective products from being marketed. Befitting a USDA program, its primary concern was to protect farmers from unscrupulous pesticide producers (Bosso 1987). In a similar vein, under the 1958 FDA-administered Delaney Clause, pesticides found to be carcinogenic on processed foods were deemed unsafe for such goods (for example, Vogt 1995), but the Delaney Clause was not too great an obstacle in the pre-EPA period because agricultural interests were preeminent. Although "the FDA could set spray tolerances and the [USDA] could perform some research . . . the [USDA] still dominated regulation" (Bosso 1987, 108).

Yet, despite the positive attributes of pesticides, many view the publication of Rachel Carson's book *Silent Spring* in 1962 as the beginning of modern environmentalism (recall Chapter 3). The book details the harmful impacts of pesticides such as DDT (dichlorodiphenyl-trichloroethane) on birds and fish.[1] Certainly, Carson's work fueled a public uproar and came to symbolize the redefinition of pesticides from an effective tool to an environmental problem threatening public welfare.

In this vein, principal authority for pesticide policy was transferred from the USDA to the EPA after 1970. This move signified an important change because authority shifted from an agricultural assistance agency to another with an environmental protection mandate. Revitalized with the passage of the Federal Environmental Pesticide Control Act in 1972, FIFRA provided the EPA with authority to regulate the distribution, labeling, sale, and use of pesticides. In typical environmental policy fashion, the new FIFRA reflected a compromise between agricultural and environmental interests, brokered by the Nixon administration, that ultimately satisfied neither. Although authority was now vested in the EPA, agricultural interests had a variety of protections built into the new legislation, such as congressional oversight remaining in more sympathetic agricultural committees (Flippen 1997). Despite the policy shift to the EPA, agricultural committees maintained congressional oversight authority and, as their members are more pro-agriculture and anti-environment than average, have proved not to be supporters of using FIFRA aggressively as a means of limiting pesticide availability.

Operationally, pesticide policy involves registration of pesticides. The stated policy goal, with some modifications in recent years, is "reasonable certainty of no harm," although that for cancellation of an approved pesticide is actually "unreasonably adverse effects." Costs to pesticide manufacturers or users are not supposed to be carefully considered, and the EPA retains much authority with only modest state involvement (generally, states only train others and enforce use of EPA-approved pesticides). More specifically, under FIFRA the EPA decides whether or not to allow a pesticide's marketing for a given purpose (for example, on a crop) against a given pest. FIFRA dictates that efficacy be demonstrated, that the pesticide be shown to work against the pest, and that health effects be considered. Health effects are determined by first generating a residue level for a pesticide in question and determining if the risk is acceptable. In practice, the big distinction employed by the EPA—in conjunction with the FDA for food and food products—in regard to risk has involved whether, as is frequently the case, a pesticide is carcinogenic, because carcinogenic pesticides are held to a stricter standard. In implementing this policy, environmentalists and their political allies have been successful in pushing the agency toward adopting rather conservative ranges of allowable pesticides and putting the burden of proof on the manufacturer for new pesticides. Although older pesticides can be canceled only if bureaucrats generate new information, producers have the burden of establishing the safety of new products.

Like most environmental policy, pesticide policy reflects many basic themes of fragmentation and lack of integration.

> Pesticide law has evolved in a way that compounds the problem of knowing the exposure and risks. Pesticides have been licensed individually, and contamination standards were set for separate environmental media such as water, food, or air. Law has therefore neglected the risks posed by chemical mixtures commonly dispersed into the environment, and instead has directed scientific attention toward very narrow questions—such as the potential for a single pesticide to contaminate a single medium and to induce a single type of effect such as cancer. The history of incremental decision making leaves little optimism that public officials know which pesticides pose the greatest risks, how we accumulate risks, how risks are distributed, or even if use prohibition will result in a pattern of pesticide substitution that poses greater or lesser peril. (Wargo 1996, 14).

Demand for environmental policy that reduces the harm of pesticides has almost certainly increased (with a countervailing response from pesticide producers and associated agricultural interests)—often in a manner that many would find poorly informed because understanding pesticide risks can be extremely difficult—but the nature of supply has unusual qualities. The instrument, registration, adopted to deal with the problem is not consistent with one that policy analysts would advance, such as taxation integrating the social costs of usage as well as perhaps informational provisions to educate consumers about the health costs of pesticide exposure and consumption (for example, J. Kahn 1998). The lack of rationalization and integration, problems associated with political fragmentation, run throughout discussions of pesticide policy.

For example, fragmentation is felt in common turf battles among the EPA, despite its principal authority, the FDA, and the USDA, which also retain jurisdictional claims. Illustratively, in 1998, responding to the concerns of agricultural growers and chemical manufacturers, Vice President Albert Gore sent the EPA a memorandum directing it to work more closely with the USDA and with stakeholders in the implementation of the Food Quality Protection Act (FQPA), which had been passed to replace the Delaney Act's prohibition on any harmful food pesticide residues by establishing a variety of standards for such residues (Schierow 1996; for a critical discussion see Byrd 1997).

Also, as pesticides affect air, land, and water, its cross-media impacts cause a variety of complications at the EPA. Critics contend that different parts of the agency dealing with water, air, and waste issues work at cross-purposes (for example, Fagin, Lavelle, and the Center for Public Integrity 1999).

Additionally, despite the EPA's growth over time, the agency lacks the ability and funds to deal with the large number of pesticides, given the use of registration and reregistration as a policy instrument. Indeed, there have been many points at which legislative opponents have been willing to try to starve the program fiscally. In turn, the EPA has been lambasted for its slowness in registration and reregistration—"one of the agency's biggest, longest-running, and least forgivable failures" in the words of the Center for Public Integrity, a public interest group that focuses on government accountability (Lewis 1998, 17). For example, in 1993 the agency reported that it had reregistered only 250 of 20,000 older pesticides despite a 1998 deadline for complete reregistration (in typical fashion, 1988 amendments had prescribed strict deadlines); additionally, the GAO labeled as a substantial underestimate the EPA's claim that reregistration's deficit would be $20 million (GAO 1993; the 1988 amendments included user fees that were supposed to defray costs), and the agency was claimed to be focusing on less important and easy to reregister pesticides to appear that it was speeding the process along.

A lack of integrated policy is also reflected by EPA/FIFRA policy that tends to ban or approve substances in isolation—often without even considering what pesticide might be substituted instead (for example, Gray and Graham 1995). Consequently, newer pesticides may be forbidden even when alternative pesticides already approved, or likely to be substituted food varieties that have more [unregulated] natural toxins, might make things worse. Indeed, there has been a bias against adopting newer pesticides even if their negative effects are less than those of pesticides approved in earlier times (National Research Council 1987; obviously this makes existing pesticide producers happy and may deter development of replacements). Additionally, the effects of fragmented policy are felt in how costs are considered. As mentioned, costs are supposedly excluded from the choice process. In actuality, statistical analysis demonstrates that EPA pesticide decisions do, at least somewhat, balance risk and benefits and, indeed, generally dictums against considering costs are rather ineffectual (Cropper et al. 1992, Van Houtven and Cropper 1996). However, policy is not rationalized, because a rather high implicit value is seemingly placed on human life and occupational exposure is weighted more heavily than consumer exposure, although workers, if they had good information, would demand to be compensated for exposure with higher wages. Additionally, environmental interest groups have had some success asking the courts to stop the agency from balancing costs and benefits, for example, by ignoring instances where real but small risks were involved (notably in 1992 when it was ruled that the EPA could not sidestep the Delaney Clause by allowing pesticides causing cancer in no more than one in one million persons).

Also, in conventional fashion, reforms have been incremental. Descriptively, environmental and agricultural interests often seem to perpetuate policy deadlock. Thus, for example, even in 1988, when rather detailed amendments were passed to induce the EPA to speed up implementation of registrations, they were so limited that they were nicknamed "FIFRA LITE" by pro-environment critics. Admittedly, the FQPA's passage was more notable and has been seen as emblematic of recognition of the problems associated with pesticide policy (also it, along with the SDWA, has been viewed as reflecting a movement to build some flexibility into legislation and to prioritize risk). Still, it represents a compromise between environmentalists, aware of the shortfalls of previous policy, and business interests, looking to jettison the widely disparaged Delaney Clause in any way possible and to provide some flexibility in regard to possible exceptions and use of risk assessment, rather than a dramatic break from the past or a reorientation in how pesticides are dealt with (for a discussion, see Cross 1997).

In brief, demand for managing pesticides to limit their environmental and health effects has risen with time. But policies have been produced in a manner seemingly destined to produce frustration. Environmentalists and agricultural concerns interested in the distribution of costs and benefits have not decided upon a given level of stridency per se, but have structured compromises with a variety of built-in inefficiencies. In addition, political actors, such as the courts, have helped institutionalize these difficulties. Rather than reworking existing policies, these actors have layered changes on top of them.

Toxics

Toxic policy has probably proved to be the most symbolic of government failure in environmental policy. More specifically, the Superfund program created in 1980 as a means of addressing problems of existing toxic waste sites, has been marked by vociferous accusations of lack of efficacy, high transaction costs, and cost overruns. Indicative of the program's high profile, of the 178 environmentally oriented reports between 1996 and 2000 (including international agreements and the like) written by the GAO, a congressional research arm that typically responds to legislator directives, 47 were specific to Superfund (and others discussed Superfund issues as they related to distinct problems).

Toxics themselves are not easily defined. For example, the Emergency Planning and Community Right-to-Know Act that created the Toxic Release Inventories defined toxics as any chemical that can cause (1) significant adverse acute human health effects at concentration levels that are reasonably likely to exist;

(2) human cancers, birth defects, or serious or irreversible chronic health effects; or (3) a significant adverse effect on the environment. Well over 600 chemicals are listed as toxics. Whatever the specific definition, toxic chemicals are typically used in production processes and can harm land, water, or air.

Regardless, in the 1970s, with the growth of environmental demand and of the chemical industry, there was increasingly a belief among many concerned with the environment that current programs such as the CAA or the CWA had not adequately addressed a group of potentially harmful chemicals. Government efforts specifically dealing with toxics or hazardous wastes through the Solid Waste Disposal Act of 1965 and the Resource Recovery Act of 1970 had focused only on how to facilitate efficient disposal or to reclaim resources. Much relevant authority remained vested with the states.

Contemporary toxic policy began in 1976 with the passage of the Resource Conservation and Recovery Act, which was substantially amended in 1984. RCRA greatly heightened national government intervention by situating the EPA in an explicitly regulatory role. It stipulated a hazardous waste permit system and explicitly prohibited open dumps. Essentially, RCRA provides a "cradle to grave" approach for hazardous waste production and disposal. It explicitly defines such wastes, lays out record keeping and labeling requirements, specifies containers to be used, dictates standards to be met by transporters of hazardous wastes, and provides for a manifest system to track wastes from production to disposal. RCRA also mandates permits for treatment, storage, and disposal facilities.

Most RCRA implementation takes place under state supervision; forty-seven states had received authorization to run their programs before 1984, with many operating the post-1984 aspects of the program as well. Other states participate via so-called Cooperative Arrangements. However, as with many environmental policies purporting to devolve authority, there are strings attached: state programs must be as stringent as, and consistent with, the federal program and they must adapt when the EPA adds new requirements or risk losing their approved status.

The 1976 RCRA legislation laid out a comprehensive and typically ambitious program. Consistent with 1970s air and water quality initiatives, optimistic deadlines spearheaded by Congress went unmet. The EPA received a mere eighteen months to enact its basic regulations, with companies getting another six months for submitting required paperwork to the agency. In reality, it would take until the middle of 1982 just for the EPA to participate in the rulemaking process. Particularly after the Reagan administration took power in 1981, there was great unhappiness among many concerned with toxics regarding the exercise of agency discretion (Davis 1985). The 1984 Hazardous and Solid Waste Amendments then added an enormous amount of detail and restrictions. Essentially, the EPA went from focusing on establishing a policy framework for managing hazardous waste production, transportation, and disposal to trying to meet a long litany of detailed congressional directives with draconian sanctions for noncompliance (so-called "hammer provisions," for example, forbidding any toxic disposal in landfills if a legislative mandate went unmet; for discussions, see EPA 1990, Melnick 1997). The 1984 amendments, besides expanding RCRA, set a new standard for detailed, explicit instructions and limits on discretion, presumably at least partially a response by those feeling that little could be left to chance when dealing with the Reagan EPA (Chambers and McCullough 1995).

Predictably, current assessments of RCRA are decidedly mixed, with most complaints flowing directly from the inflexibility built into the 1984 amendments. Environmentalists are frustrated by the difficulties that are presented in producing effective policy, and business interests complain about high costs in meeting new requirements. Detailed instructions of the sort included in RCRA amendments involve a fundamental trade-off between efficiency and control. Essentially, many complain that the EPA is hamstrung by the detailed provisions written into the 1984 reauthorization and preoccupied with meeting the specified regulatory guidelines. As such, the restrictions imposed—how waste may be disposed of, what technologies must be employed, and cumbersome permitting processes, for instance—are criticized, as are resulting priorities oriented toward meeting statutory mandates rather than addressing fundamental underlying problems (EPA 1990b).

Regardless of this less than stellar assessment, whatever unhappiness and failures that are associated with RCRA are dwarfed by Superfund. Superfund principally combines two acts: the Comprehensive Environmental Response, Compensation, and Liability Act of 1980 and the Superfund Amendments and Reauthorization Act of 1986 (SARA). CERCLA passed in the waning days of the Carter administration and in the shadow of the scandal at Love Canal, New York, where the discovery of dioxins, a by-product of chemical processes using chlorine produced by chemical companies, generated national attention. In response, roughly a thousand families had to be evacuated. CERCLA authorized the EPA to respond to spills, releases, or threatened releases of hazardous substances as well as to leaking hazardous waste dumps. In other words, RCRA addresses the production of hazardous wastes, whereas Superfund deals with storage sites. The law specified a National Priority List, which the EPA has based on a Hazard Ranking System of its own. Superfund is relatively centralized, with the EPA formally in charge of NPL site and remedy selection.

Analogous to many of the statutes preceding it, Superfund is characterized by extreme optimism in the ability to get many sites cleaned up thoroughly and quickly, technology-forcing, and a high price tag not necessarily driven by cost-benefit considerations. Reflecting these costs, Figure 8-2 documents Superfund's

Figure 8-2   Superfund Expenditures, 1987–1998

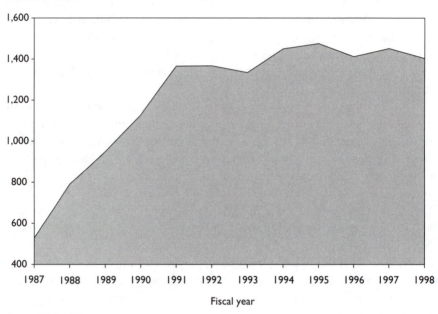

Millions of dollars

Fiscal year

Source: GAO 1999c.

growing cost to the federal government, which is far from the program's full direct costs. Contributing heavily to the overall price of the program are a rather bizarre set of liability rules. Specifically, liability is strict, joint, and retroactive, which means that EPA enforcement and cleanup costs are collectible from **potentially responsible parties** (PRPs), even if their pollution was perfectly legal at the time, even if they had only caused a small amount of the damage at a given site, and even if any offending behavior occurred before Superfund's enactment. As such, "deep pockets" polluters may be hit with bills exceeding even any legal damage that they caused.

Whatever the political or moral appeal of forcing past polluters to pay a price not only for their legal or illegal sins but for those of less-well-endowed fellow sinners, such rules become huge obstacles for site remediation, which carries an average price tag of about $30 million, because establishing liability and contributions are ready-made for laborious, expensive legalistic battles over who pays and how clean a site should be made. Transaction costs, and concomitant delays, are exceptionally high even for a program using command-and-control (Probst et al. 1995).

As such, a 1997 GAO report (1997b) found that the EPA took an average of 9.4 years from the discovery of a contaminated site not on federal government property to its NPL listing—the time taken for NPL listing had gone steadily up and was much longer than the explicit SARA requirement that this process take no more than four years. Not surprisingly, given Superfund requirements, the latter stages of the evaluation process took up the most time and involved battles over the very need for NPL listing rather than the severity of environmental ills. For sites given an NPL listing, cleanups had become lengthier and took 10.6 years (although SARA provides no explicit deadline, the EPA had a five-year, self-imposed limit), with much of the time attributable to PRP negotiations rather than the slowness of the actual remediation process. For example, by 1996, it was taking more than eight years just to select a remedy. Subsequently, the time from NPL listing to completion of the cleanup has decreased somewhat to about eight years. However, rather than a function of more administrative efficiency or streamlined procedures, this decline appears to be a product of resources being shifted away from adding to the NPL and toward cleaning listed sites. As such, only a handful of new sites are placed on the NPL annually (GAO 1999b; for example, 48 NPL sites were finalized from 1996 to 1998 compared with 107 from 1993 to 1995).

Consequently, Superfund's performance has been disappointing for all concerned. As of June 1999, roughly twenty years after the program's inauguration, 419 of the 1,231 sites on the NPL were remediated and 176 additional sites were judged as no longer needing to stay listed. Although this pace has accelerated in recent years, as "construction completion" is realized for 75 to 85 sites per year, it has been estimated that several thousand more sites remain in the NPL placement queue (GAO 1999b), meaning that two decades and many billions of dollars of effort have dealt with perhaps 15 to 20 percent of all sites.

Further complicating the funding process is that government-supplied monies have come from the Superfund Trust Fund, primarily supported by excise taxes on petroleum and chemical feedstocks and a corporate environmental income tax (up to $250 million per fiscal year could come from general Treasury revenues). However, the law allowing collection of these revenues expired at the end of calendar year 1995 and reauthorization attempts have proved unsuccessful. As of this writing, the remaining tax monies will be used up shortly (Reisch 1998), and reliance on direct contributions from the federal Treasury is increasing.[2] Whether politicians will continue to allocate such Treasury monies in this highly charged atmosphere is uncertain.

Adding to the slowness, transaction costs, and overall price have been strict cleanup standards. Business interests routinely complain about gold-plated solutions, meaning that the most expensive solutions are being chosen to achieve an economically unjustifiable cleanup level (on the EPA's rather inefficient approach to determining Superfund priorities and remediation, see Hamilton and Viscusi 1999). Regardless of an area's future use or any other factor, cleanups must be permanent and meet all legally applicable laws and requirements. Although perhaps reasonable at face value, for sites with certain types and degrees of contamination such a standard can prove difficult and expensive (Reisch 2000b). For example, a site might be recommended for a level of cleanup that would be dictated if a school were to be built but cannot be justified on economic grounds if it is to be used for another purpose, such as a warehouse. Indeed, by adopting a technology-forcing mandate, because meeting legal obligations may dictate innovation, Superfund may require that sites be cleaned far more thoroughly than is cost-effective or even possible (Reisch 1998).

To deal with existing toxics, establishing a way to determine acceptable remediation levels and to prioritize risk to citizens from toxic materials, with funding from general tax revenues, would seem a more sensible solution. However, a very different process was mandated by the legislators and Jimmy Carter when the Superfund legislation became law. A tax- and deficit-plagued national government, not looking to raise taxes or deficits, decided that previous polluters should pay the bill even if their offending behavior (or that of others) was perfectly legal at the time. Fiscal responsibilities fell disproportionately on deep pockets polluters and failed to rationalize the process in a way emphasizing the accurate assessment of risk, the extent of the population exposed to risk, and the balance between benefits and costs (Viscusi and Hamilton 1996). Given such liabilities, potentially liable companies have tended to fight the EPA every step of the way. The price of incredible delays and other transaction costs incurred by all involved parties have been enormous; legal fees alone have been estimated to be 28 to 46 percent of costs, although the percentage was smaller for larger projects (GAO 1997b), and high-end estimates of transaction costs have exceeded 80 percent. Consequently, although some of the problems associated with Superfund may be blamed on the choices of implementing bureaucrats, many are better viewed as a product of the program's liability structure and cleanup requirements.

Despite Superfund's notoriety, and although reforms have been on the table for many years, the political ability to agree has proved difficult. Indeed, the lapsing of a tax system to smooth the funding process politically offers the possibility of more damaging deadlock. One side wants relaxation of liability (both generally and especially for brownfields) and a plan to end the program, and the other wishes the program and its "polluter pays" principal to continue. In the end, Congress has again fallen prey to its own institutional proclivity to do nothing statutorily, and the EPA has been left to use administrative reforms, many of them maligned, as a way of modifying the program (on agency efforts to adjust the program, see EPA 1999b). Reforming Superfund statutorily remains the "longest-standing issue on Capitol Hill today" (Mullins 1999, 3139). Even in light of the Republican congressional landslide of 1994, much trumpeted Superfund reform legislation that would have dramatically altered liability died in Congress, a reflection of congressional Democrats making change difficult and a potentially hostile Democratic president, Bill Clinton, waiting in the wings.

SARA had one additional wrinkle worthy of mention. Title III, also known as the Emergency Planning and Community Right-to-Know Act, included provisions facilitating the ability to obtain data on toxic emissions through the creation of the Toxic Release Inventories. Specifically, manufacturers meeting certain thresholds are required to report their emissions of more than three hundred chemicals and chemical compounds (others have been added over the years). This has made information available not only to government officials but to grassroots organizations and even citizens who might have otherwise been unaware. These data are easily accessible not only through the EPA but elsewhere, such as the Internet (see, for example, http://www.rtk.net/rtkdata.html). Thus, the national government significantly incorporated informational regulation into a program best known for being extremely adversarial, and the effect seems to be providing polluters with an incentive to reduce toxic production (see Chapters 5 and 9 for further discussion).

Consequently, dealing with hazardous waste past and present would seem popular, but the policies created under the aegis of the EPA are not. In particular, Superfund appears to be an ill-designed program ripe for the kinds of deadlock and frustrations that environmental programs are often accused of creating. Once again, demand has seemingly risen and supply has increased, but in nonintuitive ways. Changes, and the lack of them, have been caught up in partisan wrangling and political infighting and have not dealt with the essential features that produce such unpopularity.

GENERAL TRENDS: RATIONALIZATION AND COMPLICATION

Beyond the specifics of given programs and their controls, there have been important general trends, tending to reflect public policy's overall evolution as well as changes found in the way environmental policy concerns are addressed. Such trends point policy in different, essentially contradictory, directions; some seemingly push toward more efficiency and greater rationalization, others toward institutionalizing even greater inefficiencies in the name of political control. Of course, policy schizophrenia is expected in an institutionally fragmented political system whose key actors have contrasting incentives for dealing with rising demands.

Thus, one prominent trend is directing policy toward both common, and more economically sensible, evaluation standards and more efficient regulatory instruments. With respect to the former, many environmental policies have benefits, such as lower levels of pollution, that appear to be less than the costs, such as increases in production costs that result in higher prices. There has been a general push toward integrating costs and risk into the regulatory process (Hahn 1998). This is consistent with pressures that have more generally been brought to bear on federal bureaucrats under the guise of a variety of initiatives, such as the Clinton administration's desire to "reinvent government" (Kettl 1998) and subsequent EPA efforts at a "Common Sense Initiative" (EPA 1999a). Consequently, the prominence of tools such as cost-benefit analysis and risk assessment, many prompted by the issuance of executive orders (see Chapter 4), has increased despite many statutes explicitly or implicitly rejecting costs from being integrated into policy choices.

Concerning more efficient policy instruments, and without overstating their prevalence, there is clearly greater receptivity toward employing informational strategies and adopting more efficient market-based policy tools than previously. For instance, with respect to information, the creation of the TRI in 1986 as part of SARA was a notable break from past practices. Congress could have mandated stricter command-and-control-style reductions in toxic releases rather than allowing citizens to respond economically and politically to data. Similarly, the government's principal response to complaints that problems associated with radon have gone undetected has been to provide information (for example, with publications like *A Citizen's Guide to Radon*), and there have been increases in available information on a variety of other environmental concerns such as safe drinking water.[3] Indeed, the United States has even supported adopting market instruments in international negotiations, notably during the December 1997 efforts in Kyoto, Japan, to arrive at a global warming treaty (Council of Economic Advisors 2000).

The push to more efficient instruments has its own problems. Most of the market-based policy instruments reflect the political process and not necessarily the choices of economists or policy analysts (Keohane, Revesz, and Stavins 1999). Also, estimated cost savings of the switch from command-and-control to market-based policies vary considerably (for example, Anderson, Carlin, McGartland, and Weinberger 1997; Congressional Budget Office [CBO] 1998). Nonetheless, the shift from command-and-control to market mechanisms domestically, in general, means a positive change for those who care about effective environmental policies (Hahn 1999). Along the same lines, the EPA has experienced a push to set its priorities better by allocating resources so that there is more environmental quality for the dollar. Thus, prominent studies directed by the agency have stressed the need to focus on issues offering the greatest return (for example, EPA 1987, 1990a). Similarly, legislative initiatives such as the Food Quality Protection Act, those parts of the Clean Air Amendments of 1990 recognizing that noncompliance areas might receive flexible treatment (although these areas also face strict regulations), and revisions to the Safe Drinking Water Act attempting to build more flexibility into the process, may be seen in a similar light. Also, there has been at least a symbolic acknowledgment of the need for better integrating the agency's responsibilities in addressing environmental issues and for focusing on pollution prevention as well as on cleanup. Most notably, although not providing much direct EPA policy-making authority or eliminating structural entities at the agency or corresponding statutes allegedly leading to misguided emphasis on pollution reduction for individual media, the Pollution Prevention Act of 1990, by emphasizing cost-effectiveness and an integrated cross-media approach, has been seen as a turning point (Schierow 1999). Specifically, the act required that the EPA establish an Office of Pollution Prevention, collect relevant data and make manufacturers report annually on source reduction and recycling, develop and coordinate a pollution prevention strategy, and develop source reduction models. Finally, although a bit more debatable, the agency's greater receptivity toward less adversarial approaches to rulemaking and implementation, such as negotiated rulemakings, may reflect a similar trend (Weber 1998; recall Chapter 5).

Additionally, the push toward devolving environmental authority, similar to the impetus in other areas of regulatory and social policy, that has highlighted politics for the last several decades can be construed as manifesting a movement toward policy rationalization. As discussed in Chapter 6, if costs and benefits of an environmental policy are localized, then there is a case for allocating responsibility to a corresponding local government as a means of increasing policy effectiveness. There are numerous political reasons why devolution might be popular, but many of the arguments voiced for it by politicians do at least articulate claims of greater efficiency.

While progress in integrating economic tools and policy instruments and generally rationalizing policy has been slow and halting, there is no compelling reason to believe that the general trend toward more sensible standards and efficient instruments will abate. Particularly given the existence of similar trends concerning other types of policy—for example, the use of auction mechanisms to sell airwave bandwidth (McAfee and McMillan 1996) and the willingness to deregulate unneeded economic regulation (Derthick and Quirk 1985)—this push is probably a function of slowly evolving secular forces, such as gradual increases in awareness of and sensitivity to the costs of environmental policy and opportunities for producing the same level of protection at a markedly lower cost. Change is not likely driven by episodic, random, conditions that may be reversed momentarily.

Curiously, however, at roughly the same time that approaches more favored by policy analysts have grown in importance, there has been a corresponding movement toward adding explicit political control, or toward more prescription, that would be the bane of the very same analysts. As already mentioned, perhaps the crucial breakpoint for environmental policy was the 1984 Hazardous and Solid Waste Amendments, which substantially transformed the RCRA program by creating more than seventy directives and giving the EPA little wiggle room in implementing policy. Presumably, detailed instructions give politicians greater control now and in the future, but their by-product is typically more policy inefficiency.

Since the mid-1980s, legislation has become more elaborate, precise, and detailed. Rather than spelling out broad goals and delegating much of the nuts and bolts to the EPA, newly enacted statutes have become more explicit in their directions to the agency. For instance, the Clean Air Act of 1970 totaled 38 pages, whereas the more than 160 explicit guidelines in the 1990 amendments exceeded 300 pages (Davies and Mazurek 1998); similarly, hazardous waste regulations, as listed in the Code of Federal Regulations, increased roughly 150 percent from 1981 to 1989 (EPA 1990b). Such detailed regulations, with their strict deadlines and their regulatory provisions, are a surefire means for reducing efficiency and raising regulatory costs (Fiorino 1995). The inefficiencies caused by detailed instructions will be greater for those current environmental issues that are more technically complex than those addressed in the 1970s. Given greater uncertainty to be resolved, more technical regulation would seem to decrease rather than increase the need for prescription (for example, Bawn 1995, Drotning and Rothenberg 1999). As political scientists Terry Moe and Michael Caldwell (1994, 173) put it, "In complex policy areas with changing social and technical environments— which is typical of modern society—[effective policy] usually calls for expert organizations that are granted much discretion and held accountable through oversight." Furthermore, the national government has not been obviously willing to increase the agency's budget despite such strict dictums. As noted, for example, budgetary strains have shown in dealing with Superfund issues, where authorization has been allowed to lapse, and with pesticide regulation, where thousands of pesticides have not been registered or reregistered. Indeed, the push for prescription coincided with the Reagan administration's attempts to reduce the EPA's budget (recall Figure 3-4).

Although prescription appeals to the desire to maintain political control, it is difficult to pinpoint the exact reasons for its increase. In particular, it is hard to determine whether this is a secular trend likely to continue unabated or a movement conditioned on specific circumstances that may be subsequently reversed. One possible reason for more prescription is that the policy process has become more politicized and, therefore, those writing statutes have more incentive to limit discretion. Without reduced politicization of policy, which most would regard as highly unlikely, a less prescriptive status quo is improbable. There may be a secular trend toward limiting discretion because a fixed number of legislators believe government should do more; for example, rising legislative workload decreases the ability to monitor a given program once enacted and heightens the desirability of limits on discretion (Epstein and O'Halloran 1999). Hence, only a workload decline would induce a prescription drop. As for episodic causes, it may be that greater prescription reflects change in levels of political uncertainty. Institutionalizing policies and limiting the ability of political successors to alter things may become more attractive if political decision makers are more uncertain about the preferences of their successors than previously (for example, Moe 1989). Claiming that uncertainty has grown is not completely unreasonable if one looks at the changes in control in Congress and the presidency in the past several decades. Alternatively, greater prescription may be a function of an increased divergence of preferences between Congress and the president so that both sides feel the need to be explicit about the negotiated bargain. Presumably, if preference divergence is crucial, legislators and a president seeing more eye-to-eye might produce statutes with more bureaucratic leeway. In short, legislators have faced presidents such as Reagan, George H. Bush, and Clinton whose preferences veered far from their own (with the potential exception of Clinton's first two years during which he had Democratic majorities in both chambers but produced no major environmental legislation), which may have increased the perceived need to write a detailed contract for bureaucrats (Epstein and O'Halloran 1999).[4]

Regardless, the basic point is that observable trends seem to be working at cross-purposes. Even in its broad contours, policy appears to be fragmented and to lack integration. Some have reacted with a desire to reduce high program costs through greater efficiency in the face of growing demand for environmental quality; although policy may improve the environment, it can be done more cheaply. But other forces may lead to more concerns about political control and distribution at the expense of efficiency. The push and pull of the desire to supply environmental quality on the one hand and to achieve other objectives on the other are seen in broad changes regarding policy evaluation and policy instruments, policy implementation, choices about which government level should have responsibility, and in whether policy should be prescriptive even for highly technical issues. The end result is that characterizing overall trends in policy is complicated, because some lead policy in one direction and some lead it in another.

REGULATION, FRAGMENTATION, AND CONTEMPORARY ENVIRONMENTAL POLICY

Before the EPA's creation, the federal role in the environmental areas that have preoccupied the agency—air, water, pesticides, and hazardous wastes—was principally technical and financial. With growing demand for environmental quality, the national government had begun to explore adopting a more explicitly regulatory stance by which it set guidelines for production and consumption choices. However, to the extent that the federal government had assumed the authority to take on an aggressive regulatory role, the agencies involved lacked enforcement capacity. But demand for environmental quality, and for the national government to take a more active part in producing it, continued to rise with greater recognition of environmental problems and heightened prosperity. Eventually, politicians responded, as symbolized by the creation of the EPA.

Reflective of this heightened demand, subsequent to the EPA's formation, the status quo changed dramatically. But the nature of these changes was driven by political supply and the numerous political interests involved in the bargaining that produces policy. A decade of statutes successively redefined the role of the national government in relation to the environment and created a stronger regulatory presence in which the national government had a profound effect on consumption and production choices. Although further changes were often slow in coming, given the policy system, eventually these policies too were adapted, revised, and rewritten in the following years, layering one set of requirements on top of those previously enacted. Initially vague and optimistic statutes were overlaid with more precise and demanding initiatives and, subsequently, a dash of flexibility. Problems were dealt with differently, various instruments were used, implementation was often made difficult by the nature of rules and regulations, and the role of local and state governments often varied for reasons beyond those suggested by externalities and public goods.

Much like land use agencies, the overriding feeling produced by surveying the evolution of EPA involvement is that demand for environmental quality, resulting in this instance in government's assuming a vigorous regulatory role, has spiraled upward but that its impact is conditioned by political supply. In this broad sense, the analysis in this chapter parallels that of land management, as greater demand gradually if unevenly produced a greater supply of environmental programs, except that policy choices for regulation of environmental quality occurred at chronologically later times than they did for land management. What has been wrought is fragmentation (despite a single, principal agency in the case of the EPA being the chief regulator), a lack of rationalization, and an absence of integration. Policies differ from one another for a variety of reasons that seem frequently more political than technical. Even if policies improve environmental quality, which they often do, the resulting inefficiencies are substantial. Adding to a schizophrenic picture, while there are some optimistic future trends, others promise to raise policy costs.

KEY TERMS

Best available technologies (p. 182)
Best practical technologies (p. 187)
Non–point source pollution (p. 187)
Point source pollution (p. 186)

Potentially responsible parties (PRPs) (p. 196)
Technology-forcing (p. 179)

9 The Costs of
Environmental Progress

This book began with a brief look at how wetlands went from being considered bogs and swamps to becoming one of the nation's most valuable environmental resources. In responding to changing demands and views of the environmental value of wetlands, government has gone from facilitating their destruction to trying to protect them. The attempt has resulted in a fragmented policy with curious, and potentially environmentally damaging, features. Yet, this very fragmented policy is not without merit—it has dramatically slowed (although not completely reversed) the rate of wetland destruction. Few would dispute that government policy has played a role in this slowdown, but many would add that more could be done, at lower cost, to reverse wetland destruction. Subsequent chapters explained how demand for environmental quality, the nature of political responses, and the relationship between the two could explain the paradox of improved, or at least the far slower decline of, environmental quality, despite increasing population and consumption, and, nonetheless, fragmented and inefficient government efforts.

Stated differently, these chapters demonstrate that wetlands policy is not an isolated example and that it is explicable. It represents what determines demand, how the United States political system supplies environmental quality in response to such demands, and how those making such demands, in turn, respond to political choices.

Indeed, in the same spirit as the wetlands example, although policy choices often vary considerably from what policy analysts recommend, environmental trends appear fairly, although not uniformly, positive. Air quality has improved, drinking water remains safe, some other elements of water quality have at least been maintained, pesticides have been somewhat controlled, and current toxic production has decreased even though attempts to address past ills have been slow-going. Although species preservation has not been as successful as might be hoped, more federal lands are protected and their environmentally damaging commercial use has declined. Yet, as evidenced by the politics and programs producing such results, the political market does not mimic the idealized economic market in providing low-cost responses to heighten demand for a good such as environmental quality. Agencies, policies, and policy instruments often seem ill-designed for the task.

Thus, with the nation's economic development and increases in consumption-based environmental pressures, demands for environmental quality have grown. Americans want to consume goods such as clean air and water, an environment not despoiled by toxics and pesticides, a climate not disrupted by global warming and holes in the ozone layer, and natural beauty and at the same time consume a variety of desirable private goods for which environmental despoliation is frequently an input.

Along with economic development and increased demand have come political development and heightened government capacity. As demand for environmental quality has grown, a variety of political choices have been made that have increasingly involved the government in environmental affairs. Myriad agencies, statutes, and other initiatives have resulted. These choices have reflected the fragmented nature of the American political system.

To some very real extent, and comparable to what is found in other advanced industrial nations, citizens have been able to consume a better environmental quality than they would have if government had remained on the sidelines. Despite this apparent progress, the nature of political choices with the purported goal of improving environmental quality is often troubling and reflects the specific constitutional features of American democracy, such as its separation of powers and federalist structure. Consequently, the policy system continues to exhibit numerous flaws. Priorities often seem misplaced, choices for achieving stated goals frequently appear ill-advised, bureaucratic structures for implementing delegated authority typically look poorly designed, and allocation of responsibilities among varying government levels many times appears haphazard. Additionally, needed policy changes often seem agonizingly painful, yet carrying out government pledges frequently appears difficult.

Thus, evidence would indicate that government policy positively, if unevenly, affects environmental quality, but that the price paid is higher than it seemingly should be. Indeed, for various policies, such as many Superfund cleanups, costs may exceed benefits. Inefficiencies associated with government efforts explain the seeming tension between quality and many political disappointments.

This final chapter underscores how American democracy does produce progress at a high price and a slow rate. Following additional detail regarding policy successes and failures, the processes driving up the costs of achieving environmental goals are summarized. The chapter also examines future trends, focusing on the **sustainability** of the current environmental situation, defined by the

Nobel Prize–winning economist Robert Solow as whether future generations will have the option of being as well off as present ones are (Solow 2000).[1]

SUCCESSES AND FAILURES

Social scientists encounter difficulties, analogous to those in many political situations, drawing causal inferences about many aspects of environmental policy. Measuring the influence on environmental policy outcomes of a political institution or an organized interest is problematic, as the world constantly changes and other relevant actors continue to respond strategically. This, in turn, further complicates the development of appropriate theoretical models and the gathering of requisite data. Similarly, both empirical and theoretical obstacles thwart attempts to make definitive conclusions about the cost of government policy and the amount that such policy helps, or hinders, the environment. For instance, requisite data for evaluating program success have frequently been lacking because governments have often made few concerted efforts even to develop appropriate measures of environmental quality. Furthermore, theoretically specifying what the world would look like without government policy is a heroic task because many changes with environmental implications take place at the same time as political intervention. Independent of government policy, societal changes such as technological innovation, the transformation from a manufacturing- to a service-based economy, population movements to the Sun Belt and the West, and the increased preference for suburban living, resulting in urban sprawl, complicate policy assessment. Beyond such major shifts, it is likely that a host of other, more subtle, changes further complicate matters. Nonetheless, most analysts would agree that environmental policy has both added economic costs and improved quality. It is also reasonable to suggest the level of costs and where the most progress has been made environmentally, at least with respect to conventional forms of pollution.

As for the economic price, although the exact cost of initiatives is debated (OMB 2000), rough estimates for environmental regulation's price tag alone are in the region of $150 billion annually. Monetized benefits are similar. These costs and benefits of environmental policy each calculate out to something more than $2,000 per year for an average family of four (as a basis of comparison, median family income in 1998 was about $39,000). Although no similar aggregate estimates for the effects of restrictions created by the land use agencies appear to exist, such limits certainly place significant economic costs on firms, governments, and citizens. Also, if more speculatively, in the immediate future the charges for environmental policy are likely to rise despite technological innovation and the possible adoption of more efficient policy instruments. Partially this inference stems

Figure 9-1 Estimates of Environmental and Risk Protection Costs, 1977–2000

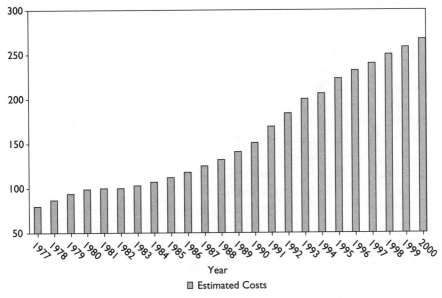

Billions of
1995 dollars

Year

□ Estimated Costs

Source: Hopkins 1998, as presented in http://www.regulation.org/keyfacts.html.
Note: The numbers presented here are typically considered high-end estimates.

from extrapolation: various advancements have been insufficient to reduce absolute costs in the past. For example, Figure 9-1 reproduces high-end estimates of costs of environmental *and* risk protection from 1977 to 2000, which display a strong upward trend over time as measured by real dollars (and this is true even in per capita terms). Similarly, real per capita pollution control and abatement expenditures increased steadily through 1994 (at which point, available estimates were no longer produced; see Council on Environmental Quality 1996). Although extrapolation is always dangerous, such an exercise clearly implies higher future price tags. Similar expectations of increasing bills stem from projected costs of proposals to maintain or to improve quality. It would seem that easier environmental targets have been addressed and more expensive ones are being turned to. Thus, for example, the EPA estimated that full (partial) attainment of its proposed particulate matter standard alone would cost $37 billion ($8.6 billion) annually by 2010. More dramatically, estimates of U.S. obligations if the Kyoto accord were implemented, while varying by many orders of magnitude depending on assumptions, typically run in the multiple billions of dollars (for example,

Schelling [1998] estimates that Kyoto would cost 2 percent of American GNP for perpetuity, or close to $200 billion dollars a year). Indeed, it is just such fears of a high economic price tag that led President George W. Bush to renounce Kyoto despite condemnation from environmentalists domestically and internationally and many governments around the world. Furthermore, there is every reason to believe that the overall costs of the policies implemented by the natural resource agencies will rise.

In the grand scheme, whatever the costs, environmental quality is seemingly better than it would have been otherwise. Uneven improvement appears to be a function of political, as well as technical and economic, factors. Such variance in quality is, quite notably, reflected in discrepancies in success regarding different elements of the EPA's jurisdiction. Thus, most agree that government has made the air cleaner by influencing fixed air pollution sources and automobile emissions. Even though many localities fail to meet government-specified clean air standards, virtually all have witnessed improvements.

Figures 9-2 and 9-3 demonstrate changes in air quality from a broad and a specific perspective. These figures are only suggestive, as nonpolicy factors affect

Figure 9-2   Air Pollution Emissions, 1970–1998

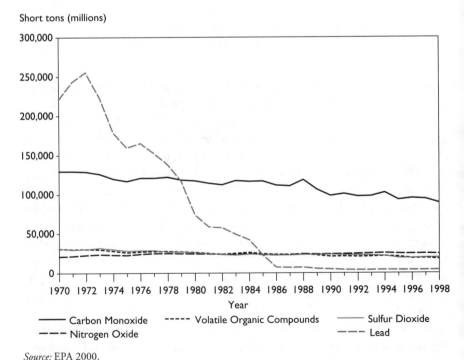

Short tons (millions)

Source: EPA 2000.

Figure 9-3   Violations of Federal Ozone Standard in the Los Angeles Basin,
1976–1998

Number of days

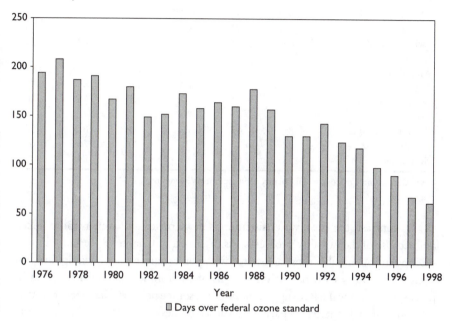

☐ Days over federal ozone standard

Source: South Coast Air Quality Management District (http://www.aqmd.gov/smog/o3trend.html).

quality. Figure 9-2 illustrates the emission rates of some major air pollutants—carbon monoxide, volatile organic compounds, lead, nitrogen oxide, and sulfur dioxide—since the EPA's creation. All declined, some more notably than others (lead, eliminated from gasoline, most dramatically), despite population and consumption increases that are most obvious in energy and automobile use (for example, even with more fuel efficient automobiles, gasoline use rose from 92 billion gallons in 1970 to 153 billion gallons in 1998). A more localized example, Figure 9-3, provides data on federal ozone standard violations in the Los Angeles basin, a metropolitan area symbolic of man-made pollution problems created by rapid growth and consumption. Well over 15 million Los Angeles residents travel more than 117 million miles daily on freeways alone in an area whose weather and geography are inclined to produce serious air quality problems. Automobile usage contributes to the ground-level ozone that is a key component of the smog haunting Southern California. Despite steep population and consumption increases, the number of annual days exceeding the federal standard has precipitously declined from more than 200 to around 50.

Table 9-1 Nation's Surface Water Quality, 1988–1998 (in percentages)

Waterway	1988	1990	1992	1994	1996	1998
Rivers						
Meet designated use	70%	69%	62%	64%	63%	65%
Fishable	86	80	66	69	85	88
Swimmable	85	75	71	77	79	72
Lakes						
Meet designated use	74	60	56	63	61	55
Fishable	95	70	69	69	65	59
Swimmable	96	82	77	81	75	80
Estuaries						
Meet designated use	89	67	68	63	62	56
Fishable	97	77	78	70	76	65
Swimmable	92	88	83	85	84	91

Source: Council on Environmental Quality 1996 and http://www.epa.gov/305b/.

By contrast, the clean water situation is more mixed—as well as more uncertain because of data quality problems. As discussed in Chapter 8, certain kinds of water pollution, notably those associated with point sources, have been significantly ameliorated. But, as worrisome discussions of environmentally sensitive estuaries such as the Chesapeake Bay suggest, non–point source pollution has been less effectively addressed. Estuaries are partially enclosed bodies of water formed where freshwater from rivers and streams flows into the ocean, mixing with the salty sea water; they are of considerable environmental importance, notably for the survival of many species. Thus, for example, of the roughly 45 percent of river miles labeled by the EPA as "impaired" (cannot support at least one designated use such as supporting aquatic life, swimming, or fish consumption), agriculture, the prototype of non–point source pollution, is the leading cause of pollution roughly 60 percent of the time. By contrast, municipal point sources are a leading problem about 10 percent of the time. Not surprisingly, although some specific water quality measures show progress (for example, frequency in which there is too much dissolved oxygen in the nation's rivers and streams), trends on the nation's surface water quality are far from uniformly positive. Table 9-1 provides some data on whether the nation's rivers, lakes, and estuaries meet a variety of goals (designated use, fishable, and swimmable) for various years and shows no clear pattern. Groundwater used for drinking is in generally good shape, although non–point source pollution makes up a substantial part of the existing problems and potential difficulties.

As discussed in Chapter 8, results for toxics have significant negative and positive elements. Overall, new toxic generation and handling seems to have been dealt with more effectively than it was before the current regulatory apparatus was

Figure 9-4 Toxic Releases—Core Chemicals and Industries, 1988, 1995–1998

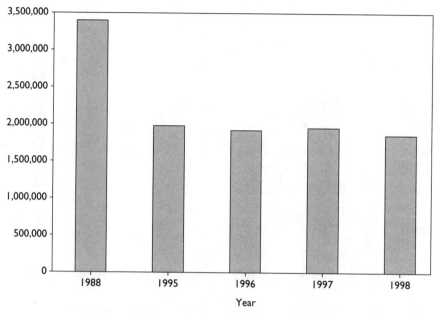

Pounds of toxics
released (thousands)

Source: Environmental Protection Agency (http://www.epa.gov/tri/tri98/data/sum8898a.pdf).
Note: Does not include chemicals delisted or added. Data do not reflect exposure to chemicals or differences in risk associated with various toxics.

in place; it is particularly striking that information dissemination about toxic production has apparently proved to be an additional disincentive to producers. To illustrate, Figure 9-4 shows the production of toxics, admittedly not controlling for features such as toxicity or exposure, for selected years after Toxic Release Inventories data collection began (and for industries and chemicals on which information was collected throughout). Clearly, output has diminished substantially. Yet, as discussed and in contrast to such optimistic news, the cleanup of hazardous waste sites has produced considerable frustration for all concerned. While some Superfund sites have been remediated, the rate has been slow and the cost high. Indeed, as seen in Figure 9-5, the National Priority List of sites that are Superfund candidates has not taken a substantial turn downward after several decades (to reiterate, these data are only suggestive, as the decline in the NPL that does appear in the 1990s may not represent increased bang for the buck but the internal shifting of EPA resources).

Figure 9-5 Number of National Priority List (NPL) Sites, 1982–1998

Number of NPL sites

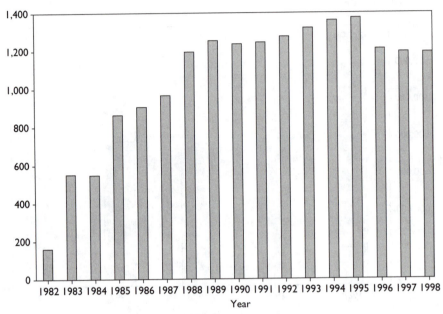

Source: Council on Environmental Quality (http://ceq.eh.doe.gov/nepa/reports/1997) and Environmental Protection Agency (http://www.crosslink.net/~cncurtis/Pollut_Trends.html).

Analogously, as mentioned, pesticide management has been a mixed bag. Clearly, certain extremely harmful pesticides, such as DDT, have been dramatically curtailed. Also, to reiterate, pesticides have clear benefits, such as increasing agricultural production and controlling disease. Nonetheless, the amount of pesticides employed have not exhibited the nice downturn of the sort found for air pollution and toxics, suggesting that policy efforts have not been as successful as might be hoped (Figure 9-6). Although there have been periods when pesticide use has tapered off, and the steep growth characterizing earlier years has not reoccurred, utilization has taken subsequent upturns. Such data must be viewed cautiously, as they neither indicate what pesticide use would be without government intervention nor weight pesticide-specific dangers. Also, as mentioned, pesticide employment contributes to other problems, such as those associated with non–point source water pollution created by agricultural runoff.

Analyses of the use of government-controlled natural resources, already considerably documented, provide similar mixed results. On the one hand, environmentally damaging resource extraction has at least been made more difficult, as

Figure 9-6   Pesticide Use for Selected U.S. Crops, 1964–1995

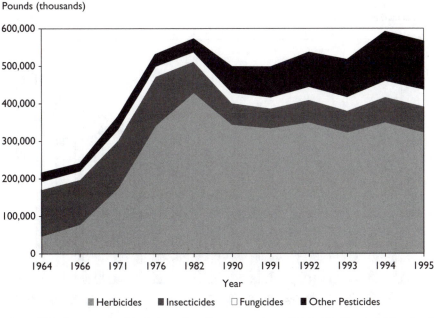

Pounds (thousands)

■ Herbicides   ■ Insecticides   □ Fungicides   ■ Other Pesticides

Source: U.S. Department of Agriculture (http://www.ers.usda.gov/Briefing/AgChemicals/Questions/pmqa4.htm).

Note: Crops include corn, soybeans, wheat, cotton, potatoes, other vegetables, citrus fruit, apples, and other fruit.

was seen with the decline of timber cutting in the national forests and a more modest fall off in rangeland grazing. Furthermore, greater emphasis given to environmental considerations has created more roadblocks to mining. Finally, additional lands have received environmental protections under a variety of programs, as symbolized by the transfer of authority away from the BLM and USFS to the FWS and NPS. On the other hand, beyond controversies swirling around remaining timber production, grazing and mining rights have not been adjusted to market levels and environmental costs have not been systematically internalized in decision making. Also, recreational demands, external development, and lack of budgetary support have put pressure, often severe, on lands and facilities in the national parks system.

Finally, even without considering the substantial costs, species preservation has been at best moderately successful. Certainly, as Figure 9-7 illustrates, the number of seemingly endangered and threatened species seems to keep growing (about 80 percent are listed as endangered rather than as threatened). Although

Figure 9-7 Threatened and Endangered Species, 1980–1999

Number of threatened
and endangered species

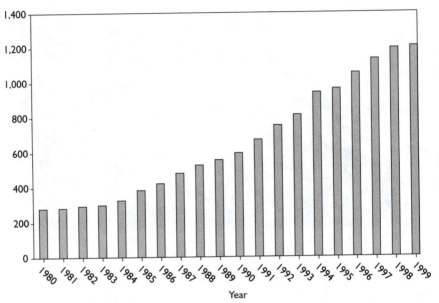

Year

Source: U.S. Fish and Wildlife Service (www.endangered.fws.gov/stats.count.pdf).

this may be a function of increased vigilance or of forces that would have had even more damaging effects without the ESA, most analyses concur that the FWS/ESA has had at best a marginal positive impact. For example, a Congressional Research Service report (Noecker 1998, 3) sums up experiences this way:

> To determine whether the ESA has been effective, one must choose a standard of measure. The primary goal of the ESA is the recovery of species. . . . As of July 31, 1997 only 11 species have been delisted due to recovery. Of the remaining species that have been removed from the endangered and threatened species list, seven have gone extinct, and nine species have been delisted due to new or improved data. . . .
>
> [A]nother standard of measure might be the number of species whose populations have stabilized or increased, even if the species is not actually delisted. Using this standard, the Act could be considered a moderate success, since a large number of the 1,676 listed species (41% according to one study) have improved or stabilized.

In short, evidence suggests uneven improvement in environmental quality, with government bearing partial responsibility. Entering costs into the equation indicates that policies' benefits do not appear to overrun vastly policies' costs or vice versa. More generally there is progress in improving environmental quality or preventing further deterioration but at a high cost.

THE HIGH COST OF PROGRESS: PROXIMATE AND FUNDAMENTAL CAUSES

Thus, American democracy has at least partially responded to its citizens' growing demands and willingness to pay for environmental quality. But U.S. citizens, firms, and governments could be getting more for their money.

By now, explanations for the reasons for such benefits and excess costs are probably familiar. Broadly, there are two levels of explanation: **proximate** and **fundamental causes.** Proximate causes essentially involve the basic features of the political system routinely targeted as reasons for success and failure. Fundamental causes principally refer to either constitutional features that induce policymakers' preferences and that influence efforts to build institutional capacity or basic characteristics largely shared by democracies.

Proximate causes of environmental policy's benefits and costs are directly related to basic features of demand and supply and the means by which they feed back onto one another. Demand has increased, both in regard to individual attitudes toward the environment and in regard to groups pressing for specific environmental goals. In the United States, economic prosperity has spurred demand for environmental quality although individuals do not typically place the environment at the top of their priority lists. The environment's increased prominence is reflected both by organizations finding various ways of overcoming collective action problems to push for heightened quality and by groups successfully mobilizing in response.

In processing various demands, supply-side institutions function as more than black boxes, meaning that they play an important role in determining how demand gets translated into supply. Elected officials have varying incentives to balance the desires of the rank-and-file citizenry and organized interests with much at stake. Some political actors have reason to care principally about distribution and others about efficiency. Certain political actors have more technical ability to process, at least partially, many of the issues involved than others do. Bureaucratic agents operate within a discretionary zone to push their own agendas, which may not correspond with those of other political actors, and may drive politicians to make choices that would otherwise appear peculiar. The ability to make the subjects of government policies comply with the laws and rules that affect them can prove difficult. And politicians do not necessarily have incentives to allocate responsibilities to what policy analysts would see as the appropriate level of government. Furthermore, supply may affect demand (for example, policy choices may influence observed mobilization and individual demands), and demand may affect institutional structures (for example, structural choices may be influenced by organized interests).

More fundamentally, the constitutional system provides policy makers incentives to worry about environmental quality, but it also fosters fragmentation and poor integration. As such, environmental issues are addressed but initiatives are not typically designed and implemented in the manner policy analysts recommend. Put differently, many of the plaudits and criticisms attributed to policy derive fundamentally from basic constitutional choices.

The constitutional system also induces credibility and commitment concerns, an inherent part of democracy even if the nature of these concerns vary with basic constitutional choices made, such as whether a presidential or a parliamentary system is selected. Credibility and commitment considerations present difficult trade-offs between stability and flexibility for those making environmental policy. Pledges of future government policies, related rewards, and punishments may lack credibility. As a result, inducing investment and generally implementing policy may prove difficult, causing apparently inefficient and inflexible institutional structures and elaborate decision-making procedures to be chosen at least partially to help solve credibility problems. Adding to the trade-off between flexibility and solutions to commitment problems, the American constitutional structure's blueprint for gridlock makes policy adjustments difficult. Thus, complaints that environmental policy lacks credibility *and* is inflexible, both at substantial cost and at the risk of goal deflection, at least partially stem from the resolution of commitment issues in the context of constitutional structure.

Consequently, the American political system has produced more environmental quality. But the interaction of supply and demand has led to increased demands for environmental quality being mediated by supply-side institutions, with these supply-side mechanisms influencing future demands and these demand-side forces affecting the nature of supply. More fundamentally, defining constitutional features and the very nature of democracy have helped generate policy that is fragmented, poorly integrated, and often characterized by problems of durability and flexibility.

FUTURE TRENDS

As difficult as establishing the relative successes and costs of environmental policy and broadly suggesting political contributions to this observed state of affairs may be, predicting the future is even harder. Given the stakes involved, making predictions is popular despite accuracy problems—the further ahead in time, the greater likelihood of gross mistakes. Nonetheless, some broad, albeit speculative, comments about the political system's ability to confront environmental issues over the next several decades are possible.

These predictions are focused only on political causes of environmental outcomes—thus, there are several basic determinants of such outcomes, related to future scientific, technological, and economic trends, which provide some reasons for future optimism that will not be addressed here:

- *Scientific and technical advancements.* Predicting the level of future scientific and technical advancements and whether, or to what degree, such progress will outrun environmental pressures and political and economic hurdles is extremely difficult. But past history indicates that significant advancements will ameliorate environmental quality, although assuming that historical trends will continue is always risky.
- *Economic progress.* Predicting future economic trends is also fraught with peril. Following Chapter 2, by certain measures increasing (declining) economic growth, and presumably heightened (reduced) demand and willingness to pay for environmental quality, will likely improve (injure) environmental quality. Thus, if American economic prosperity continues over the long haul, citizen demands will likely rise, and politicians will likely respond by supplying programs that aid the environment, if inefficiently.

Beyond such nonpolitical factors, the following discussion assumes that democracy in the United States will remain intact in its broad outlines. Although democracy seems here to stay, other nations have experienced dramatic and largely unanticipated institutional changes, such as the fall of the Soviet bloc. Nonetheless, the continuation of American democracy has more positive implications for the future than most alternatives. Although different key democratic features have implications for factors such as credibility that affect environmental policy in a variety of positive and negative ways, overall, democracies do a better job of protecting the environment than other governmental forms.

With respect to more specific political factors, and like so much about environmental quality and policy, the following comments concerning the political system's ability to improve the environment further are a mixed bag. Some suggest optimism, others pessimism, and still more have implications provoking ambivalence.

Reason for Hope: Movement toward Efficient Instruments

Perhaps the most positive trend from the standpoint of the political system's ability to handle environmental policy is the movement, albeit uneven, toward adopting more efficient policy instruments. Although the focus here is on market mechanisms, shifts toward pollution prevention, risk prioritization, and the search for greater flexibility can be viewed similarly.

Possible reasons for this trend are myriad. Environmental organizations and business representatives have been increasingly finding common ground for coordinating on more efficient solutions, allowing more environmental protection at a lower cost, and environmental organizations have gradually relented in their moral or strategic opposition to market instruments. Politicians have recognized that the instruments that policy analysts have been championing are more desirable means of delivering more environmental quality per dollar. Escalating costs of environmental intervention have brought additional pressure to bear on even those traditionally willing to tolerate less efficient results, because the "deadweight loss" by which nobody benefits rises. Actual advances in the development of market instruments (such as auction mechanisms of the sort adopted in the Clean Air Act Amendments of 1990) and initial positive experiences with market approaches have also made market instruments more palatable.

Regardless, as in other policy areas, numerous analysts have recognized a clear, if incremental, trend toward greater use of market instruments (for example, Portney 1999; Stavins 1998, 1999, 2000b). The dominant mode of intervention still remains oriented toward command-and-control, bureaucratic, and increasingly prescriptive. Furthermore, the market instruments chosen are not always exactly those recommended by policy analysts. Nonetheless, there is a recognizable movement toward market instruments and approaches.

Reason for Worry: The Internationalization of Policy

Relative to the positive spin put on greater use of economic instruments, internationalization of environmental policy provokes more worry. Concerns such as global warming, biological diversity, and protection of the world's oceans and fisheries—not to mention less purely environmental issues such as world trade and population growth—have attained higher profiles and should continue to attract growing attention. Providing public goods on a multinational scale or confronting externalities crossing national boundaries appears even more problematic than dealing with their national or subnational analogues.

In other words, applying the analytic logic introduced earlier (for example, that outlined in Chapter 6 regarding which level of government should be delegated which authority), the "right government" for handling many emerging problems exceeds national boundaries. This presents a host of interrelated complications that follow directly from the study of domestic policy:

- *Lack of a clear enforcement agent.* Although international organizations with environmental responsibilities such as the United Nations Environment Programme have been created, international structures generally lack sufficient ability to enforce environmental initiatives. International cooperation may depend more on repeated interactions between nations than on institutional structures (like enforcement on the domestic level, repeated play may induce cooperation). Related to this, establishing secure environmental property rights internationally, although attempted, is more difficult than it is nationally.

- *Overcoming nation-state free riding.* Problems of free riding may be more substantial in the international than in the national arena. Whereas domestically, small actors (for example, small producers in a highly polluting industry) may be made to pay their share of the cost of environmental quality through means such as taxation, extracting analogous international payments (for example, from small, developing nations) may prove more difficult. For instance, much of the debate over dealing with global warming can be viewed as a dialogue about who will pay (large and wealthy nations) and who will free ride (small and poor nations). Such difficulties are likely to be especially great when issues involve many diverse nations, as is the case with global warming, rather than a few homogeneous countries, such as the United States and Canada in their efforts to address acid rain.

- *Differences in cross-national demand.* A related issue is that vast discrepancies in the demand for environmental quality may complicate solutions to cross-national problems. Given huge cross-national variances in wealth, as well as differences in political systems, far more divergence in willingness to pay for environmental quality may be present than is found in the United States domestically.[2] In other words, although populations in developing countries may be concerned about the environment—not surprisingly, given the extent of degradation in some of these nations—they may be unwilling to pay for improving it.

- *Differences in national capacity.* Analogous to earlier discussions regarding federalism and reasons why some are leery about devolving authority to the states, many developing countries may lack the domestic capacity to enforce environmental agreements (or may plausibly deny knowledge of violations when they fail to enforce such agreements). For instance, a nation that agrees to prevent its populations from burning down the rainforest (rainforest deforestation being a major concern regarding global warming and worries over biodiversity) may lack the capacity to stop indigenous populations from doing so (indeed, this seems to be a real problem that mars efforts to protect the Brazilian rainforest; Eveleigh 2000).[3]

- *Interaction with domestic politics.* Finally, and related to the above, layered on top of all this are the possible difficulties associated with domestic politics. Although national leaders may wish to commit to international accords, domestic constraints may limit their ability to do so. For instance despite the great fanfare that accompanied the initial American announce ment of the Kyoto agreement, at first legislators and subsequently Georg W. Bush were unwilling to support the accord because of the substantia economic costs involved.

In short, the logic of matching environmental problems with the smalles government level that encompasses relevant costs and benefits indicates that cer tain problems are best dealt with internationally, everything else being equal. Bu there are a host of problems involved that suggest that progress is likely to be eve slower on the international than on the domestic front. Besides domestic politic mucking up the works in the international arena, enforcement will be more dif ficult, free riding more problematic, demand more variable, and capacity short falls a greater hindrance. Thus, to the degree that the mix of relevant environ mental issues is international in scope, there is reason for worry.

Reason for Hesitance: The Localization of Policy

Compared with the positive and negative aspects of increased adoption of eco nomic instruments and greater internationalization of policy, a more ambiguou trend is a movement toward devolving authority back to localities.[4] Just as con clusions regarding the current impact of federalism are mixed, so are expectation about further devolution. Specifically, a greater trend in the future toward devo lution may be substantially positive if localism rationalizes policy; indeed, civi environmentalism is often linked to the idea of using innovative instruments t solve difficult problems. Hence, one possibility is that the movement toward local ism is linked to the trend toward getting more environmental quality per unit o expenditure. Regardless, given the kinds of issues discussed in Chapter 6, there i good reason to think that devolving authority to states and regions will be a pos itive thing, since it will allow more flexibility and produce policy better reflectin; the preferences of those who benefit and suffer.

Still, such policy devolution has several pitfalls. One potential problem, flow ing directly from the analysis in Chapter 6, is that the wrong policies will b devolved, as those with localized costs and benefits remain at the national leve and those with geographically broad costs and benefits are localized. If the author ity granted to localities, states, or regions does not encompass the bulk of envi ronmental costs and benefits, bad outcomes can result, as these entities will no internalize the full consequences of their acts when making decisions. Addition ally, the achievement of environmental justice and the thwarting of environmen tal racism may also be viewed as more problematic on the subnational level

Finally, difficulties may arise if the result of devolution is simply another layer of bureaucratic inefficiencies placed on top of those already existing. Well-known environmental economist Paul Portney presents his assessment of a possible solution to this problem (1999, 381):

> [W]hile many environmental problems belong squarely in a discussion of national priority setting, we should not assume that is true for all such problems. A thoughtful reappraisal of "who should do what" in the environmental arena would be most welcome. This last point brings us back to the size of the EPA. Nearly half of the EPA's 18,000 employees are stationed in regional offices around the country, where their principal function is overseeing the activities of state and local environmental officials. This level of "supervision" may have been appropriate in the early years of the EPA, but it is arguable at best whether more states need the EPA to review permits they may have taken years to write. Although one might wish to redeploy elsewhere in the EPA these regional employees, that so many be engaged in their current activities is no longer necessary.

Nonetheless, despite these cautions, devolution can be a net positive, allowing for flexibility, innovation, and higher social welfare. It is grounds for cautious optimism.

SUSTAINING ENVIRONMENTAL QUALITY

The most ambitious task in prognostication is to predict whether the current environmental path is sustainable. Although debated, Solow's definition of sustainability is the one used here: the assurance that future generations will have the opportunity to be at least as well off as the current one (Solow 2000). Although the current generation may damage certain elements of the environment or use up exhaustible resources that cannot then be consumed by later generations, the core issue is whether these future generations will have equal or better opportunities. For example, will they be able to use technologies to deal with exploited resources or to compensate for environmental damage? Not surprisingly, there are great discrepancies in scholarly predictions about sustainability. They range from the extremely optimistic (for example, Easterbrook 1995, Simon 1999) to the extremely pessimistic (for example, Ehrlich and Ehrlich 1996).

Focusing principally on political elements of domestic environmental policy, combined with the inherent danger of predictions far into the future, makes a definitive forecast impossible. Despite the uncertainty, there is some reason for optimism in the United States. Environmental progress, even at a high price, has been the norm and the nature of demand and supply is not likely to change greatly in the coming years. Although new, more challenging environmental problems may evolve that are more difficult and expensive to fix than past difficulties (for example, Arrow et al. 1995), or other exogenous events may take place (for example, an economic depression), experience has shown that sustainability is not an unreasonable expectation for the immediate future and beyond.

FINAL THOUGHTS

This book has established that environmental policies are not unique and can be understood in terms of demand and supply. As in all advanced industrial countries, American concern with environmental quality has risen and, indeed, there has been progress, if expensive progress, that provides some optimism for the future. Furthermore, unlike many policies in which governments get involved, there is a strong justification for environmental intervention.

But although government capacity has increased for well over a century, this growth has reflected the general fragmentation and lack of integration of the American political system. Growth and fragmentation are seen in the nature of demand-side forces, such as the large but highly diverse interest group community, and in supply, such as the multiplicity of institutional forces that influence environmental policy. They are felt in the awkward way in which policy is implemented and in the disjointed manner in which the federal structure affects environmental policy. Growth and fragmentation are also evident in the multiplicity of overlapping and disjointed land management agencies and in the ill-structured EPA, their seemingly always expanding and sometimes conflicting policy responsibilities, and the instruments and procedures that they employ to carry out their tasks. To the degree that environmental quality has been delivered, it has been at a high price.

The future would appear to include growing demand for environmental quality within the context of fragmented political supply and pressures from local and international forces. Although environmental quality has been improved by a number of conventional measures, and there are grounds for optimism, this does not translate into an environmental nirvana. Consumption and congestion pressures will continue to stress the environment. Supply-side institutions and the nature of democracy itself, interacting with demand-side forces, will continue to strain how government translates demand into output. And new challenges, for example, the rise of international environmental concerns such as global warming, are daunting. Nonetheless, the short- to medium-term future is not without optimism. Growing consumption and increasingly internationalized policies will bring additional pressures to bear (with consumption also potentially increasing calls for environmental quality). Conversely, growing societal demands, technological innovation, and the seeming willingness of government to innovate, however haltingly, in its means of addressing problems provide reasons to think that all is not lost.

While understanding future changes will be challenging as well as fascinating, the distinctive approach to environmental policy offered in this book should make it easier to make sense of new developments in the environmental field. If the past is a guide, it should be possible to conceptualize the policy choices made, their impact on environmental quality, and their economic costs as a function of the interaction of economic demand with political supply.

KEY TERMS

Fundamental causes (p. 217)
Proximate causes (p. 217)
Sustainability (p. 207)

Notes

I. Environmental Policy in Context

1. For example, political scientist Ronald Inglehart (for example, 1995) emphasizes the importance of individuals being inculcated with so-called post-materialist values—values reflecting the desire for goods beyond those satisfying basic human needs such as housing and shelter that have allegedly become more important as economic security has become less problematic—as an additional determinant of demand beyond ability to pay. Nevertheless, as will be discussed in more depth, whatever the validity of such assertions (the utility of the post-materialist framework has been widely contested, see Duch and Taylor 1993), the evidence that a significant and positive relationship exists between economic growth and government and between the demand for environmental quality and the ability to pay for it is strong and unambiguous (for example, Grossman and Krueger 1995, Holsey and Borcherding 1997, Rothenberg 2000).

2. Statements that more environmental quality is demanded with growth and prosperity should not be construed as endorsing the more extreme proposition, which some on the political right espouse, that economic activity is the best policy for a clean environment. (For a particularly controversial example of such environmental optimism see Easterbrook 1995; for critiques, see Arrow et al. 1995; Oppenheimer, Wilcove, and Bean 1995.) For present purposes, noting that demand for environmental quality seems to rise with prosperity and that this demand collides with political, economic, and technical realities to produce environmental policy and quality is sufficient.

3. Kahn (1998) discusses this process and reactions to cleaning up air pollution in the Los Angeles basin, while Chay and Greenstone (1998) analyze the relationship between air pollution and housing prices. Such behavior designed to avoid pollution's negative effects is partially responsible for concerns that environmental ills fall disproportionately on the poor and the disenfranchised. For instance, as will be discussed further, many activists, scholars, and political figures decry what they consider to be a system of environmental injustice and racism by which the poor inhabit high pollution areas (see Bullard 1993, 1994; Hamilton 1995b; Hamilton and Viscusi 1999). Analogously, many find that those who are better situated politically, and typically better-off financially, are more adept than those with little political clout at preventing activities that cause or dispose of pollution and, therefore, might improve quality of life generally but impose costs on those located nearby (this is the NIMBY, or Not in My Backyard, syndrome; for a discussion, see Rabe 1994). Indeed, environmental justice concerns were politically sanctioned by Bill Clinton in February 1994 when he signed Executive Order 12898, "Federal Actions to Ensure Environmental Justice in Minority and Low Income Communities," which ordered seventeen federal agencies to develop strategic plans to address environmental justice (for an analysis of environmental justice issues, see Foreman 1998).

4. Residentially, radon is most commonly found in the air at high levels in structures providing little ventilation, such as in many energy-efficient buildings constructed during the last several decades, that are built on granite, shale, or phosphate-bearing geological formations.

Occupational exposure is most associated with uranium mining. Although inexpensive detection kits identify radon dangers fairly cheaply, remediation costs, such as those of substantially improving ventilation, can run into thousands of dollars (Cole 1993, Reitze and Carof 1998).

5. Establishing secure and well-defined property rights is deemed essential for generating productive economic activity, as the creation of value is commonly thought to be diminished if property rights are undefined, unclear, or unenforced (North and Thomas 1973, Eggertsson 1996).

6. Indeed, the 1996 passage of the Food Quality Protection Act (FQPA), which established a variety of standards for pesticide residues on food, formally recognized this fact (Schierow 1996; for a critical discussion see Byrd 1997). Previously, under the 1958 Delaney Clause, pesticide traces were not allowed in processed foods (Vogt 1995), leading to the paradox that acceptable amounts of pesticides on raw foods were unacceptable after processing.

7. It would be unsurprising to discover that people in poorer countries consider the environment to be problematic, especially because quality is objectively worse in such nations on many dimensions, even if they are unwilling or unable to pay the same amount per capita for environmental attributes. (On comparing opinions of those in poor and rich nations on the environment, see Dunlap, Gallup, and Gallup 1993; Dunlap and Mertig 1995.) Also, particularly for a good with costs and benefits spilling over to so many others, asking people hypothetical questions often raises validity issues (are responses actually measuring what they seem to?); indeed, a huge literature considers how to measure willingness to pay for public goods such as the environment (for example, Mitchell and Carson 1989). In this book, therefore, most opinion data are viewed as suggestive, and measures of actual behavior are considered stronger indications of how to classify environmental quality as a good.

8. Although green parties are important forces in certain western European countries, America's version is a pale imitation (for example, Green Party presidential candidate Ralph Nader received 685,000 votes, or 0.71 percent of the popular vote, in 1996 and 2,878,000 votes or 2.73 percent in 2000). The discrepancy in green party success is almost certainly a function of the advanced democracies of Europe being parliamentary systems, which typically encourage multiple parties, and America being a presidential system biased toward two principal parties (for the classic work, see Duverger 1954).

9. For instance, only 17.3 percent of General Social Survey respondents answer that they have a great deal of confidence in the people running the executive branch of the federal government (51 percent say that have "only some" confidence, 27.3 percent have "hardly any" confidence, and 2.8 percent simply "don't know" if they have confidence). Perhaps more ironically, by producing pressures to make government even more inert and inflexible (for example, Kagan 1995), this tension between the mistrust of government and the demands on it may exacerbate pathologies associated with American public policy.

10. Kahn and Matsusaka actually make the stronger claim that preferences are *unimportant* determinants of behavior once income is controlled; however, their measures of preferences (voter registration and vote for president) are incomplete, and their measures of production costs (for example, agricultural production in a county) may tap some of the effects of preferences, particularly if mobility is important (that is, similar types of people may deliberately congregate together). Additionally, Kahn and Matsusaka do discover that income has a declining effect for some referenda, which they attribute, probably reasonably, to "crowding" behavior by which wealthy individuals purchase private goods, such as an isolated house in the midst of pristine surroundings, rather than contribute to public provision, such as parks open to all, thereby displacing the production of public goods with that of private goods.

11. Consistent with this discussion (although other factors are relevant), while the United States virtually eliminated its emissions fairly quickly once international efforts to reduce CFCs gained momentum (industrial nation production declined by roughly 90 percent from 1989 to 1995), a variety of developing nations continue to use them and have actually increased production.

12. In a related vein, whether unifying authority in a single party across both chambers of the U.S. Congress and the office of the president makes for more effective or decisive government is vigorously debated (Mayhew 1991, Fiorina 1996, Epstein and O'Halloran 1999, Laver 1999).

13. In this framework, second-tier explanations focus on fundamental differences with separation of powers or parliamentary systems related to regime or government type, and third-tier explanations include a plethora of other considerations not directly tied to legislative-executive relations.

14. Also, interestingly, there was a recent movement in judicial circles to revive the so-called nondelegation doctrine, which had been presumed dead since the 1930s, with specific application to environmental issues (on nondelegation, see Lowi 1979). Under this doctrine, delegating broad discretion to agencies like the Environmental Protection Agency (EPA) is deemed unconstitutional; notably, in *American Trucking Associations* v. *Environmental Protection Agency,* the District of Columbia Court of Appeals ruled that regulatory efforts to promulgate new ozone and particulate standards violated Article I of the Constitution vesting legislative powers in Congress. However, in *Whitman* v. *American Trucking Associations,* the Supreme Court put a stop to this potential assault on agency delegation (see also Chapter 6).

15. Another form of commitment that government may find more difficult to solve and which will be covered in Chapter 5, involves implementing sanctions to punish those not behaving in a prescribed manner. Although durability may solve commitment problems related to expectations about a policy's longevity, it will not solve those stemming from expectations about whether government will have the nerve to punish transgressors (for example, manufacturers not meeting prescribed standards) even at the risk of, for example, throwing employees out of work.

2. Environmental Action, Environmental Caution

1. Another typical justification for intervention, notably for economic regulation by which government decides issues such as firm entry, exit, and pricing, is imperfect competition stemming from market concentration, that is, government steps in when a monopoly or an oligopoly gives economic actors market power. However, concentration is not especially relevant for social regulation of consumption and production choices generally or for environmental policy specifically. Although imperfect competition can have environmental repercussions justifying intervention in selected instances, such as with respect to public utilities where economies of scale may make competition difficult and harm the environment, other market failures weigh far more heavily. (Economies of scale involve the reduction of the average cost of a product when it is made by a single producer.) As such, monopoly and oligopoly will be largely ignored.

2. One argument heard for discounting smokers' utility is that those with high chemical sensitivities, such as asthmatics, suffer through no fault of their own, whereas smoking is more or less voluntary. Also, along the lines that smokers should be harshly penalized, another possible justification for discounting smokers' utility is that symbolic gestures such as bans or the

condemnation of other forms of environmentally damaging behavior might change attitudes in the population more generally and result in a more favorable state of affairs through a process of stigmatization; in other words, ostracizing smokers can be good (on stigma, which has been principally analyzed with application to means-based programs such as welfare, see Besley and Coate 1992).

3. Although not obviously what Sandel has in mind, as implied, an instrumental perspective on moral stigma could suggest that it helps reduce policy enforcement costs by internalizing beliefs that harming the environment is wrong (similar arguments are found, for example, in Glazer and Rothenberg 2001). However, moral stigma likely works far more on individuals than on larger economic decision makers, such as corporations, who are the primary focus of many environmental market mechanisms. Additionally, the positive effects of moral stigma would have to be quite large to justify eschewing markets on instrumental grounds.

4. For instance, Keohane, Revesz, and Stavins (1999) suggest a wide variety of reasons for hesitancy in adopting market instruments: legislators may find command-and-control more comfortable, familiar, better for hiding costs, more symbolically attractive, and better for distributing benefits; firms may be wary of market instruments if they push more costs onto their industry or undo established rights, undo barriers for new entrants into the industry, or eliminate a cost advantage relative to other firms in complying with regulations; besides philosophical objections, environmental organizations may be suspicious of market instruments if they threaten their ability to attract members, if they are more difficult to alter than command-and-control policy (which, frankly, would not seem to be the case), or because group leaders believe market mechanisms will be less effective in practice than theory.

5. In the spirit of the earlier discussion, the Coasian solution can only be realized with clearly defined and easily transferable property rights. The ability to make effective bargains is undermined if rights or their exchange are in question—for example, proper choices will not be made if those involved are worried that government will step in and appropriate rights by fiat.

3. A Brief History of U.S. Environmental Policy

1. The definition of multiple use cited here is from the Federal Land and Policy Management Act of 1976.

2. Passage of the 1960 Multiple Use and Sustained Yield Act codified the linkage between multiple use and sustained yield.

3. These groups were the Environmental Defense Fund, the Environmental Policy Institute, the Friends of the Earth, the Izaak Walton League of America, the Natural Resources Defense Council, the National Audubon Society, the National Parks and Conservation Association, the National Wildlife Federation, the Sierra Club, and the Wilderness Society.

4. Illustrative of the increasing attention to brownfields was the Clinton administration's 1997 announcement of a Brownfields National Partnership (Bartsch 1997) and, despite some complaints that it is statutorily inappropriate, the EPA's decision to employ some Superfund monies to help clean up selected brownfield sites ($91.3 million in fiscal year 2000; see, for example, General Accounting Office [GAO] 1998c, Reisch 2000a).

Climate change issues principally concern worries that increasing emissions of atmospheric greenhouse gases, such as of carbon dioxide, cause global warming. They are highlighted by the 1997 Kyoto, Japan, multinational agreement—although meaningful implementation of this accord has proven difficult. As mentioned earlier, ozone depletion involves worries about how gases, such as CFCs, might deplete stratospheric ozone, potentially resulting in changes such as increases in skin cancer. Besides prompting domestic efforts, worries about climate seemingly precipitated nations to sign the Montreal Protocol in 1987 (Benedick 1998). Although not completely alleviating broader concerns, as other chemicals threaten the ozone layer and developing nations increase their CFC production and consumption, this accord greatly reduced CFC production and usage, particularly in the industrial countries.

5. The United States had developed significant pollution problems by the end of the nineteenth century, such as waterborne diseases, particularly in urban areas, caused by a lack of sewers and water treatment (Melosi 1980, Andrews 1999), and urban air pollution produced by America's industrial engine (Hays 1959).

6. Perhaps even more surprising, unlike the soon-to-be-discussed General Revision Act, Congress has never revoked this authority. An obvious reason is that presidents have exercised caution in using these powers in ways that would alienate Congress. However, there are exceptions. For instance, in 1996 Bill Clinton created the Grand Staircase Escalante National Monument in Utah in a transparent election-time gesture to skeptical environmentalists. Lacking much local support—for example, both Utah senators opposed it—this action provoked unsuccessful cries for repealing the act. Predictably, the president then abstained from using the act in such incendiary ways until near his administration's end, when, because his worries about legislative retribution were marginal, he produced a torrent of lame-duck initiatives.

7. Separating agencies that are, intuitively, best served by coordination between different executive departments with contrasting orientations reflects and reinforces institutional and policy fragmentation. Although such differences should not be exaggerated, those favoring preservationist goals have historically found the DOI more receptive than the USDA.

8. Providing ranchers with grazing rights over specific lands eliminated the commons, but moral hazard remains problematic to the extent that ranchers worry that their rights may be adjusted or taken away after their leases expire. More generally, as will be discussed in Chapter 7, the guardianship of the Grazing Service and the BLM, although producing lands that are better than previously, comes under considerable attack from all sides.

9. As Kaufman's seminal analysis illustrates, the USFS had a reputation for developing mechanisms to keep producer interests at arm's length. It became known for its highly professional employees, decentralized decision making, and mission orientation. For many years the USFS was claimed to be one of the best managed American organizations—public or private (see Clarke and McCool 1996). However, although perhaps not as reviled as the BLM, the USFS would ultimately be subject to claims of special interest capture (for example, Hodges 1996).

10. Specifically, Nixon's executive order transferred two DOI bureaus—the Federal Water Quality Administration and the Office of Research on Effects of Pesticides on Wildlife and Fish—five Health, Education and Welfare agencies (Bureau of Water Hygiene, Bureau of Solid Waste Management, National Air Pollution Control Administration, Bureau of Radiological Health, and the Office of Pesticides Research), the Pesticides Regulation Division from the USDA, the Division of Radiation Standards from the Atomic Energy Commission, and the Interagency Federal Radiation Council.

11. Delegating authority locally over various environmental issues may be sensible. However, one can also convincingly argue that tasks that were locally delegated—and the nature of the defined intergovernmental relationship—do not correspond to those suggested by a rationalized treatment of environmental policy (see Chapter 6).

4. National Political Influences on Environmental Policy

1. Public interest groups and business-commercial organizations may overlap financially. A variety of grassroots organizations, for example, many wise use groups, are substantially bank-rolled by the corporate sector; similarly, more conservative interests frequently complain about government support for environmental organizations (to be discussed in more detail later).

2. Reiterating an earlier point, business and corporate interests have, at times, pushed for more efficient policy (for example, adopting market instruments) to meet goals more cheaply. But such preferences are often overwhelmed by incentives of specific corporations or business sectors to pursue their narrow self-interest.

3. Assertions that structural choice is exclusively the province of organized interests should be made cautiously because voters care about environmental conditions and their financial well-being. By this logic, elected officials will be penalized if mistakes in agency design cause poor environmental quality or high costs. A balance must be struck between narrow, concentrated interests and inefficiency (Becker 1983; Grossman and Helpman 1994; and Keohane, Revesz, and Stavins 1999 provide arguments consistent with this assertion).

4. In contrast, scholars such as Berry (1999) emphasize the influence of liberal environmental interest groups on congressional policy choices.

5. Somewhat counter to claims of legislative venality, others maintain that congressional impact is limited because large numbers of members deter effective organization for pursuing collective goals because of high transaction costs, leaving more nimble political actors such as the president with a strategic advantage (Moe and Howell 1999). However, the repeated nature of congressional activity and the coordination mechanisms, such as political parties, that legislators have created should substantially mitigate such obstacles. (The increasing complexity of institutions such as the presidency may also produce problems in getting subordinates to march in lockstep.) Thus, for example, legislators representing various concerns have little problem organizing around mutual concerns; in illustration, those interested in protecting auto producers effectively mobilize when air pollution standards threaten, as do western Republicans combating attempts to raise grazing fees.

6. The most notable recent threat occurred in 1993, when the House and Senate passed contrasting royalty payment schemes. The two chambers failed to reconcile their differences, and the legislation died in a House/Senate conference committee charged with forging a compromise. Currently, legislators, environmentalists, and mining interests are fighting over how much of a given parcel can be used as a mill site, with smaller sites reducing environmental damage and mining profitability.

7. These processes are frequently nuanced, with political actors anticipating each other's actions. Executive orders may be circumvented by strategic legislators passing statutes; vetoes may be rendered unnecessary by strategically amended bills; and presidential nominations of candidates mutually acceptable to all sides may defuse hostile conferral battles.

8. Although the following discussion focuses on federal courts (since the EPA's formation for the most part), state courts have jurisdiction over intrastate pollution issues and concerns of state regulatory agencies and the like.

9. Justices may also invite statutory reversal when they believe that the law ties their hands. Perhaps the best known example is the Supreme Court's ruling in *TVA* v. *Hill* (437 U.S. 153 [1978]) in which the ESA unambiguously required that a dam threatening the existence of a species of snail darter not be built regardless of the desirability of an exception.

10. The next section shows how this confluence of preferences could have given agencies such as the EPA a zone of discretion; essentially, these agencies could change the status quo, and statutory reversion would be difficult as these agencies had presidential support.

11. Workload is an additional capacity issue. Interestingly, while the lower federal courts are overwhelmed by growing caseloads—a situation exacerbated after 1994, when squabbling between Republican senators and a Democratic president left both sides willing to leave judgeships unfilled at the expense of increasing delay and transaction costs (for example, in April 1997, twenty-three positions had been vacant for at least eighteen months)—the Supreme Court has not found restrictions in the number of cases that it can handle annually constraining in the sense of not being able to hear cases for reasons of workload as its present composition has made it more passive than in the past.

Also, a caveat is that the District of Columbia Court of Appeals handles more environmental cases than other courts (for example, the EPA litigates about two-thirds of its cases in the court) and thus its justices have become somewhat more familiar with environmental issues (Wald 1992). However, administrative cases are still a small absolute percentage of the court's workload, and judicial expertise regarding the environment remains modest (Banks 1999).

5. Developing and Enforcing Environmental Policy

1. For those interested in the importance of program areas, for the EPA in fiscal 1997 there were 89 air cases, 111 water cases, 154 CERCLA cases, 49 RCRA cases, and 23 toxics/pesticide cases. For the states, the numbers were 151 water, 164 air, and 64 RCRA.

2. A similar movement concerns environmental management systems and involves efforts to survey and improve firms' environmentally relevant activities.

3. This does not mean that CAFE standards are good public policy. Indeed, from an economist's perspective they are far from ideal and could be improved by simpler taxes; for example CAFE is estimated to be seven to ten times more expensive than a petroleum tax and is claimed to have possibly *reduced* average fuel efficiency in the 1980s by shifting automobile sales toward low fuel efficiency cars (Kleit 1990, Crandall 1992, Thorpe 1997).

6. National or Local Control

1. Although a stable federal system helps check the abrogation of property rights—which is essential if markets are to function and, for that matter, if policies requiring investment are to succeed—establishing the processes preventing national government usurpation of authority is complex (for example, Weingast 1993, 1995; Qian and Weingast 1997; see also, Riker 1987). Put differently, since national political actors need to devise mechanisms for credibly committing to preserving federalism, they can be viewed as party to any bargain allowing local control.

2. Specifically, Tiebout's model suggests that, if different bundles of public goods are offered in different geographic polities, those with homogenous preferences will separate themselves through residential choice by "voting with their feet."

3. Another complicating factor in stopping a bidding war is that the national government may find itself having to reserve vast arrays of policies as local leaders, faced with having to maintain a single national standard, may respond by manipulating others. For example, local leaders wishing to reduce business costs may respond to a national rule setting a strict environmental standard by relaxing local worker safety rules.

4. For instance, in the spirit of the analysis emphasizing the relationship between ability to pay and demand for environmental quality, Henry Butler and Jonathan Macey (1996b, 20), scholars of law and economics, argue that income effects may produce more environmental

quality in high-income states: "In fact, competition between jurisdictions may lead to greater increases in environmental quality. It is often argued that environmental quality is a luxury good, in that individuals develop a greater concern for environmental issues as their incomes rise. If this is true, the key to increases in environmental quality may be found in higher incomes. This point has implications for the desirability of jurisdictional competition." In reality, although they might be more proactive if the devolution of authority were less constraining, states only exceed current national environmental standards with modest frequency.

5. Politically, there may also be an imbalance in regard to costs if they are disproportionately borne by those outside the district; for example, midwestern automakers do not vote in California, providing the latter with an incentive to pass legislation that makes the former pay for cleaner air in their state (Elliott, Ackerman, and Millian 1985).

6. This inference is conditioned on assuming that national policies would be identical in centralized and federated systems. Intuitively, national standards might be stricter if local leaders could not exceed them when demand warrants, although prominent economist Wallace Oates (1997) speculates that national regulators tend toward excessively stringent standards.

7. The commission's domain includes areas of Connecticut, Delaware, Maine, Maryland, Massachusetts, New Hampshire, New Jersey, New York, Pennsylvania, Rhode Island, Vermont, parts of Virginia, and the District of Columbia (one criticism is that this area is not comprehensive for covering all externalities) and involves representatives from each state's environmental quality bureaucracy and the three relevant EPA regions. The commission may recommend initiatives, by majority vote, that the EPA may or may not approve. To date, the commission has passed two initiatives successfully, one regarding the use of low-emission vehicles and the other concerning the production of nitrogen oxide from power plants and large boilers (for a discussion of the commission, see Trinkle 1995).

8. One exception, already discussed, is setting designs and standards for automobile tailpipe emissions, given large economies of scale. Here, the national government almost certainly plays a positive coordinating role.

7. Land Use Agencies

1. Although these environmental policies substantially affect land quality and value (for example, areas covered with toxics are diminished and devalued), this chapter concentrates on how land is directly managed, whereas Chapter 8 provides additional insight into the effect on lands of EPA regulatory policies.

2. Illustrative of the reasoning of skeptics is the policy advice furnished by the conservative, market-oriented Cato Institute in its manual designed for members of Congress: "[L]ands that have recreational or historical value should be sold or given to private conservation groups such as the Nature Conservancy or the Audubon Society. Such groups would surely do a better job of preserving those lands than has the federal government. Lands that have commercial value—such as timber and grazing lands—should be sold to the private business concerns that currently lease them from the federal government or to environmentalists who wish to buy them for conservation purposes." (Stansel 2001, 176)

3. The Army Corps of Engineers and the Bureau of Reclamation could also fall into this group and would reinforce many analytic themes. They are excluded only for the sake of brevity. These agencies, long associated with water projects such as dam construction, control about 21 million acres of land (almost 9 million by the bureau and over 12 million by the corps). Tra-

ditionally identified with economically inefficient, pork barrel projects, environmental pressures have recently made them more environmentally sensitive (for example, Clarke and McCool 1996). Also, the Department of Defense (DOD) is excluded, as its goals are geared neither toward conservation nor toward preservation. Nonetheless, the DOD owns about one percent of the total land in the United States, takes actions with significant environmental consequences, and spends billions of dollars annually on environmental programs.

4. This battle engulfed three of the four principal land management agencies, the courts, Congress, and several presidents (for a detailed description covering the period until 1993, see Yaffee 1994). It was highlighted by a summit called by Bill Clinton that ultimately led to a compromise—putting substantial environmental safeguards in place and transferring more than $1 billion to the region to ease the economic pain—that left both sides dissatisfied and appears to have contributed to the substantial decline of logging in the Northwest.

5. Bidder collusion over timber rights may also reduce prices received by the USFS (Brannman 1996; Baldwin, Marshall, and Richard 1997). Such collusion is facilitated by relying on oral auctions (where behavior is observable) rather than on sealed bids.

6. Claims of below market pricing are sometimes challenged on the grounds that (1) public land quality is poor, and (2) grazing rights have a capital value for which ranchers not originally receiving rights have to pay, that is, after the initial allocation of who could purchase grazing rights was decided, the windfall for ranchers subsequently controlling these rights was not as great as might appear, since they had to be purchased from the original grantees.

7. The National Marine Fisheries Service (part of the Department of Commerce's National Oceanic and Atmospheric Administration) also has some responsibility for implementing the ESA.

8. The EPA

1. DDT became commercially important after World War II because it was cheap, killed mosquitoes and lice carrying malaria and typhus, and had other desirable properties. But the slow rate at which it metabolizes means that it builds up in those consuming it directly or indirectly. Consequently, widespread DDT application threatened the ability of birds such as the American bald eagle and the peregrine falcon to reproduce successfully because it deformed embryos, thinned eggshells, and lowered hatching rates. The EPA banned DDT in 1973 (Dunlap 1981).

2. Also, although Superfund is heavily centralized, for those cleanups that require program monies because PRPs are not picking up the tab, states may influence which sites get cleaned up and how vigorously because, among other requirements, they must pay 10 percent of the costs.

3. Harking back to the discussion in Chapter 2 of indoor air pollution and justifications for intervention, it is not intuitively clear that radon involves a market failure. As no obvious public goods or externality problems exist, it must be argued that the market is incapable of furnishing information.

4. This discussion is related in spirit to that of divided government (where the presidency and control of Congress are split between the two major parties). Divided government may accentuate preference divergences between presidents and Congress and, therefore, give all involved an incentive to write a detailed contract, everything else being equal. However, as indicated by the fact that much key environmental legislation in the 1970s was written under divided government (notably with the Republican Richard Nixon in the White House and a

Democratic Congress), the obstacle is obviously not divided government per se but preference divergence (see Krehbiel 1998).

9. The Costs of Environmental Progress

1. Solow (2000) makes clear that there are more restrictive definitions of sustainability. However, his view is intuitive, sensible, and consistent with this analysis.

2. Not only are democracies likely to be more receptive to the production of environmental quality than other forms of government but the correlation between democracy and sociodemographic factors, such as wealth, that produce demand for environmental quality may further widen the gap between high- and low-demand countries.

3. Ironically, there are only small returns to populations burning rainforests, as the land's agricultural value is exhausted quickly (inducing still more burning), making a Coasian type contract by which payments are made to maintain the rainforest an obvious solution if enforceable.

4. Others now discuss this movement under the rubric of sustainability (for example, Kraft and Mazmanian 1999), but in this chapter the word *sustainability* is used in accordance with the precise definition offered earlier.

References

Abbey, Edward. 1975. *The Monkey Wrench Gang.* New York: Avon.

Ackerman, Bruce A., and William T. Hassler. 1981. *Clean Coal, Dirty Air.* New Haven, Conn.: Yale University Press.

Adler, Jonathan. 1998. "Bean Counting for a Better Earth." *Regulation* 21:40–48.

Allen, John L. 1995. *Annual Editions: Environment.* 14th edition. Guilford, Conn.: Dushkin.

Amacher, Gregory S., and Arun S. Malik. 1998. "Instrument Choice When Regulators and Firms Bargain." *Journal of Environmental Economics and Management* 35:225–241.

Anderson, Mikael Skou. 1994. *Governance by Green Taxes: Making Pollution Prevention Pay.* Manchester, England: Manchester University Press.

Anderson, Robert C., Alan Carlin, Albert M. McGartland, and Jennifer B. Weinberger. 1997. "Cost Savings from the Use of Market Incentives for Pollution Control." In *Market-Based Approaches to Environmental Policy: Regulatory Innovations to the Fore.* Edited by Richard F. Kosobud and Jennifer M. Zimmerman. New York: Van Nostrand Reinhold.

Anderson, Terry L., and Peter J. Hill. 1997. "Environmental Federalism: Thinking Smaller." In *Environmental Federalism.* Edited by Terry L. Anderson and Peter J. Hill. Lanham, Md.: Rowman and Littlefield.

Anderson, Terry L., and Donald R. Leal. 1997. *Enviro-capitalists: Doing Good while Doing Well.* Lanham, Md.: Rowman and Littlefield.

Anderson, Terry L., and Randy T. Simmons, eds. 1993. *The Political Economy of Customs and Culture: Informal Solutions to the Commons Problem.* Lanham, Md.: Rowman and Littlefield.

Ando, Amy Whitenour. 1997. "Delay on the Path to the Endangered Species List: Do Costs and Benefits Matter?" Resources for the Future Working Paper 97-44. Washington, D.C.: Resources for the Future.

———. 1999. "Waiting to Be Protected under the Endangered Species Act: The Political Economy of Regulatory Delay." *Journal of Law and Economics* 42:29–60.

Andrews, Richard N. L. 1999. *Managing the Environment, Managing Ourselves: A History of American Environmental Policy.* New Haven, Conn.: Yale University Press.

Arnold, Ron. 1993. *Ecology Wars: Environmentalism as If People Mattered.* Bellevue, Wash.: Free Enterprise Press.

———. 2000. *Undue Influence: Wealthy Foundations, Grant-Driven Environmental Groups, and Zealous Bureaucrats That Control Your Future.* Bellevue, Wash.: Merril Press.

Arora, Seema, and Timothy N. Cason. 1996. "Why Do Firms Volunteer to Exceed Environmental Regulation? Understanding Participation in EPA's 33/50 Program." *Land Economics* 72:413–432.

———. 1999. "Do Community Characteristics Influence Environmental Outcomes? Evidence from the Toxics Release Inventory." *Southern Economic Journal* 65:691–716.

Arrow, Kenneth J., and others. 1995. "Economic Growth, Carrying Capacity, and the Environment." *Science* 268 (April 28):520–521.

Bacot, A. Hunter, and Roy A. Dawes. 1997. "State Expenditures and Policy Outcomes in Environmental Program Management." *Policy Studies Quarterly* 25:355–370.

Badrinath, S. G., and Paul J. Bolster. 1996. "The Role of Market Forces in EPA Enforcement Activity." *Journal of Regulatory Economics* 10:165–181.

Bailey, Christopher J. 1998. *Congress and Air Pollution: Environmental Politics in the U.S.* Manchester, England: Manchester University Press.

Baldwin, Laura H., Robert C. Marshall, and Jean-Francois Richard. 1997. "Bidder Collusion at Forest Service Timber Sales," *Journal of Political Economy* 105:657–699.

Baldwin, Pamela. 2000. "Federal Grazing Regulations: *Public Lands Council* v. *Babbitt.*" CRS Issue Brief RS20453. Washington, D.C.: Congressional Research Service.

Banks, Christopher P. 1999. *Judicial Politics in the D.C. Circuit Court.* Baltimore, Md.: Johns Hopkins University Press.

Bardach, Eugene, and Robert A. Kagan. 1982. *Going by the Book: The Problem of Regulatory Unreasonableness.* Philadelphia, Pa.: Temple University Press.

Barro, Robert J. 1996. *Getting It Right: Markets and Choices in a Free Society.* Cambridge: MIT Press.

Bartsch, Charles. 1997. "New Life for Brownfields." *Issues in Science and Technology* 14:35–36.

Baumgartner, Frank R., and Bryan D. Jones. 1993. *Agendas and Instability in American Politics.* Chicago: University of Chicago Press.

Baumgartner, Frank R., and Beth L. Leech. 1998. *Basic Interests: The Importance of Groups in Politics and Political Science.* Princeton, N.J.: Princeton University Press.

Baumol, William J., and Wallace E. Oates. 1988. *The Theory of Environmental Policy.* Cambridge: Cambridge University Press.

Bawn, Kathleen. 1995. "Political Control versus Expertise: Congressional Choices about Administrative Procedures." *American Political Science Review* 89:62–73.

Bearden, David M. 1999. *Air Quality and Emissions Trading: An Overview of Current Issues.* CRS Report 98-563. Washington, D.C.: Congressional Research Service.

Becker, Gary S. 1983. "A Theory of Competition among Pressure Groups for Political Influence." *Quarterly Journal of Economics* 98:371–400.

Bendor, Jonathan B. 1985. *Parallel Systems: Redundancy in Government.* Berkeley: University of California Press.

Benedick, Richard Elliot. 1998. *Ozone Diplomacy: New Directions in Safeguarding the Planet.* Enlarged edition. Cambridge: Harvard University Press.

Berry, Jeffrey M. 1977. *Lobbying for the People: The Political Behavior of Public Interest Groups.* Princeton, N.J.: Princeton University Press.

———. 1999. *The New Liberalism: The Rising Power of Citizen Groups.* Washington, D.C.: Brookings Institution.

Besley, Timothy, and Stephen Coate. 1992. "Understanding Welfare Stigma: Taxpayer Resentment and Statistical Discrimination." *Journal of Public Economics* 48:165–183.

———. 1999. "Centralized versus Decentralized Provision of Local Public Goods: A Political Economy Analysis." NBER Working Paper No. W7084. Cambridge, Mass.: National Bureau of Economic Research.

Biener Lois, and Michael Siegel. 1997. "Behavior Intentions of the Public after Bans on Smoking in Restaurants and Bars." *American Journal of Public Health* 87:2042–2044.

Blodgett, John E., Larry B. Parker, and James E. McCarthy. 1997. *Air Quality: EPA's Proposed New Ozone and Particulate Matter Standards.* CRS Issue Brief 97-8ENR. Washington, D.C.: Congressional Research Service.

Blume, Lawrence, Daniel L. Rubinfeld, and Perry Shapiro. 1984. "The Taking of Land: When Should Compensation Be Paid?" *Quarterly Journal of Economics* 99:71–92.

Boerner, Christopher, and Jennifer Chilton Kallery. 1995. *Restructuring Environmental Big Business*. Center for the Study of American Business Policy Study No. 124. St. Louis, Mo.: CSAB.

Bosch, J. C., E. Woodrow Eckard, and Insup Lee. 1998. "EPA Enforcement, Firm Response Strategies, and Stockholder Wealth: An Empirical Examination." *Managerial and Decision Economics* 19:167–177.

Bosso, Christopher J. 1987. *Pesticides and Politics: The Life Cycle of a Public Issue*. Pittsburgh, Pa.: University of Pittsburgh Press.

Brady, David W., and Craig Volden. 1998. *Revolving Gridlock: Politics and Policy from Carter to Clinton*. Boulder, Colo.: Westview Press.

Brannman, Lance Eric. 1996. "Potential Competition and Possible Collusion in Forest Service Timber Auctions." *Economic Inquiry* 34:730–745.

Breyer, Stephen G. 1993. *Breaking the Vicious Circle: Toward Effective Risk Regulation*. Cambridge: Harvard University Press.

Brooks, Nancy, and Rajiv Sethi. 1997. "The Distribution of Pollution: Community Characteristics and Exposure to Air Toxics." *Journal of Environmental Economics and Management* 32:233–250.

Bryner, Gary C. 1987. *Bureaucratic Discretion: Law and Policy in Federal Regulatory Agencies*. New York: Pergamon.

———. 1994. "Social Regulation." In *Handbook of Regulation and Administrative Law*. Edited by David H. Rosenbloom and Richard D. Schwartz. New York: Marcel Dekker.

———. 1995. *Blue Skies, Green Politics: The Clean Air Act of 1990 and Its Implementation*. 2d edition. Washington, D.C.: Congressional Quarterly Press.

Buck, Eugene H., M. Lynne Corn, and Pamela Baldwin. 2001. *Endangered Species: Difficult Choices*. CRS Report IB1072. Washington, D.C.: Congressional Research Service.

Bullard, Robert. 1994. *Dumping in Dixie: Race, Class, and Environmental Quality*. 2d edition. Boulder, Colo.: Westview.

———, ed. 1993. *Confronting Environmental Racism: Voices from the Grassroots*. Boston: South End Press.

Butler, Henry N., and Jonathan R. Macey. 1996a. "Externalities and the Matching Principle: The Case for Reallocating Environmental Regulatory Authority." *Yale Law and Policy Review* 14:23–66.

———. 1996b. *Using Federalism to Improve Environmental Policy*. Washington, D.C.: American Enterprise Institute.

Byrd, Daniel M. 1997. "Whither Pesticides? The Food Quality Protection Act of 1996." *Regulation* 20:57–62.

Cahn, Robert, ed. 1985. *An Environmental Agenda for the Future by Leaders of America's Foremost Environmental Organizations*. Washington, D.C.: Island Press.

Caldeira, Gregory A., and John R. Wright. 1988. "Organized Interests and Agenda Setting in the U.S. Supreme Court." *American Political Science Review* 82:1109–1127.

Caldwell, Lynton Keith. 1998. *The National Environmental Policy Act: An Agenda for the Future*. Bloomington: Indiana University Press.

Calvert, Randall, Mathew McCubbins, and Barry Weingast. 1989. "A Theory of Political Control and Agency Discretion." *American Journal of Political Science* 33:588–611.

Cammisa, Anne Marie. 1995. *Governments as Interest Groups: Intergovernmental Lobbying and the Federal System*. Westport, Conn.: Praeger.

Campos, Jose Edgardo L. 1989. "Legislative Institutions, Lobbying, and the Endogenous Choice of Regulatory Instruments." *Journal of Law, Economics and Organization* 5:333–353.

Carlson, Dale A., and Anne M. Sholtz. 1994. "Designing Pollution Market Instruments: Cases of Uncertainty." *Contemporary Economic Policy* 14:114–125.

Carson, Rachel. 1962. *Silent Spring.* Boston: Houghton Mifflin.

Cawley, R. McGreggor. 1993. *Federal Land, Western Anger: The Sagebrush Rebellion and Environmental Politics.* Lawrence: University of Kansas Press.

Center for Public Integrity. 1998. *Unreasonable Risks: The Politics of Pesticides.* Washington, D.C.: Center for Public Integrity.

Center for Responsive Politics. 1999. *The Big Picture: The Money behind the 1998 Elections.* Washington, D.C.: Center for Responsive Politics.

Chambers, John C., and Mary S. McCullough. 1995. "From the Cradle to the Grave: An Historical Perspective on RCRA." *Natural Resources and Environment* 10:21–23, 73–74.

Chay, Kenneth Y., and Michael Greenstone. 1998. "Does Air Quality Matter? Evidence from the Housing Market." NBER Working Paper No. 6826. Boston: National Bureau of Economic Research.

Church, Thomas W., and Robert T. Nakamura. 1993. *Cleaning Up the Mess: Implementation Strategies in Superfund.* Washington, D.C.: Brookings Institution.

Cigler, Beverly A. 1995. "Not Just Another Special Interest: Intergovernmental Representation." In *Interest Group Politics.* 4th edition. Edited by Allan J. Cigler and Burdett A. Loomis. Washington, D.C.: Congressional Quarterly Press.

Clark, Ray, and Larry Canter, eds. 1997. *Environmental Policy and NEPA: Past, Present, and Future.* Boca Raton, Fla.: St. Lucie Press.

Clarke, Jeanne Nienaber, and Daniel McCool. 1996. *Staking out the Terrain: Power and Performance among Natural Resource Agencies.* 2d edition. Albany: State University of New York Press.

Clary, David A. 1986. *Timber and the Forest Service.* Lawrence: University of Kansas Press.

Coase, Ronald. 1960. "The Problem of Social Cost." *Journal of Law and Economics* 3:1–44.

Cody, Betsy, and Pamela Baldwin. 1997. *Grazing Fees and Rangeland Management.* CRS Issue Brief 96006. Washington, D.C.: Congressional Research Service.

Coglianese, Cary. 1994. *Challenging the Rules: Litigation and Bargaining in the Administrative Process.* Ph.D. diss., Department of Political Science, University of Michigan, Ann Arbor.

———. 1997. "Assessing Consensus: The Promise and Performance of Negotiated Rulemaking." *Duke Law Journal* 46:1255–1349.

Cohen, Linda R., and Matthew L. Spitzer. 1994. "Solving the *Chevron* Puzzle." *Law and Contemporary Problems* 57:65–110.

———. 1996. "Judicial Deference to Agency Action." *Southern California Law Review* 69: 431–476.

Cole, Leonard A. 1993. *Element of Risk: The Politics of Radon.* Oxford: Oxford University Press.

Conlan, Timothy J. 1988. *New Federalism: Intergovernmental Reform from Nixon to Reagan.* Washington, D.C.: Brookings Institution.

Cooper, Joseph. 1970. *The Origins of the Standing Committees and the Development of the Modern House.* Houston, Texas: Rice University.

Cooter, Robert D. 1982. "The Cost of Coase." *Journal of Legal Studies* 11:1–33.

Copeland, Claudia. *Clean Water Act: A Summary of the Law.* CRS Issue Brief RL30030. Washington, D.C.: Congressional Research Service.

Costain, W. Douglas, and James P. Lester. 1995. "The Evolution of Environmentalism." In *Environmental Politics and Policy.* 2d edition. Edited by James P. Lester. Durham, N.C.: Duke University Press.

Couch, Jim F., Keith Atkinson, and William H. Wells. 1997. "Environmental Pressure Groups and State Environmental Expenditures." *Journal of Private Enterprise* 13:60–67.

Council of Economic Advisors. 2000. *Economic Report of the President.* Washington, D.C.: Government Printing Office.

Council on Environmental Quality. 1996. *25th Anniversary Report.* Washington, D.C.: Government Printing Office.

Council of State Governments. 1999. *Resource Guide to State Environmental Management.* 5th edition. Lexington, Ky.: Council of State Governments.

Coursey, Don. 1992. "The Demand for Environmental Quality." Washington University, St. Louis.

———. 1994. "The Revealed Demand for a Public Good: Evidence from Endangered and Threatened Species." University of Chicago.

Crandall, Robert W. 1992. "Policy Watch: Corporate Average Fuel Economy Standards." *Journal of Economic Perspectives* 6:171–180.

Crandall, Robert W., Frederick H. Rueter, and Wilbur A. Steger. 1997. "Clearing the Air: EPA's Self-Assessment of Clean-Air Policy." *Regulation* 4:35–46.

Cronon, William, ed. 1995. *Uncommon Ground: Rethinking the Human Place in Nature.* New York: Norton.

Cropper, Maureen L., William N. Evans, Stephen J. Beradi, Maria M. Ducla-Soares, and Paul R. Portney. 1992. "The Determinants of Pesticide Regulation: A Statistical Analysis of EPA Decision Making." *Journal of Political Economy* 100:175–197.

Cropper, Maureen L., and Wallace E. Oates. 1992. "Environmental Economics: A Survey." *Journal of Economic Literature* 30:675–740.

Cross, Frank B. 1997. "The Consequences of Consensus: Dangerous Compromises of the Food Quality Protection Act." *Washington University Law Quarterly* 75:1155–1206.

———. 1999. "Shattering the Fragile Case for Judicial Review of Rulemaking." *Virginia Law Review* 85:1243–1334.

Cross, Frank B., and Emerson H. Tiller. 1998. "Judicial Partisanship and Obedience to Legal Doctrine: Whistleblowing on the Federal Courts of Appeals." *Yale Law Journal* 107: 2155–2176.

Cubbage, Frederick W., Jay O'Laughlin, and Charles S. Bullock III. 1993. *Forest Resource Policy.* New York: Wiley.

Culhane, Paul J. 1981. *Public Lands Politics: Interest Group Influence on the Forest Service and the Bureau of Land Management.* Baltimore, Md.: Johns Hopkins University Press.

Dalton, Russell J. 1994. *The Green Rainbow: Environmental Groups in Western Europe.* New Haven, Conn.: Yale University Press.

Dana, Samuel Trask, and Sally K. Fairfax. 1980. *Forest and Range Policy: Its Development in the United States.* 2d edition. New York: McGraw-Hill.

Davies, J. Clarence, and Jan Mazurek. 1997. *Regulating Pollution: Does the System Work?* Washington, D.C.: Resources for the Future.

———. 1998. *Pollution Control in the United States: Evaluating the System.* Washington, D.C.: Resources for the Future.

Davies, Terry. 1998. "Critically Evaluating America's Pollution Control System." *Resources* 130:17–18.

Davis, Charles. 1985. "Implementing the Resource Conservation and Recovery Act of 1976: Problems and Prospects." *Public Administration Quarterly* 9:218–236.

De Figueiredo, Rui J. 1996. "The Structure of Reciprocity: A Formal Theory of Electoral Uncertainty." Stanford University.

Deily, Mary E., and Wayne B. Gray. 1991. "Enforcement of Pollution Regulations in a Declining Industry." *Journal of Environmental Economics and Management* 21:260–274.

DelRossi, Alison F., and Robert P. Inman. 1999. "Changing the Price of Pork: The Impact of Local Cost Sharing on Legislators' Demands for Distributive Public Goods." *Journal of Public Economics* 71:247–273.

Denzau, Arthur T., and Michael C. Munger. 1986. "Legislators and Interest Groups: How Unorganized Interests Get Represented." *American Political Science Review* 80:89–106.

Derthick, Martha, and Paul Quirk. 1985. *The Politics of Deregulation.* Washington, D.C.: Brookings Institution.

Dietz, Nathan, and Lawrence S. Rothenberg. 2000. "The Institutional Basis of Non-Market Pricing: Modeling Valuations of Grazing Lands." University of Rochester.

Dijkstra, Bouwe R. 1999. *The Political Economy of Environmental Policy: A Public Choice Approach to Market Instruments.* Cheltenham, England: Edward Elgar.

Dixit, Avinash K. 1996. *The Making of Economic Policy: A Transaction-Cost Politics Perspective.* Cambridge: MIT Press.

Dobra, John L. 1994. "Reform of the 1872 Mining Law: A Primer." In *Multiple Conflicts over Multiple Uses.* Edited by Terry L. Anderson. Bozeman, Mont.: Political Economy Research Center.

Dowie, Mark. 1995. *Losing Ground: American Environmentalism at the Close of the Twentieth Century.* Cambridge: MIT Press.

Downs, Anthony. 1972. "Ups and Downs with Ecology: The Issue-Attention Cycle." *Public Interest* 28:38–50.

Drotning, Lucy, and Lawrence S. Rothenberg. 1999. "Predicting Bureaucratic Control: Evidence from the 1990 Clean Air Act Amendments." *Law and Policy* 29:1–20.

Duch, Raymond, and Michael A. Taylor. 1993. "Postmaterialism and the Economic Condition." *American Journal of Political Science* 37:737–769.

Dudley, Susan E., and Angela Antonelli. 1997. "Congress and the Clinton OMB: Unwilling Partners in Regulatory Oversight," *Regulation* 20:17–23.

Dunlap, Riley E. 1995. "Public Opinion and Environmental Policy." In *Environmental Politics and Policy: Theories and Evidence.* 2d edition. Edited by James P. Lester. Durham, N.C.: Duke University Press.

Dunlap, Riley E., George H. Gallup Jr., and Alec M. Gallup. 1993. "Of Global Concern: Results of the Health of the Planet Survey." *Environment* 35:6–22.

Dunlap, Riley E., and Angela G. Mertig. 1995. "Global Concern for the Environment: Is Affluence a Prerequisite?" *Journal of Social Issues* 51:121–137.

Dunlap, Thomas R. 1981. *DDT: Scientists, Citizens, and Public Policy.* Princeton, N.J.: Princeton University Press.

Durant, Robert F. 1992. *The Administrative Presidency Revisited: Public Lands, the BLM, and the Reagan Revolution.* Albany: State University of New York Press.

Duverger, Maurice. 1954. *Political Parties, Their Organization and Activity in the Modern State.* New York: Wiley.

Easterbrook, Gregg. 1995. *A Moment on the Earth: The Coming Age of Environmental Optimism.* New York: Viking.

Echeverria, John D., and Raymond Booth Eby, eds. 1995. *Let the People Judge: Wise Use and the Private Property Rights Movement.* Washington, D.C.: Island Press.

Eggertsson, Thrainn. 1996. "A Note on the Economics of Institutions." In *Empirical Studies of Institutional Change.* Edited by Lee J. Alston, Thrainn Eggertsson, and Douglass C. North. Cambridge: Cambridge University Press.

Ehrlich, Paul R., and Anne H. Ehrlich. 1996. *Betrayal of Science and Reason: How Anti-environmental Rhetoric Threatens Our Future.* Washington, D.C.: Island Press.

Elliott, E. Donald, Bruce A. Ackerman, and John C. Millian. 1985. "Toward a Theory of Statutory Evolution: The Federalization of Environmental Law." *Journal of Law, Economics and Organization* 1:313–340.

Environmental Defense Fund. 1999. *1998 Annual Report.* Washington, D.C.: Environmental Defense Fund.

Epple, Dennis, and Thomas Romer. 1991. "Mobility and Redistribution." *Journal of Political Economy* 99:828–858.

Epstein, David, and Sharyn O'Halloran. 1999. *Delegating Powers: A Transaction Cost Politics Approach to Policy Making under Separate Powers.* Ann Arbor: University of Michigan Press.

Epstein, Lee, and Jack Knight. 1998. *The Choices Justices Make.* Washington, D.C.: Congressional Quarterly Press.

Epstein, Lee, and C. K. Rowland. 1991. "Debunking the Myth of Interest Group Invincibility in the Courts." *American Political Science Review* 85:205–217.

Epstein, Richard A. 1993. *Bargaining with the State.* Princeton, N.J.: Princeton University Press.

Erikson, Robert S., and Thomas R. Palfrey. 1998. "Campaign Spending and Incumbency: An Alternative Simultaneous Equations Approach." *Journal of Politics* 60:355–373.

Eskridge, William N., Jr. 1991. "Overriding Supreme Court Statutory Interpretation Decisions." *Yale Law Journal* 101:331–455.

Eskridge, William N., Jr., and John Ferejohn. 1992. "Making the Deal Stick: Enforcing the Original Constitutional Structure of Lawmaking in the Modern Regulatory State." *Journal of Law, Economics and Organization* 8:165–189.

Esty, Daniel C. 1996. "Revitalizing Environmental Federalism." *Michigan Law Review* 95:570–653.

Eveleigh, Robin. 2000. "Amazon Timber Stewards Busted for Bribes." Available: http://www.enn.com/news/enn–stories/2000/10/10112000/loggingbribes_32413.asp?site=email.

Fagin, Dan, Marianne Lavelle, and the Center for Public Integrity. 1999. *Toxic Deception: How the Chemical Industry Manipulates Science, Bends the Law, and Endangers Your Health.* Monroe, Me.: Common Courage Press.

Farber, Daniel A. 1997a. "Environmental Federalism in a Global Economy." *Virginia Law Review* 83:1283–1329.

———. 1997b. "Parody Lost/Pragmatism Regained: The Ironic History of the Coase Theorem." *Virginia Law Review* 83:397–428.

Farrell, Joseph. 1987. "Information and the Coase Theorem." *Journal of Economic Perspectives* 1:113–129.

Ferejohn, John A. 1999. "Independent Judges, Dependent Judiciary: Explaining Judicial Independence." *Southern California Law Review* 72:353–384.

Ferejohn, John A., and Charles Shipan. 1990. "Congressional Influence on Bureaucracy." *Journal of Law, Economics and Organization* 6:1–20.

Ferejohn, John A., and Barry R. Weingast. 1997. "Can the States Be Trusted?" In *The New Federalism: Can the States Be Trusted?* Edited by John Ferejohn and Barry R. Weingast. Stanford, Calif.: Hoover Institution Press.

Fiorina, Morris P. 1989. *Congress, Keystone of the Washington Establishment.* 2d edition. New Haven, Conn.: Yale University Press.

———. 1996. *Divided Government.* 2d edition. Boston: Allyn and Bacon.

Fiorino, Daniel J. 1995. *Making Environmental Policy.* Berkeley: University of California Press.

Fischel, William A. 1995. *Regulatory Takings: Law, Economics, and Politics.* Cambridge: Harvard University Press.

Fishback, Price V. 1992. *Soft Coal, Hard Choices: The Economic Welfare of Bituminous Coal Miners, 1890–1930.* Oxford: Oxford University Press.

Flippen, J. Brooks. 1995. "Pests, Pollution, and Politics: The Nixon Administration's Pesticide Policy." *Agriculture History* 71:442–456.

Foreman, Christopher H., Jr. 1998. *The Promise and Peril of Environmental Justice.* Washington, D.C.: Brookings Institution.

Foster, Vivien, and Robert W. Hahn. 1995. "Designing More Efficient Markets: Lessons from Los Angeles Smog Control," *Journal of Law and Economics* 38:19–48.

Fowler, Linda L., and Ronald G. Shaiko. 1987. "The Grass Roots Connection: Environmental Activists and Senate Roll Calls." *American Journal of Political Science* 31:484–510.

Frater, Elisabeth. 2000. "Adding up Pollution Prosecutions." *National Journal* 32 (October 21): 3330.

Freedman, Allan. 1998. "GOP's Secret Weapon against Regulations: Finesse." *Congressional Quarterly Weekly Report* 56 (September 5): 2305, 2314.

Freemuth, John C. 1991. *Islands under Siege: National Parks and the Politics of External Threats.* Lawrence: University of Kansas Press.

Friends of the Earth. 1999. *1998 Annual Report.* Washington, D.C.: Friends of the Earth.

Gaddie, Ronald Keith, and James L. Regens. 2000. *Regulating Wetlands Protection: Environmental Federalism and the States.* Albany: State University of New York Press.

Garrett, Theodore I. 1998. "Reinventing EPA Enforcement." *Natural Resources and Environment* 12:180–182, 223–224.

Gersbach, Hans, and Amihai Glazer. 1999. "Markets and Regulatory Hold-Up Problems." *Journal of Environmental Economics and Management* 37:151–164.

Glazer, Amihai. 1989. "Politics and the Choice of Durability." *American Economic Review* 79:1207–1213.

Glazer, Amihai, and Lawrence S. Rothenberg. 2001. *The Causes of Governmental Success and Failure.* Cambridge: Harvard University Press.

Goklany, Indur M. 1999. *Clearing the Air: The Real Story of the War on Air Pollution.* Washington, D.C.: Cato Institute.

Goodin, Robert E. 1994. "Selling Environmental Indulgences." *Kyklos* 47:573–596.

Gore, Albert. 1992. *Earth in the Balance: Ecology and the Human Spirit.* Boston: Houghton Mifflin.

Gorte, Ross W., and Betsy A. Cody. 1995. *The Forest Service and Bureau of Land Management: History and Analysis of Merger Proposals.* CRS Issue Brief 95-117ENR. Washington, D.C.: Congressional Research Service.

Gray, George M., and John D. Graham. 1995. "Regulating Pesticides." In *Risk vs. Risk: Tradeoffs in Protecting Health and the Environment.* Edited by John D. Graham and Jonathan Baert Wiener. Cambridge: Harvard University Press.

Gray, Virginia, Russell L. Hanson, and Herbert Jacob. 1999. *Politics in the American States: A Comparative Analysis.* 7th edition. Washington, D.C.: Congressional Quarterly Press.

Gray, Wayne B., and Mary E. Deily. 1996. "Compliance and Enforcement: Air Pollution Regulation in the U.S. Steel Industry." *Journal of Environmental Economics and Management* 31:96–111.

Greve, Michael S. 1996. *The Demise of Environmentalism in American Law.* Washington, D.C.: American Enterprise Institute.

Grier, Kevin B., Michael C. Munger, and Brian E. Roberts. 1991. "The Industrial Organization of Corporate Political Activity." *Southern Economic Journal* 57:727–738.

———. 1994. "The Determinants of Industry Political Activity, 1978–1986." *American Political Science Review* 88:911–926.

Grossman, Gene M., and Elhanan Helpman. 1994. "Protection for Sale." *American Economic Review* 88:833–860.

———. 1999. "Economic Models of Political Processes: Rent-seeking, Elections, Legislatures, and Voting Behavior." *American Economic Review* 89:501–524.

Grossman, Gene M., and Alan B. Krueger. 1995. "Economic Growth and the Environment." *Quarterly Journal of Economics* 110:353–377.

Hahn, Robert W. 1990. "The Political Economy of Environmental Regulation: Towards a Unifying Theory." *Public Choice* 65:21–47.

———. 1998. "Policy Watch: Government Analysis of the Benefits and Costs of Regulation." *Journal of Economic Perspectives* 12:201–210.

———. 1999. "The Impact of Economics on Environmental Policy." AEI-Brookings Joint Center for Regulatory Studies Working Paper No. 99-4. Washington, D.C.: American Economics Institute and Brookings Institution.

Hahn, Robert W., and John A. Hird. 1991. "The Costs and Benefits of Regulation: Review and Synthesis." *Yale Journal of Regulation* 8:233–278.

Haider, Donald H. 1974. *When Governments Come to Washington: Governors, Mayors, and Intergovernmental Lobbying.* New York: Free Press.

Hall, Bob, and Mary Lee Kerr. 1991. *1991–1992 Green Index.* Washington, D.C.: Island Press.

Hall, Richard L. 1996. *Participation in Congress.* New Haven, Conn.: Yale University Press.

Halper, Julie Edelson. 2001. "Company Names Are Busting Out All Over." *New York Times,* February 18, C1.

Hamilton, James T. 1993. "Politics and Social Costs: Estimating the Impact of Collective Action on Hazardous Waste Facilities." *Rand Journal of Economics* 24:101–125.

———. 1995a. "Pollution as News: Media and Stock Market Reactions to the Toxics Release Inventory Data." *Journal of Environmental Economics and Management* 28:98–113.

———. 1995b. "Testing for Environmental Racism: Prejudice, Profits, Political Power?" *Journal of Policy Analysis and Management* 14:107–132.

Hamilton, James T., and Christopher H. Schroeder. 1994. "Strategic Regulators and the Choice of Rulemaking Procedures: The Selection of Formal vs. Informal Rules in Regulating Hazardous Waste." *Law and Contemporary Problems* 57:111–160.

Hamilton, James T., and W. Kip Viscusi. 1999. *Calculating Risks: The Spatial and Political Dimensions of Hazardous Waste Policy.* Cambridge: MIT Press.

Hansen, John Mark. 1985. "The Political Economy of Group Membership." *American Political Science Review* 79:79–96.

———. 1991. *Gaining Access: Congress and the Farm Lobby, 1919–1981.* Chicago: University of Chicago Press.

Hardin, Garrett. 1968. "The Tragedy of the Commons." *Science* 162:1243–1248.

Hardin, Russell. 1982. *Collective Action.* Baltimore, Md.: Johns Hopkins University Press.

Harrington, Winston. 1988. "Enforcement Leverage When Penalties Are Restricted." *Journal of Public Economics* 37:29–53.

Harrison, Kathryn. 1995. "Is Cooperation the Answer? Canadian Environmental Enforcement in Comparative Perspective." *Journal of Policy Analysis and Management* 14:221–244.

Harter, Philip J. 1982. "Negotiating Regulations: A Cure for Malaise." *Georgetown Law Journal* 71:1–118.

———. 2000. "Assessing the Assessors: The Actual Performance of Negotiated Rulemaking." *New York University Environmental Law Journal* 9:32–59.

Hawkins, George S. 1997. "Compliance and Enforcement Changes in Congress and EPA." *Natural Resources and Environment* 11:42–47.

Hays, Samuel P. 1959. *Conservation and the Gospel of Efficiency: The Progressive Conservation Movement, 1890–1920.* Cambridge: Harvard University Press.

———. 1998. *Explorations in Environmental History: Essays by Samuel P. Hays.* Pittsburgh, Pa.: University of Pittsburgh Press.

Hays, Scott P., Michael Esler, and Carol E. Hays. 1996. "Environmental Commitment among the States: Integrating Alternative Approaches to State Environmental Policy." *Publius* 26:41–58.

Heclo, Hugh. 1978. "Issue Networks and the Executive Establishment." In *The New American Political System.* Edited by Anthony King. Washington, D.C.: American Enterprise Institute.

Helland, Eric. 1998a. "The Enforcement of Pollution Control Laws: Inspections, Violations, and Self-Reporting," *Review of Economics and Statistics* 80:141–153.

———. 1998b. "Environmental Protection in the Federalist System: The Political Economy of NPDES Inspections." *Economic Inquiry* 36:305–319.

———. 1998c. "The Revealed Preferences of State EPAs: Stringency, Enforcement, and Substitution." *Journal of Environmental Economics and Management* 35:242–261.

Helvarg, David. 1994. *The War against the Greens: The "Wise Use" Movement, the New Right, and Anti-Environmental Violence.* San Francisco: Sierra Club Books.

Hermalin, Benjamin E. 1995. "An Economic Analysis of Takings." *Journal of Law, Economics and Organization* 11:64–86.

Hess, Karl, Jr., and Jerry L. Holechek. 1995. "Beyond the Grazing Fee: An Agenda for Rangeland Reform." Policy Analysis No. 234. Washington, D.C.: Cato Institute.

Heyes, Anthony G. 1998. "Making Things Stick: Enforcement and Compliance." *Oxford Review of Economic Policy* 14:50–63.

Heyes, Anthony, and Neil Rickman. 1999. "Regulatory Dealing: Revisiting the Harrington Paradox." *Journal of Public Economics* 72:361–378.

Hill, Jeffrey S., and John E. Brazier. 1991. "Constraining Administrative Decisions: A Critical Examination of the Structure and Process Hypothesis." *Journal of Law, Economics and Organization* 7:355–372.

Hird, John A. 1990. "Superfund Expenditures and Cleanup Priorities: Distributive Politics or the Public Interest?" *Journal of Policy Analysis and Management* 9:455–483.

Hodges, Glenn. 1996. "Dead Wood." *Washington Monthly* 28:12–18.

Holsey, Cheryl M., and Thomas E. Borcherding. 1997. "Why Does Government's Share of the National Income Grow? An Assessment of the Recent Literature on the U.S. Experience." In *Perspectives on Public Choice: A Handbook.* Edited by Dennis C. Mueller. Cambridge: Cambridge University Press.

Hopkins, Thomas D. 1998. "Regulatory Costs in Profile." *Policy Sciences* 31:301–320.

Horn, Murray J. 1995. *The Political Economy of Public Administration: Institutional Choice in the Public Sector.* Cambridge: Cambridge University Press.

Hula, Kevin W. 1999. *Lobbying Together: Interest Group Coalitions in Legislative Politics.* Washington, D.C.: Georgetown University Press.

Humphries, Marc. 1997. *The 1872 Mining Law: Time for Reform?* CRS Issue Brief 89130. Washington, D.C.: Congressional Research Service.

Hunter, Susan, and Richard W. Waterman. 1996. *Enforcing the Law: The Case of the Clean Water Acts.* Armonk, N.Y.: Sharpe.

Huntington, Samuel P. 1953. "The Marasmus of the ICC: The Commission, the Railroads, and the Public Interest." *Yale Law Journal* 61:467–509.

Inglehart, Ronald. 1995. "Public Support for Environmental Protection: The Impact of Objective Problems and Subjective Values in 43 Societies." *PS: Political Science and Politics* 28:57–71.

Ingram, Helen M., David H. Colnic, and Dean E. Mann. 1995. "Interest Groups and Environmental Policy." In *Environmental Politics and Policy: Theories and Evidence.* Edited by James P. Lester. Durham, N.C.: Duke University Press.

Inman, Robert P., and Daniel L. Rubinfeld. 1997a. "Rethinking Federalism." *Journal of Economic Perspectives* 11:43–64.

———. 1997b. "The Political Economy of Federalism." In *Perspectives on Public Choice.* Edited by Dennis C. Mueller. Cambridge: Cambridge University Press.

Innes, Robert. 1997. "Takings, Compensation, and Equal Treatment for Owners of Developed and Undeveloped Property." *Journal of Law and Economics* 40:403–432.

Israelsen, Brent. 2000a. "Activists for Roadless Forests Converge on Utah." *Salt Lake Tribune,* July 18, B8.

———. 2000b. "Cutthroat Battle: Colorado River Trout Endangered, Says Suit." *Salt Lake Tribune,* November 18, D2.

Jacobson, Peter D., and Jeffrey Wasserman. 1997. *Tobacco Control Laws: Implementation and Enforcement.* Santa Monica, Calif.: Rand.

Jaffee, Adam B., Steven R. Peterson, Paul R. Portney, and Robert Stavins. 1995. "Environmental Regulation and the Competitiveness of U.S. Manufacturing." *Journal of Economic Literature* 33:132–163.

John, DeWitt. 1994. *Civic Environmentalism: Alternatives to Regulation in States and Communities.* Washington, D.C.: Congressional Quarterly Press.

Johnson, Ronald N., and Gary D. Libecap. 1994. *The Federal Civil Service System and the Problem of Bureaucracy: The Economics and Politics of Institutional Change.* Chicago: University of Chicago Press.

Johnson, Scott Lee, and David M. Pekelney. 1996. "Economic Assessment of the Regional Clean Air Incentives Market: A New Emissions Trading Program for Los Angeles." *Land Economics* 72:277–297.

Jones, Charles O. 1975. *Clean Air: The Policies and Politics of Pollution Control.* Pittsburgh, Pa.: University of Pittsburgh Press.

Jordan, Grant, and William Maloney. 1997. *The Protest Business? Mobilizing Campaign Groups.* Manchester, England: Manchester University Press.

Jordan, Richard N. 1994. *Trees and People: Forestland Ecosystems and Our Future.* Washington, D.C.: Regnery.

Joskow, Paul L., and Richard Schmalensee. 1998. "The Political Economy of Market-Based Environmental Policy: The U.S. Acid Rain Program." *Journal of Law and Economics* 41: 37–83.

Joskow, Paul L., Richard Schmalensee, and Elizabeth R. Bailey. 1998. "The Market for Sulfur Dioxide Emissions." *American Economic Review* 88:669–685.

Kagan, Robert A. 1995. "Adversarial Legalism and American Government." In *The New Politics of Public Policy.* Edited by Marc K. Landy and Martin A. Levin. Baltimore, Md.: Johns Hopkins University Press.

———. 1997. "Political and Legal Obstacles to Collaborative Ecosystem Planning." *Ecology Law Quarterly* 24:871–875.

———. 1999. "Trying to Have It Both Ways: Local Discretion, Central Control, and Adversarial Legalism in American Environmental Regulation." *Ecology Law Quarterly* 25: 718–732.

Kahn, James R. 1998. *The Economic Approach to Environmental and Natural Resources.* 2d edition. Orlando, Fla.: Dryden Press.

Kahn, Matthew E. 1998. "Does Smog Regulation Replace Private Self Protection?" Columbia University.

———. 2000. "United States Pollution Intensive Trade Trends from 1972 to 1992." Tufts University.

Kahn, Matthew E., and John G. Matsusaka. 1997. "Demand for Environmental Goods: Evidence from Voting Patterns on California Initiatives." *Journal of Law and Economics* 40: 137–173.

Kaufman, Herbert. 1960. *The Forest Ranger, a Study in Administrative Behavior.* Baltimore, Md.: Johns Hopkins University Press.

Kelman, Steven. 1981. *What Price Incentives? Economics and the Environment.* Boston: Auburn House.

Keohane, Nathaniel O., Richard L. Revesz, and Robert N. Stavins. 1999. "The Positive Political Economy of Instrument Choice in Environmental Policy." In *Environmental and Public Economics: Essays in Honor of Wallace Oates.* London: Edward Elgar.

Kerwin, Cornelius. 1999. *Rulemaking: How Government Agencies Write Law and Make Policy.* 2d edition. Washington, D.C.: Congressional Quarterly Press.

Kettl, Donald F. 1998. *Reinventing Government: A Fifth Year Report Card.* Washington, D.C.: Brookings Institution.

Khanna, Madhu, Wilma Rose H. Quimio, and Dora Bojilova. 1998. "Toxics Release Information: A Policy Tool for Environmental Protection." *Journal of Environmental Economics and Management* 36:243–266.

Kingdon, John W. 1995. *Agendas, Alternatives, and Public Policies.* 2d edition. New York: HarperCollins.

Kleit, Andrew N. 1990. "The Effect of Annual Changes in Automobile Fuel Economy Standards." *Journal of Regulatory Economics* 2:151–172.

Kline, Benjamin. 2000. *First Along the River: A Brief History of the U.S. Environmental Movement.* 2d edition. San Francisco: Acada Books.

Klyza, Christopher McGrory. 1996. *Who Controls Public Lands? Mining, Forestry, and Grazing Policies, 1870–1990.* Chapel Hill: University of North Carolina Press.

Knott, Jack H., and Gary J. Miller. 1987. *Reforming Bureaucracy: The Politics of Institutional Choice.* Englewood Cliffs, N.J.: Prentice-Hall.

Konar, Shameek, and Mark A. Cohen. 1997. "Information as Regulation: The Effect of Community Right to Know Laws on Toxic Emissions." *Journal of Environmental Economics and Management* 32:109–124.

Kovacic, William E. 1991. "The Reagan Judiciary and Environmental Policy: The Impact of Appointments to the Federal Court of Appeals." *Boston College Environmental Affairs Law Review* 18:669–713.

Kraft, Michael E. 1996. *Environmental Policy and Politics: Toward the Twenty-first Century.* New York: HarperCollins.

Kraft, Michael E. 2000a. "Environmental Policy in Congress: Revolution, Reform, or Gridlock?" In *Environmental Politics.* 4th edition. Edited by Norman J. Vig and Michael E. Kraft. Washington, D.C.: Congressional Quarterly Press.

———. 2000b. "U.S. Environmental Policy and Politics: From the 1960s to the 1990s." *Journal of Policy History* 12:17–42.

Kraft, Michael E., and Daniel Mazmanian, eds. 1999. *Toward Sustainable Communities: Transition and Transformation in Environmental Policy.* Cambridge: MIT Press.

Krehbiel, Keith. 1996. "Committee Power, Leadership, and the Median Voter: Evidence from the Smoking Ban." *Journal of Law, Economics and Organization* 12:234–256.

———. 1998. *Pivotal Politics: A Theory of U.S. Lawmaking.* Chicago: University of Chicago Press.

Krugman, Paul. 1997. "Earth in the Balance Sheet: Economists Go for the Green." Available: http://www.mit.edu./krugman/www/green.html.

Kunioka, Todd, and Lawrence S. Rothenberg. 1993. "The Politics of Bureaucratic Competition: The Case of Natural Resource Policy." *Journal of Policy Analysis and Management* 12:700–725.

Kuznets, Simon S. 1961. *Capital in the American Economy: Its Formation and Financing.* Princeton, N.J.: Princeton University Press.

Ladd, Everett Carl, and Karlyn H. Bowman. 1995. *Attitudes toward the Environment: Twenty-five Years after Earth Day.* Washington, D.C.: American Enterprise Institute.

———. 1996. "Public Opinion on the Environment." *Resources* 124:5–7.

Landau, Martin. 1969. "Redundancy, Rationality, and the Problem of Duplication and Overlap." *Public Administration Review* 29:346–358.

Landy, Marc K. 1995. "The New Politics of Environmental Policy." In *The New Politics of Public Policy.* Edited by Marc K. Landy and Martin A. Levin. Baltimore, Md.: Johns Hopkins University Press.

Landy, Marc K., Marc J. Roberts, and Stephen R. Thomas. 1994. *The Environmental Protection Agency: Asking the Wrong Questions from Nixon to Clinton.* 2d edition. New York: Oxford University Press.

LaRue, James B., and Lawrence S. Rothenberg. 1992. "Institutional Features of Congressional Decisions: The Fight to Prohibit Smoking on Airlines." *Public Choice* 18:301–318.

Laver, Michael. 1999. "Divided Parties, Divided Government." *Legislative Studies Quarterly* 24: 5–30.

Lear, Kelly Kristen, and John W. Maxwell. 1998. "The Impact of Industry Structure and Penalty Policies on Incentives for Compliance and Regulatory Enforcement." *Journal of Regulatory Economics* 14:127–148.

Lee, Martin R. 1999. *Summaries of Environmental Laws Administered by the Environmental Protection Agency (Updated).* CRS Report RL30022. Washington, D.C.: Congressional Research Service.

Lehmann, Scott. 1995. *Privatizing Public Lands.* Oxford: Oxford University Press.

Leshy, John D. 1998. "Putting the Antiquities Act in Perspective." In *Visions of the Grand Staircase-Escalante: Examining Utah's Newest National Monument.* Edited by Robert B. Keiter, Sarah B. George, and Joro Walker. Salt Lake City: University of Utah Press.

Lester, James P. 1995. "Federalism and State Environmental Policy." In *Environmental Politics and Policy.* Edited by James P. Lester. Durham, N.C.: Duke University Press.

Lester, James P., and Joseph Stewart Jr. 2000. *Public Policy: An Evolutionary Approach.* 2d edition. Belmont, Calif.: Wadsworth.

Leventhal, Harold. 1974. "Environmental Decisionmaking and the Role of the Courts." *University of Pennsylvania Law Review* 122:509–555.

Levinson, Arik. 1996. "Environmental Regulations and Manufacturers' Location Choice: Evidence from the Census of Manufactures." *Journal of Public Economics* 62:5–29.

———. 1997. "A Note on Environmental Federalism: Interpreting Some Contradictory Results." *Journal of Environmental Economics and Management* 33:359–366.

———. 1999. "NIMBY Taxes Matter: The Case of State Hazardous Waste Disposal Taxes." *Journal of Public Economics* 74:31–51.

Lewis, Charles. 1998. *Unreasonable Risk: The Politics of Pesticides.* Washington, D.C.: Center for Public Integrity.

Libby, Ronald T. 1998. *Eco-Wars: Political Campaigns and Social Movements.* New York: Columbia University Press.

Libecap, Gary D. 1981. *Locking up the Range: Federal Lands Control and Grazing.* Cambridge, Mass.: Ballinger.

———. 1992. "Bureaucratic Issues and Environmental Concerns: A Review of the History of Federal Land Ownership and Management." *Harvard Journal of Law and Public Policy* 15:467–487.

Lowi, Theodore J. 1979. *The End of Liberalism: The Second Republic of the United States.* 2d edition. New York: Norton.

Lowry, Robert C. 1997. "The Private Production of Public Goods: Organizational Maintenance, Managers' Objectives, and Collective Goods." *American Political Science Review* 91:308–323.

———. 1999. "Foundation Patronage toward Citizen Groups and Think Tanks: Who Gets Grants?" *Journal of Politics* 61:758–776.

Lowry, William R. 1992. *The Dimensions of Federalism: State Governments and Pollution Control.* Durham, N.C.: Duke University Press.

———. 1994. *The Capacity for Wonder: Preserving National Parks.* Washington, D.C.: Brookings Institution.

———. 1998. "Public Provision of Intergenerational Goods: The Case of Preserved Lands." *American Journal of Political Science* 42:1082–1107.

Magat, Wesley A., and W. Kip Viscusi. 1990. "Effectiveness of the EPA's Regulatory Enforcement: The Case of Industrial Effluent Standards." *Journal of Law and Economics* 33: 331–360.

———. 1992. *Informational Approaches to Regulation.* Cambridge: MIT Press.

"Managing Paradise: National Parks." 1993. *Economist,* February 6, A31.

Manus, Peter. 1999. "Wild Bill Douglas's Last Stand: A Retrospective on the First Supreme Court Environmentalist." *Temple Law Review* 72:111–196.

Mashaw, Jerry L. 1990. "Explaining Administrative Process: Normative, Positive, and Critical Stories of Legal Development." *Journal of Law, Economics and Organization.* 6:267–298.

Matlack, Carol, with *National Journal* staff. 1988. "What Reagan Promised, What Reagan Delivered." *National Journal* 30 (May 14): 1298.

Mayhew, David R. 1991. *Divided We Govern: Party Control, Lawmaking, and Investigations, 1946–1990.* New Haven, Conn.: Yale University Press.

McAfee, Preston, and John McMillan. 1996. "Analyzing the Airwaves Auction." *Journal of Economic Perspectives* 10:159–175.

McCarthy, James E. 1999. *Clean Air Act Issues.* CRS Issue Brief 97007. Washington, D.C.: Congressional Research Service.

McCarty, Nolan. 2000. "Presidential Pork: Executive Veto Power and Distributive Politics." *American Political Science Review* 94:117–130.

McCarty, Nolan, and Lawrence S. Rothenberg. 1996. "Contributors, Candidates, and the Nature of Electoral Support." Paper presented at W. Allen Wallis Conference on Political Economy, University of Rochester, October 4.

———. 2000. "The Time to Give: PAC Motivations and Electoral Timing." *Political Analysis* 8:239–259.

McConnell, Virginia D., and Robert M. Schwab. 1990. "The Impact of Environmental Regulation on Industry Location Decisions: The Motor Vehicle Industry." *Land Economics* 66:67–81.

McCubbins, Mathew, Roger Noll, and Barry Weingast. 1989. "Structure and Process, Politics and Policy: Administrative Arrangements and the Political Control of Agencies." *Virginia Law Review* 74:431–482.

McGarity, Thomas O. 1991. "The Internal Structure of EPA Rulemaking." *Law and Contemporary Problems* 54:57–111.

McKelvey, Richard D., and Peter C. Ordeshook. 1985. "Sequential Elections with Limited Information." *American Journal of Political Science* 29:480–512.

———. 1986. "Information, Electoral Equilibria, and the Democratic Ideal." *Journal of Politics* 48:909–937.

McKelvey, Richard D., and Talbot Page. 1997. "The Coase Theorem with Private Information." California Institute of Technology.

———. 1999. "Taking the Coase Theorem Seriously." *Economics and Philosophy* 15:235–247.

McKinnon, Ronald, and Thomas Nechyba. 1997. "Competition in Federal Systems: The Role of Political and Financial Constraints." In *The New Federalism: Can the States Be Trusted?* Edited by John Ferejohn and Barry R. Weingast. Stanford, Calif.: Hoover Institution Press.

McSpadden, Lettie. 1995. "The Courts and Environmental Policy." In *Environmental Politics and Policy.* 2d edition. Edited by James P. Lester. Durham, N.C.: Duke University Press.

Medema, Steven G. 1999. "Legal Fiction: The Place of the Coase Theorem in Law and Economics." *Economics and Philosophy* 15:209–233.

Meiners, Roger, and Andrew Morriss, eds. 1999. *The Common Law and the Environment: Rethinking the Statutory Basis for Modern Environmental Law.* Lanham, Md.: Rowman and Littlefield.

Melnick, R. Shep. 1983. *Regulation and the Courts: The Case of the Clean Air Act.* Washington, D.C.: Brookings Institution.

———. 1992. "Pollution Deadlines and the Coalition for Failure." In *Environmental Politics: Public Costs, Private Rewards.* Edited by Michael S. Greve and Fred L. Smith Jr. New York: Praeger.

———. 1997. "The Political Roots of the Judicial Diilemma." *Administrative Law Review* 49:585–598.

———. 1998. "Strange Bedfellows Make Normal Politics: An Essay." *Duke Environmental Law and Policy Forum* 9:75–93.

Melosi, Martin. 1980. *Pollution and Reform in American Cities, 1870–1930.* Austin: University of Texas Press.

Meltz, Robert, and James E. McCarthy. 1999. *The D.C. Circuit Remands the Ozone and Particulate Matter Clean-Air Standards: American Trucking Associations v. EPA.* CRS Issue Brief RS20228. Washington, D.C.: Congressional Research Service.

————. 2001. *The Supreme Court Upholds EPA Standard-Setting under the Clean Air Act: Whitman v. American Trucking Ass'ns.* CRS Report RS20860. Washington, D.C.: Congressional Research Service.

Mendelsohn, Robert, William D. Nordhaus, and Daigee Shaw. 1994. "The Impact of Global Warming on Agriculture: A Ricardian Analysis." *American Economic Review* 84:753–771.

Merrill, Thomas W. 1997. "Golden Rules for Transboundary Pollution." *Duke Law Journal* 46:931–1019.

Meyer, Harvey. 1999. "When the Cause Is Just." *Journal of Business Strategy* 20:27.

Milgrom, Paul, and John Roberts. 1992. *Economics, Organization and Management.* Englewood Cliffs, N.J.: Prentice Hall.

Miller, Gary J. 1992. *Managerial Dilemmas: The Political Economy of Hierarchy.* Cambridge: Cambridge University Press.

Mintz, Joel A. 1995. *Enforcement at the EPA: High Stakes and Hard Choices.* Austin: University of Texas Press.

Misakian, A. L., and L. A. Bero. 1998. "Publication Bias and Research on Passive Smoking: Comparison of Published and Unpublished Studies." *Journal of the American Medical Association* 280:250–253.

Mitchell, Neil J., Wendy Hansen, and Eric Jepsen. 1997. "The Determinants of Domestic and Foreign Corporate Political Activity." *Journal of Politics* 59:1096–1113.

Mitchell, Robert Cameron, and Richard T. Carson. 1989. *Using Surveys to Value Public Goods: The Contingent Valuation Method.* Baltimore, Md.: Johns Hopkins University Press.

Mixon, Franklin G., Jr. 1995. "Public Choice and the EPA: Empirical Evidence on Carbon Emissions Violations." *Public Choice* 83:127–137.

Moe, Terry M. 1989. "The Politics of Bureaucratic Structure." In *Can the Government Govern?* Edited by John Chubb and Paul Peterson. Washington, D.C.: Brookings Institution.

————. 1990. "Political Institutions: The Neglected Side of the Story." *Journal of Law, Economics and Organization* 6:213–253.

Moe, Terry M., and Michael Caldwell. 1994. "The Institutional Foundations of Democratic Governments—A Comparison of Presidential and Parliamentary Systems." *Journal of Institutional and Theoretical Economics* 150:171–195.

Moe, Terry M., and William G. Howell. 1999. "The Presidential Power of Unilateral Action." *Journal of Law, Economics and Organization* 15:132–179.

Moe, Terry M., and Scott A. Wilson. 1994. "Presidents and the Politics of Structure." *Law and Contemporary Problems* 57:1–44.

Moulin, Herve, and Alison Watts. 1997. "Two Versions of the Tragedy of the Commons." *Economic Design* 2:399–421.

Mueller, Dennis C. 1989. *Public Choice II.* Cambridge: Cambridge University Press.

Mullins, Brody. 1999. "After a Decade of Toxic Talk—Congress Is (Maybe) About to Turn to Revising the Superfund Hazardous-Waste Cleanup Program." *National Journal* 31 (October 30): 3139–3140.

Mundo, Philip A. 1992. *Interest Groups: Cases and Characteristics.* Chicago: Nelson-Hall.

Munger, Michael C., and Dennis Coates. 1995. "Strategizing in Small Group Decision Making: Host State Identification in the Southeast Compact." *Public Choice* 82:1–15.

Murdoch, James C., and Todd Sandler. 1997. "The Voluntary Provision of a Pure Public Good: The Case of Reduced CFC Emissions and the Montreal Protocol." *Journal of Public Economics* 63:331–349.

Musgrave, Richard A. 1997. "Devolution, Grants, and Fiscal Competition." *Journal of Economic Perspectives* 11:65–72.

Nadeau, Louis W. 1997. "EPA Effectiveness at Reducing the Duration of Plant-Level Non-compliance." *Journal of Environmental Economics and Management* 34:54–78.

National Audubon Society. 1999. *Annual Report 98.* Washington, D.C.: National Audubon Society.

"National Park Status Sought for Paterson Waterfall Site." 2001. *New York Times* February 19, B8.

National Performance Review. 1993. *Environmental Protection Agency: Accompanying Report of the National Performance Review.* Washington, D.C.: Office of the Vice President.

National Research Council. 1986. *Environmental Tobacco Smoke in the United States.* Washington, D.C.: National Academy Press.

———. 1987. *Regulating Pesticides in Food: The Delaney Paradox.* Washington, D.C.: National Academy Press.

———. 1995. *Science and the Endangered Species Act.* Washington, D.C.: National Academy Press.

———. 2001. *Compensating for Wetlands Loss under the Clean Water Act.* Washington, D.C.: National Academy Press.

Neal, Jennifer. 1999. "Paving the Road to Wetlands Mitigation Banking." *Boston College Environmental Affairs Law Review* 27:161–192.

Nice, David C. 1994. *Policy Innovation in State Government.* Ames: Iowa State University Press.

Niskanen, William A., Jr. 1971. *Bureaucracy and Representative Government.* Chicago: Aldine-Atherton.

Noecker, Robert J. 1998. *Endangered Species List Revisions: A Summary of Delisting and Downlisting.* CRS Report 98-32 ENR. Washington, D.C.: Congressional Research Service.

North, Douglass C. 1990. *Institutions, Institutional Change, and Economic Performance.* Cambridge: Cambridge University Press.

North, Douglass C., and Robert P. Thomas. 1973. *The Rise of the Western World: A New Economic History.* Cambridge: Cambridge University Press.

Nowell, Clifford, and Jason Shogren. 1994. "Challenging the Enforcement of Environmental Regulation." *Journal of Regulatory Economics* 6:265–282.

Nownes, Anthony J. 1996. "Public Interest Group Entrepreneurship and Theories of Group Mobilization." *Political Research Quarterly* 49:119–146.

Nugent, John Douglas. 1998. *Federalism Attained: Gubernatorial Lobbying in Washington as a Constitutional Function.* Ph.D. diss., Department of Political Science, University of Texas, Austin.

Oates, Wallace E. 1997. "On Environmental Federalism." *Virginia Law Review* 83:1321–1329.

———. 1998. "Thinking about Environmental Federalism." *Resources* 130:14–16.

Oates, Wallace E., and Robert M. Schwab. 1988. "Economic Competition among Jurisdictions: Efficiency Enhancing or Distortion Inducing." *Journal of Public Economics* 33:333–354.

———. 1992. "The Theory of Regulatory Federalism: The Case of Environmental Management." In *The Economics of the Environment.* Edited by Wallace E. Oates. Aldershot, England: Edwin Elgar.

Olson, Mancur. 1965. *The Logic of Collective Action.* Cambridge: Harvard University Press.

Oppenheimer, Michael, David S. Wilcove, and Michael J. Bean. 1995. "Review: *A Moment on the Earth: The Coming of Age of Environmental Optimism.*" *Environmental Law* 25:1293–1325.

Ostrom, Elinor. 1990. *Governing the Commons: The Evolution of Institutions for Collective Action.* Cambridge: Cambridge University Press.

Ostrom, Elinor, Roy Gardner, and James Walker. 1994. *Rules, Games, and Common-Poo. Resources.* Ann Arbor: University of Michigan Press.

Ostrom, Elinor, and James Walker. 1997. "Neither Markets nor States: Linking Transforma-tion Processes in Collective Action Arenas." In *Perspectives on Public Choice: A Handbook.* Edited by Dennis C. Mueller. Cambridge: Cambridge University Press.

O'Toole, Randal. 1988. *Reforming the Forest Service.* Washington, D.C.: Island Press.

————. 1995. "The National Pork Service." *Forbes* November 20, 160–165.

Palfrey, Thomas R., and Jeffrey E. Prisbrey. 1997. "Anomalous Behavior in Public Goods Ex-periments: How Much and Why?" *American Economic Review* 87:829–846.

Parker, Larry B., and John E. Blodgett. 1999. *Air Quality: EPA's Ozone Transport Rule, OTAG and Section 126 Petitions—A Hazy Situation?* CRS Report ENR98-236. Washington D.C.: Congressional Research Service.

Pashigan, Peter. 1985. "Environmental Regulation: Whose Self-Interests Are Being Protected?" *Economic Inquiry* 23:551–584.

Percival, Robert V. 1995. "Environmental Federalism: Historical Roots and Contemporary Models." *Maryland Law Review* 54:1141–1182.

Persson, Torsten, and Guido Tabellini. 1990. *Macroeconomic Policy, Credibility, and Politics.* Chur, Switzerland: Harwood.

Petersen, Shannon. 1999. "Congress and Charismatic Megafauna: A Legislative History." *Envi-ronmental Law* 29:463–491.

Peterson, Mark A. 1992. "The Presidency and Organized Interests: White House Patterns of Interest Group Liaison." *American Political Science Review* 86:612–625.

Peterson, Paul E. 1981. *City Limits.* Chicago: University of Chicago Press.

————. 1995. *The Price of Federalism.* Washington, D.C.: Brookings Institution.

Pierce, Richard J. 2000. "The Inherent Limits on Judicial Control of Agency Discretion: The D.C. Circuit and the Nondelegation Doctrine." *Administrative Law Review* 52:63–96.

Pigou, Arthur C. 1920. *The Economics of Welfare.* London: Macmillan.

Pildes, Richard H., and Cass R. Sunstein. 1999. "Reinventing the Regulatory State." *Univer-sity of Chicago Law Review* 62:1–129.

Polasky, Stephen, and Holly Doremus. 1998. "When the Truth Hurts: Endangered Species Pol-icy on Private Land with Imperfect Information." *Journal of Environmental Economics and Management* 35:22–47.

Polsky, Claudia, and Tom Turner. 1999. "Justice on the Rampage." *Amicus Journal* 21:34–35.

Poole, Keith T., Thomas Romer, and Howard Rosenthal. 1987. "The Revealed Preferences of Political Action Committees." *American Economic Review* 77:298–302.

Poole, Keith T., and Howard Rosenthal. 1997. *Congress: A Political-Economic History of Roll Call Voting.* Oxford: Oxford University Press.

Pope, Charles. 2000. "Congress Likely to Take Piecemeal Approach Again to Environmental Legislation." *Congressional Quarterly Weekly Report* 58 (January 29): 191.

Portney, Paul. 1999. "Environmental Policy in the Next Century." In *Setting National Priori-ties: The 2000 Election and Beyond.* Edited by Henry J. Aaron and Robert D. Reischauer. Washington, D.C.: Brookings Institution.

————. 2000. "Looking Ahead to 2050. Environmental Problems and Policy: 2000–2050." *Resources* 138:6–10.

Potters, Jan, Randolph Sloof, and Frans van Winden. 1997. "Campaign Expenditures, Con-tributions and Direct Endorsements: The Strategic Use of Information and Money to Influence Voter Behavior." *European Journal of Political Economy* 13:1–31.

Powell, Mark R. 1999. *Science at EPA: Information in the Regulatory Process.* Washington, D.C.: Resources for the Future.

President's Advisory Council on Executive Organization. 1971. *A New Regulatory Framework: Report on Selected Independent Regulatory Agencies.* Washington, D.C.: Government Printing Office.

Primm, Steven A., and Tim W. Clark. 1996. "The Greater Yellowstone Policy Debate: What Is the Policy Problem?" *Policy Sciences* 29:137–166.

Pritchard, Paul. 1997. "National Park Service Burdened by Politics." *Forum for Applied Research and Public Policy* 12:28–32.

Probst, Katherine, Don Fullerton, Robert E. Litan, and Paul R. Portney. 1995. *Footing the Bill for Superfund Cleanups: Who Pays and How?* Washington, D.C.: Brookings Institution and Resources for the Future.

Qian, Yingyi, and Barry R. Weingast. 1997. "Federalism as a Commitment to Preserving Market Incentives." *Journal of Economic Perspectives* 11:83–92.

Quigley, John M., and Daniel L. Rubinfeld. 1996. "Federalism and Reductions in the Federal Budget." *National Tax Journal* 49:289–302.

Rabe, Barry G. 1994. *Beyond NIMBY: Hazardous Waste Siting in Canada and the United States.* Washington, D.C.: Brookings Institution.

———. 1995. "Integrating Environmental Regulation: Permitting Innovation at the State Level." *Journal of Policy Analysis and Management* 14:467–472.

———. 1996. "An Empirical Examination of Innovations in Integrated Environmental Management: the Case of the Great Lakes Basin." *Public Administration Review* 56:372–381.

———. 1999a. "Federalism and Entrepreneurship: Explaining American and Canadian Innovation in Pollution Prevention and Regulatory Integration." *Policy Studies Journal* 27: 288–306.

———. 1999b. "Sustainability in a Regional Context: The Case of the Great Lakes Basin." In *Toward Sustainable Communities: Transition and Transformations in Environmental Policy.* Edited by Daniel A. Mazmanian and Michael E. Kraft. Cambridge: MIT Press.

———. 2000. "The Promise and Pitfalls of Decentralization." In *Environmental Policy: New Directions for the Twenty-First Century.* 4th edition. Edited by Norman J. Vig and Michael E. Kraft. Washington, D.C.: CQ Press.

Rabin, Robert L., and Stephen D. Sugarman. 1993. "Overview." In *Smoking Policy: Law, Politics, and Culture.* Edited by Robert L. Rabin and Stephen D. Sugarman. Oxford: Oxford University Press.

"Rangeland Reform '94: A Proposal to Improve Management of Rangeland Ecosystems and the Administration of Livestock Grazing on Public Lands." 1994. Washington, D.C.: Departments of Agriculture and Interior.

Rauber, Paul. 1996. "Bill Clinton: Does He Deserve Your Vote?" *Sierra* 81:38–39.

Raymond, Mark. 1999. "Enforcement Leverage When Penalties Are Restricted: A Reconsideration under Asymmetric Information." *Journal of Public Economics* 73:289–295.

Rechtschaffen, Clifford. 1998. "Deterrence vs. Cooperation and the Evolving Theory of Environmental Enforcement." *Southern California Law Review* 71:1181–1271.

Reisch, Mark. 1998. *Superfund Reauthorization Issues in the 105th Congress (I and II).* CRS Report 97025. Washington, D.C.: Congressional Research Service.

———. 2000a. *Superfund and the Brownfields Issue.* CRS Report 97-731. Washington, D.C.: Congressional Research Service.

———. 2000b. *Superfund Reauthorization Issues in the 106th Congress.* CRS Report IB10011. Washington, D.C.: Congressional Research Service.

Reisch, Mark, and David Michael Bearden. 2000. *Superfund Fact Book.* CRS Report 97312. Washington, D.C.: Congressional Research Service.

Reitze, Arnold W., Jr., and Sheryl-Lynn Carof. 1998. "The Legal Control of Indoor Air Pollution." *Boston College Environmental Affairs Law Review* 25:247–345.

Revesz, Richard L. 1992. "Rehabilitating Interstate Competition: Rethinking the 'Race to the Bottom' Rationale for Federal Environmental Regulation," *New York University Law Review* 67:1210–1254.

———. 1996. "Federalism and Interstate Environmental Externalities." *University of Pennsylvania Law Review* 144:2341–2416.

———. 1997a. "Environmental Regulation, Ideology, and the D.C. Circuit." *Virginia Law Review* 83:1717–1772.

———. 1997b. "Federalism and Environmental Regulation: A Normative Critique." In *The New Federalism: Can the States Be Trusted?* Edited by John Ferejohn and Barry R. Weingast. Stanford, Calif.: Hoover Institution Press.

Richer, Jerrell. 1995. "Green Giving: An Analysis of Contributions to Major U.S. Environmental Groups." Resources for the Future Discussion Paper 95/39. Washington, D.C.: Resources for the Future.

Riker, William H. 1987. *The Development of American Federalism.* Boston: Kluwer.

Ringquist, Evan J. 1993. *Environmental Protection at the State Level: Politics and Progress in Controlling Pollution.* Armonk, N.Y.: Sharpe.

Rivlin, Alice M. 1992. *Reviving the American Dream: The Economy, the States, and the Federal Government.* Washington, D.C.: Brookings Institution.

Rodriguez, Daniel B. 1996. "Testing Federalism Inside Out: Intrastate Aspects of Interstate Regulatory Competition." *Yale Law and Policy Review* 14:149–176.

Romer, Thomas, and James M. Snyder Jr. 1994. "An Empirical Examination of the Dynamics of PAC Contributions." *American Journal of Political Science* 38:745–769.

Rose-Ackerman, Susan. 1994. "Changing Images of the State: American Administrative Law under Siege: Is Germany a Model?" *Harvard Law Review* 107:1279–1302.

———. 1995. *Controlling Environmental Policy: The Limits of Public Law in Germany and the United States.* New Haven, Conn.: Yale University Press.

Rothenberg, Lawrence S. 1992. *Linking Citizens to Government: Interest Group Politics at Common Cause.* Cambridge: Cambridge University Press.

———. 1994. *Regulation, Organizations, and Politics: Motor Freight Policy at the Interstate Commerce Commission.* Ann Arbor: University of Michigan Press.

———. 2000. "Democracy, Economic Growth, and Environmental Quality." University of Rochester.

Rothman, Hal K. 1998. *The Greening of a Nation? Environmentalism in the United States Since 1945.* New York: Harcourt Brace.

Sabatier, Paul A., ed. 1999. *Theories of the Policy Process.* Boulder, Colo.: Westview.

Sabatier, Paul A., and Hank Jenkins-Smith. 1993. *Policy Change and Learning: An Advocacy Coalition Approach.* Boulder, Colo.: Westview.

Sagoff, Mark. 1981. "At the Shrine of Our Lady of Fatima, or Why Political Questions Are Not All Economic." *Arizona Law Review* 23:1283–1298.

Sandel, Michael J. 1997. "It's Immoral to Buy the Right to Pollute." *New York Times* December 15, A23.

Sanders, Elizabeth. 1999. *Roots of Reform: Farmers, Workers, and the American State, 1877–1917.* Chicago: University of Chicago Press.

Satchell, Michael. 1995. "Trouble in Paradise." *U.S. News and World Report,* June 19, 24–32.

Scheberle, Denise. 1997. *Federalism and Environmental Policy: Trust and the Politics of Implementation.* Washington, D.C.: Georgetown University Press.

Schelling, Thomas C. 1997. "The Costs of Combatting Global Warming." *Foreign Affairs* 76:8–21.

———. 1998. *Costs and Benefits of Greenhouse Gas Reduction.* Washington, D.C.: American Enterprise Institute.

Schierow, Linda Jo. 1993. *A Directory of Some Interest Groups and Governmental Organizations Concerned with National Environmental Policies.* CRS Report 93-831ENR. Washington, D.C.: Congressional Research Service.

———. 1996. *Pesticide Policy Issues.* CRS Report 95016. Washington, D.C.: Congressional Research Service.

———. 1999. *Pollution Prevention Act of 1990.* CRS Report RL30022. Washington, D.C.: Congressional Research Service.

Schoenbrod, David. 1993. *Power without Responsibility: How Congress Abuses the People through Delegation.* New Haven, Conn.: Yale University Press.

———. 1996. "Behind the Green Curtain." *Regulation* 19:18–25.

———. 1999. "Putting the "Law" Back into Environmental Law." *Regulation* 22:17–23.

Scholz, John T. 1984. "Voluntary Compliance and Regulatory Enforcement." *Law and Policy* 6:385–404.

———. 1994. "Managing Regulatory Enforcement in the United States." In *Handbook of Regulation and Administrative Law.* Edited by David Rosenbloom and Richard Schwartz. New York: Marcel Dekker.

Scholz, John T., and Wayne B. Gray. 1997. "Can Government Facilitate Cooperation? An Informational Model of OSHA Enforcement." *American Journal of Political Science* 41:693–717

Scholz, John T., and Feng Heng Wei. 1986. "Regulatory Enforcement in a Federalist System." *American Political Science Review* 80:1249–1270.

Schroeder, Christopher H. 1998. "The Political Origins of Modern Environmental Law: Rational Choice versus Republican Moment-Explanations for Environmental Laws." *Duke Environmental Law and Policy Forum* 9:29–59.

Scruggs, Lyle A. 1999. "Institutions and Environmental Performance in Seventeen Western Democracies." *British Journal of Political Science* 29:1–32.

Segal, Jeffrey A., Charles M. Cameron, and Albert D. Cover. 1992. "A Spatial Model of Roll Call Voting: Senators, Constituents, Presidents, and Interest Groups in Supreme Court Confirmations." *American Journal of Political Science* 36:96–121

Seldon, Barry J., Euel Elliott, James L. Regens, and Charles G. Hunter. 1994. "The Effect of EPA Enforcement Funding on Private-Sector Pollution-Control Investment." *Applied Economics* 26:949–955.

Shaiko, Ronald G. 1989. *The Public Interest Dilemma: Organizational Maintenance and Political Representation in the Public Interest Sector.* Ph.D. diss., Department of Political Science, Syracuse University.

———. 1998. *Voices and Echoes for the Environment: Public Interest Representation in the 1990s and Beyond.* New York: Columbia University Press.

Shanley, Robert A. 1992. *Presidential Influence and Environmental Policy.* Westport, Conn.: Greenwood Press.

Shapiro, Marc Douglas. 2000. *The Impact of Community Characteristics and State Policy on Changes in Education and Risk from Toxic Airborne Chemicals.* Ph.D. diss. Department of Political Science, University of Rochester.

Shaw, Robinson. 2000. "Groups Lobby to Get Work Load off Park Service's Back." *ENN News,* June 19, 1–2. Available: http://www.enn.com/news/enn–stories/2000/06/06192000/parkphotos_13936.asp.

Shepsle, Kenneth A., and Mark S. Bonchek. 1997. *Analyzing Politics: Rationality, Behavior, and Institutions.* New York: Norton.

Simon, Julian. 1999. *Hoodwinking the Nation.* New Brunswick, N.J.: Transaction.

Skea, Jim. 1999. "Flexibility, Emissions Trading and the Kyoto Protocol." In *Pollution for Sale: Emissions Trading and Joint Implementation.* Edited by Steve Sorrell and Jim Skea. Cheltenham, England: Edward Elgar.

Skocpol, Theda. 1992. *Protecting Soldiers and Mothers: The Political Origins of Social Policy in the United States.* Cambridge: Harvard University Press.

Skowronek, Stephen. 1982. *Building a New American State: The Expansion of National Administrative Capacities, 1877–1920.* Cambridge: Cambridge University Press.

Sloof, Randolph. 1999. "Campaign Contributions and the Desirability of Full Disclosure Laws." *Economics and Politics* 11:83–107.

Slovic, Paul. 1986. "Informing and Educating the Public about Risk." *Risk Analysis* 6:403–415.

Smith, Troy Ellis. 1998. *When States Lobby.* Ph.D. diss., Department of Political Science, State University of New York, Albany.

Soden, Dennis L., and Brent S. Steel. 1999. "Evaluating the Environmental Presidency." In *The Environmental Presidency.* Edited by Dennis L. Soden. Albany, N.Y.: State University of New York Press.

Solow, Robert M. 2000. "Sustainability: An Economist's Perspective." In *Economics of the Environment: Selected Readings.* 4th edition. Edited by Robert N. Stavins. New York: Norton.

Spiller, Pablo T. 1996. "A Positive Political Theory of Regulatory Instruments—Contracts, Administrative Law or Regulatory Specificity." *Southern California Law Review* 69: 477–515.

Spiller, Pablo T., and Emerson H. Tiller. 1996. "Invitations to Override: Congressional Reversals of Supreme Court Decisions." *International Review of Law and Economics* 16: 503–521.

Stansel, Dean. 2001. "Costly Agencies." In *Cato Handbook for Congress, 107th Congress.* Washington, D.C.: Cato Institute.

Starr, Kenneth W. 1986. "Judicial Review in the Post-*Chevron* Era," *Yale Journal on Regulation* 3:283–312.

Stavins, Robert N. 1998. "What Can We Learn from the Grand Policy Experiment? Lessons from SO_2 Allowance Trading." *Journal of Economic Perspectives* 12:69–88.

———. 1999. "Experience with Market-based Environmental Policy Instruments." Cambridge, Mass.: John F. Kennedy School of Government.

———, ed. 2000a. *Economics of the Environment.* 4th edition. New York: Norton.

———. 2000b. "Market-Based Environmental Policies." In *Public Policies for Environmental Protection.* Edited by Paul R. Portney and Robert N. Stavins. Washington, D.C.: Resources for the Future.

Steel, Brent S., John C. Pierce, and Nicholas P. Lovrich. 1996. "Resources and Strategies of Interest Groups and Industry Representatives Involved in Federal Forest Policy." *Social Science Journal* 33:401–419.

Stewart, Richard B. 1975. "The Reformation of American Administrative Law." *Harvard Law Review* 88:1667–1813.

———. 1977. "Pyramids of Sacrifice? Problems of Federalism in Mandating State Implementation of National Environmental Policy." *Yale Law Journal* 86:1668–1813.

———. 1993. "Environmental Regulation and International Competitiveness." *Yale Law Journal* 102:2039–2106.

———. 1997. "Environmental Quality as a National Good in a Federal State." *University of Chicago Legal Forum* 97:199–229.

Stroup, Richard L. 1995. "Endangered Species Act: Making Innocent Species the Enemy." Policy Series Paper No. PS-3. Bozeman, Mont.: Political Economy Research Center.

Susskind, Lawrence, and Gerard McMahon. 1985. "The Theory and Practice of Negotiated Rulemaking." *Yale Journal on Regulation* 3:133–165.

Svendsen, Gerg Tinggaard. 1999. "U.S. Interest Groups Prefer Emission Trading: A New Perspective." *Public Choice* 101:109–128.

Swire, Peter P. 1996. "The Race to Laxity and the Race to Undesirability: Explaining Failures in Competition among Jurisdictions in Environmental Law." *Journal of Law and Policy Review* 14:67–110.

Switzer, Jacqueline Vaughn. 1997. *Green Backlash: The History and Politics of the Environmental Opposition in the U.S.* Boulder, Colo.: Lynne Rienner.

Taylor, Ronald A. 1982. "Why Reagan Is on Griddle over Environment." *U.S. News and World Report*, August 30, 57–59.

Taylor, Serge. 1984. *Making Bureaucracies Think: The Environmental Impact Assessment Strategy of Administrative Reform.* Stanford, Calif.: Stanford University Press.

Taylor, Steven T. 1994. *Sleeping with the Industry: The U.S. Forest Service and Timber Interests.* Washington, D.C.: Center for Public Integrity.

Teles, Steven M. 1997. "Think Local, Act Local: Environmentalists Are Shifting Their Focus." *New Statesman,* August 22, 28–31.

Templet, Paul H. 1995. "Grazing the Commons: An Empirical Analysis of Externalities, Subsidies and Sustainability." *Ecological Economics* 12:141–159.

Thompson, Barton H., Jr. 1997. "The Endangered Species Act: A Case Study in Takings and Incentives." *Stanford Law Review* 49:305–380.

Thompson, Margaret Susan. 1985. *The Spider Web: Congress and Lobbying in the Age of Grant.* Ithaca, N.Y.: Cornell University Press.

Thorpe, Steven G. 1997. "Fuel Economy Standards, New Vehicle Sales, and Average Fuel Efficiency." *Journal of Regulatory Economics* 11:311–326.

Tiebout, Charles M. 1956. "A Pure Theory of Local Expenditures." *Journal of Political Economy* 64:416–424.

Tiemann, Mary E. 1996. *Safe Drinking Water Act: Implementation and Reauthorization.* CRS Issue Brief 91041. Washington, D.C.: Congressional Research Service.

———. 1999. *Safe Drinking Water Act.* CRS Report RL 30022. Washington, D.C.: Congressional Research Service.

Tiller, Emerson H. 1998. "Controlling Policy by Controlling Process: Judicial Influence on Regulatory Decision Making." *Journal of Law, Economics and Organization* 14:114–135.

Tiller, Emerson H., and Pablo T. Spiller. 1999. "Strategic Instruments: Legal Structure and Political Games in Administrative Law." *Journal of Law, Economics and Organizations* 15: 349–377.

Trinkle, Daniel B. "Cars, Congress, and Clean Air for the Northeast: A Separation of Powers Analysis of the Ozone Transport Commission." *Boston College Environmental Affairs Law Review* 23:169–201.

U.S. Bureau of Land Management (BLM). 2000. *Public Land Statistics 1999.* Washington, D.C.: Government Printing Office.

U.S. Congressional Budget Office (CBO). 1995. *The Safe Drinking Water Act: A Case Study of an Unfunded Federal Mandate.* Washington, D.C.: Congressional Budget Office.

———. 1997a. *Federalism and Environmental Protection: Case Studies for Drinking Water and Ground-Level Ozone.* Washington, D.C.: Congressional Budget Office.

————. 1997b. *Reducing the Deficit: Spending and Revenue Options.* Washington, D.C.: Congressional Budget Office.

————. 1998. *Factors Affecting the Relative Success of EPA's NO$_X$ Cap-and-Trade Program.* Washington, D.C.: Congressional Budget Office.

————. 1999. *Maintaining Budgetary Discipline: Spending and Revenue Options.* Washington, D.C.: Congressional Budget Office.

U.S. Department of Agriculture (USDA). 1997. *Forest Management Program Annual Report: Fiscal Year 1996.* Report FS-591. Washington, D.C.: Government Printing Office.

U.S. Department of Health and Human Services (HHS). 1986. *The Health Consequences of Involuntary Smoking: A Report of the Surgeon General.* Washington, D.C.: Government Printing Office.

U.S. Department of the Interior (DOI). 1998. "Babbitt Challenges Congress to Pass Mining Law Reform." Press release. Washington, D.C.: Office of the Secretary, Department of the Interior, April 28.

U.S. Department of Transportation (DOT). 2000. *Automotive Fuel Economy Program: Twenty-fourth Annual Report to Congress Calendar Year 1999.* Washington, D.C.: Government Printing Office.

U.S. Environmental Protection Agency (EPA). 1987. *Unfinished Business: A Comparative Assessment of Environmental Problems.* Washington, D.C.: Environmental Protection Agency.

————. 1990a. *Reducing Risk: Setting Priorities and Strategies for Environmental Protection.* Washington, D.C.: Environmental Protection Agency.

————. 1990b. *The Nation's Hazardous Waste Management Program at a Crossroads: The RCRA Implementation Study.* Washington, D.C.: Environmental Protection Agency.

————. 1998. *Enforcement and Compliance Assurance Accomplishments Report FY 1997.* Washington, D.C.: Environmental Protection Agency.

————. 1999a. *Reinventing Environmental Protection: 1998 Annual Report.* Washington, D.C.: Environmental Protection Agency.

————. 1999b. *Superfund Reforms: Annual Report FY 1998.* Washington, D.C.: Environmental Protection Agency.

————. 1999c. *Twenty-five Years of the Safe Drinking Water Act: History and Trends.* Washington, D.C.: Environmental Protection Agency.

————. 2000. *National Air Pollutant Emission Trends, 1900–1998.* Washington, D.C.: Environmental Protection Agency.

U.S. Fish and Wildlife Service (FWS). 2000. *Status and Trends of Wetlands in the Conterminous United States, 1986–1997.* Washington, D.C.: Fish and Wildlife Service.

U.S. General Accounting Office (GAO). 1993. *Pesticides: Reregistration Delays Jeopardize Success of Proposed Policy Reforms.* GAO/T-RCED-94-48. Washington, D.C.: Government Printing Office.

————. 1995a. *Forest Service: Distribution of Timber Sales Receipts, Fiscal Years 1992–94.* GA0/RCED-95-237FS. Washington, D.C.: Government Printing Office.

————. 1995b. *Federal Lands: Information on Land Owned on Acreage with Conservation Restrictions.* GAO/RCED-95-73FS. Washington, D.C.: Government Printing Office.

————. 1996. *Federal Land Management: Information on Efforts to Inventory Abandoned Hard Rock Mines.* GAO/RCED-96-30. Washington, D.C.: Government Printing Office.

————. 1997a. *Clean Water Act: Nine States' Experience with the Clean Water State Revolving Fund.* GAO/T-RCED-97-152. Washington, D.C.: Government Printing Office.

————. 1997b. *Hazardous Waste: Remediation Waste Requirements Can Increase the Time and Cost of Cleanups.* GAO/RCED-98-4. Washington, D.C.: Government Printing Office.

———. 1997c. *Times to Complete the Assessment and Cleanup of Hazardous Waste Sites.* GAO/RCED-97-20. Washington, D.C.: Government Printing Office.

———. 1998a. *Environmental Protection: EPA's and States' Efforts to "Reinvent" Environmental Regulation.* GAO/RCED-98-33T. Washington, D.C.: Government Printing Office.

———. 1998b. *National Park Service: Maintenance Backlog Issues.* GAO/T-RCED-98-61. Washington, D.C.: Government Printing Office.

———. 1998c. *Superfund: EPA's Use of Funds for Brownfield Revitalization.* GAO/RCED-98-97. Washington, D.C.: Government Printing Office.

———. 1999a. *Drinking Water Research: Better Planning Needed to Link Needs and Resources.* GAO/T-RCED-00-15. Washington, D.C.: Government Printing Office.

———. 1999b. *Superfund: Half the Sites Have All Cleanup Remedies in Place or Completed.* GAO/RCED-99-245. Washington, D.C.: Government Printing Office.

———. 1999c. *Superfund: Information on the Program's Funding Status.* GAO/RCED-00-25. Washington, D.C.: Government Printing Office.

———. 2000a. *Acid Rain: Emissions Trends and Effects in the Eastern United States.* GAO/RCED-00-47. Washington, D.C.: Government Printing Office.

———. 2000b. *Clean Water Act: Proposed Revisions to EPA Regulations to Clean Up Polluted Waters.* GAO/RCED-00-206R. Washington, D.C.: Government Printing Office.

———. 2000c. *Environmental Protection: More Consistency Needed among EPA Regions in Approach to Enforcement.* GAO/RCEDB00-108. Washington, D.C.: Government Printing Office.

U.S. Office of Management and Budget (OMB). 2000. *Report to Congress on the Costs and Benefits of Federal Regulations.* Washington, D.C.: Office of Management and Budget.

Van Houtven, George, and Maureen L. Cropper. 1996. "When Is a Life Too Costly to Save? The Evidence from U.S. Environmental Regulation." *Journal of Environmental Economics and Management* 30:348–368.

Vig, Norman J. 2000. "Presidential Leadership and the Environment: From Reagan to Clinton." In *Environmental Politics.* 4th edition. Edited by Norman J. Vig and Michael E. Kraft. Washington, D.C.: Congressional Quarterly Press.

Vileisis, Ann. 1997. *Discovering the Unknown Landscape: A History of America's Wetlands.* Washington, D.C.: Island Press.

Viscusi, James T., and James T. Hamilton. 1996. "Cleaning up Superfund." *The Public Interest* 124:52–60.

Viscusi, W. Kip, John M. Vernon, and Joseph E. Harrington Jr. 1996. *Economics of Regulation and Antitrust.* 2d edition. Cambridge: MIT Press.

Vogel, David. 1989. *Fluctuating Fortunes: The Political Power of Business in America.* New York: Basic Books.

———. 1993. "Representing Diffuse Interests in Environmental Policymaking." In *Do Institutions Matter? Government Capabilities in the United States and Abroad.* Edited by R. Kent Weaver and Bert Rockman. Washington, D.C.: Brookings Institution.

———. 1995. *Trading Up: Consumer and Environmental Regulation in a Global Economy.* Cambridge: Harvard University Press.

Vogt, Donna U. 1995. *The Delaney Clause Effects on Pesticide Policy.* CRS Report 95-514 SPR. Washington, D.C.: Government Printing Office.

Wald, Patricia M. 1992. "The Role of the Judiciary in Environmental Protection." *Boston College Environmental Affairs Law Review* 19:519–546.

Walker, Jack L., Jr. 1991. *Mobilizing Interest Groups in America: Patrons, Professions, and Social Movements.* Ann Arbor: University of Michigan Press.

Wargo, John. 1996. *Our Children's Toxic Legacy: How Science and Law Fail to Protect Us from Pesticides.* New Haven, Conn.: Yale University Press.

Warren, Melinda, and Murray Weidenbaum. *The Rise of Regulation Continues: An Analysis of the Budget for the Year 2000.* Center for the Study of American Business Regulatory Budget Report 22. St. Louis, Mo.: CSAB.

Watts, Myles J., and Jeffrey T. Laurence. 1994. "Cows, Cowboys, and Controversy: The Grazing Fee Issue." In *Multiple Conflicts over Multiple Uses.* Edited by Terry L. Anderson. Bozeman, Mont.: Political Economy Research Center.

Weaver, R. Kent. 1986. "The Politics of Blame Avoidance." *Journal of Public Policy* 6:371–398.

Weaver, R. Kent, and Bert Rockman, eds. 1993. *Do Institutions Matter? Government Capabilities in the United States and Abroad.* Washington, D.C.: Brookings Institution.

Weber, Edward P. 1998. *Pluralism by the Rules: Conflict and Cooperation in Environmental Regulation.* Washington, D.C.: Georgetown University Press.

Weingast, Barry R. 1993. "Constitutions as Governance Structures: The Political Foundations of Secure Markets." *Journal of Institutional and Theoretical Economics* 149:286–311.

———. 1995. "The Economic Role of Political Institutions: Market-Preserving Federalism and Economic Development." *Journal of Law, Economics and Organization* 11:1–31.

Wells, Donald T. 1996. *Environmental Politics: A Global Perspective for the Twenty-first Century.* Upper Saddle River, N.J.: Prentice Hall.

Wenner, Lettie McSpadden. 1982. *The Environmental Decade in Court.* Bloomington: Indiana University Press.

———. 1990. *U.S. Energy and Environmental Interest Groups: Institutional Profiles.* Westport, Conn.: Greenwood Press.

———. 1993. "Wetlands Preservation in the United States: A Case of Fragmented Authority." *Northern Illinois University Law Review* 14:589–609.

Wenner, Lettie M., and Cynthia Ostberg. 1994. "Restraint in Environmental Cases by Reagan-Bush Judicial Appointees." *Judicature* 77:217–220.

Wilcox, Geoffrey L. 1996. "New England and the Challenge of Interstate Ozone Pollution under the Clean Air Act of 1990." *Boston College Environmental Affairs Law Review* 24:1–101.

Wildavsky, Aaron. 1995. *But Is It True? A Citizen's Guide to Environmental Health and Safety Issues.* Cambridge: Harvard University Press.

Wilson, James Q. 1989. *Bureaucracies: What Government Agencies Do and Why They Do It.* New York: Basic Books.

Wise, Charles R. 1994. "Regulatory Takings." In *Handbook of Regulation and Administrative Law.* Edited by David H. Rosenbloom and Richard D. Schwartz. New York: Marcel Dekker.

Wittman, Donald. 2000. "Candidate Quality, Pressure Group Endorsements, and Uninformed Voters." University of California, Santa Cruz.

Wood, B. Dan. 1988. "Principals, Bureaucrats, and Responsiveness in Clean Air Enforcements." *American Political Science Review* 82:213–234.

———. 1991. "Federalism and Policy Responsiveness: The Clean Air Case." *Journal of Politics* 53:851–859.

———. 1992. "Modeling Federal Implementation: The Clean Air Case." *American Journal of Political Science* 36:40–67.

Wood, B. Dan, and Richard W. Waterman. 1991. "The Dynamics of Political Control of the Bureaucracy." *American Political Science Review* 85:801–828.

———. 1994. *Bureaucratic Dynamics: The Role of Bureaucracy in a Democracy.* Boulder, Colo.: Westview Press.

Wright, John R. 1990. "Contributions, Lobbying, and Committee Voting in the U.S. House of Representatives." *American Political Science Review* 84:417–438.

Yaffee, Steven Lewis. 1994. *The Wisdom of the Spotted Owl: Policy Lessons for a New Century.* Washington, D.C.: Island Press.

Yandle, Bruce. 1989. *The Political Limits of Environmental Regulation: Tracking the Unicorn.* New York: Quorum.

Zinn, Jeffrey A. 2001. "Managing Growth and Related Issues in the 107th Congress." CRS Issue Brief 10015. Washington, D.C.: Congressional Research Service.

Zinn, Jeffrey A., and Claudia Copeland. 2001. "Wetlands Issues." CRS Issue Brief 97014. Washington, D.C.: Congressional Research Service.

Zywicki, Todd J. 2000. "Industry or Environmental Lobbyists: Enemies or Allies?" In *The Common Law and the Environment: Rethinking the Statutory Basis for Modern Environmental Law.* Edited by Roger Meiners and Andrew Morriss. Lanham, Md.: Rowman and Littlefield.

Index